Legal Perspectives on State Power

Legal Perspectives on State Power:

Consent and Control

Edited by

Chris Ashford, Alan Reed
and Nicola Wake

Cambridge
Scholars
Publishing

Legal Perspectives on State Power: Consent and Control

Edited by Chris Ashford, Alan Reed, Nicola Wake

This book first published 2016

Cambridge Scholars Publishing

Lady Stephenson Library, Newcastle upon Tyne, NE6 2PA, UK

British Library Cataloguing in Publication Data
A catalogue record for this book is available from the British Library

ISBN (10): 1-4438-9944-5
ISBN (13): 978-1-4438-9944-4

TABLE OF CONTENTS

PREFACE

The contributing authors bring to bear a range of interdisciplinary perspectives on the various topics and views herein presented. The matters with which this edited collection monograph concerns itself are important and timely, with the law relating to Consent and State Control in a state of flux, and the work sets out to address some of the problematic aspects in this arena, and to provide a platform for further research and policy reform.

The contributions range from the academic and theoretical to the more practice and policy focused, and one of the aims of the collection is to achieve a balance in this respect. So far as practicable, the chapters are arranged thematically, in order to assist the reader in navigating the different topics addressed. The volume is intended to form a coherent whole, connected by an overarching theme, and it can be read as such, or more selectively by those interested by particular themes or chapters. To this end, there are cross-references between the chapters where appropriate, but these are kept to a minimum.

As editors, we would like to take this opportunity to thank the contributors to this volume, both for their excellent chapters and for the professional and timely manner in which they completed. These factors have made the editing process a relatively straightforward one. It has been a pleasure to receive, and to have the opportunity to edit, such a fine collection of work. We hope the readers will find the chapters, and the monograph as a whole, a useful and interesting addition to the expanding literature in this area. In addition, we would like to thank Beth Stuart-Cole, a Doctoral Candidate of Northumbria, for her invaluable assistance in formatting the chapters, and the University of Northumbria's Centre for Evidence and Criminal Justice Studies and Signature Area in Law and Society for their support. It has also been a pleasure to work with the superb editorial team at Cambridge Scholars Publishing towards final publication.

Chapter One

Introduction

Consent and Control: Legal Perspectives on State Power

Chris Ashford, Alan Reed and Nicola Wake

The Consent Crucible

Power, Lukes tells us, is essentially a contested concept with three dimensions: influencing the making of decisions, shaping the political agenda to prevent decisions being made, and controlling people's thoughts.[1] Social control, organised through the ways in which society regulates and responds to behaviour that might be considered deviant or troubling,[2] is one way through which power is exercised by the state and this control is often as legal as it is social. This legal control of the deviant or troubling typically manifests itself as criminal law. This body of law defines those actions or activities that the state seeks to prohibit, and enables the punishment of those offenders who transgress these legal rules. At the core of this is the issue of consent and control: those actions and behaviours that one can consent to and those that are controlled.

Debates about consent can act as a crucible in which the citizen and state powers are thrown together, and the new truth(s) constructed by this process are read, understood, and debated through the criminal law.

---

[1] Steven Lukes, *Power: A Radical View* (Palgrave 1974) *passim*.
[2] See more generally: Stanley Cohen, *Visions of Social Control* (Polity 2005).

Since the start of the twenty-first century, Western socio-legal discourse has arguably focused upon 'rights-based' narratives and cultures. These narratives have sought to re-cast the power of the state, re-framing liberal democracy and the power of the citizen. This shift was codified through the Human Rights Act 1998. The then British Prime Minister Tony Blair was to later remark that the Act and the accompanying policy changes 'were not just changes in policy; they were radical departures in the way Britain was governed, in the constitution and in attitude.'[3]

Concomitant to this re-casting of the citizen, the criminal law has faced new interventions from technology, science and culture, all of which have served, at least in part, to re-cast and re-form doctrinal and theoretical debates about consent. Consent, on the one hand, a right-derived discourse, comes into growing conflict with state sanctioned or mandated control and in doing so, tells us much about contemporary society and the state that seeks to govern that society.

Legal Perspectives

In this edited collection, twenty-one authors over the course of the following fifteen chapters seek to offer legal perspectives on consent, recognising and interrogating the often complex relationship that consent has with state control and the expression of state power. This relationship, present pre-, during and post-trial, is analysed in this collection from a range of perspectives including, for example, doctrinal, socio-legal, medico-legal and queer, and draws upon authors from a range of practice and disciplinary backgrounds to offer multi- and inter-disciplinary perspectives on consent and control. The book commences with chapters that seek to understand the broader theoretical and doctrinal landscape of consent.

Ben Livings, in his chapter *Private Authorisation and Public Censure: Negotiating the Limits of Consensual Harm* explores non-sexual violence

---

[3] Tony Blair, *A Journey* (Hutchinson 2010) 26. It is worth noting, as the then Home Secretary Jack Straw subsequently noted, that just eleven months after the Human Rights Act came into force, the terrorist attacks of 11 September took place, ensuring fear became the dominant emotion and national security took priority over individual rights. New criminal sanctions would be rapidly introduced to temper the rights agenda. See, Jack Straw, *Last Man Standing: Memoirs of a Political Survivor* (Macmillan 2012) 282. See more generally, Shami Chakrabarti, *On Liberty* (Allen Lane 2014).

and consent in order to consider what Livings describes as the dichotomy that underlines consent's relation to the criminal law; that 'the significance of consent depends upon the private authorisation of the victim to excuse or justify what would otherwise amount to a public wrong.' His chapter provides a useful framework for engagement with the chapters that follow, considering the theoretical limits of consensual harm that are (re)negotiated. Livings provides us with a foundation, reflecting the inherent challenges in understanding consent within the confines of the symbiotic expression of state power.

Tanya Palmer considers *State Control of Consensual Behaviour through the Sexual Offences Act 2003* and in doing so covers an important overview of the statutory landscape of sexual offences law in England and Wales. The debates contained here, about the limits of sexual autonomy constructed by the State and the constructions of vulnerability, give practical meaning to the dichotomy outlined by Livings in the preceding chapter. Moreover, these debates are cross-jurisdictional in their applicability.

Palmer advocates a radical re-thinking of sexual offences against vulnerable people and in doing so, reimagines the relationship between the state and the individual.

Jess Elvin and Claire de Than consider *Consent to Death*, perhaps an area where the limits on individual freedom and consent and the application of state power is particularly stark and emotive. The authors note that academics along with legal and medical practitioners have long debated this, but in this chapter, the authors seek to move beyond the narrow analysis that has dominated so much of this debate, and offer a comprehensive and thought-provoking appraisal of consensual killing issues from a doctrinal perspective. They compellingly argue that the criminal law is in need of significant reform.

Jonathan Herring explores, in *The Age of Consent in an Age of Consent*, how the law seeks to balance protecting children from abuse, on the one hand, with a desire to 'avoid criminalising "everyday" consensual sexual behaviour between teenagers,' on the other. Herring offers a thoughtful and thought-provoking intervention in this debate, providing a measured discussion of what age any age of consent might be along with a discussion of capacity to consent and capacity as constructed within a broader social and values-based framework. Ultimately, Herring questions the ultimate practical value of an age of consent but if one does exist, that it should be 'high', such as sixteen.

Chris Ashford, in the first of two chapters that seek to draw upon a queer theory perspective to consent, continues the discussion of the age of consent. In *Queering Consent: (Re)evolving Constructions of the Age of Consent and the Law*, Ashford notes the recent re-interest in the origins of the UK socio-legal paedophile activist movement and its connections with the gay rights movement. Set against a background of the ongoing Goddard Inquiry, Ashford explores our shifting understandings and constructions of consent in recent decades and suggests that the conflation of these two political movements for legal change is itself misleading, but that the insights this conflation offers for our (re)evolving constructions of consent remain valid and pertinent for queer radicals in broader agendas of resistance to the contemporary expressions of state power and limits on individual consent.

In *Queering Fear: Pro-LGBTI Refugee Cases*, Senthorun Raj continues this queer political re-appraisal of law, noting the increasing number of jurisdictions that have apparently recognised asylum claims based on sexual orientation and gender identity. Raj notes the dominance of heteronormative frameworks in how LGBTI refugees must demonstrate intimacy, identity and injury, and considers the limitations that such a dominance has for progressive assumptions in this area. Moreover, Raj considers how the concept of fear has been mobilised both in the granting of asylum but also in the responses to the adjudication of it.

In *Rethinking Rape-By-Fraud*, Vera Bergelson offers the first chapter of a number in this collection that seek to examine fraud and deception issues in the context of consent and state power. Starting with the Gayle Newland trial in which Newland was convicted for lying to her female partner about her biological sex, Bergelson explores the question of 'in what circumstances should deception turn the apparently consensual sex into rape?' Bergelson revisits the traditional doctrine of rape-by-fraud and rejects its historical rationales, arguing instead for a different framework which recognises contemporary society and values. The author suggests that the right to sexual autonomy is absolute and yet a violation of this autonomy may not be punishable. Whether it ought to be punishable should, Bergelson suggests, be determined by the interplay of harm and culpability.

Natalia Hanley and Philip Rumney challenge another area sexual consent and rape. In *Perceptions of Consent in Adult Male Rape: Evidence-based and Inclusive Policy Making*, Hanley and Rumney argue that criminal justice policy continues to fail to incorporate research evidence. They argue that policy responses to sexual violence have failed 'to counter rape myths, heteronormative sexual scripts and sexist attitudes.' Hanley and Rumney draw on a series of focus groups which they conducted to explore these attitudes, concluding that there are specific rape scripts that are attached to adult male sexual victimisation and that these scripts are often gendered.

Ben Fitzpatrick contemplates recent controversies surrounding undercover policing in which gender has also been a dynamic factor. In *#Spycops: Undercover Policing, Intimate Relationships and the Manufacture of Consent by the State*, Fitzpatrick explores how key state actors – namely the Police – might raise additional issues of consent through the relationships, particularly intimate relationships, that they might engage in during undercover operations.

Fitzpatrick highlights recent controversies surrounding the practice which has arguably led to what he describes as 'a spectacular unravelling of the fabric of undercover policing.' Fitzpatrick suggests that our collective tolerance of cultivating intimate relationships – such as those in the Mark Kennedy case – should be restricted to exceptional circumstances, if at all.

David Hughes and Alan Reed turn to the issue of criminalisation of *HIV transmission: Anglo-North-American Comparative Perspectives and Optimal Reforms to Failure of Proof Defences*. They note the 2015 review by Law Commission (England and Wales) of the Offences Against the Person Act 1861 and associated offences. Whilst that report held back from offering radical reform of the law pertaining to HIV transmission, the authors put forward an argument for a fresh and urgent legislative intervention in this area. Their analysis focuses upon failure of proof defences and draw upon Anglo-North-American comparative perspectives to advance their analysis. They conclude with legislative proposals that would enable the law to recognise greater management of risk, specifically in relation to condom usage and viral load management.

Rajan Nathan and Keith JB Rix ask if the distinctions between personality disorder and mental illness in clinical and legal practice are justified. In the first of our final section of chapters, each addressing broad themes of treatment or diversion and consent, Nathan and Rix ask: *A Special Case for Personality Disorder: Are the Distinctions between Personality Disorder and Mental Illness in Clinical and Legal Practice Justified?* The authors question the distinction between personality disorders and mental illness, and conclude by pondering the continued advantageous case that is made for legal and clinical approaches to personality disorder in contrast to mental illness. They also note that continuing to make this distinction 'goes against the ride of the theoretical and empirical evidence.'

Linda Steele considers *Diversion of Individuals with Disability from the Criminal Justice System: Control Inside or Outside Criminal Law?* Steele offers an analysis of a specific diversion scheme and ultimately concludes that there does seem to be a relationship 'between law, disability and coercion (and *consent* and *incapacity*) which is central to the way in which the state intervenes in the lives of individuals with disability.'

Ann Creaby-Attwood and Chris Ince consider *Sex Offenders with Autistic Spectrum Conditions*, providing an important intervention in the debate surrounding sex offenders with high functioning autism and offender treatment programmes. They conclude that medical diagnosis is 'now sitting as an uncomfortable bed-fellow with criminal law and sentencing' in cases involving individuals on the autistic spectrum. They highlight the complexities that sex offenders in this category present for law, medicine and ultimately policy making, suggesting that at the very least, greater understanding of these complexities is needed.

In *Consent, Compulsion and Sex offenders: An Ethical and Rights Based Approach to the Treatment and Management of Sex Offenders*, Karen Harrison and Bernadette Rainey consider the 'treatment' response landscape in relation to those who sexually offend. Harrison and Rainey consider two specific responses enabled by law: that of the use of drugs such as libido suppressants (chemical castration) in custody, and managing behaviour upon release. The authors take a rights-based approach to an often emotive and challenging area of law. They note that in considering rights, we must also contemplate risk and explore alternative approaches to the treatment and management of sex offenders such as 'Circles of Support and Accountability.' The authors ultimately argue that policy and legal responses to sex offending need to be more nuanced, and in seeking strategy that effectively reduces risk of offending behaviour, we should engage much more with right-based responses.

Finally, Astrid Birgden offers a practical exploration of sex offender rehabilitation, and notes that in assessing *Consent Versus Coercion: Offender Rights and Community Rights in Sexual Offender Rehabilitation* one needs a more sophisticated analysis that understands the continuum of coercion and consent. Birgden argues that community rights and offender rights need to be balanced, and the various legal and societal actors involved in the rehabilitation process have roles in ensuring this effective balancing.

Together, these chapters highlight the ways that issues of consent and control permeate through our society and criminal justice system, and through a series of theoretical and practical engagements with these themes, offer powerful interventions for our thinking on the application of state power. Collectively, we are forced to re-examine the 'consent crucible' and what that means, not just for the criminal law, but the society that (re)creates and exists within that law.

CHAPTER TWO

PRIVATE AUTHORISATION
AND PUBLIC CENSURE:
NEGOTIATING THE LIMITS
OF CONSENSUAL HARM

BEN LIVINGS

Introduction

The potential relevance of consent to the criminal law spans property
offences such as theft and criminal damage, and sexual and non-sexual
offences of violence,[1] in each of which the consent of the 'victim'[2] may
operate to vitiate the *prima facie* liability of the defendant. A considerable
body of legal doctrine has developed around consent, particularly in
relation to the way in which it is construed, and the conditions under
which apparent consent will translate into legal force. For instance,
minimum age requirements might pertain in order for a person's consent
to be considered legally relevant,[3] or there may be numerous other
demands relating to capacity.[4] Where coercion or deception is used in
order to procure apparent consent, this may be deemed invalid, echoing
the maxim that 'every consent involves a submission; but it by no means

---

[1] Elliott and De Than describe consent as 'a concept that has general application
across the spectrum of criminal law' (Catherine Elliot and Claire de Than, 'A Case
for Rational Reconstruction of Consent in Criminal Law' (2007) 70 Modern Law
Review 225, 228).

[2] The dynamics of consent mean that 'victim' is arguably an inappropriate term in
this context, but it is used in the absence of a better alternative.

[3] See, for example, the age-related provisions of the Sexual Offences Act 2003 and
the Tattooing of Minors Act 1969.

[4] See, for example, the Mental Capacity Act 2005.

follows that a mere submission involves consent'.[5] In the case of consensual physical harm, the availability of consent has proven problematic; that is, what level of consensual harm can be inflicted lawfully, and in what circumstances. This difficulty stems from an inherent dichotomy that underlies consent's relation to the criminal law: the significance of consent depends upon the private authorisation of the victim in order to excuse or justify what would otherwise amount to a public wrong. This chapter looks at this dichotomy in the context of offences of non-sexual violence,[6] and appraises some of the organising principles that have been propounded as a means by which to negotiate the resultant tensions.

The chapter begins by setting out why consent is important for the criminal law, as an expression of private authorisation, before moving to questions about its proper function in light of the public censuring role of the criminal law. People routinely expose themselves to the risk of interpersonal contact and injury, whether this is walking along a crowded street, electing to undergo invasive surgery, or taking part in contact sports, and here consent might override the technical application of the criminal law. Calibrating the availability of consent to harms depends upon public policy judgements, which seek to balance autonomy and the social utility of some risky activities against countervailing priorities in relation to protecting individuals and society. Attempts to develop clear legal rules have raised a fundamental question about the treatment of consent: whether its function is inculpatory (nonconsent as a constituent element of the offence) or exculpatory (consent as a defence, to be applied once the formal requirements of the *prima facie* offence have been made out).[7] At first sight, this may appear a distinction of little significance, beyond procedural demands in relation to allocating evidential burdens at

---

[5] May CJ in R v Dee (1884) 15 Cox CC 579.

[6] That is, where the offence committed is not a sexual offence. Offences of non-sexual violence can be committed in a sexual context, without amounting to a sexual offence (see, for example: *R v Dica* [2004] EWCA Crim 1103; [2004] QB 1257).

[7] In its reflections on the role of consent in relation to interpersonal violence, the Law Commission clearly felt this to be an unresolved issue and, in approaching the question, used what it termed 'neutral expressions' (Law Commission, *Consent and Offences Against the Person* (Law Com CP No 134, 1994) 1).

trial,[8] but the majority judgments in *Brown*, and commentators such as Bergelson and Gardner, posit this distinction as one that can be of assistance when it comes to understanding and imposing the proper limits to consensual violence and injury.

Consent as Private Authorisation

Some of the difficulties associated with devising a comprehensive rule system in relation to consent stem from the breadth of its meaning. To say that a person 'consents' may signify any of a range of mental states, such as desire, permission, or acquiescence; or it may denote the communication or expression of these. For instance, the consent of a patient may be said to exist where they accede to the treatment offered by a doctor following diagnosis, or where they actively pursue a course of treatment. In *Bree*, the Court of Appeal described consent to sexual intercourse as extending from 'passionate enthusiasm to reluctant or bored acquiescence'. [9] Whilst the similarities may be sufficient for the overarching term to cover such expansive territory, it is clear that, from an ontological or semiotic perspective, 'there is no single "essence of consent"'. [10] Westen writes of 'a single concept with a multiplicity of competing conceptions', [11] while, for Cowling, consent is best understood as comprising 'an overlapping series of meanings'. [12]

Howsoever its 'overlapping meanings' are construed and accommodated by the criminal law, the effect of consent is roughly synonymous with authorisation, and this renders it an intuitively significant concept. Consent has the potential to affect the quality of relationships in a profound way, and the private authorisation it represents means that its presence can be morally relevant and legally transformative when it comes to interpersonal conduct. Hurd offers a powerful and widely cited characterisation of the 'moral magic' of consent in legitimising otherwise wrongful conduct:

---

[8] As Kell notes, this is not itself insignificant (David Kell, 'Social Disutility and the Law of Consent' (1994) 14 Oxford Journal of Legal Studies 121, 132-33).

[9] *R v Bree* [2007] EWCA Crim 804, [2008] QB 131, 139 (Lord Judge LJ).

[10] Mark Cowling, *Date Rape and Consent* (Ashgate 1998) 82.

[11] Peter Westen, *The Logic of Consent: The Diversity and Deceptiveness of Consent as a Defence to Criminal Conduct* (Ashgate 2004) 309.

[12] Cowling (n 10).

[C]onsent can function to transform the morality of another's conduct – to make an action right when it would otherwise be wrong. For example, consent turns a trespass into a dinner party; a battery into a handshake; a theft into a gift; an invasion of privacy into an intimate moment; a commercial appropriation of name and likeness into a biography.[13]

The transformative power with which Hurd imbues consent is closely related to, and derives from, the important liberal value of autonomy, which has been described as 'the unifying principle that underpins the concept of consent'.[14] Feinberg asserts that 'the kernel of the idea of autonomy is the right to make choices and decisions',[15] and consent is an important and useful concept because it can facilitate the exercise of 'personal sovereignty'.[16]

In making his claims about the significance of the role of consent, Feinberg draws on the 'harm principle', a foundational concept when it comes to the political basis of the criminal law, and to demarcating its legitimate scope according to liberal principles. In his original iteration of the harm principle, Mill wrote that 'the only purpose for which power can be rightfully exercised over any member of a civilized community, against his will, is to prevent harm to others. His own good, either physical or moral, is not a sufficient warrant'.[17] In the centuries since this statement, the harm principle has been appraised and criticised on many occasions,[18] and more sophisticated articulations have been developed.[19] Nevertheless,

---

[13] Heidi Hurd, 'The Moral Magic of Consent' (1996) 2 Legal Theory 121, 121.

[14] Elliot and de Than (n 1) 231.

[15] Joel Feinberg, *The Moral Limits of the Criminal Law: Harm to Self* (Oxford University Press 1986) 54.

[16] ibid.

[17] John Stuart Mill, *On Liberty* (Longman, Green & Co 1865) 6.

[18] John Stanton-Ife points out: 'it is a little misleading to speak of the "Harm Principle" as one principle shared by all the leading thinkers associated with the principle' (John Stanton-Ife, 'The Limits of Law', *The Stanford Encyclopedia of Philosophy* (Winter edn, 2014) <http://plato.stanford.edu/archives/win2014/entries/law-limits/> accessed 12 January 2015).

[19] See, for example: Joel Feinberg, *The Moral Limits of the Criminal Law: Harm to Others* (Oxford University Press 1984); Joel Feinberg, *The Moral Limits of the Criminal Law: Offense to Others* (Oxford University Press 1985); Feinberg (n 15); Joel Feinberg, *The Moral Limits of the Criminal Law: Harmless Wrongdoing* (Oxford University Press 1988). For contrasting perspectives on the harm

the base proposition remains influential in liberal conceptions of the limits
of the criminal law.

Adherence to the harm principle offers strong *prima facie* support for the
significance of consent, as its anti-paternalistic invocations favour
autonomy,[20] and this naturally includes control over 'what contacts with
my body to permit'.[21] If a person wishes to engage in an activity that
entails injury, or the risk thereof, this can be construed as the exercise of
personal sovereignty. The authorising effect of consent might even be held
to extend to a person's right to consent to conduct on the part of another
that will lead to their own death; Roberts asserts: 'It is entirely in keeping
with respect for autonomy that a person should be able to consent to his or
her own death; indeed, autonomy demands that such a choice should be
respected'.[22] A strict interpretation of the concept of personal sovereignty
can serve to authorise some extreme conduct: German Armin Meiwes was
tried and convicted in 2004, following his apparently consensual killing
and eating of Bernd Juergen Brandes.[23] A libertarian adherent to the harm
principle may argue that, even where it leads to such drastic consequences,
Brandes's autonomy, and thus his consent, should be respected. Under this
view, Meiwes's conduct should be judged in light of the quality of the
consent offered by Brandes; if it is given freely, the exercise of personal
sovereignty his consent represents renders inappropriate the imposition of
criminal liability.

Balancing Consent and Public Wrongs

Consent is a powerful force when it comes to the pursuit of liberal goals,
but there are evident tensions between the private function of consent and
the public role of the criminal law when it comes to censuring conduct.
Whatever the moral force of consent in denoting acquiescence or desire,

principle, see: John Gardner, *Offences and Defences* (Oxford University Press
2007); Douglas Husak, *Overcriminalization: The Limits of the Criminal Law*
(Oxford University Press 2008).

[20] Paul Roberts writes of it as 'underpinned by the liberal value of autonomy' (Law
Commission, *Consent in the Criminal Law* (Law Com CP No 139, 1995) para
C.54).

[21] Feinberg (n 15).

[22] Law Commission, *Consent in the Criminal Law* (Law Com CP No 139, 1995)
para C.54.

[23] http://news.bbc.co.uk/1/hi/world/europe/4752797.stm.

and creating private authorisations between individuals, the criminal law is ostensibly concerned with public wrongs and harms. Since a crime is nominally committed against the State,[24] the consent of the person who suffers injury is of questionable importance; conduct that is privately authorised may nevertheless legitimately invite public censure. In making this point, Dempsey marks the distinction between the private relationships that lie at the heart of tortious disputes, and the relationship to the State that is invoked by the criminal law:

> In criminal law, as distinct from tort, the party with standing to complain against wrongful conduct is the State—not the injured party. Thus, if B consents to A's punching him, the fact that B's consent strips B of standing to complain against A is of no consequence to criminal law—for, in criminal law, B has no standing to complain against A in any event.[25]

Dempsey provides a sceptical account of the significance of consent in the criminal law, and its ability to affect the quality of the defendant's conduct, since the private authorisation it represents does not affect the State's 'standing' when it comes to the imposition of criminal liability; it is 'of no consequence for the criminal law'.

The potential otiosity of consent to the question of criminal liability is regularly noted by the criminal courts, and was addressed in the following terms by the Court of Appeal in *Donovan*: 'If an act is unlawful in the sense of being in itself a criminal act, it is plain that it cannot be rendered lawful because the person to whose detriment it is done consents to it. No person can license another to commit a crime'.[26] In *Donovan*, where a man had caned a woman for his own sexual fulfilment, this meant that where an act was 'likely or intended to do bodily harm',[27] there was no need to prove consent, since the fact that it was consensual could not alter the criminal nature of the conduct.

Cases such as *Donovan* illustrate a limitation on the power of consent: the State may retain an interest in criminalising behaviour even where it is

---

[24] See Grant Lamond, 'What is a Crime?' (2007) Oxford Journal of Legal Studies 609.

[25] Michelle Madden Dempsey, 'Victimless Conduct and the Volenti Maxim: How Consent Works' (2013) 7 Criminal Law and Philosophy 11, 13.

[26] *R v Donovan* [1934] 2 KB 498 (CA), 507 (Swift J).

[27] ibid.

consensual and therefore privately authorised by the injured party. The dichotomy between the private 'licensing' of behaviour and the public nature of the concept of crime means that the application of the harm principle to the criminal law is commonly held to be subject to qualifications and compromise, and even Feinberg's avowedly liberal interpretation allows for a number of 'mediating maxims' and 'liberty-limiting principles'.[28] The application of such restraints on the availability and operation of consent seeks to acknowledge and accommodate within the criminal law the deeper personal and social harms that can result from consensual violence and injury.[29]

There are many forms of conduct that are criminalised by virtue of an absolute bar on consensual activity. For instance, if a surgeon (or indeed any other person) is performing an act of female genital mutilation, the consent of the parties will not serve to vitiate the criminality of the conduct.[30] Further examples include illegal abortion,[31] and the continuing criminality of voluntary euthanasia and assisting suicide.[32] Other conduct is not criminalised *per se*, but certain classes of persons may be prohibited from engaging in it; for example, the absolute ineffectiveness of consent to sexual intercourse where the person is under the age of 13,[33] or the prohibition on the tattooing of minors.[34]

As these examples illustrate, the criminal law 'takes the position that there are numerous harms that all persons are incompetent to inflict or allow to

---

[28] Feinberg (n 15) xvi.

[29] Anderson points out that in considering the question of when and to what a person should be able to consent, Feinberg's sophisticated account of the harm principle is infused with a core of 'soft paternalism' that cannot but look to the social utility of the activity in question when making the judgement as to how it is to be treated by the criminal law (Jack Anderson, *The Legality of Boxing: A Punch-Drunk Love?* (Birkbeck Law Press 2007) 144).

[30] Female Genital Mutilation Act 2003.

[31] Abortion Act 1967. See: http://www.chroniclelive.co.uk/news/north-east-news/county-durham-mum-jailed-diy-10618161.

[32] Suicide Act 1961, s 2. See: http://www.itv.com/news/westcountry/2015-12-17/assisted-suicide-man-charged-with-helping-a-person-die-in-exeter/. There have been repeated attempts to change the law in this respect, the most recent of which is the Assisted Dying Bill, introduced by Lord Falconer, and which received its first reading in the House of Lords in June 2015.

[33] Sexual Offences Act 2003, s 5.

[34] Tattooing of Minors Act 1969.

be inflicted upon themselves, regardless of how much they consciously desire them'.[35] The concerns outlined above suffuse the House of Lords' judgment in *R v Brown*, the leading statement of the current limits of consensual harm under the criminal law, and are reflected in Lord Templeman's objection to the appellants' argument that 'every person has a right to deal with his person as he pleases':

> I do not consider that this slogan provides a sufficient guide to the policy decision which must now be made. It is an offence for a person to abuse his own body and mind by taking drugs. Although the law is often broken, the criminal law restrains a practice which is regarded as dangerous and injurious to individuals and which if allowed and extended is harmful to society generally.[36]

The rationale of this passage reflects the earlier view of Stephen J in *Coney*, who noted that consent to an injury would not be effective where the nature or circumstances of that injury mean that 'its infliction is injurious to the public as well as to the person injured'.[37]

The moral values and principles underpinning policy moves which proscribe consensual behaviour are often unclear; as Westen points out, '[i]t is difficult to determine whether Anglo-American law bases the prohibitions upon the view that the underlying conduct is not good for [the victim] (…), or upon the view that the conduct violates shared morality'.[38] Constraints on the freedom of individuals to engage in consensual harm may be characterised as examples of paternalism or of legal moralism,[39] and the State may view such limitations as necessary, notwithstanding the potential impact upon a person's autonomy. These limitations depend upon the quality of the conduct to which the consent is being offered and its effect on the victim, and are informed by a moral view of the consensual harm, and concomitant public policy concerns. The extent to which consensual harm will be considered lawful is therefore inevitably shaped by contingent factors, and will vary

---

[35] Westen (n 11) 129.

[36] *R v Brown* [1994] 1 AC 212 (HL), 235 (Lord Templeman).

[37] *R v Coney* (1882) 8 QBD 534, 549 (Stephen J).

[38] Westen (n 11) 129.

[39] See, for example: Paul Roberts, 'Philosophy, Feinberg, Codification, and Consent: A Progress Report on English Experiences of Criminal Law Reform' (2001-02) 5 Buffalo Criminal Law Review 173.

according to prevailing social mores.[40]

Negotiating the Limits of Consensual Harm

Consent is a potentially powerful force, but the private authority it represents is limited insofar as it can vitiate or otherwise affect criminal liability. The dichotomy at the heart of consent means that it must draw its authority from a broader source than simply that which might be gleaned from the views and perspectives of the individuals involved. The question of how to decide upon the nature and degree of limitations to the availability of consent is of fundamental importance to the coherence and operation of the criminal law, and there have been attempts to formulate clear criteria that can be used in order to establish definitive legal rules. In *Brown*, Lord Slynn enunciated this requirement in straightforward terms: '[a] line has to be drawn as to what can and as to what cannot be the subject of consent'.[41] In addressing this task, the Law Lords set out to organise principles by which to assess the operation of consent in different contexts.

Before examining these organising principles, it is worth noting that such concerns are not unique to consent; the availability of other 'defences' – such as duress, necessity and self-defence[42] – is also subject to public policy limitations. Where a defendant has committed a violent act against another, and is relying upon one of these defences in order to vitiate liability, it is necessary but not sufficient for the defendant to argue that he was in a position where he felt under duress, or that he considered a course of action necessary, or that a course of action was undertaken in self-defence. In addition to the requisite subjective belief, it must also be established that the 'reasonable man' placed in the defendant's position would, or might, also behave in this way, in order for any of these

---

[40] The Court of Appeal has held that 'the categories of activity [involving consensual harm] regarded as lawful are not closed, and equally, they are not immutable', and their expansion and contraction is inevitable (*Dica* (n 6) 1269 (Judge LJ)).

[41] *Brown* (n 36) 279.

[42] Whether consent is properly described as a 'defence' is often unclear. Likewise, it can be argued that duress, necessity and self-defence are not 'true' defences, since the onus on establishing that they do not pertain remains on the prosecution.

defences to succeed.[43] Thus, the availability of duress, necessity and self-defence is restricted by reference to an objective normative standard. This requirement reflects the status of (in this case violent) crime as constituting a public wrong, and is designed to calibrate the respective defences according to social standards, in order to preclude their use where it would be against the public interest.

When it comes to consent to injury, or risk thereof, it might be argued that the need for calibration of its availability and operation against social standards is no less important, and attempts have been made to realise this. One means by which the court in *Brown* seeks to achieve harmonisation between social standards and the criminal response to consensual violence is by reference to the quantum of harm suffered; by allowing consent to injury which is less serious, but denying it where more serious injury has been caused. Adopting this approach allowed the Law Lords to differentiate along the lines of the offences, which are also stratified *inter alia* according to the severity of injury caused.[44] Lord Templeman stated: 'When no actual bodily harm is caused, the consent of the person affected precludes him from complaining. There can be no conviction for the summary offence of common assault if the victim has consented to the assault'.[45] Lord Lowry deemed this uncontroversial, asserting: 'Everyone agrees that consent remains a complete defence to a charge of common assault'.[46] Under this general rule, therefore, a threshold is set whereby violence towards another will not bring criminal liability where it is consensual, and where it causes injury that is no more than 'merely transient and trifling'.[47]

---

[43] This, of course, is a simplification of the operation of duress, necessity and self-defence. On self-defence, see: *R v Wilson* [2005] Crim LR 108.

[44] As Lord Templeman noted: 'There are now three types of assault in ascending order of gravity, first common assault, secondly assault which occasions actual bodily harm and thirdly assault which inflicts grievous bodily harm' (*Brown* (n 36) 230).

[45] ibid 231.

[46] ibid 248.

[47] Lord Templeman invoked the judgment of Swift J in *R v Donovan*: '"bodily harm" has its ordinary meaning and includes any hurt or injury calculated to interfere with the health or comfort of the prosecutor. Such hurt or injury need not be permanent, but must, no doubt, be more than merely transient and trifling' ([1934] 2 KB 498, 509, cited in *Brown* (n 36) 230).

The House of Lords held that injury below the threshold of 'actual bodily harm' could be the subject of consent without qualification, and suggested that, in such sub-threshold cases, nonconsent on the part of the victim is inculpatory; that is, the absence of consent is necessary in order to fulfil the offence requirements. This approach can be traced through the case law relating to consensual physical harm. In the middle of the nineteenth century, Lord Denman CJ considered it 'a manifest contradiction in terms to say that the defendant assaulted the plaintiff by his permission',[48] and this was taken up in the prizefighting case of *Coney*, in which Hawkins J was of the view that an assault could only be described as such if there was no consent on the part of the victim:

> As a general proposition it is undoubtedly true that there can be no assault unless the act charged as such be done without the consent of the person alleged to be assaulted, for want of consent is an essential element in every assault, and that which is done by consent is no assault at all.[49]

Later, Williams wrote that it is 'inherent in the conception of assault and battery that the victim does not consent',[50] and, in *Attorney-General's Reference (No 6 of 1980)*, the Court of Appeal considered the 'absence of consent' to be 'part of the definition of assault',[51] so that 'ordinarily an act consented to will not constitute an assault'.[52]

In *Brown*, the House of Lords considered the availability of consent to minor harm to be uncontroversial, and universally applicable. Where this is so, it is arguably unproblematic to consider nonconsent to be a constituent part of the offence, since the universal availability of consent does not impinge unduly upon the offences by introducing complexity, nor does it overly moralise or politicise them. Its inclusion within the offence definition can be used to promote coherence and predictability of application when it comes to the offence requirements. This Norrie refers to the aspiration for a 'technical offence core', whereby *offences* are constituted by reasonably robust and consistent legal principles; and moral considerations that might pertain in exceptional situations can be

---

[48] *Christopherson v Bare* (1848) 11 QB 473, 477.

49 *Coney* (n 37) 549.

[50] Glanville Williams, 'Consent and Public Policy' [1962] Criminal Law Review 74, 75.

[51] *A-G's Reference (No 6 of 1980)* (1981) 1 QB 715 (CA), 717 (Lord Lane CJ).

[52] ibid 719 (Lord Lane CJ).

categorised as separate *defences*, contained in what Norrie terms the 'moral defence periphery'.[53]

Qualifying Harm and Exceptional Categories

Although the quantitative distinction outlined above is approved in *Brown*, its use when deciding upon the availability of consent has been criticised. As Roberts notes, 'criminal wrongs cannot be reduced to the *degree,* or severity, of bodily injury inflicted or suffered'.[54] Instead, it is necessary to look at the circumstances in which that injury has been inflicted.

> If for no other reason than to relieve your boredom you come up to me in the street and deliberately kick me in the shins, that is a (relatively minor) criminal offense even though it causes me little if any discomfort. Yet the surgeon who with my consent cuts open my gums, gouges out my wisdom teeth and stitches up the wound, causing me (…) considerable pain, commits no offense. As Lord Mustill wisely observed in his dissenting judgment in *Brown*: 'Circumstances must alter cases'.[55]

A distinction founded in quantity of injury does not capture satisfactorily the normative difference between these two examples, since it takes no account of the broader context in which the consent was given.

The sado-masochistic practices under discussion in *Brown* involved the infliction of injuries that exceeded the quantitative threshold of the general rule outlined above, and the House of Lords was faced with the question of whether they should be considered as lawful notwithstanding this.[56] By analogy, the Law Lords considered the lawfulness of a variety of activities in which there is an inevitability or likelihood of injury amounting to or exceeding the threshold of actual bodily harm. Lord Templeman spoke for the majority in saying:

> Even when violence is intentionally inflicted and results in actual bodily harm, wounding or serious bodily harm the accused is entitled to be acquitted if the injury was a foreseeable incident of a lawful activity in

---

[53] Alan Norrie, *Crime, Reason and History* (3rd edn, Cambridge University Press 2014); Alan Norrie, *Punishment, Responsibility and Justice* (Oxford University Press 2000).
[54] Roberts (n 39).
[55] ibid 219.
[56] *Brown* (n 36).

which the person injured was participating. Surgery, (...) ritual
circumcision, tattooing, ear-piercing and violent sports including boxing
are lawful activities.[57]

Lord Templeman therefore marks out particular activities as deserving of
an exceptional status; a status that allows those activities that qualify to
involve lawful consensual violence that causes injury at or above the level
of actual bodily harm.[58] This demarcation of a category of lawful activities
operates to exclude those practices that cannot be brought within its
confines, and precludes all other forms of consensual violence that involve
causing injury at or above the threshold level of actual bodily harm.

Whereas the implementation of the quantitative test works by reference to
the offence definitions, and therefore allows for a *legal* distinction to be
made, the demarcation of a category of 'lawful activities' is an overtly
moral and *political* calculation, and the value judgements that lie at the
heart of this are open to criticism on a number of grounds. Kell describes
the approach as constituting a 'social utility' test, the basis of which is
fundamentally opposed to what he perceives as the properly liberal basis
of the criminal law, under which there is a presumption of legality.[59]
Roberts takes a similar view, and argues that the exceptionary approach
'reverses the traditional common law presumption, that everything is
lawful unless expressly proscribed, by extending criminal sanctions to
conduct simply because the legislature has not (yet) had occasion to
consider the case for exemption'.[60] For Roberts, this constitutes 'a
disturbingly expansionist tendency in the criminal law'.[61] To ameliorate
this particular flaw, he suggests 'the formulation of particularistic rules to
proscribe only those *specific forms* of consensual injury deemed worthy of
criminal prohibition'.[62] As Kell explains, this means reversing the

---

[57] *Brown* (n 36) 231.

[58] To this list can be added 'general horseplay' (see *R v Aitken and Others* (1992) 1
WLR 1006 (C-MAC)), an unwieldy category that Lord Mustill justified as follows:
'The law recognises that community life (...) such as exists in the school
playground, in the barrack-room and on the factory floor, may involve a mutual
risk of deliberate physical contact in which a particular recipient (...) may come
off worst, and that the criminal law cannot be too tender about the susceptibilities
of those involved'.

[59] Kell (n 8).

[60] Roberts (n 39) 239.

[61] ibid 239.

[62] ibid. On this, see also: Marianne Giles, 'R v Brown: Consensual Harm and the

presumption; he advocates a 'social disutility' model whereby consent to harm would be effective, 'unless the prosecution is able to provide persuasive reasons for prohibiting particular conduct'.[63] Kell points out that the adoption of a social disutility test presents a lower explanatory hurdle for practices that should not be criminalised; he offers tattooing and ear-piercing as examples of activities that are difficult to justify as 'needed in the public interest', but notes that it is 'equally difficult to state why the public interest would require their prohibition'.[64]

Kell's and Roberts's shared preference for presumptive lawfulness is a matter of liberal principle, but the exceptionary approach elucidated by Lord Templeman is also susceptible to criticism on the grounds of imprecision, as the example of contact sports demonstrates: it is to be presumed that formal iterations of mainstream sports are included as 'lawful activities', but there is little guidance when it comes to the less formal manifestations that might occur during training sessions, or in ad hoc, informal games between friends in a park or schoolyard. As Roberts observes, 'one can always envisage forms of nontraditional medicine or new leisure pursuits which might end up criminalized, simply through oversight'.[65] Under this analysis, the lawfulness of benign and even socially beneficent activities is potentially unclear, and they may be under threat from discriminatory or capricious prosecution.

Offence-Types and Non/Violation of Prohibitory Norms

There are evident difficulties in the application of the organising principles propounded by the House of Lords in *Brown*, and it is worthwhile looking to the attempts of others who have tried to make sense of the limits on consent in this context. Bergelson and Gardner are amongst commentators who have also attempted to rationalise and enunciate the relationship

---

Public Interest' (1994) 57 Modern Law Review 101; Sue Streets, 'S & M in the House of Lords' (1993) 18 Alternative Law Journal 233; Brian Bix, 'Assault, Sado-Masochism and Consent' (1993) 109 Law Quarterly Review 540; Kell (n 8).

[63] Kell (n 8) 127.

[64] Kell (n 8) 128. This is not to say that these are uncontested moral issues, particularly when it comes to minors. Although the tattooing of minors is unlawful, the criminal law is largely silent when it comes to piercing, aside from the application of indecent assault in the event of genital - or (for females) nipple-piercing.

[65] Roberts (n 39) 239.

between consent and harm under the criminal law.[66] Their respective arguments are framed differently to those advanced in the majority judgments in *Brown*. Instead of constructing rules based upon the quantum of injury caused, supplemented by categories of 'lawful activity', Bergelson and Gardner look to 'offence-types', and distinguish those which constitute the violation of a 'prohibitory norm' from those which do not. Bergelson writes:

> Compare cases of rape, kidnapping, or theft on the one hand, and cases of killing or maiming on the other. In the first group of cases, the *act itself* does not violate a prohibitory norm. Having sex, transporting someone to a different location, or taking other people's property is not bad *in itself*. It becomes bad *only* due to the absence of consent.[67]

Depending on the type of offence, Bergelson suggests that whether nonconsent is inculpatory or consent exculpatory depends upon whether or not the conduct in question is construed as violating a prohibitory norm. Where the conduct does not violate a prohibitory norm, Bergelson proposes that nonconsent is inculpatory: 'no matter how we draft the statute, in cases of theft, rape, or kidnapping, the absence of consent is *inculpatory* – nonconsent is a part of the definition of the offense'.[68] In contrast, for offences where the act violates a prohibitory norm, such as violent offences, consent acts as an exculpatory defence.

Gardner uses a similar distinction when he writes that 'there is no general reason not to have sexual intercourse', and contrasts this with offences where physical injury is an inherent element: 'Actual bodily harm is *per se* an unwelcome turn of events, even when consensual; sexual intercourse is not *per se* an unwelcome turn of events, but becomes one by virtue of being non-consensual'.[69] Gardner draws the same conclusion as Bergelson, and argues that the distinction 'is captured in the law's treatment of consent under the "defence" heading in assault occasioning actual bodily harm, but under the "offence" heading in rape'.[70] According

---

[66] Vera Bergelson, 'Consent to Harm' in Franklin Miller and Alan Wertheimer, *The Ethics of Consent: Theory and Practice* (Oxford University Press 2010); Gardner (n 19).

[67] Bergelson (n 66) 171.

[68] ibid.

[69] Gardner (n 19) 144.

[70] ibid.

to both Bergelson and Gardner, therefore, the type of offence dictates whether its commission violates a prohibitory norm. This, in turn, indicates whether consent functions as an exculpatory defence, or whether its absence is a constituent element of the offence.

The analytical frameworks that Bergelson and Gardner present offer an appealingly straightforward means by which to structure the role of consent, and from here to work out rules relating to its availability and operation. The application of such a distinction can be seen in *Dica*,[71] which concerned the appeal of a man who had been convicted as a result of recklessly transmitting HIV to multiple partners through sexual intercourse. In the facts of *Dica*, there lay the potential issue of consent in two respects: that of consent to sexual intercourse, and that of consent to (the risk of) being infected with HIV. There is no suggestion in *Dica* that the consent to sexual intercourse was invalid (which would raise the possibility of rape), but there was considerable discussion by the Court of Appeal as to whether consent would be available to counter a charge under section 20 of the Offences Against the Person Act 1861, where the defendant had recklessly infected the victim with HIV. The separability of the consent involved here is notable, as is the fact that it is referred to as a 'defence' in the context of the section 20 offence.

Dica lends support to the usefulness of prohibitory norm violation as an aid to structuring consideration of consent, and, in that particular case, this involved the appraisal of consent against different types of offence. However, tying the delineation of the boundaries of prohibitory norms to 'offence-types' will often rely upon drawing arbitrary distinctions in much the same way as the demarcation based on quantum of injury. This can be demonstrated by reference to rape, an offence-type that both Bergelson and Gardner suggest derives from behaviour that does not violate a prohibitory norm. However, sexual intercourse with a person under the age of 13 is a form of rape that amounts to an absolute liability offence for which consent, or indeed a mistake as to consent or age, will not avail the defendant.[72] Here, to say that 'having sex (...) is not bad *in itself*',[73] or that 'there is no general reason not to have sexual intercourse',[74] is surely not

---

[71] *Dica* (n 6).
[72] Sexual Offences Act 2003, s 5.
[73] Gardner (n 19).
[74] Bergelson (n 66) 171.

true. Whilst the offence of 'rape of a child under 13' could be categorised as in itself violating a prohibitory norm, and therefore as a different offence-type from other instances of rape, to do so undermines the clear categorisation and demarcation that Gardner and Bergelson present. Similarly, it seems strange to characterise 'actual bodily harm' as *'per se* an unwelcome turn of events'* where it takes the form of necessary and beneficent surgical interference, such as the removal of a tumorous growth, or a wart.

Conclusion

Setting the boundaries of consensual harm is a difficult task, complicated by the dichotomy between private authorisation and public censure that lies at the heart of consent and its application to the criminal law. The formulation of legal rules depends upon policy judgements that seek to strike a balance between 'personal sovereignty' and the broader public interest. The realities of quotidian human interaction demand an acceptance of the risk of harm; in *Collins v Wilcock*,[75] the Court of Appeal suggested that 'the physical contacts of ordinary life' are 'not actionable because they are impliedly consented to by all who move in society and so expose themselves to the risk of bodily contact'. Beyond this, socially useful endeavours such as surgical treatment or contact sports subject those involved to the risk or inevitability of (sometimes serious) physical injury. This is well accepted by the criminal courts; in *Brown*, Lord Templeman stated that 'the courts have accepted that consent is a defence to the infliction of bodily harm in the course of some lawful activities'.[76]

The majority judgments in *Brown* purport to set out technical legal rules as to the availability and operation of consent to physical violence and injury. Under the quantitative approach laid out in *Brown*, valid consent is generally permissible where it is to injury that falls short of actual bodily harm, even when caused recklessly or intentionally. This offence-based and pragmatic distinction cannot tell the whole story, and the Law Lords held that this threshold did not apply to exceptional 'lawful activities', thus reintroducing a moral and political calculation. Taking a different approach, Bergelson and Gardner point to the normative difference in how consent should operate, according to whether or not the conduct violates a

---

[75] *Collins v Wilcock* [1984] 1 WLR 1172 (DC).
[76] *Brown* (n 36) 234 (Lord Templeman).

'prohibitory norm'. They suggest that this standard can be construed so as to correlate to 'offence-types', thereby also implying a legal basis for the availability of consent. The analysis of the relationship between prohibitory norms and the operation of consent is promising, but this simply in terms of offence-types will often rely upon making arbitrary distinctions. The contours of prohibitory norms are contingent upon those of social norms, and classifying something as 'not bad *in itself*' or an 'unwelcome turn of events' is a moral calculation that does not always fall to be judged according to legal categories. As Norrie points out, 'all moral judgments are "all things considered" judgments'.[77]

---

[77] Alan Norrie, *Punishment, Responsibility and Justice* (Oxford University Press 2000) 154.

CHAPTER THREE

STATE CONTROL OF CONSENSUAL SEXUAL BEHAVIOUR THROUGH THE SEXUAL OFFENCES ACT 2003

TANYA PALMER

Introduction

The Sexual Offences Act 2003 prohibits non-consensual sexual activity through the offences of rape and sexual assault. This reflects an emphasis on autonomy as a key value at stake in sexual offences, and a construction of consent as the hallmark of autonomous action. Alongside the non-consensual offences, the Act also prohibits ostensibly consensual sexual behaviour in a range of circumstances. These additional offences centre on objectivist criteria including the identity of the victim (children and persons with mental disorders), the relationship between the parties (familial relationships and other positions of trust), and the exchange of money for sexual services. State intrusion into these activities through the criminal law is justified on the basis that it protects vulnerable people from harm, a claim which abrogates the need for proof of non-consent. Despite claims of a new approach to vulnerability that would move away from the status-based approach of the old law, the 2003 Act continues to categorise specific groups of people as 'vulnerable' and to subject their sexual behaviour to increased scrutiny and control.

In the first part of this chapter I introduce the non-consensual offences, which are straightforwardly constructed as violations of sexual autonomy. In the second part of the chapter I give an overview of the sexual exploitation offences involving children, people with mental disorders, familial sexual relationships and commercial sex, and demonstrate that the rationale of protection from harm is used to justify greater state intrusion in these contexts, to an extent that is in some cases draconian and oppressive. In the third part I draw out some commonalities between the exploitation offences, exploring some of the negative consequences for those affected. Whilst explicitly recognizing that these offences criminalise much behaviour that is genuinely abusive and worthy of criminalization, I question the way that this behaviour is organized between the different offences and advocate a re-examination of the relationship between non-consent and exploitation. In the final part, I locate the uneasy relationship between the different groups of sexual offences as reflective of overarching conceptions of the liberal subject and its incompatibility with the notion of vulnerability. Drawing on the work of Martha Fineman, I advocate a radical rethinking of legal and political subjectivity which recognises vulnerability as a universal human condition rather than an attribute of particular populations. Rethinking the sexual offences against vulnerable people is thus part of a broader reimagining of the relationship between the state and the individual.

Consent and the Sexual Offences Act 2003

In 2000, the Sex Offences Review published the report of its comprehensive evaluation of sexual offences in England and Wales.[1] The recommendations of the Review, with some adjustments, formed the basis of the Sexual Offences Act 2003. The Review set out two key 'guiding principles' to steer its proposals. The first, which I have termed *protection from harm*, states that, 'what is right and wrong [as embodied in sexual offences law] should be based on an assessment of the harm done to the individual (and through the individual to society as a whole).'[2] The second, which I have termed *freedom from state interference*, states that, 'the criminal law should not intrude unnecessarily into the private life of adults.'[3] The concept of consent plays a central role in operationalizing both of these principles.

In relation to the principle of protection from harm, the Sexual Offences Act 2003 prohibits a range of non-consensual sexual activity under the offences of rape, assault by penetration, sexual assault and causing sexual activity without consent.[4] According to the Sex Offences Review, which preceded the 2003 Act:

---

[1] Home Office, 'Setting the Boundaries: Reforming the Law on Sexual Offences' (Home Office Communication Directorate 2000).

[2] ibid iv.

[3] ibid iv.

[4] Sexual Offences Act 2003 ss1-4.

> Consent is the crucial issue for these offences because the lack of consent is the essence of the criminal behaviour. It is one individual forcing another to undergo an experience against their will. It is a violation of the victim's autonomy and freedom to decide how and with whom she (or he) would want to share any kind of sexual experience.[5]

Consent here is treated as the hallmark of autonomous action, while non-consensual sexual activity is treated as a violation which individuals should be protected from.

With regard to the principle of freedom from state interference, the Review recommended the repeal or reframing of several offences which prohibited consensual sexual behaviour. The clearest example of this is the recommendation that the offences of buggery and indecency between men,[6] which prohibited same sex sexual behaviour between men in specified circumstances, be repealed. This recommendation was adopted in the Sexual Offences Act 2003. By the time the 2003 Act was passed, the circumstances in which consensual activity between men was prohibited had in fact been severely curtailed by a series of amendments.[7] In addition, the review asserted that 'those aspects of the offences providing protection for children, vulnerable people and animals would be replaced by our other proposals.'[8] Thus the significance of repealing the offences was as much rhetorical as substantive: any behaviour currently encompassed by these offences which ought to remain criminal should be framed so as to emphasise the harm caused, as opposed to being framed around the idea that same sex activity is deviant or wrongful in and of itself.

In summary then, consent in the Sexual Offences Act 2003 functions as a barrier to physical interference by other individuals, and as a barrier – or at least a hurdle – to interference in one's sexual relationships by the state. I refer to the latter as a hurdle rather than a barrier because the principle against state interference is not absolute. It provides only a general rule against legal intrusion, one which can be disregarded where 'necessary'.[9] As a result, the 2003 Act in fact prohibits ostensibly consensual sexual

---

[5] Home Office (n 1) 9.
[6] Sexual Offences Act 1956 ss12-13.
[7] Sexual Offences (Amendment) Act 2000 ss1-2; Criminal Justice and Public Order Act 1994 s143; Sexual Offences Act 1967 s1.
[8] Home Office (n 1) vii.
[9] ibid iv.

behaviour in a wide range of circumstances, as I explore in the following section.

Protection from Harm and the Prohibition of Consensual Sexual Activity

Much of the discussion in the Sex Offences Review focuses on striking a balance between the two guiding principles described above – protection from harm and freedom from state interference. Arguably however, these two principles were not placed on equal footing. The principle of freedom from state interference is explained in the review as follows:

> Our other key guiding principle was that the criminal law should not intrude unnecessarily into the private life of adults. Applying the principle of harm means that most consensual activity between adults in private should be their own affair, and not that of the criminal law. But the criminal law has a vital role to play where sexual activity is not consensual, or where society decides that children and other very vulnerable people require protection and should not be able to consent. It is quite proper to argue in such situations that an adult's right to exercise sexual autonomy in their private life is not absolute, and society may properly apply standards through the criminal law which are intended to protect the family as an institution as well as individuals from abuse.[10]

Despite setting out a general rule against prohibition of consensual sexual behaviour, this explanation devotes considerably more attention to the exceptions to that rule. These exceptions are characterized here in broad terms – consensual sexual behaviour can, it seems, be prohibited whenever this is deemed necessary to protect individuals from abuse, or from some other unspecified harm, or to protect the institution of the family. The principle of freedom from state interference is therefore secondary to and effectively subsumed by the principle of protection from harm, which allows prohibition of all harmful behaviour but not behaviour that causes no harm. Thus the exercise in which the Review is engaged is not so much a balancing act between two principles, but rather a process of deciding what sexual activity is harmful, and for whom.

Non-consensual sexual acts are prohibited on the basis that they are violations of autonomy, and that this is a harm in and of itself. In addition, non-consensual sex can involve a range of associated or consequential

---

[10] Home Office (n 1) iv.

harms including physical injury, psychological trauma, unwanted pregnancy and relationship breakdown. However, the Sexual Offences Act 2003 contains numerous other offences which do not turn on the presence or absence of consent. These can be divided into four categories: sexual activity with children and young people,[11] sexual activity between family members,[12] sexual activity with persons with a mental disorder,[13] and exploitation of commercial sex.[14] Each of these groups of offences criminalises some ostensibly consensual sexual activity. Below, I give a brief overview of each of these groups of offences before drawing out some common themes.

Offences against Children and Young People

Offences against children and young people can be divided into three distinct age bands: below thirteen years, thirteen to fifteen years, and sixteen to seventeen years. Children aged below thirteen years are deemed entirely incapable of consent to sex (though paradoxically, they can be liable for rape and other sexual offences at age ten[15]), and all sexual activity with children in this age group is criminalized under sections 5-8 of the 2003 Act. These four offences parallel the nonconsensual offences under sections 1-4 of the Act, and are referred to as 'rape *of a child*', 'assault *of a child* by penetration' and so on.[16] In each case, the requirement to prove that the victim did not consent is replaced with a requirement to prove that the victim was aged below thirteen. The sections 1-4 requirement to prove that the defendant lacked a reasonable belief in consent has no corresponding *mens rea* element in the sections 5-8 offences. Higher sentences are available compared to the sections 1-4 offences. The offences against this age group are thus constructed as embodying the same harm as the offences of rape and sexual assault, but exacerbated by the age and associated vulnerability of the victim.

---

[11] Sexual Offences Act 2003 ss5-29.

[12] ibid ss25-26 and 64-65.

[13] ibid ss30-51.

[14] ibid ss45-60.

[15] Heather Keating, 'When the kissing has to stop: children, sexual behaviour, and the criminal law' in Michael Freeman (ed.), *Law and Childhood Studies* (Oxford University Press 2012).

[16] This represents a change from the Review's original recommendation that the terms 'rape' and 'assault' be reserved for offences where lack of consent was specifically proven in court, Home Office (n1) 43.

Children aged thirteen to fifteen are not deemed incapable of consent, but sexual activity with them is prohibited nonetheless. Section 9 of the Sexual Offences Act 2003 prohibits all sexual activity with children aged below sixteen, whilst sections 10-15 prohibit related conduct such as causing, inciting and arranging child sexual activity and exposing children to the sexual activity of others.[17] These offences do not require proof of non-consent and have lower penalties than the offences contained in sections 1-4 and sections 5-8. Therefore, the conduct prohibited by these offences includes consensual sexual activity involving children aged below sixteen.[18] This is consistent with a trend of increasing adult power over children's sexuality, identified by Michel Foucault.[19] Indeed, the Sex Offences Review strongly implied that the target of these offences was to protect children not from non-consensual sex, but from sex itself. It stressed that where there was evidence that sexual activity involving young teenagers was not consensual, the more serious charges under ss1-4 of the Act should be used.[20] Moreover, the offences under ss9-15 were justified on the basis that sex at too early an age carried risks of emotional, psychological and physical harm, including the contraction of sexually transmitted diseases and the specific risks associated with early pregnancy, and thus children 'ought not to have sex' under sixteen.[21] Thus the prohibition of consensual sexual behaviour involving children aged below sixteen could be said to rest on an assumption that sexuality at this age is dangerous in and of itself and needs to be controlled.

This rationale is somewhat muddied, however, by the statement from the Review that the ss9-15 offences should not be used in cases of mutually agreed sexual experimentation, but only 'where behaviour was not mutually agreed, but exploitative and coercive.'[22] In addition, the availability of lower penalties for defendants aged below eighteen suggests

---

[17] Sexual Offences Act 2003 ss9-15. All of these offences apply to all children aged under sixteen, and thus overlap with the offences under ss5-8 in cases where the victim is aged under 13. However, Crown Prosecution Service guidance states ss5-8 should always be applied in these cases, due to the higher maximum penalties available, unless there is any difficulty in proving the age of the victim.

[18] Provided one accepts that at least some children aged below sixteen are capable of consenting to some sexual activity in some circumstances.

[19] Michel Foucault, *The History of Sexuality* (Penguin 1976). See also Keating (n 15) for further context.

[20] Home Office (n 1) 51.

[21] ibid 38.

[22] ibid 55.

that exploitation by an older (and thus more powerful) party is the primary target. This casts the offences in a different light, as a safety net for addressing sexual behaviour that is not really consensual (i.e. behaviour that is coercive and not mutually agreed), but where lack of consent and lack of reasonable belief in consent may be difficult to prove. To use ss9-15 in this way delegates to prosecutors the complex task – particularly in cases where the parties are similar in age – of identifying incidents that are sufficiently abusive to justify criminalization, but where there is insufficient evidence to prosecute for a non-consensual offence. As John Spencer has argued, if there is a principled distinction between the behaviour that is to be criminalized and that which is not, this should be stated in the substance of the Act, not left to prosecutorial discretion.[23] In any event, whatever the rationale of ss9-15, the result is that all sexual activity involving children aged below sixteen is criminal, at least in theory, even where it is consensual and even where both parties are within the thirteen to fifteen age bracket. If this criminalization is only theoretical, it may promote a perception that the criminal law consists of 'empty threats'.[24] If this behaviour is criminalized in practice, it constitutes a particularly draconian exercise of state power to control teenage sex.

Consensual sexual activity with young people in the third age band – ages sixteen and seventeen – is generally permitted. There are exceptions, however. Sexual activity involving children and young people up to the age of eighteen is criminalized regardless of consent where the actor is in a specified position of responsibility or power over the victim, including family relationships, [25] or alternatively where sexual services are performed by the victim for payment.[26] In addition, it is an offence to take 'indecent' photographs of any person aged below eighteen.[27] The Sexual Offences Act 2003 thus treats this age group as capable of consent, but nevertheless susceptible to manipulation and not entirely capable of exercising that consent appropriately. Moreover, while thirteen to fifteen year olds are constructed as needing protection from all sexual activity, sixteen and seventeen year olds are constructed as needing protection from certain suspect sexual activities (prostitution and pornography) and

---

[23] John Spencer, 'The Sexual Offences Act 2003: (2) Child and Family Offences' [2004] *Criminal Law Review* 347, 354.

[24] Keating (n 15) 276.

[25] Sexual Offences Act 2003 ss16-19 and 25-26.

[26] ibid ss47-50.

[27] Protection of Children Act 1978 as amended by Sexual Offences Act 2003 ss45-46.

relationships (with people in positions of trust or authority). As with the offences against thirteen to fifteen year olds, these offences arguably capture some genuinely exploitative and abusive sexual activity. However, they also capture some fully consensual sexual activity. For example, they prohibit two seventeen year olds, who can legally have sex with each other, from photographing that sexual activity. Again, this is arguably an unnecessarily oppressive exercise of state power over young people's sexuality.

Sexual Activity Involving Adults with a Mental Disorder

The Sex Offences Review viewed mentally disordered individuals as particularly vulnerable, on the basis of evidence that they may be 'easily induced or persuaded into a sexual relationship and are targeted by others for their own sexual gratification.'[28] While there were existing offences addressing sexual activity with mentally disordered persons, there were a number of problems with these offences. The offences applied unevenly to men and women, were limited to victims with severe mental impairment, were subject to very low sentences, and employed archaic and offensive language, describing the victims as 'defective'.[29] In order to address these problems, the review sought to enact more robust, gender neutral protection for a wider group of mentally disordered individuals.

The 2003 Act prohibits engaging in or inciting sexual activity with a person whose mental disorder impedes their ability to make a choice about engaging in sexual activity, as well as engaging in sexual activity in the presence of such persons or causing them to watch a sexual act, provided that the defendant knows or could reasonably be expected to know that the victim is unlikely to be able to refuse due to a mental disorder.[30] As the case of *R v Cooper* makes clear, the question for courts in such cases is whether the victim's mental disorder rendered them unable to refuse the specific sexual act that is the subject of the charge at that time and in those circumstances, not whether it rendered them generally incapable of making choices about sexual activity.[31] This is a welcome step forward from the previous status-based approach to capacity, under which all sexual activity with women classed as 'defectives'[32] or 'imbeciles'[33] was

---

[28] Home Office (n 1) 63.
[29] Sexual Offences Act 1956 s45.
[30] Sexual Offences Act 2003 ss30-33.
[31] *Cooper* [2009] UKHL 42 per Baroness Hale.
[32] Sexual Offences Act 1956 ss6, 7, 14(3) and 15(3).

prohibited. It does, however, raise questions about the relationship between the section 30 offence and the offences of rape and sexual assault under ss1-4 of the Act, an issue highlighted by Baroness Hale in her judgment in *Cooper*.[34] Arguably, if a person 'lacks the capacity to choose whether to agree' to sexual activity,[35] or to communicate their choice,[36] they do not consent to the activity, and it is appropriate to call the perpetrator a rapist.

Two justifications have been offered for the existence of a separate offence specifically targeting sexual activity with mentally disordered victims: that they act as a fail-safe where rape would be difficult to prove, and that they in fact capture a distinct wrong. The Sex Offences Review originally envisaged the offence as a safety net where a non-consensual offence would be 'too severe for the circumstances' or 'where there is real difficulty in prosecuting for the more serious offence.'[37] There is, however, little evidence that section 30 is any easier to prove than rape or sexual assault. Moreover, difficulties in prosecuting rape might best be dealt with by reforming this offence rather than introducing alternative routes to conviction for the same conduct.[38] Furthermore, the recommended starting points for sentencing section 30 are higher than if the equivalent conduct was prosecuted as rape. This approach further undermines the construction of these offences as a safety net where a rape charge cannot be pursued. The higher penalties instead suggest that section 30 captures a different, and more serious, wrong. David Ormerod has argued that the culpability of the offender differs between section 30 and section 1 and that this is expressed in the distinct *mens rea* requirements of the two offences: A defendant who sexually penetrates another when they know (or ought to know) that that person is likely to be unable to refuse due to a mental disorder commits a different wrong to a defendant who rapes.[39] With respect, I do not find this argument convincing. Knowledge that a person likely lacks the capacity to refuse sexual activity because of

---

[33] Criminal Law Amendment Act 1885 s5(2).

[34] *Cooper* (n 31) per Baroness Hale.

[35] Sexual Offences Act 2003 s30(2)(a).

[36] ibid s30(2)(b).

[37] Home Office (n 1) 74; see also David Ormerod, 'Case Comment: R. v C: sexual offences: Sexual Offences Act 2003 s.30(2) – sexual touching – complainant suffering from mental disorder' [2010] (1) *Criminal Law Review* 75.

[38] Gerry Maher, 'Case Comment: Rape and other things: sexual offences and people with mental disorder' (2010) 14(1) Edinburgh Law Review 129.

[39] Ormerod (n 37).

their mental disorder is not compatible with a reasonable belief in consent, thus proof of the *mens rea* of section 30 amounts to proof of the *mens rea* of rape.

The offences against victims with a mental disorder impeding choice are supplemented by two further groups of offences. The same range of sexual activity is prohibited with a person with *any* mental disorder where agreement to engage in the activity is procured by inducement, threat or deception[40] or where the defendant is a care worker for the complainant.[41] These offences are largely positive additions to the array of sexual offences. There is a general consensus among professionals in the learning disability field that sexual relationships between careworkers and those in their care are always seriously wrongful, even with victims who are capable of consent to sex in some circumstances, because, 'So great are the power dynamics between staff and people with learning disabilities, that it is difficult to imagine a scenario of a person with learning disabilities ever being an equal sexual partner.'[42] Meanwhile the offences involving inducement, threat or deception provide a means of criminalizing predatory behaviour by individuals who are not careworkers, without disqualifying individuals with mental disabilities or disorders from legitimately consenting to sex across the board.[43]

Taken together, the three groups of offences against mentally disordered victims are a positive step forward. As they do not rely on proof of non-consent, there is some danger that they may criminalise behaviour that is genuinely consensual and mutually desired, especially as offences can be reported by third parties and prosecuted on the basis of psychiatric evidence without any testimony from the alleged victim. However, this danger is limited. The offences are drafted so as to target behaviour that is predatory and abusive. Nevertheless, my concern about these offences is the way they separate out mentally disordered individuals as a separate class of victim whose sexual activity is subject to a different regime of

---

[40] Sexual Offences Act 2003 ss34-37.

[41] ibid ss38-41.

[42] Michelle McCarthy and David Thompson, 'People with Learning Disabilities: Sex, the Law and Consent' in Mark Cowling and Paul Reynolds (eds.), *Making Sense of Sexual Consent* (Ashgate 2004) 231.

[43] Janine Benedet and Isobel Grant, 'Sexual Assault of Women with Mental Disabilities: A Canadian Perspective' in Clare McGlynn and Vanessa Munro (eds.) *Rethinking Rape Law: International and Comparative Perspectives* (Routledge 2010).

protection and scrutiny from non-disabled individuals. As I explore below, the paradigmatic sexual offences of rape and sexual assault continue to be structured around the experiences of a theoretical rational, consenting, liberal subject. Victims who do not fit this mold are treated as exceptional, rather than paradigmatic, and the existence of specific offences against mentally disordered victims is a key example of this.[44] Constructing different categories of victimisation avoids more radically reassessing the concept of consent and its central role in sexual offences law.

Sex with Family Members

The Sexual Offences Act 2003 criminalises sexual abuse of children and young people by family members, as well as sexual activity between adult relatives. The familial child sex offences duplicate the generic child sex offences with an additional requirement to prove a relevant family relationship, and that the defendant could reasonably be expected to be aware of that relationship.[45] Family relationship is broadly defined for the purpose of these offences to include a range of members of the child's household; it is not limited to close blood relatives.[46] The presence of a family relationship is constructed as an extra layer of culpability over and above the generic offences as it involves the subversion of relationships and spaces (the home) which should be safe and nurturing rather than abusive. In the case of under sixteens, the additional wrongfulness is reflected in higher recommended sentence starting points,[47] while for sixteen and seventeen year olds, it manifests in the criminalization of behaviour that would otherwise be consensual.

The offences prohibiting sex with adult relatives are more problematic. Sections 64 and 65 of the 2003 Act criminalise penetration and consenting to penetration respectively, with specified blood relatives.[48] According to the Sex Offences Review, the rationale for these offences is based on 'the fact that many adult incestuous relationships are based on long term grooming and pressure from childhood, and are not genuinely

---

[44] ibid.

[45] Sexual Offences Act 2003 ss25-26.

[46] ibid s27.

[47] Crown Prosecution Service, 'Sentencing Manual: s25 Sexual Activity with a Child Family Member (Adult Defendant Only)' January 2010 <http://www.cps.gov.uk/legal/s_to_u/sentencing_manual/s25__sexual_activity_wit h_a_child_family_member_(adult_defendant_only)/> accessed 3 February 2016.

[48] Sexual Offences Act 2003 ss64-65.

consensual.'[49] However, there is nothing to prevent the prosecution of individuals for fully consensual sexual activity with adult relatives; for example, relationships between siblings of a similar age who did not meet until adulthood. Moreover, the limited scope of the offence, which prohibits only penetrative sex and only between blood relatives, evokes the historical rationale of concerns about the genetic makeup of any children produced – a rationale which the Review stated was not a significant consideration.[50] These offences thus criminalise some fully consensual and harmless sexual activity between consenting adults.[51] This is achieved by rhetorically aligning the taboo of familial sex with abuse, and then using that presumption of abuse to sidestep the thorny issue of consent.[52]

Sex Work

The rhetoric of abuse and vulnerability has also played a key role in recent developments in prostitution law. The Sex Offences Review considered the question of whether the purchase and/or sale of sexual services itself should be criminal to be beyond its remit. It did, however, examine a range of existing offences related to prostitution 'insofar as they link to the sexual exploitation of others.'[53] As a result, the Sexual Offences Act 2003 includes offences criminalizing the abuse of children through prostitution and pornography. As with the familial child sex offences, the commercial nature of the sexual activity adds an extra layer of culpability such that higher sentences are recommended compared to the equivalent generic child sex offences,[54] and the offences apply to children and young people aged up to eighteen, rather than sixteen.

---

[49] Home Office (n 1) 95.

[50] ibid 82.

[51] James Roffee, 'No Consensus on Incest? Criminalisation and Compatibility with the European Convention on Human Rights' (2014) 14 Human Rights Law Review 541.

[52] James Roffee, 'The Synthetic Necessary Truth Behind New Labour's Criminalisation of Incest' (2014) 23(1) Social & Legal Studies 113.

[53] Home Office (n 1) 105.

[54] Crown Prosecution Service, 'Sentencing Manual: s47: Paying for Sexual Services of a Child' January 2012
<http://www.cps.gov.uk/legal/s_to_u/sentencing_manual/s47__paying_for_sexual _services_of_a_child/ accessed> 3 February 2016.

The Act also contains a number of offences concerned with the exploitation of adults through commercial sex.[55] The focus within these offences on 'pimps' and clients as wrongdoers represents a marked shift in prostitution policy in England and Wales, influenced by radical feminist approaches and the Nordic model that aims to abolish prostitution by ending demand.[56] Within this discourse, individuals (usually women specifically) who perform sexual services for money are constructed as vulnerable victims in need of rescue.[57] This rhetoric of vulnerability allows the framework of consent to be sidestepped in favour of concepts such as 'incitement', 'control' and 'force'. These concepts suggest a high degree of coercion on the part of offenders – arguably higher than mere non-consent – but have in fact been drawn more broadly. For example, in *R v Massey*,[58] it was held that, for the purposes of the offence of 'controlling a prostitute for gain',[59] 'control' did not require evidence of coercion or compulsion, and could apply to activities such as setting up a website and making bookings with clients.[60] Meanwhile, the strict liability offence of 'paying for sexual services of a prostitute subject to force etc.' requires evidence of 'exploitative conduct' by a third party, defined as 'force, threats (whether or not relating to violence) or any other form of coercion, or (…) any form of deception.'[61] Such conduct is undoubtedly wrongful, but not all such conduct would vitiate consent to sex according to the leading cases.[62] Thus the context of sex work and assumptions about the vulnerability of sex workers are used to lower the threshold of coercion or deception that renders a particular instance of sexual activity criminal, when compared with sex in non-commercial contexts.

These offences provide an easier route than ss1-4 for convicting abusive individuals who force others into prostitution,[63] as well as 'clients' who

---

[55] Sexual Offences Act 2003 ss51A-53A and offences of trafficking for the purposes of sexual exploitation ss57-59.

[56] Jane Scoular and Anna Carline, 'A Critical Account of a 'Creeping Neo-abolitionism': Regulating Prostitution in England and Wales' (2014) 14(5) Criminology & Criminal Justice 608.

[57] ibid.

[58] *Massey* [2007] EWCA Crim 2664.

[59] Sexual Offences Act 2003 s53(1).

[60] *Massey* (n 58).

[61] Sexual Offences Act 2003 s53A(3)(a)-(b).

[62] See for example *R v McNally* [2013] EWCA Crim 1051 where it was held, per Leveson LJ, that 'some deceptions (…) would obviously not be sufficient to vitiate consent.'

[63] This appears to have been the case in *Massey* itself.

pay for sex with men or women whom they know have no choice. They are also drawn widely enough to criminalise individuals who engage in or facilitate sexual activity that would be legally classed as consensual. It is not only those individuals directly targeted by the legislation that are affected; the offences have several problematic consequences for sex workers themselves. Criminalisation of clients[64] negatively impacts sex workers' livelihoods and personal safety. It encourages sex workers to drop prices and/or offer a wider range of services, reduces time and opportunity for screening clients, and pushes workers to accompany clients to more remote locations to avoid discovery.[65] These offences add little to sex workers' bargaining power, instead causing them to absorb the increased risk to clients. Similarly, offences targeting 'pimps' and brothel-keepers[66] make it difficult for sex workers to work with others, despite the risks of social isolation and physical danger associated with loan working.[67] In addition, an array of anti-trafficking provisions equip police to raid premises and remove sex workers against their will, a notable example being the 2013 Soho raids in which sex workers were dragged from their flats before a crowd of press photographers who had reportedly been given prior notice by the Metropolitan Police.[68] Such 'rescue' missions expose sex workers to a high degree of scrutiny, and have

---

[64] Sexual Offences Act 2003 s51A and s53A.

[65] Arna Nord and Tila Rosenberg, 'Rapport: Lag mot köp av sexuella tjänster. Metodutveckling avseende åtgärder mot om förbud prostitution. Malmö: Polismyndigheten i Skåne' (2001) in Phil Hubbard, Roger Matthews and Jane Scoular 'Regulating Sex Work in the EU: Prostitute Women and the New Spaces of Exclusion' (2008) 15(2) Gender, Place and Culture 137; see also, Molly Smith 'For Sex Workers in Scotland, Life May be About to get Safer' *The Guardian* 17 September 2015 <http://www.theguardian.com/commentisfree/2015/sep/17/scotland-life-safer-sex-workers-decriminalisation-scottish-parliament> accessed 3 February 2016; Jay Levy and Pye Jakobsson 'Sweden's Abolitionist Discourse and Law: Effects on the Dynamics of Swedish Sex Work and on the Lives of Sweden's Sex Workers' (2014) 14(5) Criminology & Criminal Justice 593; Hilary Kinnell, 'Murder Made Easy: The Final Solution to Prostitution?' in Rosie Campbell and Maggie O'Neill (eds.), *Sex Work Now* (Routledge 2006).

[66] Sexual Offences Act 2003 ss52-53 and Sexual Offences Act 1956 ss33-36.

[67] Jane Pitcher and Marjan Wijers, 'The Impact of Different Regulatory Models on the Labour Conditions, Safety and Welfare of Indoor Sex Workers' (2014) 14(5) Criminology & Criminal Justice 549; Kinnell ibid.

[68] Molly Smith, 'Soho Police Raids Show Why Sex Workers Live in Fear of Being 'Rescued'', *The Guardian* 11 December 2013 <http://www.theguardian.com/commentisfree/2013/dec/11/soho-police-raids-sex-workers-fear-trafficking> accessed 3 February 2016.

resulted in individuals initially identified as potential trafficking victims
being detained, deported, and separated from their children.[69] Measures
designed to protect sex workers from abuse by private individuals thus
paradoxically justify their exposure to a complex architecture of state
power, itself experienced as oppressive, controlling and abusive.

Criminalising Consensual Sex: Common Themes

Each of the four groups of offences discussed above was constructed, at
least in part, as a safety net to capture behaviour that was abusive and not
'genuinely' consensual, but where proving non-consent within the terms of
ss1-4 would be too difficult. In order to have this fail-safe quality, each
offence must prohibit an objective/external wrong that is easier to prove
than non-consent. Broadly speaking, the 2003 Act identifies such prima
facie wrongs where one party to a sexual encounter is part of a class of
persons deemed 'vulnerable', where the circumstances in which the sexual
activity takes place are deemed particularly exploitative, or both. It could
be argued then, that the fact these offences do not rely on consent is
inconsequential; they serve an important purpose and target behaviour that
is wrongful and worthy of criminalisation. It is certainly the case that
much of the conduct captured by these offences should properly be treated
as criminal. Nevertheless, I have three major concerns about the current
structure of the offences.

First, the offences each cover a wide spectrum of behaviour, some of
which *should not* be criminalised (for example two sex workers working
from the same flat, or two fifteen-year-olds engaging in consensual sex). It
may be thought that this would be addressed by victims choosing not to
report and/or prosecutors electing not to pursue cases in such
circumstances. However, the fact that third parties such as parents,
psychiatrists and police can report offences and provide witness testimony,
and that testimony from the victim is not required, means much is left to
prosecutorial discretion without clear legal guidance on which cases
should be pursued. Second, I am not convinced by the way that conduct
which should properly be regarded as criminal is organized between the
offences of rape and sexual assault and the various offences involving
exploitation of vulnerable people discussed above. The current structure
has a number of problematic consequences, which I explore below, and

---

[69] Niki Adams, 'Anti-trafficking Legislation: Protection or Deportation?' (2003) 73
Feminist Review 135. See also Hubbard et al (n 65).

potentially falls foul of principles of fair labelling and proportionate sentencing. Third, as I discuss in the final section of this paper, these offences reflect larger underlying issues about the construction of different types of subjects and the level of scrutiny and control they are subject to by the state.

The Relationship between Non-consent Offences and Exploitation Offences

The Sex Offences Review envisaged that offences against children and mentally disordered persons and those involving familial sexual relationships, abuse of trust and exploitation through prostitution and pornography would provide *additional* protection to particularly vulnerable groups. The existence of these offences does provide an additional chance that abusers will be convicted of *an* offence, but it may not be an offence that adequately reflects the nature or seriousness of the wrong committed. For example, the violation at the heart of ss64-65 of the 2003 Act was identified by the Review as sexual activity induced by long term grooming by an older family member, such as where an adult woman 'consents' to sex with her father having been manipulated and abused by him since childhood. This wrong is hardly reflected in the offence label – 'sex with an adult relative' – or in the maximum available penalty of two years imprisonment. Similarly, paying for the sexual services of a prostitute subject to exploitation or force is punished by a maximum £1000 fine.

Other pertinent examples of downgrading include the cases of *Massey* and *Cooper*, discussed above. In *Massey*, the defendant was convicted of controlling a prostitute for gain. The complainant also testified that he had raped and assaulted her occasioning actual bodily harm, crimes for which he was unsuccessfully prosecuted. [70] In *Cooper*, the defendant was originally charged with rape. The charge of sexual activity with a person with a mental disorder impeding choice was substituted at a later stage, and resulted in a conviction. [71] In one sense, these cases demonstrate the value of the separate offences, without which justice may have eluded the two victims. They should also, however, give us pause to consider what obstacles impeded convictions for rape. In addition, *Cooper* highlights the potentially stigmatizing nature of separate offences for vulnerable people.

---

[70] *Massey* (n 58).
[71] *Cooper* (n 31).

The majority of the court's discussion focuses not on the offender's wrongdoing, but on the complainant, her diagnosis, and its relationship to her 'irrational fears' and capacity to consent, despite the fact that, as Baroness Hale notes in her judgment, 'some of this complainant's fears may have been all too rational.'[72]

Stigmatising victims was an issue that concerned the authors of the Sex Offences Review. With this in mind, they removed the 'demeaning and derogatory' term 'defective' from the lexicon of sexual offences law,[73] along with the term 'incest', which was thought to 'taint' victims and portray them as complicit.[74] However, while the terminology has been changed, the retention of separate offences arguably reinforces taboos about the kinds of people who can and cannot legitimately be sexual. It also constructs sex work as inherently problematic (in ways that work in general, and sex in general are not), regardless of the specific circumstances. A framework which defines offences on the basis of the victim's identity (as a child or a person with a mental disorder) implies that the central wrong is having sex with particular categories of people, rather than imposing sexual activity on a person against their will. One answer to this is that these offences do in fact capture distinct wrongs.

A case could perhaps be made that at least some of these offences cover forms of sexual violation which are different from non-consensual sex.[75] Nothing I claim in this chapter is intended to rule out this possibility. Nevertheless, it should be clear from the above discussion that distinct and coherent wrongs have not been expressed through the offences as currently enacted. It is beyond the scope of this paper to engage in a thorough review of the various activities currently prohibited in order to ascertain whether they do embody any distinct wrongs seriousness enough to justify criminal sanction, or to articulate what those wrongs might be. It is, however, possible to identify two themes which may provide a starting point for reconsidering the relationship between rape and other forms of sexual violation: 'taking advantage' and ongoing abuse.

---

[72] ibid per Baroness Hale at [32].

[73] Home Office (n 1) 62.

[74] ibid 83. Notably the term 'prostitute' is retained, even where the 'prostitute' in question is a child or an adult subject to force.

[75] David Ormerod has made such an argument in relation to the offence of sexual activity with a person with a mental disorder impeding choice, Ormerod (n 37).

Many of the offences discussed target offenders who take advantage of an aspect of the victim that makes them vulnerable, or a position of power over the victim. Future research could fruitfully explore whether this kind of exploitation is conceptually distinct from non-consensual sex. If it is, a further question for investigation, posed by Lucy Series, is whether offences prohibiting sexual activity with specific categories of victims and in specified relationships of trust (as per current practice) are necessary, or whether 'a general offence of sex under undue influence or pressure' could be formulated.[76] Are there legally relevant differences between a person who exploits the compliant nature of an individual with learning difficulties, and someone who exploits the physical dependence of a person with a physical disability? Between someone who takes advantage of an undocumented migrant's need for money and lack of access to mainstream labour opportunities, and someone who exploits another's financial dependence upon them when that person is their partner, or their employee? Elsewhere, I have developed a concept of 'freedom to negotiate' as a starting point for thinking through these complex questions in an inclusive manner.[77]

A related theme in the existing offences is ongoing abuse. The types of conduct that the Sex Offences Review sought to target often include an element of gaining compliance through grooming behaviours over a period of time (even where no such course of conduct is required by the offences as ultimately enacted). For example, an ongoing pattern of control and exploitation by a pimp, or abuse of a position of responsibility – such as teacher or careworker – that endures over a period of time. By contrast, rape and sexual assault have traditionally been conceptualized as individual incidents. However, the distinction is not clear cut. Recent developments in the legal formulation of consent introduce some slippage between one-off assaults and ongoing courses of conduct. The statutory definition of consent foregrounds 'freedom and capacity to make a choice',[78] and recent case law suggests this freedom and capacity may be

---

[76] Lucy Series, 'Framing the Test of Capacity to Consent to Sex' *The Small Places* 24 January 2014 <http://thesmallplaces.blogspot.co.uk/2014/01/framing-test-of-capacity-to-consent-to.html> accessed 3 February 2016.

[77] Tanya Palmer, *Renegotiating Sex and Sexual Violation in the Criminal Law* (Hart, forthcoming); Tanya Palmer 'Distinguishing Sex from Sexual Violation: Consent, Negotiation and Freedom to Negotiate' in Alan Reed, Michael Bohlander, Nicola Wake and Emma Smith (eds.) *Consent: Domestic and Comparative Perspectives* (Routledge 2017, forthcoming).

[78] Sexual Offences Act 2003 s74.

compromised by a pattern of behaviour over a period of time (particularly where deception is involved).[79] It is unclear whether the current definition of consent is flexible enough to include the behaviours currently captured by exploitation offences. A further question is whether it should. If it is concluded that there is a distinction to be made between one-off or 'acute' incidents of sexual violation and ongoing or 'chronic' forms of sexual violation, should the relevant offences not be built more explicitly around this idea, rather than around specific 'suspect' categories of victims, relationships and practices? What of individuals who experience chronic violations of their sexual autonomy falling outside of these categories, such as those subject to ongoing domestic abuse or coercive control? These questions implicate the definition of consent itself.

The need for additional offences and the form they should take is intertwined with the way consent is understood for the purposes of rape and sexual assault.[80] I have argued elsewhere that consent is not an effective way to distinguish between sex and sexual violation.[81] Thus, in identifying problems with the exploitation offences, I do not claim that they are simply unnecessary and that the state should only interfere where sexual activity is non-consensual. My argument is that the relationship between sex and sexual violation needs to be radically rethought so that state power is applied in an equal and principled manner. At present, this power is applied unevenly in ways that subject particular groups of people who are already marginalised – children, sex workers, individuals with mental disorders – to an increased level of state scrutiny and control. In the final section of this chapter, I argue that the reason for this unevenness is derived from a liberal concept of subjecthood that struggles to incorporate vulnerability.

The Liberal Subject and the Vulnerable Subject

The splitting of sexual offences into those involving lack of consent and those involving alternative forms of exploitation of vulnerable people, stems from the adherence in English and Welsh legal discourse to two incompatible notions of subjectivity: the liberal subject and the vulnerable subject. The Kantian liberal subject is a central figure in English law. This

---

[79] *R v Newland* (Chester Crown Court, 12 November 2015); *McNally* (n 62); *R v Jheeta* [2007] EWCA Crim 1699.

[80] Jonathan Herring, 'Case Comment: *R v C:* Sex and Mental Disorder' (2010) 126 Law quarterly Review 36.

[81] Palmer (n 77).

figure is defined by two key features: the mental capacity for reason and the physical integrity of the body, i.e. its wholeness, physical separateness from other bodies, and impermeability. This notion of integrity finds expression in sexual offences law through the repeated privileging of penetrative sexual activity, i.e. the penetration of bodily boundaries, as the worst form of violation. As Nicola Lacey argues, the image of the bounded body as normative 'informs the construction of the bodies of gay men and all women, of small children, the disabled, the elderly, as exceptional and marginal to legal subjectivity.'[82] Bodies understood as open to penetration, or as weak and dependent are not a comfortable fit with the liberal legal subject. However, as Ngaire Naffine notes, these constructions are based on a selective reading of bodily integrity in which typically masculine experiences of being penetrated, such as piercing by weapons on the battlefield, are understood as toughening, rather than weakening, bodily boundaries.[83]

The liberal subject's capacity for making rational judgements about his or her own best interests and how to pursue them is the capacity for autonomy. Autonomy has come to be seen as the central interest at stake in rape and sexual assault, and consent is the mechanism by which autonomy is exercised. For Kant, autonomy required a conscious weighing of factors and the capacity to articulate reasons for one's choice. Where autonomy is invoked in discussions of sexual offences, however, it tends to be equated with a somewhat vague notion of 'meaningful choices'. The malleability of the concept of autonomy allows it to be applied in ways that are similarly exclusionary to the concept of bodily integrity. The Sexual Offences Act 2003 defines consent in the loose terms of 'freedom', 'capacity' and 'choice' which allow many decisions to engage in sexual activity to be regarded as autonomous, even where the decision-making process is more visceral than cerebral.[84] However, parties that are understood as lacking a rational will, such as children and people with mental disorders, as well as those who choose the 'wrong things' (sex work, incest), face a higher level of scrutiny of their choices and stricter

---

[82] Nicola Lacey, 'Unspeakable Subjects, Impossible Rights: Sexuality, Integrity and Criminal Law' in Nicola Lacey (ed.) *Unspeakable Subjects: Feminist Essays in Legal and Social Theory* (Hart 1998) 115.

[83] Ngaire Naffine, 'The Body Bag' in Ngaire Naffine and Rosemary Owen (eds.) *Sexing the Subject of Law* (Sweet & Maxwell 1997).

[84] See discussion of this point in *In re. M* [2014] EWCA Civ 37.

tests of autonomy.[85] Thus the lack of rational reflection is only made visible in relation to people already constructed as lacking reason, or making unreasonable choices. The supposedly neutral autonomous subject is therefore understood and applied selectively in a way that excludes some parties from full legal subjectivity.

Martha Albertson Fineman's groundbreaking work on vulnerability has identified this tendency to designate particular populations as 'vulnerable' when they are not easily accommodated within liberal notions of the subject. [86] While the liberal subject is constructed as universal, vulnerability is viewed as a characteristic of specified populations. According to Fineman, political and legal responses to populations that are designated as 'vulnerable' tend to be either punitive and stigmatising, or paternalistic and stigmatizing (approaches which can both be identified in the discussion of sexual offences against vulnerable people, above). Fineman further explains, 'Their perceived vulnerability marks them as lesser, imperfect, and deviant, and places them somehow outside of the protection of the social contract as it is applied to others.'[87]

Children and mentally disordered adults are two groups to which the condition of vulnerability has long been specifically attached, particularly in the context of sexuality. The idea of children, and particularly girl children, as vulnerable to sexual exploitation was cemented in the public consciousness by the social reformers of the latter half of the nineteenth century,[88] and has been reiterated through the 'paedophile panics' of the 1990s, and the recent coverage of organized child sexual abuse in Rotherham and Rochdale and the findings of Operation Yewtree. At the same time, children continue to occupy a double status, in need of both protection and control.[89] Mentally disordered individuals, and particularly people with learning difficulties, have occupied a similarly doubled status, lacking rights but subject to various forms of state control for their own

---

[85] Suzanna Doyle, 'The Notion of Consent to Sexual Activity for Persons with Mental Disabilities' (2010) 31 Liverpool Law Review 111. But see acknowledgement of this point in *M* ibid.
[86] Martha Albertson Fineman, 'Equality, Autonomy and the Vulnerable Subject in Law and Politics' in Martha Albertson Fineman and Anna Grear, *Vulnerability: Reflections on a New Ethical Foundation for Law and Politics* (Ashgate 2013).
[87] ibid 16.
[88] Matthew Waites, 'The Age of Consent and Sexual Consent' in Mark Cowling and Paul Reynolds (eds.), *Making Sense of Sexual Consent* (Ashgate 2004).
[89] Keating (n 15).

and others' protection. The disability rights movement has led a critique of this approach which has shifted the discourse towards a balancing of rights, support and protection, embodied in the UN Convention on the Rights of Persons with Disabilities.[90] It is striking that children and persons with mental disorders are the same groups that have been legally classed as vulnerable in sexual offences legislation dating back to the nineteenth century, and that the approach to protecting them is still to formulate separate offences against these classes of potential victims. The Sex Offences Review placed a great deal of emphasis on protecting the vulnerable, but it ultimately failed to think radically or creatively about vulnerability or protection for vulnerable groups.

By contrast, incest and prostitution have historically been constructed as deviant activities and subject to punitive and restrictive legal measures. The rise of autonomy as a key value underpinning sexual offences militates against the prohibition of sexual activities on the basis of moral deviance. In light of this development, consenting adults engaged in familial sexual relationships and sex work have been recast as vulnerable victims and abusers. Criminalisation of the latter is thus justified on the basis of protecting the former. There is no doubt that abuse does sometimes take place in both these contexts. However, in the case of sexual relationships between adult relatives, this should direct our attention to the inadequacies of consent and to why there is a need for separate offences structured around the deviant nature of familial sexual relationships rather than around the presence of coercion. In the case of prostitution, attention should be paid to the wider political and legal factors which produce vulnerability (e.g. gender inequality, migrant rights, labour rights, benefit cuts, poverty, war, lack of services for substance abusers) that constrains choice and makes sex work the most viable option for some people.[91] After all, if individuals are vulnerable due to a lack of choice, constraining that choice further through criminal law is not particularly helpful.

The present approach of the Sexual Offences Act 2003, in which 'universal' offences of rape and sexual assault sit alongside specific offences against vulnerable victims, expresses the broader relationship between the supposed neutrality of the liberal subject and the particularity of the vulnerable subject, who stand in different relationships to the state

---

[90] Doyle (n 85).
[91] Scoular and Carline (n 56); Hubbard et al (n 65).

and are subject to different regimes of protection and control. The vulnerability thesis developed by Fineman and others explicitly rejects this construction of vulnerability as a characteristic of particular populations.[92] Fineman views vulnerability as at the core of what it means to be human, whilst still recognizing that it varies across individual experiences.[93] It is 'the characteristic that positions us in relation to each other.'[94] She thus advocates a radical rethinking of political and legal subjectivity in which the liberal subject is replaced by the vulnerable subject, a subject which prioritises connection and dependence over autonomy and independence. Under this formulation, the role of the state would be to foster resilience rather than freedom. Fineman's 'responsive state' would monitor societal institutions and adjust them when they are harmful to individuals or society.[95] A thorough reformulation of sexual offences law that treats vulnerable victims as paradigmatic, rather than exceptional,[96] would thus be a partial step towards a more comprehensive reevaluation of the relationship between the state and the individual.

Conclusion

The Sexual Offences Act 2003 criminalises non-consensual sexual behaviour alongside a variety of consensual sexual activities under the guise of prohibiting various forms of sexual exploitation. The latter category covers a wide spectrum of sexual encounters, from behaviour that is genuinely voluntary and non-abusive, e.g. mutually desired sex between two fifteen year olds, to serious forms of sexual violation such as the deliberate targeting and grooming of adults with learning difficulties in order to secure compliance from individuals who do not understand that they can say no.

The exploitation offences are defined with reference to the status of the victim (as a child or person with a mental disorder), the status of the parties in relation to each other (family relationships and positions of trust), the commercial nature of the sexual activity, or a combination thereof. This, coupled with the wide spectrum of behaviour covered, has several negative results. It curtails the positive autonomy of individuals

---

[92] Anna Grear, 'Vulnerability, Advanced Global Capitalism and Co-Symptomatic Injustice' in Martha Albertson Fineman and Anna Grear (n 86).

[93] Fineman (n 86).

[94] ibid 13.

[95] ibid.

[96] Benedet and Grant (n 43).

whose consensual sexual activity is caught by the provisions; it stigmatizes sexual activity involving the features described above, even where no abuse is involved; and it subjects particular categories of individuals – children, people with mental disorders, sex workers – to a coercive architecture of state scrutiny and power, even while they are simultaneously classed as victims. The deportation of victims of sex trafficking is a stark example of this. It also provides a mechanism for downgrading some serious forms of sexual violation from rape or sexual assault to specific exploitation offences, most of which involve lower sentences and less stigmatizing labels for the offender. The relationship between the non-consensual offences and the exploitation offences raises important questions about the legal standard of consent, if it is unable to recognize some of the serious forms of sexual violation targeted by the exploitation offences. It also raises questions about the nature of sexual exploitation, and its status as a distinct wrong, and calls for further research to comprehensively review the relationship between non-consent and exploitation.

Finally, I have argued that the uneasy relationship between the non-consensual offences and the exploitation offences stems from an attachment to a liberal construction of the subject and its incompatibility with the condition of vulnerability. The Sexual Offences Act 2003 expresses this incompatibility by subjecting liberal subjects and vulnerable subjects to alternative regimes of protection or control. Addressing the problems outlined in this chapter requires a re-evaluation of concepts central to sexual offences, particularly consent, in ways that centralize rather than marginalise the experiences of so-called vulnerable victims. At a broader level, it calls for a more radical rethinking of the legal subject.

CHAPTER FOUR

CONSENT TO DEATH

JESSE ELVIN AND CLAIRE DE THAN

Introduction

This chapter will consider how the law should deal with cases where people consent to be killed. Academics and legal and medical practitioners have long debated how the law should deal with 'mercy killing': cases where people wish to die because they are suffering from terminal or chronic medical conditions that cause, or will inevitably lead to, extreme physical or mental anguish. Indeed, the Supreme Court has recently dealt with this issue in *R v Ministry of Justice*.[1] However, the issue is much larger than this type of scenario, and involves a wide range of situations. There are cases where defendants have killed a person who they claimed had wanted to die for financial reasons. For instance, in 1919, an English court convicted William Adams of murder: Adams had argued that the person he killed had requested death as a result of major income tax problems.[2] Furthermore, there are also cases concerning cannibalism, where defendants have claimed that people consented to be killed and eaten. In 2004, a German court convicted a defendant, Armin Meiwes, who killed and ate a willing person. More recently, the BBC reported that 'A former German policeman [had] been convicted of murdering a businessman he met on a website for cannibalism fetishists'.[3] A notorious English case, *R v Dudley and Stephens*,[4] is also relevant here. In this case, two defendants were convicted of murder for killing and eating a cabin boy in order to survive while they drifted in a lifeboat following a

---

[1] *R (on the application of Nicklinson and another) v Ministry of Justice* [2014] UKSC 38.
[2] See National Archives, PCOM 8/351.
[3] BBC, 'Germany "Cannibal" Trial: Former Policeman is Sentenced'
<www.bbc.co.uk/news/world-europe-32146031> accessed 7 October 2015.
[4] *R v Dudley and Stephens* (1884) 14 QBD 273.

shipwreck. In the related judgment, Huddleston B. noted a previous case involving shipwrecked sailors who killed and ate a person after the drawing of lots, the lot having fallen on the person who had proposed it. Moreover, consent to death is relevant in relation to organ donation: the debate here is whether the law should allow the donation of vital organs prior to death in certain circumstances, even though the donation would cause death. We shall consider all of the above situations in examining how the law on homicide should deal with consent. Our argument is that the law should take a principled rather than an ad hoc approach to cases of consensual death, but that each case should be considered on its particular facts. We conclude that consent to the deliberate infliction of death should be a defence to a murder charge in at least certain cases where it is not currently allowed, i.e. that reform is advisable. Our focus here is not on the definition of 'consent', which is a subject in itself;[5] rather, it is on the relevance of consent. For the purposes of this article, when we refer to 'consent to death' or 'consensual killing', we are simply referring to situations where V either agreed to be killed or to the drawing of lots to determine whether this would happen.[6] What we are considering in this chapter is where people ought to be able to give legally relevant consent in criminal law cases of these types, not what counts as consent for these purposes.

Current Law

We will begin with a very brief outline of the current English criminal law approach to consent to death so that the analysis which follows can be better understood in its context. The law in this area is beguilingly simple, at least on the face of it.[7] The general rule is that 'consent to the deliberate infliction of death is no defence to a charge of murder'.[8] The only explicit exception to this is in the context of suicide pacts, where V's consent reduces what would be murder to manslaughter.[9] As the Law Commission put it in 2005:

---

[5] On this issue, see Catherine Elliott and Claire de Than, 'The Case for a Rational Reconstruction of Consent in Criminal Law' (2007) 70 Modern Law Review 225.

[6] We use the term V here simply as a form of convenient shorthand, not to imply that the person who died was necessarily exploited by D.

[7] *Airedale NHS Trust v Bland* [1993] AC 789, 892 (Lord Mustill).

[8] ibid.

[9] Homicide Act 1957, s 4. It must be recognised that the law is more complex than it might first appear in relation to cases involving the provision of medical treatment. The law allows a person to consent to the withdrawal of medical

'Euthanasia' is, in law, murder. Even so, if someone kills another person as part of a suicide pact, but then does not (for whatever reason) kill themselves, they are only guilty of manslaughter. If they simply helped the other person to die they may be convicted of the lesser offence of 'assisting suicide', contrary to section 2 of the Suicide Act 1961.[10]

How should Criminal Law Deal with Consensual Killing?

Although the law in this context is easy to state, it is controversial and the issues relating to it are complex. There has been much debate of the issues of euthanasia and assisted suicide; indeed, this matter was debated in Parliament in relation to the Assisted Dying Bill 2014-15 and the subsequent short-lived Assisted Dying Bill 2015.[11] While these are important matters, we have chosen not to restrict ourselves to them but to

---

treatment even where this will lead to death. The rule is that 'it is unlawful, so as to constitute both a tort and the crime of battery, to administer medical treatment to an adult, who is conscious and of sound mind, without his consent (...) Such a person is completely at liberty to decline to undergo treatment, even if the result of his doing so will be that he will die' (*Bland* (n 7) 857 (Lord Keith)). This rule 'extends to the situation where the person, in anticipation of his, through one cause or another, entering into a condition such as P.V.S. [persistent vegetative state], gives clear instructions that in such [an] event he is not to be given medical care, including artificial feeding, designed to keep him alive' (ibid). This means that 'a patient of sound mind may, if properly informed, require that life support should be discontinued' (ibid 864 (Lord Goff)). In cases like this, the common law contentiously characterises the withdrawal of medical treatment as an omission rather than an act, and concludes: 'there is no question of the patient having committed suicide, nor therefore of the doctor having aided or abetted him in doing so. It is simply that the patient has, as he is entitled to do, declined to consent to treatment which might or would have the effect of prolonging his life, and the doctor has, in accordance with his duty, complied with his patient's wishes' (ibid (Lord Goff)).

[10] The Law Commission, *A New Homicide Act for England and Wales?* (Law Com CP 177, 2006) 1.82. For recent case law in this area, see *R (Pretty) v Director of Public Prosecutions (Secretary of State for the Home Department intervening)* [2001] UKHL 61, *R. (on the application of Purdy) v DPP* [2009] UKHL 45, and *R (on the application of Nicklinson) v Ministry of Justice* [2014] UKSC 38.

[11] For recent relevant discussion, see, for example, Emily Jackson and John Keown, *Debating Euthanasia* (Hart Publishing 2011); John Coggon, 'The Wonder of Euthanasia: A Debate that's Being Done to Death' (2013) 33 Oxford Journal of Legal Studies 401; Sam Halliday, 'Comparative Reflections Upon the Assisted Dying Bill 2013' (2013) 13 Medical Law International 135; Carman Draghici, 'The Blanket Ban on Assisted Suicide: Between Moral Paternalism and Utilitarian Justice' (2015) European Human Rights Law Review 286.

also consider issues which have received less attention and which are therefore ripe for further exploration. Indeed, the majority of our discussion is not about so-called 'mercy killings', although it is informed by the debate relating to euthanasia. We argue that the law should take a principled approach to cases of consensual death, but that each case should be considered on its particular facts. Our unique contribution to this field is to develop a three-stage approach to apply to cases in this area, and to explore how this approach might apply to a range of particular types of case which have received relatively little legal academic attention. In this way, we aim to significantly enhance the field in two respects: first, by proposing a general approach; and secondly, by suggesting answers in relation to particular legal questions raised by case law.

Academic work on defences to homicide tends to start from the blanket position that killing is wrong, and hence the focus is placed upon whether there are good legal, societal or moral grounds for the existence of a defence or exemption from liability. Contrary to this, our starting point is the methodology recommended by Paul Roberts. His view is that:

> In order to determine whether a particular form of conduct should be criminalized it is always necessary to pose two quite separate questions:
> (1) Is there a good (moral) reason to justify extending the criminal law to this particular conduct?
> (2) Should this conduct be criminalized all things considered (with particular reference to other moral principles and the pragmatics of law enforcement)?[12]

This is a sensible general method to determine whether conduct should be criminalised. The first stage deals with matters of principle, considering any relevant clashes of philosophical perspectives.[13] If a proposed criminal prohibition 'passes muster at the level of principle it is necessary to consider whether there is a compelling case for criminalisation all things considered',[14] considering matters such as 'general principles of law-making, criminal procedure, and the ethics and practicalities of law

---

[12] Law Commission, *Consent in the Criminal Law* (Law Com CP 139, 1995), C.18. This quotation is from Appendix C of a Law Commission report on consent. Roberts did not write this Appendix, but it reflects the advice that he gave to the Commission about a philosophical approach to issues in this context. He defends this approach in Paul Roberts, 'The Philosophical Foundations of Consent in the Criminal Law' (1997) 17 Oxford Journal of Legal Studies 389.

[13] Roberts ibid 401.

[14] ibid.

enforcement'.[15] Roberts' scheme is rightly premised on the idea that conduct should be lawful unless its prohibition would be justified.[16] Moreover, it recognises not only that 'criminal wrongs cannot be reduced to the degree of injury suffered by a "victim"'[17] and that '[c]ircumstances must alter cases',[18] but also that the law should not assume 'that all injuries (including consensually inflicted injuries) above a certain level of gravity constitute criminal harms, unless they can be brought within some pre-ordained protected category'.[19] This might not sound contentious to non-criminal lawyers, but English law adopts what Roberts calls 'the quantitative-rule-plus-exceptions approach'[20] in relation to offences to the person;[21] indeed, as discussed above, the general rule is that consent is no defence to a charge of murder. Thus, Roberts' approach does not reflect the law; moreover, the Law Commission rejected it in their 1995 consultation paper on consent,[22] and implicitly in their 2015 paper on the reform of offences against the person.[23]

---

[15] ibid. These matters are sketched out in Appendix C of the Law Commission's 1995 consultation paper (n 12).

[16] As Andrew Simester and Graham Sullivan put it in *Criminal Law: Theory and Doctrine* (3rd ed. Hart Publishing 2007) 5: 'No-one, including the State, should coerce others without good reason. The constriction of people's conduct calls for justification, especially when it is accompanied by censorious and punitive treatment of those who do not comply. Unless there are compelling reasons, the criminal law should not be deployed (…).'

[17] Roberts (n 12) 402.

[18] *R v Brown* [1994] 1 AC 212, 270e (Lord Mustill), quoted approvingly by Roberts, ibid.

[19] Roberts, ibid 404.

[20] ibid.

[21] The general rule is that 'the line [between criminalisation and non-criminalisation is] (…) between assault at common law and the offence of assault occasioning actual bodily harm created by s 47 of the Offences against the Person Act 1861, with the result that consent of the victim is no answer to anyone charged with the latter offence or with a contravention of s 20 unless the circumstances fall within one of the well-known exceptions such as organised sporting contests and games, parental chastisement or reasonable surgery' (*Brown* (n 18) 244-245 (Lord Jauncey)). It is arguable that consent of the victim is also no answer to anyone charged with assault or battery who intended to cause injury (see Alan Reed and Ben Fitzpatrick, *Criminal Law* (4th ed. Sweet and Maxwell 2009) 409, and the discussion in the recent Law Commission paper, *Reform of Offences Against the Person,* Law Com 3611, 2015).

[22] See Roberts (n 12) 404-405, criticising the Law Commission for not adopting his recommended approach.

[23] Law Commission (n 21).

A further benefit of Roberts' scheme is that its second stage takes account of pragmatic considerations. As he puts it, 'Even moral prohibitions with firm philosophical foundations should not be translated into criminal laws if in practice they would, for example, produce evil side-effects that are morally worse than the conduct to be prohibited'.[24] In addition, Roberts' proposed structure brings transparency to the process at hand. 'It demands that any assertion or position should be backed up by arguments, in the form of reasons, for holding the beliefs and commitments which underpin it'.[25] The point here is not that Roberts' two stage approach simplifies matters, but that it facilitates open debate.[26] However, a limitation with the framework developed by Roberts is that it cannot deal with the matter at hand in this chapter without modification.[27] In this chapter, we are not simply interested in *whether* conduct should be criminalised, but also in *how* the law should deal with cases where criminalisation is appropriate. The choice here is not a binary one between liability and non-liability; if criminalisation is merited, it is also important to choose between different possible offences in imposing liability. There are presently only two such relevant forms of homicide in English law: murder and manslaughter.[28] Nonetheless, English law could in principle develop a new offence to deal with consensual killing in some or all cases, if this were appropriate. For example, for reasons of 'fair labelling', English law could introduce an

---

[24] Roberts (n 12) 402.

[25] Law Commission (n 12) C4.

[26] As the Law Commission summarised his position, ibid C3: 'Philosophical investigation cannot reconcile competing ethical commitments, efface moral dilemmas, reduce the need to work out solutions to moral problems under conditions of uncertainty or put an end to moral argument and debate'.

[27] This is not intended as a criticism of Roberts' approach as it is summarised by the Law Commission in their paper and his related article, discussed above. His framework is not designed to deal with such matters but rather focused upon a single, albeit extremely complex, issue: whether conduct should be criminalised.

[28] Manslaughter is relevant because one possible approach is to amend the law so that a partial defence dealing with consensual killing could reduce what would be murder to voluntary manslaughter. This defence could operate in the same way as the current partial defences to murder of loss of control and diminished responsibility, but in different contexts. Indeed, it is worth noting here that the Law Commission did consider expanding the defence of diminished responsibility to cover some cases of consensual killing (Law Commission (n 10) 8.36 and 8.89-8.94). We have proposed elsewhere that a remodelled diminished responsibility defence would remove disability discrimination issues from the current law, and we will examine such as defence in the current context later in this chapter.

offence of 'killing upon request'.[29] German criminal law has such an offence, which applies where 'a person is induced to kill by the express and earnest request of the victim' and is punishable by a maximum of five years imprisonment.[30] 'The rationale for the penalty is that the victim's consent reduces the wrongfulness of the wrongdoing'.[31] It is because there are different potential forms of liability in this context that we will adapt Roberts' test for our own purposes by adding a third stage to it. Our test consists of Robert's first two stages in addition to a third question to be considered if the answer to each of the first two is affirmative: *How* should this conduct be criminalised, all things considered?

At this stage, we should explain why we reject two possible extreme positions on consensual killings. First, we reject the current English position that consent is only a 'defence'[32] to a charge of murder in the context of suicide pacts where a person kills or is party to a killing in pursuance of a suicide pact. The fundamental problem with this approach is that it pays insufficient respect to autonomy: by adopting an inflexible approach, English law does not sufficiently recognise that circumstances may alter cases.[33] We agree with Heidi Hurd that consent is morally transformative because it facilitates autonomy by giving the individual 'the ability to create and dispel rights and duties'.[34] As she says:

> Consent can function to transform the morality of another's conduct – to make an action right when it would otherwise be wrong (...). By consenting to another's intrusion onto one's land, one dispels a duty that antecedently obligated that person to keep off private property'.[35]

---

[29] On the importance of fair labelling generally, see James Chalmers and Fiona Leverick, 'Fair Labelling in Criminal Law' 71 (2008) Modern Law Review 217.

[30] German Criminal Code, S 216.

[31] George Fletcher, *Rethinking Criminal Law* (Little, Brown and Company 1978) 332.

[32] There is of course debate as to whether consent is a defence to offences against the person, or whether its absence is part of the actus reus of a relevant offence; see Law Commission (n 21) 5.20.

[33] On the importance of considering the facts of the case in issue, see Julia Tolmie, 'Consent to Harmful Assaults: The Case for Moving Away from Category Based Decision Making' [2012] Criminal Law Review 656.

[34] Heidi Hurd, 'The Moral Magic of Consent' (1996) 2 Legal Theory 121, 124.

[35] ibid 123.

Where law disregards consent, it interferences with autonomy because it restricts what Hurd calls 'the capacity for self legislation'.[36] English law does not allow the capacity for self-legislation in cases where people consent to be killed. Thus, it does not 'respect persons as autonomous' in this context because it does not recognize them as 'the givers and takers of rights and duties' as far as their lives are concerned.[37] As we will argue below, this approach is not justified.

However, we also reject the view that where there is consent there should be an absolute right to be killed, or, to put it another way, that the criminal law should always respect an individual's autonomy by not imposing liability on a party who carries out a consensual killing. Respecting an individual's choices is not all-important; there are other considerations which may be relevant. It may be true to say that each person should have 'a right to have the final say over what happens to him and his body',[38] and thus the right to commit suicide. Nonetheless, this does not mean that there should be no criminal liability where a person kills another individual who wishes to die:

> The fact that one has the right to the final say over what happens to one's body does not imply that anyone else has the right to go along with one's preferences or accede to one's requests. It merely means that others may not positively interfere against one's wishes, and there might still be certain things that Jones has no right to do to Smith irrespectively of whether Smith has consented to or even requested them.[39]

It also does not mean that V can expect a willing D to be provided by the state in order to help V to die. Our position is that there may be a good moral reason to justify extending the criminal law to a consensual killing, and it may be that such a killing should be criminalised, all things considered. For instance, we argue below that the law should continue to criminalise killings where D intended to help V make a deception in relation to a life insurance policy. What follows is a consideration of various kinds of cases of consensual killing. We will briefly describe these cases for the sake of clarity, considering each of them according to the themes which they raise. However, our focus is on how the law should

---

[36] ibid 124.
[37] ibid.
[38] Ian Brassington, 'Five Words for Assisted Dying' (2008) 27 Law and Philosophy 415, 422, summarising autonomy-based arguments for the legalisation of suicide.
[39] ibid 418.

address the issues that they raise. Although we will consider these cases in clusters, we shall explain that it is necessary to bear in mind that there may be important distinctions between cases within each category and that the appropriate legal response cannot be determined here simply by deciding the category into which a case falls. A more sophisticated and subtle approach is required for the intricacies of human life and death.

Cannibalism

In our introduction, we referred to three consensual cannibalism cases: first, two cases in which a fetish for human flesh is an issue, and, secondly, a case in which cannibalism occurred because of hunger after a shipwreck. Our view is that there is a significant distinction between these two types of case based on the circumstances and the motivations of the parties involved, but that consent should be a complete defence in both of them, albeit for different reasons.

Let us begin with the first type of cannibalism. This is exemplified by the case of Armin Miewes, a German man who killed and ate Bernd Brandes, another German. They met via the internet after the latter responded to an advertisement placed by Miewes on cannibalism websites. This advertisement requested a volunteer to be killed and eaten. Miewes had 'a lifelong desire to eat another human being; (...) [Brandes had a] lifelong desire to be eaten'.[40] Miewes killed and ate Brandes with the latter's enthusiastic agreement. 'They exchange[d] consent not once, but repeatedly, videotaping their consent, signing a formal "willingness agreement," and performing other acts making clear the total resolve of the victim as well as the cannibal'.[41] Miewes regarded such cannibalism as 'a genuine bonding of spirit and mind'[42] between him and a willing participant, 'a sacred communion with a [willing] sacrificial offering'.[43] The precise nature of the motives of Miewes and Brandes is a matter of dispute, particularly in relation to whether there was a sexual character to

---

[40] Charles Reid, 'Eat What You Kill: Or, A Strange and Gothic Tale of Cannibalism by Consent' (2013-14) 39 North Carolina Journal of International Law and Commercial Regulation 423.

[41] ibid.

[42] ibid 469, citing Lois Jones, *Cannibal: The True Story Behind the Maneater of Rotenburg* (Berkley Books 2005) 151-54.

[43] Reid ibid.

the behaviour concerned.[44] However, what is clear is that both parties concerned acted on the basis of long-standing cravings.

How should the law deal with consent in this kind of case? It might be objected that Brandes was not rational and competent and thus unable to consent. However, we cannot assume this simply because he agreed to be killed and eaten. Under English law, he is presumed to have capacity unless and until it is proved otherwise, and emotional problems do not necessarily deny capacity. 'It is highly likely that Brandes did indeed have "emotional problems," but if every person with emotional problems were denied the right to determine what is in his own interests, none of us would be self-determining in the eyes of the law, except those of us who had no emotions to have problems with'.[45] The issue here is how the law should deal with D, assuming that Brandes was mentally competent. One view is that D should be convicted for murder, since 'One of the basic moral principles of our society is that one should not take another human life, and to do so with the intention of eating that person's flesh seems to further compound such an act.'[46] Nonetheless, this is a conclusion rather than a fully-developed argument: it is true that it is a basic moral principle that one should not take another human life, but there are exceptions to this principle, e.g. in relation to self-defence. Thus, the basic principle does not in itself determine the matter at hand.

An alternative approach is to focus upon the autonomy rights of V, since 'the claim would be that it is his right to sexual autonomy and [the] right to die that would be violated by the unavailability of the consent defense in the Meiwes case'.[47] Adopting this approach, Youngjae Lee argues that granting D a defence in a case like this would not protect a freedom that was worth protecting:

> Intimate relationships are important aspects of human flourishing and well-being, and the government accordingly has an interest in promoting a

---

[44] For detailed consideration of this and other related factual issues, see Reid (n 40).

[45] Theodore Dalrymple, 'The Case for Cannibalism' <www.city-journal.org/html/eon_01_05_04td.html> accessed 6 October 2015. See too Vera Bergelson, 'The Right to Be Hurt: Testing the Boundaries of Consent' (2006-07) 75 George Washington Law Review 165, 186; Youngjae Lee, 'Valuing Autonomy' (2006-07) Fordham Law Review 2973, 2986.

[46] W. McQuillan, 'Challenging our Aversion to Anthropophagy' [2005] University College London Jurisprudence Review 180, 195.

[47] Lee (n 45) 2984.

culture in which people are (and feel) free to enter into relationships that
are important for living good lives. No analogous argument can be made
about killing and eating a human being or being killed and eaten.[48]

Lee's position is unsatisfactory. Firstly, such an approach in any context
risks a paternalistic judgment about the choices of others, and a severe
encroachment on the freely chosen behaviour of adults. There is no single
morality concept, as the European Court of Human Rights has noted
repeatedly.[49] Further, Lee's argument seems to overlook the point. What is
at stake in this kind of case is the right to die for a particular reason rather
than live in a particular way. Societies glorify death 'for one's country', or
in 'noble self-sacrifice', such as throwing oneself in front of V to protect
him from a natural disaster, when the former is not necessarily a free
choice and the latter does not represent an overall gain for society; at best
it is a substituted loss. For Brandes, it was crucial to be killed for the
purposes of cannibalism. Adopting arguments that may be called at least
partially 'moralistic' in nature, some theorists have argued for
criminalisation in such a case. By 'moralism', we mean interfering with a
person's autonomy in the service of 'the interests a person ought to
recognize or choose for herself, whether or not she knows she has them or
ought to have them'.[50] Vera Bergelson argues that 'by killing Brandes,
Meiwes (…) used Brandes as an object, a means of obtaining a desired
experience, and thus disregarded his dignity.'[51] The claim here is that 'no
matter how respectfully Armin Meiwes treated his victim, cannibalism by
its very terms denies people equal moral worth and thus assaults the
victim's dignity'.[52] Nonetheless, this argument about objectification is not
convincing. As Jeremy Wisnewski states: 'If I have as an end to be
consumed by someone who wants to consume me (as Brandes did), it
might well be a sign of respect for my agency to carry out this action'.[53] It
is not obvious that granting somebody their life-long wish is assaulting
their dignity. Similarly, it is also hard to understand arguments based upon
the need to protect society at large in this context. Bergelson's view is that:

> [W]e should recognize that every time we use the 'dignity' argument to
> criminalize consensual behavior, we override an individual's liberty –

---

[48] ibid 2987.

[49] See for example *Muller v Switzerland* [1988] ECHR 5 [36].

[50] Roberts (n 12) 393.

[51] Bergelson (n 45) 221.

[52] ibid 217.

[53] Jeremy Wisnewski, 'Murder, Cannibalism, and Indirect Suicide: A Philosophical
Study of a Recent Case' (2007) 14 Philosophy in the Contemporary World 11, 20.

partly paternalistically, but mostly for the benefit of society at large. Therefore, as with any imposition on individual liberty, the threat to society should be serious enough to warrant the use of criminal sanctions.[54]

However, it is not clear how society at large might be threatened by some people choosing to be killed for the purposes of cannibalism, at least where such people are competent and the killings take place in private and there is therefore no 'likelihood of tangible harm to society by disturbance being caused by witnessing the events'.[55] It is true that such killings might provoke outrage amongst the community at large, but this is neither inevitable nor a reason why it should be criminalised.[56] It is now almost impossible to obtain a conviction for an obscenity offence under the Obscene Publications Acts; outrage changes with time, and many events which cause outrage are not crimes.

Touching upon the point of harm to society, Victor Tadros has argued that there are two reasons why 'a person must treat her own life and body as sacred'.[57] First, 'When a person treats her own life or body as worthless, she may contribute to a culture in which lives and bodies are more generally regarded as worthless'.[58] Secondly, 'she may contribute to a culture that undermines the tendency that other people have to develop attitudes of self-respect'.[59] However, Tadros offers no empirical evidence in support of these two claims. Furthermore, it is arguable that Brandes did not regard his own life or body as worthless: on the contrary, it may be that he regarded himself as making a valuable sacrifice. The opposite assertion could equally be true: perhaps people make decisions in their own lives not merely as sheep or trend-followers, but by rejecting examples set by others. Arguments about cultural harm were made in support of the extreme pornography legislation, again without supporting

---

[54] Bergelson (n 45) 218.

[55] David Ormerod, 'Consent and Offences against the Person: Law Commission Consultation Paper No. 134' (1994) 57 MLR 928, 939, making a general point about a possible distinction between consensual injuries in private and public.

[56] See Wisnewski (n 53) 19, pointing out that 'People are sometimes outraged by perfectly innocuous things' and that 'there have, after all, been societies that routinely practiced cannibalism'.

[57] Victor Tadros, 'Consent to Harm' (2011) 64 Current Legal Problems 23, 43.

[58] ibid.

[59] ibid.

evidence, and were met with sustained criticism.[60] Thus, Tadros' points are not necessarily relevant in this kind of case.

Our view is that there is not a good moral reason to justify extending the criminal law to this particular conduct where it takes place in private and V has capacity, i.e. the ability to understand the choice he is making and its consequences. Indeed, from an animal rights perspective, it can be argued that 'since Meiwes sought consent (...) it seems far better than the millions of us who simply purchase the end result of countless suffering animals'[61] or those who take the lives of non-human sentient creatures for food, fun or profit. We acknowledge that, since partial cannibalism is possible through, for example, the consensual donation of a limb or flesh, there would also need to be a consent defence available under non-fatal offences, which would require reform to the *Brown*[62] principle that consent cannot exculpate intentional infliction of harm. However, our view does not mean that there should be no safeguards in this context to protect those who might lack capacity. For example, we would argue that there should be criminal liability where V did not give explicit enthusiastic consent[63] and had not been evaluated by several independent psychiatrists. Even if there is a 'good moral reason' to criminalise consensual cannibalism, such as public health, then it does not follow that it should be murder. There are already other relevant crimes – preventing a lawful burial at common law, for example. If the 'good moral reason' is related to outrage, then it stems from the cannibalism rather than the killing, and should be labelled appropriately with a specific offence.

---

[60] See, for example, Erica Rackley and Clare McGlynn, 'The Cultural Harm of Rape Pornography' <freespeechdebate.com/en/discuss/the-cultural-harm-of-rape-pornography/> accessed 31 January 2016, stating: 'one common response to the cultural harm argument is to suggest that it is nothing more than assertion. (...) But (...) our inability to prove [that rape pornography causes cultural harm] is not in itself a reason for thinking that these connections do not exist'.

[61] Tauriq Moosa, 'Murders, Monsters and Mirrors: The Ethics of Killing and Cannibalism' <www.3quarksdaily.com/3quarksdaily/2010/12/murders-monsters-mirrors.html> accessed 7 October 2015.

[62] *Brown* (n 18).

[63] We have written elsewhere about consent, capacity and enthusiastic consent to serious harm, arguing that enthusiastic consent should be a defence to serious injury in certain circumstance: Claire de Than and Jesse Elvin, 'The relationship between capacity and consent' in Alan Reed and Michael Bohlander (eds), *Consent: Domestic and Comparative Perspectives* (Routledge 2017) Chapter 3 (forthcoming).

The second type of cannibalism case which we wish to consider involves killings and cannibalism which occurred because of hunger after a shipwreck. There are many historical examples of such a case, often involving victims who agreed to the drawing of lots to determine who would be killed.[64] Such cases raise issues relating to two potential defences: consent and necessity. Our view in this context is that these two doctrines should be developed in combination with each other to provide a complete defence in appropriate circumstances. We believe that there may not be a good moral reason to justify criminalising D's conduct where V was competent to make a decision and agreed to be killed in order to save the lives of others. In *Re A (Children) (Conjoined Twins: Surgical Separation)*, Brooke LJ controversially held that the doctrine of necessity could be a defence where a proposed operation to separate conjoined twins, who were only a few weeks old and thus lacking the capacity to give consent in law, would lead to the death of the weaker twin.[65] He stated:

> [T]here are three requirements for the application of the doctrine of necessity: (i) the act is needed to avoid inevitable and irreparable evil; (ii) no more should be done than is reasonably necessary for the purpose to be achieved; (iii) the evil inflicted must not be disproportionate to the evil avoided.[66]

This is not the place to explore the appropriate general parameters of the necessity defence.[67] However, we would like to explore how it should apply where V was competent to make a decision and agreed to be killed in an emergency in order to save the lives of others. Bergelson argues that V's consent is essential in this context, and that 'no amount of saved lives' would justify a non-consensual killing.[68] Regardless of whether or not this is true, we argue that consent is at least relevant, and that the doctrine of necessity should apply where valid consent is present and the three requirements outlined by Brooke LJ are satisfied.

---

[64] See Alfred Simpson, 'Cannibals at Common Law' (Crosskey Lectures No. 5, 1981) 6. Simpson argues that 'maritime survival cannibalism, preceded by lot drawing and killing, was, in fact, a socially accepted practice among seamen until the end of the days of sail'.

[65] *Re A (Children) (Conjoined Twins: Surgical Separation)* [2001] Fam 147.

[66] ibid 240.

[67] This is a field of study in itself.

[68] Bergelson (n 45) 229.

We agree with Bergelson that consent is relevant here because its presence is necessary to ensure that there is no violation of V's right to life: 'the consensual killing would not involve a certain kind of harm, namely, violation of rights',[69] since V would have chosen to sacrifice his or her life. Nonetheless, we do not agree with Bergelson's use of the concept of 'dignity' here. Discussing a hypothetical lifeboat scenario 'in which all will die unless a few sacrifice their lives',[70] Bergelson argues that it would be legitimate for D to push any volunteers overboard who were unable to move themselves, since doing so would not violate 'their rights nor (...) [disregard] their dignity and, in addition (...) [save] numerous human lives which otherwise would have been lost'.[71] As explained by Bergelson, violation of dignity occurs where treatment denies 'the victim the respect to which every person is entitled just by virtue of being a human being'.[72] This might sound like a vague concept, but it appears that its application would in fact be partially determined by how many members of a community regard the treatment as unacceptable, since Bergelson claims: 'To be morally convincing, this understanding of dignity has to be shared by the community at large'. [73] The obvious problem with this approach is that it would make law a popularity contest where the majority could criminalise consensual activity conducted by the minority by reference to the concept of dignity. Berlgeson would only allow 'the "dignity" argument' to criminalise consensual behaviour where 'the threat to society (...) [would] be serious enough to warrant the use of criminal sanctions'.[74] However, it is not clear in what sense violations of dignity could ever be a threat to society at large if dignity is concerned with the respect to which individuals are entitled by virtue of being a human being. Bergelson's approach explicitly builds upon Anthony Duff's notions of dignity and humanity.[75] Duff argues that 'that there are more ways to deny or radically fail to respect humanity than by violating autonomy. We (...) therefore have good reason – reason of the same kind as we have to criminalize violations of autonomy – to criminalize other modes of conduct that deny or radically fail to respect the humanity of those against or on whom they

---

[69] ibid 222.
[70] ibid.
[71] ibid 228.
[72] ibid 218.
[73] ibid.
[74] ibid.
[75] ibid 218-219.

are perpetrated'.[76] Nonetheless, Duff's argument seems to be focused upon the need to protect the individual, rather than society. His point seems to be that the protection of a person's dignity can be a valid reason for interfering with that person's autonomy in the person's own interest, not to save others; being shoved off a lifeboat is not in the volunteers' own interests, since they are likely to die either way, but will now die alone. Moreover, Duff concludes that the fact that we might have good reason to criminalise 'these kinds of conduct (…) [does not mean] that we should in the end and on balance criminalize them'.[77] Thus, Duff's argument does not provide strong support for Bergelson's position about dignity.

Where D Killed V because V Wished to be Killed for the Purposes of a Fraud

Let us now consider cases where V wanted D to kill him or her for the purposes of a fraud in relation to a life insurance policy; for example, by V hiring D as a hitman to kill V. There are several cases which are relevant here.[78] The facts of some of them are a matter of dispute, but in a United States case involving a killing in 2009, it is clear 'that the decedent sought the defendant's assistance to help him accomplish his goal of ending his life and making it look like he was killed'.[79] According to this defendant, the decedent explained that the killing 'needed to look like a robbery so his family could get the life insurance benefits'.[80] There was a dispute in this case about whether D stabbed V or whether V impaled himself on a knife held by D.[81] Nonetheless, for the purposes of argument, let us assume that the former occurred. As far as English law is concerned, a defendant in such a case has committed conspiracy to defraud by agreeing

---

[76] Anthony Duff, 'Harms and Wrongs' (2001) 5 Buffalo Criminal Law Review 13, 44.

[77] ibid 45.

[78] See, for example, Linda Stratman, 'Murder by Consent' <www.lindastratmann.com/articles/the-long-pack-murder-by-consent.aspx> accessed 7 October 2015, discussing two cases which occurred in South Africa in the 1960s.

[79] *People v Minor* 2013 NY Slip Op 06444. Decided on October 3, 2013. Appellate Division, First Department.

[80] ibid.

[81] An appeal court ordered a retrial, holding that D's conviction for murder was unsafe because the jury's decision had not been based upon proper legal instruction.

to a plan to defraud an insurance company.[82] Moreover, D would be liable for murder for carrying out this plan.[83] However, the issue here is what approach English law *should* take in relation to such a case.

It is the law in relation to the implementation of the plan in which we are interested. Adopting our three-stage methodology outlined above for determining how the criminal law should approach consensual killing, we would argue that there is a good reason to justify extending the criminal law to a defendant who carries out a plan to make a deception in relation to a life insurance policy, and that this conduct should always be criminalised, all things considered. The difficult issue here is whether D should be liable for a homicide offence for carrying out this agreement. Our view is that such liability is only appropriate in certain cases. Thus, we do not agree with the current English law, which would always make D liable for murder.

A good reason for extending the criminal law to this particular conduct is the need to discourage those who might otherwise assist a person who intends to commit fraud in relation to a life insurance policy; a second good reason is to punish those who participate in such fraud. This is one situation where even liberals would accept that there are good reasons to justify extending the criminal law. Liberals are hostile to state intervention but accept it in the interests of the prevention of harm to others; 'that there must be limits to individual freedom is implicit in the liberal's own position'.[84] Moreover, there is a compelling reason for criminalisation, all things considered. In particular, there is no state action short of criminalisation which might be effective in controlling or eradicating the conduct in question, since there is no other action which might act as a deterrent here. Moreover, there is 'a realistic prospect of the prohibition being enforced';[85] it would not be 'aimed at very trivial harms or at activities that many thoughtful law-abiding people regard as doing no harm to anyone'.[86] Thus, we need to consider *how* this conduct should be criminalised.

---

[82] See the definition of conspiracy to defraud in *Scott v Metropolitan Commissioner* [1975] AC 819, 839 (Viscount Dilhorne).

[83] D could also have committed an offence under the Serious Crime Act 2007; e.g. contrary to section 45.

[84] Law Commission (n 12) [C40].

[85] Law Commission ibid [C104], discussing one of the requirements for criminal prohibition in relation to consensual harm.

[86] ibid.

Our view is that V's consent means that D should not be liable for a homicide offence in this context where V had the chance to consider matters in the light of his or her long-term goals. However, we believe that English law should introduce some kind of 'killing upon request' offence to deal with other cases where D's moral wrongdoing was reduced but not extinguished. We stated above that there is no violation of V's right to life where V has chosen to sacrifice his or her life to save the lives of others in an emergency. However, we believe that a limited paternalism model could legitimately be extended to cover certain situations where V agreed to be killed as part of a fraud in relation to a life insurance policy. We have adopted this idea from Andrew Von Hirsch, who has stated that a 'limited-paternalism model' could be applied to all cases where V had asked D to terminate his or her life.[87] Von Hirsch's point is that D could 'be called upon to allow (…) [V] a waiting period for reflection and reconsideration, before permissibly acting on his request.'[88] As Hirsch says, 'Humans are fallible, and are tempted in moments of stress to take actions that lead to drastic and irreversible consequences to themselves. In such situations, a refusal ever to intervene could frustrate the achievement of the person's own longer-term goals'.[89] The type of case at hand is one where V is under considerable stress because of financial problems. For instance, in the 2009 United States case mentioned above, the victim 'was drowning in debt and in early 2009 had been ordered to return over $121,000 in gains he had received in an investment that turned out to be a Ponzi scheme'.[90] Thus, Hirsch's observations are relevant here.

Making D liable for a homicide offence in all non-emergency situations where s/he did not allow V a waiting period for reflection and reconsideration might encourage individuals not to act until it became reasonably clear that death really was V's considered wish. Moreover, it could punish D appropriately for wrongfully killing V: '[D] acts wrongfully, it may be argued, if he does the killing without giving (…) [V] adequate opportunity for reflection and reconsideration'.[91] This wrongful

---

[87] Andrew von Hirsch, 'Direct Paternalism: Criminalizing Self-Injurious Conduct' (2008) 27 Criminal Justice Ethics 25, 31.

[88] ibid.

[89] ibid 26, explicitly drawing upon the work of John Kleinig, *Paternalism* (Rowman & Allanheld, 1983) 67-73, and Gerald Dworkin, 'Paternalism' (1972) 56 The Monist 64.

[90] Walter Pavlo, 'When White Collar Crime Involves Murder – The Case of Jeffrey Locker' *Forbes* (Jersey City, New Jersey) March 4 2011.

[91] Andrew von Hirsch (n 87) 31-32.

killing is in addition to the wrong which D does in participating in an actual or attempted fraud in relation to a life insurance policy. Thus, there is a need for an additional punishment to reflect this. However, V's agreement means that D deserves a lesser punishment and to be convicted for an offence which reflects the nature of his wrongdoing. A 'killing upon request' offence could apply here, with the punishment being a maximum sentence of life imprisonment to deal with a range of possible circumstances, e.g. depending upon the time that D gave V for opportunity for reflection.[92] Our proposals on enthusiastic consent also feed in here: enthusiastic consent requires a reasonable time for reflection.

Life-and-Death Medical Decision-Making

For the reasons outlined in the Introduction, assisted suicide and mercy killing are not the main focus of this chapter; indeed they have been considered in detail by others elsewhere, including the sources listed in footnote 11. We shall therefore make only brief reference to the current very complicated law and recent case developments, before applying the three-stage process. The scenario we will examine is where a person wishes (and freely consents) to die because of the physical or mental anguish which their life-threatening or life-limiting medical condition will cause. This scenario has tested many courts recently, including those of Canada,[93] England,[94] France[95] and Ireland[96] as well as the European Court of Human Rights. The approach of current English law, and indeed the law of many other countries, is that a person with capacity may refuse treatment at any stage, including the withdrawal of treatment which has already been begun (the negative right to be free from medical intervention), or may commit suicide unaided. However, a person who has capacity but whose physical disability prevents them from committing suicide unaided has only a stark choice: to spend some of their remaining

---

[92] A period for reflection would not be suitable in relation to the emergency situations which we discussed above in relation to cannibalism, which is why we would not propose that such a 'cooling off' period should apply to them. As Gerald Dworkin puts it in considering the merits of introducing a 'cooling off' period in relation to decisions made under extreme pressure, 'it may be that if no practical arrangements were feasible then we would have to conclude that there should be no restriction at all on this kind of action' (Dworkin (n 89) 81).
[93] *Carter v Canada* [2015] SCC 5.
[94] *Nicklinson (*n 1).
[95] *Lambert v France* [2015] ECHR 185.
[96] *Fleming v Ireland* [2013] IESC 19.

time travelling to a country where assisted suicide is legal, such as the Benelux countries, or to use their negative right to freedom from medical intervention to refuse treatment, hydration and nutrition, with death as a result. What they cannot do is require anyone else to kill them, nor obtain any legal assurance that D who assists their suicide in the UK will not be prosecuted for either assisting suicide or murder, depending on the facts.[97] Courts have struggled to fit 'right to die' cases within existing frameworks of both criminal law and human rights law, when what V is essentially arguing is not a right to die or the right to life, but a right to a 'good death'. In *Lambert v France*[98] the European Court of Human Rights held that the decision to withdraw artificial hydration and nutrition from V, who was in a minimally conscious state but whose life was not in imminent danger, did not violate the right to life: it was not an intentional killing since V would die from his condition; and the safeguards under French law were sufficient for the positive obligation to protect human life under Article 2, particularly considering the wide margin of appreciation given to States as to end-of-life decisions. Recent English cases have also given a strong interpretation to the right to refuse treatment. For example, in *King's College Hospital NHS Foundation Trust v C and another*, the Court of Appeal upheld V's decision to refuse dialysis after suffering kidney failure as a result of a suicide attempt.[99] The hospital trust had argued that this refusal demonstrated a lack of mental capacity, but the court rightly states that adults have the absolute right to refuse medical treatment, and that mental capacity cannot be assessed by looking at whether a person appears to have made a bad, unwise or irrational decision. Even where V lacks mental capacity, his refusal of medical treatment should be upheld, as it was in *Wye Valley NHS Trust v V*,[100] where the court held that it was not in V's best interests to remove his remaining independence and dignity through amputation of a gangrenous limb against his wishes. The difficulty under the sum total of the current English law is that what is legally permissible (refusal of treatment and sustenance) is not a 'good death' in circumstances of V's choosing. V must either die earlier than they wish, while still able to commit suicide, or in suffering. Arguments based on disability discrimination have failed in England, Ireland and the European Court of Human Rights so far. For example, in *Fleming* the Supreme Court of Ireland stated that the law was neutral and that it was

---

[97] *Nicklinson* (n 1).

[98] *Lambert v France* (n 95)

[99] *King's College Hospital NHS Foundation Trust v C and another* [2015] EWCOP 80, which the media have dubbed the 'Sparkle' case.

[100] *Wye Valley NHS Trust v V* [2015] EWCOP 60.

the fact of F's own disability which prevented her from committing suicide, rather than the legal ban on assisted suicide, since she could legally have committed suicide unaided when she was healthier.[101] Similarly, the European Court of Human Rights held that the applications in *Nicklinson and Lamb v UK*[102] were inadmissible, it being Parliament's role to make appropriate rules on assisted suicide, and Mr Lamb having not yet exhausted all domestic remedies in relation to his argument that there should a procedure by which courts could authorise voluntary euthanasia in appropriate cases.

For the first limb of our Roberts-based process, the good/moral reasons generally argued to justify the ban on voluntary euthanasia are preservation of the sanctity and dignity of life, protection of the vulnerable, and protection of the medical professions from coercion into acts which would breach their most basic ethical principle of 'do no harm'. The last of these will be discussed in the next section of this chapter for practical reasons, and the first has been discussed above in the context of cannibalism. For both, we reject the assertion that they justify criminalising consensual killing where V is an adult, has capacity and gives free informed consent, for the reasons we give elsewhere in this chapter.[103] With regards to protection of the vulnerable, there is no need to criminalise *all* consensual killings of this type: V will not be vulnerable if he or she is an adult, gives free informed consent, and, applying the limited paternalism model, has had reasonable time for reflection. Support for the argument that there is no good moral reason for criminalising *all* physician-assisted suicide can be taken from *Carter v Canada*,[104] where the Canadian Supreme Court found that the section 241(b) of Canada's Criminal Code's prohibition on assisted suicide violated the right to life, liberty and security of the person under Article 7 of the Canadian Charter of Rights and Freedoms.[105] Specifically, the Canadian Supreme Court stated that physician-assisted death should be lawful[106] for 'a competent adult person who (1) clearly consents to the termination of life and (2) has

---

[101] Fleming (n 4).

[102] *Nicklinson* (n 1).

[103] Cf Bergelson (n 45); Tadros (n 57).

[104] *Carter v Canada* (n 93).

[105] The Supreme Court's references to the underlying values of Article 7 of the Charter as individual dignity and autonomy, the right to make fundamental personal choices free from state interference [64], would position their argument comparatively within Article 8 of the ECHR.

[106] Subject to strict safeguards, including independent scrutiny.

a grievous and irremediable medical condition[107] (including an illness, disease or disability) that causes enduring suffering that is intolerable to the individual in the circumstances of his or her own care'.[108] The ruling was suspended until 2016 to give time for implementation. Emily Jackson's argument that 'where we can be certain that a human being's future contains no experiences at all, or only pain or suffering which has become unbearable, death may no longer be an instrumental harm'[109] has therefore found judicial force in Canada. Although the majority of the English Supreme Court in *Nicklinson*[110] found itself unable to balance V's right to respect for private life under Article 8 of the ECHR against the need to protect vulnerable people from being pressured into suicide, the Canadian Supreme Court found no such difficulty in *Carter*, confirming that not every person who wishes to commit suicide is vulnerable, and that a blanket prohibition on physician-assisted suicide was overly broad since in at least some cases nobody vulnerable needed to be protected.[111] The minority in *Nicklinson* would similarly have found the present English law to be incompatible with human rights due to the lack of exceptions.[112] Perhaps the forthcoming proposals for a British Bill of Rights, with the tantalising hints of a constitutional court, would bridge the gap between the two positions.

Moving to the second stage of the process, other principles will sometimes work in favour of interference with autonomy via criminalisation, such as where there is a need to protect a specific V, applying Duff's reasoning on dignity as discussed above. This runs parallel to the arguments that the elderly and terminally ill might face indirect social pressure, real or imagined, to commit suicide, as mooted in *Nicklinson*[113] and in the debates on both recent Assisted Dying Bills. The safeguards insisted upon by the Canadian Supreme Court would address that possibility. But in the general scenario, when there is no specific vulnerability to external pressures, there is another argument to consider. As one of us has argued

---

[107] 'Irremediable does not require a person to undertake treatments that are not acceptable to the individual' Carter (n 1) [127].

[108] ibid [127].

[109] Emily Jackson, 'Secularism, Sanctity, and the Wrongfulness of Killing' (2008) 2 Biosocieties 125, 139.

[110] *Nicklinson* (n 1).

[111] ibid [86].

[112] *Nicklinson* (n 1) [299].

[113] ibid [228].

elsewhere,[114] a case can be made in human rights law that when a person (here V) cannot access a right due to a physical disability which prevents them from using a body part, then D's actions should be lawful if they merely consensually 'lend' a corresponding part of the body to compensate for the effects of the disability. Under that analysis, assisted suicide should be lawful between consenting adults where V is unable to commit suicide unaided. So, viewed in the round, the first two stages of the process do not point towards criminalisation of voluntary euthanasia. Even if our arguments on the first two stages of the process fail, there is room under the third stage for further discussion of how criminalisation should operate. Our earlier proposal of a reworked non-discriminatory diminished responsibility defence[115] would be a way forward, since it could apply to assisted suicide and mercy killing and provide much greater flexibility of disposal, but it is our view that the three-stage process would not point to criminal liability for D at all.

Vital Organ Donation

Our final category of consensual killings for analysis is where V participates in a transplant of a vital organ as a living donor, and again this may be split into two subcategories: where V has an incurable life-threatening medical condition and the donation will speed their death; and where V has no such condition but chooses to donate and hence to die in order to save another who needs a transplanted organ urgently. At present, both situations are subject to the same rule: vital organs may only be donated after brain death (the 'dead donor rule'), to comply with both the current criminal law and with medical ethics. However, both legally and medically, the lines do blur under closer analysis. Deliberately taking a vital organ from a person, who is not brainstem dead, in order to transplant it into another person, would indeed be murder by the physician in spite of consent under the *Bland* principle.[116] Yet there are narrow distinctions on causation and double effect which protect physicians from criminal liability and from breaching their ethical imperatives in situations related

---

[114] Claire de Than, 'Capacity and Consent' Jersey and Guernsey Law Review, forthcoming 2016.

[115] Claire de Than and Jesse Elvin, 'How Should Criminal Law Deal with People who have "Partial Capacity"?' in Alan Reed, Nicola Wake and Ben Livings (eds), *Mental Condition Defences and the Criminal Justice System: Perspectives from Law and Medicine* (Ashgate 2015) 295, 315-317.

[116] *Bland* (n 7).

to patient death: when they switch off life-support machines;[117] prescribe and administer potentially lethal doses of drugs such as morphine in order to reduce pain, while hastening death;[118] or withdraw treatment in a manner which will lead to death through an omission rather than an act.[119] Contrary to both current legal doctrine and medical ethics, Mike Collins has argued that doctors do cause death in legal terms when they remove a brainstem dead V from life-support.[120] Further, the doctrine of double effect has much clearer backing in medical ethics than in law,[121] leading to the appearance that such cases are de facto decriminalised through a combination of an unarticulated defence without binding case authority and prosecutorial discretion. Dealing first with living donors who have life-threatening conditions, whether or not they are currently on life-support, we will apply our three-stage test. Firstly, is there a good moral reason to criminalise consensual living donation of vital organs when V has no prospect of recovery from their existing medical condition? The current understanding of the 'do no harm' ethical imperative could be one moral reason since reform might lead to an expectation on doctors to violate their medical ethics, but that could be countered in various ways. Firstly, medical ethics contain contradictions. Some children are born in order to become living donors of non-vital organs, stem cells and so on for their siblings with life-limiting and life-threatening conditions, and parental consent overrules the wishes of the child; medical ethics allow this, and so are more flexible than some would assert. Secondly, the ethical position is at least murky, and hence may not meet the threshold required for a moral reason:

> The fact that taking vital organs from living patients on life support, prior to treatment withdrawal, would cause their death does not suffice to make this practice unethical .... Given that it is ethical to cause death by withdrawing life-sustaining treatment, it cannot be presumed that it is necessarily unethical to procure vital organs from living patients prior to withdrawing treatment.[122]

---

[117] *Malcherek v Steel* [1981] 1 WLR 690.

[118] Patrick Devlin, *Easing the Passing: The Trial of Dr Bodkin Adams* (2nd edn Bodley Head 1985).

[119] *Bland* (n 7).

[120] Mike Collins, 'Reevaluating the Dead Donor Rule' (2010) 35 Journal of Medicine and Philosophy 154, 166.

[121] Law Commission (n 10).

[122] Franklin Miller et al, 'The Dead Donor Rule: Can It Withstand Critical Scrutiny?' 299, 305.

Miller et al contend that consensual living donation where V is on life-support is ethical (the consent could be given via an Advance Directive). We submit that where V is not on life-support but has no realistic prospect of recovery from an incurable life-threatening condition, and has given informed and enthusiastic consent for living donation of a vital organ, although medical ethics may be a moral reason according to the first stage of the test, they fall within the 'good death' argument and so a physician who assists them should not be criminalised according to the second stage.

A second possible 'good reason' for criminalisation is protecting the vulnerable: many people towards the end of their lives could be regarded as vulnerable. Yet the requirement of consent as we have framed it (informed, free and enthusiastic, from an adult V with capacity, in advance and with legally-acceptable evidence) would prevent such exploitation. It is important not to classify all people with disabilities as vulnerable, since to do so risks violating human rights law. Alternatively, preventing suffering could be argued as the reason for criminalisation: living donation of vital organs could cause pain, suffering and indignity meeting the threshold of inhuman and degrading treatment or punishment under Article 3 of the European Convention on Human Rights. Such suffering could be prevented through palliative care for V and through a code of measures designed to ensure the dignity, comfort and respect of living donors. Such a package of measures would counter the argument made by Rodríguez-Arias et al that the dead donor rule maintains public trust in organ donation,[123] and would remove the desperate artificiality of the current position, where doctors attempt 'to orchestrate (...) death in the operating room, waiting for cardiac death as (...) vital organs are starved of oxygen.'[124]

With regards to the second limb of the test, other moral and pragmatic principles within the bigger picture would work against criminalisation. Medicine does not have a single goal, preserving life; it also aims to heal people, promote health, and help patients to achieve a dignified death[125], all of which are relevant to the present discussion. The arguments which we have made above in the context of cannibalism are also relevant (and

---

[123] David Rodríguez-Arias et al, 'Donation After Circulatory Death: Burying the Dead Donor Rule' (2011) 11 The American Journal of Bioethics 36, 41.
[124] Collins (n 120) 164.
[125] Franklin Miller and Howard Brody, 'Professional Integrity and Physician-Assisted Death' (1995) 25 The Hastings Center Report 8, 13.

probably less controversial) here: allowing living donation demonstrates respect for the autonomy and dignity of V. Further, it respects V's choice of a good death on their own terms and of their own choosing, dying in the knowledge that he or she is making a difference and has saved a life rather than that he or she potentially might save a life through post-mortem donation. In practical terms, and for the health of the donee, organs donated while V was alive are more likely to lead to successful transplants since they have not been starved of oxygenated blood. Hence in relation to living donors with life-threatening conditions, our view is that there should be no criminal liability for D, subject to the above requirements.

Where V does not have a life-threatening condition, but wishes to become a living donor in circumstances which will cause his own death, the situation is almost parallel to that of our first category of consensual cannibalism. The difference is that D will not be acting for his own reasons in carrying out the transplant – the mutuality of benefit is absent. However, where V is an adult, has capacity, and gives enthusiastic informed consent, and D freely and willingly performs the transplant, we would argue that medicine's goals are broad enough to find such donations ethical, and hence there is no good reason to prevent them. Miller and Brody note the practical implications:[126] it would be extremely rare for there to be a competent medical team willing to perform such surgery, but the law needs to deal with the rare and unlikely, as well as the commonplace. However, we would find very strong good reasons against the use of substituted consent (e.g. parental consent), not least the requirements of the United Nations Convention on the Rights of Persons with Disabilities and the Law Commission's recent proposals[127] to reform the Mental Capacity Act towards supported decision-making, not substitute decision-making, for those who lack capacity to make a particular decision.

Conclusion

Having taken a systematic approach to examining the arguments behind criminal liability for consensual killing, and having concluded that in at least some such situations there should be no criminal liability at all, we think that English criminal law is in need of substantial reform. The

---

[126] Miller and Brody ibid 308.
[127] Law Commission, *Mental Capacity and Deprivation of Liberty* (Law Com CP 222, 2015) Chapter 12.

current legal regime is too blunt a tool to deal with the situations we have examined, and the blanket ban on consensual killing does not stand up to closer scrutiny. We agree with Ian Brassington that 'there is no readily apparent reason to suppose that legalising some forms of killing would put us on the road to legalising all of them'.[128] As we have said above, we believe that English law should introduce some kind of 'killing upon request' offence to deal with cases where D's moral wrongdoing was reduced but not extinguished by V's request. Like infanticide,[129] this would operate both as an offence in itself and a defence to murder, but in different circumstances. This is not the place to outline the details of how such a reform would work in practice. However, we can say that such a hybrid offence/defence could enable fair labelling in cases where D's responsibility was substantially reduced by V's request, and that a judge could have a wide sentencing discretion so that D's punishment could reflect the circumstances. Secondly, if enthusiastic consent became a defence to the infliction of serious injury in non-fatal offences, then it would logically also be the minimum standard required for consensual killing. Thus, V would have to remain enthusiastic throughout.[130] Sadly we were not able to cover all possible situations of consensual killing in this chapter for reasons of space, but we hope that our chapter will influence the intellectual debate on this significant area of law.

---

[128] Brassington (n 38) 429.

[129] See the Infanticide Act 1938.

[130] See Clare de Than and Jesse Elvin (n 63) for further details on the issue of 'enthusiastic consent'.

CHAPTER FIVE

THE AGE OF CONSENT IN AN AGE OF CONSENT

JONATHAN HERRING

Introduction

The prevalence of child abuse is hard to ascertain precisely, but the statistics available are horrifying. We live in a world in which 150 million girls, 14% of the world's girl population, are sexually abused each year.[1] Child trafficking has become an international phenomenon.[2] It has been estimated that at least one million children are involved in the sex industry in Asia alone.[3] The European Commission has estimated that one in five children in Europe is sexually abused.[4]

In relation to England, a major study by the National Society for the Protection of Cruelty to Children[5] found that 21% of girls and 11% of boys aged under 16 had experienced sexual abuse during childhood. Another NSPCC survey found that 11.3% of those aged 18-24 reported contact sexual abuse during childhood.[6] 38% of all rapes recorded by the police are committed against children (mainly girls) under 16 years of age.[7] While the stereotype portrayed in the media is of the child abuser

---

[1] Paulo Pinheiro, *World Report on Violence Against Children* (UNICEF, 2006) 12.
[2] Michelle Madden Dempsey, 'Sex Trafficking and Criminalization: In Defense of Feminist Abolitionism' (2010) 158 University of Pennsylvania Law Review 1729.
[3] Ben Spiecker and Jan Steutel, 'A Moral-Philosophical Perspective on Paedophilia and Incest' (2000) 32 Educational Philosophy and Theory 283, 284.
[4] A Child is Crying, *Statistics* (A Child is Crying, 2015) 1.
[5] Pat Cawson, Corinne Wattam and Sue Brooker, *Child Maltreatment in the United Kingdom: A Study of the Prevalence of Child Abuse and Neglect* (NSPCC 2000).
[6] Lorraine Radford et al, *Child Abuse and Neglect in the UK Today* (NSPCC 2011).
[7] HM Government, *Government Response to the Stern Review* (The Stationery Office 2011).

being the "dirty old man" in the park, the reality is that most child abusers are young or middle aged, and are far more likely to be family members, neighbours or friends of the victim, rather than strangers.[8] One part of the stereotype which has validity is that the vast majority of sexual abuse is undertaken by men, and girls are more likely than boys to be victims.[9]

It is a natural instinct to respond to such statistics with an urge to protect children with the strongest protections under the criminal law. A popular option is a statute making it an offence to have sex with anyone under a certain age. Making a clear statement that anyone who has sex with a child below a stated age has its attractions. It means that an unambiguous message is sent: never have sex with a child below age X, no arguments. It makes conviction much easier. It simply needs to be demonstrated that the defendant had sex with the victim and the victim is below the statutory age. The difficulties of proof of consent, which bedevil rape trails where the victim is an adult, can be set to one side.

Yet, as is well known, age of consent provisions carry problems of their own. If we set the age of consent at 16 then we criminalise large sections of the population. The latest National Survey of Sexual Attitudes and Lifestyles found that 31% of men and 29% of women first had sexual intercourse before age 16.[10] Many others would have engaged in some form of sexual touching with someone else. Their partners would all be guilty of sexual offences.

And here we have the familiar problem in this area of the law. How can we balance the desire to provide effective protection to children from sexual abuse with the desire to avoid criminalising 'everyday' consensual sexual behaviour between teenagers? Before discussing that further, I will briefly make a few points on the current law.

---

[8] Lorraine Radford et al, *Child Abuse and Neglect in the UK Today* (NSPCC 2011).
[9] Michael Freeman, 'The Sexual Abuse of Children' in Belinda Brooks-Gordon, Loraine Gelsthorpe, Martin H Johnson, Andrew Bainham (eds), *Sexuality Repositioned* (Hart 2004) 320.
[10] Welcome Trust, 'Survey examines changes in sexual behaviour and attitudes in Britain' (Welcome Trust 2013).

The Current Law

Historically, the age of consent has varied significantly. It was 10 in 1576, but increased to 14 in the late 19th century. The late Victorian age, with its concerns about child prostitution, saw the Criminal Law Amendment Act 1885 raise the age of consent of girls to 16. The age for male same sex behaviour was lowered from 21 to 18 in 1994 and from 18 to 16 to produce equality between gay and straight sex in the Sexual Offences (Amendment) Act 2000.[11]

The Sexual Offences Act 2003 includes the following offences in relation to children:

(1) Rape of a child under 13;[12]
(2) Assault of a child under 13 by penetration;[13]
(3) Sexual assault of a child under 13;[14]
(4) Causing or inciting a child under 13 to engage in a sexual activity.[15]
(5) Sexual activity with a child;[16]
(6) Causing or inciting a child to engage in a sexual activity;[17]
(7) Engaging in sexual activity in the presence of a child;[18]
(8) Causing a child to watch a sexual act;[19]
(9) Child sex offences committed by children or young persons;[20]
(10) Arranging or facilitating the commission of a child sex offence;[21]
(11) Meeting a child following sexual grooming, etc.[22]

This chapter is not designed to give a complete assessment of these offences, and there are many others. However, a number of points are worth highlighting.

---

[11] See Sarah Beresford, 'The Age of Consent and the Ending of Queer Theory' (2014) 4 Laws 759, for further discussion.
[12] Sexual Offences Act 2003, s 5.
[13] Sexual Offences Act 2003, s 6.
[14] Sexual Offences Act 2003, s 7.
[15] Sexual Offences Act 2003, s 8.
[16] Sexual Offences Act 2003, s 9.
[17] Sexual Offences Act 2003, s 10.
[18] Sexual Offences Act 2003, s 11.
[19] Sexual Offences Act 2003, s 12.
[20] Sexual Offences Act 2003, s 13.
[21] Sexual Offences Act 2003, s 14.
[22] Sexual Offences Act 2003, s 15.

The first is that it is rare in the criminal law to distinguish between offences based on a characteristic of the victim. Theft is theft, whether the victim is a toddler or awaiting their telegram from the queen. In some offences (such as racially aggravated offences), the characteristic of the victim may create an aggravated version of the offence, but not a different offence as such. But in the Sexual Offences Act 2003, we have offences which can only be committed if it is shown that the victim was below a certain age. Parliament could, for example, have stated in the detailed provisions relating to the offence of rape, that a child under 13 could not give consent for the purposes of rape. However, rather than doing this, it created a separate offence of rape of a child under 13. Clearly Parliament thought it necessary to mark out the rape of a child as a distinct offence to the rape of an adult.

Second, it is no defence to prove that the victim consented to the activity in relation to some of the more serious offences. Where the victim is under 13, his or her consent is irrelevant to these offences. It is not even a defence if the defendant reasonably believed the victim to be over the age of 13 and to have consented.[23]

Third, the law covers sexual touching as well as full intercourse. As Victor Tadros[24] observes, this has some surprising consequences:

> [T]he criminal law prohibits 15-year-old children from kissing sexually. We must assume that kissing can be sexual, for were it not sexual a 50-year-old man could not be found guilty of an offence if he sexually kisses a 10 year old. Similarly, if one 15-year-old child encourages another 15-year-old child sexually to kiss her 15-year-old boyfriend sexually, the former child is guilty of an offence under section 13.

Fourth, unusually, distinctions are drawn depending on the age of the defendant. Under s 13, defendants under the age of 18 face a lower sentence than older defendants committing the same act.

Fifth, although it is commonly thought that the age of consent in England and Wales is 16, as set out in section 9 of the Sexual Offences Act 2003, to say that would be a little misleading. It is children under the age of 13 who do not have the legal capacity to consent. Children between 13 and 16 can

---

[23] *R v G* [2003] UKHL 50.
[24] Victor Tadros, 'The Ideal of the Presumption of Innocence' (2014) 8 Criminal Law and Philosophy 449.

give consent and so a sexual penetration of a consenting 13-16 year old is not necessarily rape, although it can be if non-consent is proved. However, even if consensual, it is still a crime. This, as we shall see is significant. It highlights the fact that wrong, in sexual activities of those between the ages of 13 and 16, is not specifically the lack of valid legal consent, but lies elsewhere.

In 2013, the Number 10 Policy Unit suggested the age of consent be reduced to 14.[25] A media outcry (at least in the usual quarters) resulted[26] and the proposal was quickly dropped.[27] There were some interesting features of the media response. The most widely reported arguments in favour of the reform were those suggesting it would encourage teenagers to seek medical and contraceptive advice, rather than being deterred for fear of revealing a criminal offence.[28] It was also notable that a widespread view was that changing the law would not have any impact on the sexual behaviour of teenagers. However, it was the fear that altering the age of consent would give a "green light" to paedophiles which was the dominant response. The kinds of arguments which are more prevalent in the academic literature – debates over the nature of children's rights; fears of over-criminalisation; and constructions of childhood vulnerability – had little role to play.

It seems that in the academic literature, the majority opinion is in favour of a change in the law.[29] It is widely seen as being based on a fiction (many under 16 year olds are perfectly mature enough to consent); as punishing perfectly harmless activities (sexual experimentation with an under 16 year old becomes a serious criminal offence); and perpetuating an image of children being innocent and vulnerable.

---

[25] The Daily Telegraph. 'No 10 Policy Unit "Suggested Lowering Age of Consent to 14".' 11 January 2013.

[26] James Chapman, 'Lower the Age of Consent to just Fourteen, say Civil Servants' *The Daily Mail*, 10 January 2013.

[27] Nicholas Watt, 'No 10 Rejects Call to Lower Age of Consent' *The Guardian*, 17 November 2013.

[28] Adam Withnall, 'Health Expert Calls for Age of Consent to be Lowered to 15." *The Independent*, 17 November 2013.

[29] For example, John Spencer, 'Child and Family Offences' [2004] Criminal Law Review 347) and Michelle Goodwin, 'Law's Limits: Regulating Statutory Rape Law' (2013) Wisconsin Law Review 418.

This chapter makes a case in favour of its retention. It will proceed as follows. First, I will set out the idea of "line drawing" in the criminal law. The reasons for this are not often appreciated in the context of the debate over age of consent. Second, I will discuss why these arguments are particularly appropriate in debates over age of consent and why they could support an age of sixteen.

Drawing Lines in the Criminal Law Generally

It is the curse, and the blessing, of the criminal law that it has to draw lines. The rule of law requires that the boundaries of what is or is not criminal are clearly defined, so that a person can predict with a degree of certainty whether their conduct will be criminal or not.[30] Clearly defined boundaries are also necessary to enable courts to deal with cases effectively. A good example is a speed limit. If the speed limit is set at 30 mph, then the driver knows precisely what speed they need to drive at to avoid a ticket. Similarly, if the driver exceeds that limit, the case can be easily dealt with at court. With modern technology, the speed of the driver is readily proved and a conviction or acquittal follows with the upmost efficiency. Contrast the alternative, an offence of 'travelling at a dangerous speed'. A driver would not know for sure if the speed they thought safe would be accepted as safe by a court. A police officer would have considerable discretion in deciding whom to arrest and court hearings would get bogged down with lengthy disputes over whether or not the speed was dangerous. Those kinds of arguments have persuaded legislatures in many countries to use "line drawing" offences in several ways.

Of course, such offences have a serious draw back. They can be seen as punishing harmless conduct in some cases. To return to the driving example, a person may be driving perfectly safely at 35mph but still receive a ticket. Less often noticed, but also important, is that people may pose a harm but they may be on the "right side" of the line. A driver may be travelling at 26mph, but that may be dangerously fast for those road conditions. In short, the clarity and efficiency of the bright line comes with 'errors' on either side of it.

The age of consent can be seen as a good example of a bright line criminal rule. Baroness Hale in *R v G* explained:

---

[30] Joseph Raz, *The Authority of Law* (Oxford University Press 1979) ch1.

> Even if a child is fully capable of understanding and freely agreeing to such sexual activity, which may often be doubted, especially with a child under 13, the law says that it makes no difference. He or she is legally disabled from consenting.[31]

As she emphasises, with such a legal presumption there is no claim that every child under a particular age *in fact* has capacity to consent (although she may well), but rather that there are sound policy reasons justifying the presumption.

Bright legal line drawing based on age is common in the law generally. Age is regularly used by the law to mark out when a person may or may not be permitted to engage in activities ranging from buying alcohol to getting married.[32] While not always explicitly stated, this is normally done on the basis that the child is legally presumed to lack the capacity to make the decision.[33] Whenever they are used, it must be accepted (as it usually is in cases of legal line drawing) that there will be cases where people below the particular age are deemed to lack the capacity to consent, even though in fact they do have that capacity. Why are such presumptions used, if we know that there are cases where they will be incorrect?

I suggest that line drawing of this kind with regard to age requires us to consider the following:

1. Is this a situation which is better resolved by individual assessment in the particular circumstance, rather than drawing a line?
2. At what age should the line be drawn?

Is it Justifiable to Line Draw in Relation to Age?

Obviously, a fifteen year old on the day before her 16th birthday does not magically acquire the knowledge and experience in the next day so as to grant her maturity to consent. Indeed, most legal systems recognise that children under the age of 16 can be as mature as adults and therefore be entitled to make decisions.[34] Indeed, there can be a large range of

---

[31] *R v G* [2008] UKHL 37 (HL) [44].

[32] Jonathan Herring, 'Children's Rights for Grown Ups' in Sandra Fredman and Sarah Spencer (eds) *Age as an Equality Issue* (Hart 2003).

[33] There may be other considerations at play too. For example, it might be claimed that alcohol is more harmful to younger people than to older people.

[34] *Gillick v West Norfolk & Wisbech Area Health Authority* [1986] *AC* 112.

understanding, maturity and intelligence among adolescents. Does this not mean that an individual assessment of age is preferable to line drawing?

It certainly does in some cases. In English law, for example, a child who is below the age of 16 can give effective consent to receive medical treatment if she is able to persuade a doctor that she has sufficient maturity to understand the issues raised (*Gillick* competence, as it known).[35] The child who is assessed by the doctor to have sufficient maturity and understanding can give consent to legal treatment just like an adult. Why not apply the same approach to sexual offences?

The answer is fairly obvious. There are three key differences between a doctor treating a minor patient and a person wanting to have sex with a minor. The first is that a medical professional has the expertise to make the kind of nuanced assessment of the capacity of the person that we would want. Indeed, if the question of a minor's capacity to understand an issue were to go to court, the evidence of a medical professional would be key. By contrast, an ordinary person who wants to have sex with a minor has no skills or expertise to make an assessment of their minor partner's capacity.

The second is that while the medical professional, we might take it, has no personal stake in whether their patient does or does not have capacity, they will want what is best for their patient and will make their assessment in the best way they can, while having nothing to gain from the outcome. By contrast, the person who wants to have sex with an underage partner is obviously biased in their assessment of capacity.

The third is that the doctor has the time, clarity of thought and space to make the necessary assessment. The person at the start of a sexual encounter is unlikely to have the kind of cool detachment to make a full assessment of capacity.[36] A doctor will have a set of professional guidelines to follow in order to ensure she has made an appropriate assessment. The person wishing to have sex with an underage child has little to go on to perform his assessment.

With these points in mind, it becomes clear that saying to a person who wants to have sex with a minor, 'well you should make an assessment of

---

[35] ibid.

[36] David Archard, *Children, Family and the State* (Ashgate 2003) 25.

their capacity', is unlikely to result in an accurate assessment or to provide sufficiently clear guidance to the would-be participant in sexual penetration. Antony Duff,[37] arguing in favour of such bright lines, provides a detailed analysis in support of them. He explains that there are certain dangerous activities where people cannot be trusted and should not trust themselves to decide whether the activity is safe. He writes:

> A man excited at the prospect of sex with a young woman is ill placed to judge her maturity; a driver in a hurry is ill placed to judge how fast it is safe for her to drive; and someone relaxing in a pub is ill placed to judge whether another drink might impair his capacity to drive safely. We recognise the need for some kind of regulation in these spheres, because we cannot trust each other, or ourselves, to decide in these contexts whether we can safely engage in a proposed action (having sexual intercourse with this young person; driving at this speed, or after having this many drinks).[38]

He goes on to say that there will be defendants who insist that their partner is below the age of consent but that they have the maturity to make the decision nevertheless. Yet he says of such a defendant, 'he does not know that he knows this' and if he goes ahead based on his own judgement, he takes an unjustified risk that he is wrong and

> arrogantly claims the right to decide for himself on matters which he, like the rest of us, should not trust himself to decide. His claim is arrogant because it is unjustified — but also because it seeks to set him above his fellow citizens, in matters which affect their legally protected interests; and that is what merits the censure of the criminal law.[39]

I find Duff's explanation compelling. If, then, individual assessment is not possible, we need an alternative marker. Any marker leading to a presumption of lack of capacity would need to satisfy three demands: it must have ease of use and be well known to roughly match levels of competence. Age fits these requirements. With ID readily used, age can be checked easily; the concept of an age of consent is well known; and age is a rough indicator of maturity.[40] Other criteria that could be used might include puberty or intellectual ability, but these are unlikely to be as effective or as readily assessable as age.

---

[37] Antony Duff, 'Crime, Prohibition, and Punishment' (2002) 19 Journal of Applied Philosophy 97.

[38] ibid 103.

[39] ibid.

[40] David Archard, *Children, Family and the State* (Ashgate 2003) 30.

I believe that these points make a powerful argument that justifies the law having an age of consent. But, that still leaves open the question what that age should be.

What Should the Age Be?

This is not a straightforward question. That is reflected by the fact that there is no agreement between jurisdictions as to the age of consent. David Archard claims that the average within Europe is 15, although some countries use the age of 12 (with certain qualifications, e.g. that there not be a significant age disparity between the parties).[41]

I suggest the factors that are to be taken into account in assessing the age.

The Gravity of the Issue

Let us imagine (and these figures are simply guesswork) we are persuaded that at the age of 13: 25% of children have capacity to consent to sex, and 75% do not; at 14, 45% do and 55% do not; at 15, 75% do and 25% do not; and at 16, 98% do and 2% do not.[42] Which proxy should be selected? Should we choose (using my figures) 15, because by then it will be correct in the majority of cases?

I think not. Choosing the appropriate age requires a weighing up of the wrong done to those deemed to have capacity to consent, who in reality do not; and the wrong done to those deemed not to have capacity to consent, who in reality do. They are not equal.

Let us consider, first, those deemed not to have capacity, but in fact do. There will, then, be interference in their private life. Anyone who has sex with them will be treated as committing a criminal offence. This may mean that there will be people who will not be able lawfully to have the sexual encounter they wish, because of the legal provision. Plenty of those under the age of consent who in fact have capacity will have no wish to engage in sexual activity and so there will be no effective interference in their rights. Further, of those who wish to, some will not find a partner who wishes to engage in sexual activity with them. So, again, for them,

---

[41] ibid 30.
[42] Of course, it is highly simplistic to suggest capacity is straightforwardly something you do or do not have.

there is no interference in their rights. But there will be a group who are deemed incompetent, but in fact have capacity, who want to have sex and find a partner who wants to have sex with them. Their rights will be interfered with. But, I suggest, this interference is not severe. First, it is a time-limited interference, in that it will cease at the time they reach the age of consent.[43] Second, the interference in their rights can be justified by the protection of the rights of those in their age group who lack the capacity to consent, and those with capacity to consent, but who do not in fact consent to a particular sexual encounter.

On the other hand, there are those who might be deemed to have capacity, but in reality will lack it. The law here will be doing what it can to protect their rights. In part, this is an acknowledgement of a point to be explored later, that the law of rape generally, is not efficient in protecting victims from rape and an age based statute will provide a stronger deterrent and easier route for the prosecution of those who have sex with a non-consenting child under the age of consent.

In short, then, it is not simply a matter of setting an age which will be a correct assessment of capacity for the majority of children. That is because the harm done to a group assessed as having capacity when in fact they do not is far greater than the group assessed as lacking capacity when in fact they do. The former are put at risk of rape, the latter at risk having to put off lawful sexual experiences for a short time. We should be far happier to err on the side of deeming the competent incompetent, than of deeming the incompetent competent.[44]

Children Rights

The debate over the age of consent reflects the broader issue of whether there is legitimacy in the law being protectionist towards children in a way which it is not towards adults. Children's liberationists, who were particularly vocal in the 1970s, argued that children needed to be liberated from the tyranny of childhood.[45] The argument went that children's ability to make decision for themselves was underestimated; deliberately so, it

---

[43] Diane Richardson, 'Constructing sexual citizenship: theorizing sexual rights' (2000) 62 Critical Social Policy 105.

[44] For a broader examination of this argument, see Stephen Gilmore and Jonathan Herring, 'No is the hardest word: Consent and Children's Autonomy' (2011) 23 Child and Family Law Quarterly 3.

[45] For example, John Holt, *Escape from Childhood* (Pelican 1974).

was claimed, because it meant that children could be kept as super-pets or super-slaves for the convenience of others. The child liberationist argument, then, went that children should have the same legal rights that adults had. For example, John Holt[46] argued for children having the right to vote, work, own property, receive minimum state education, use drugs and be able to consent to sexual relations.

Few commentators would now take such a position. There is a recognition that giving the same rights to children and adult fails to recognise the slower rate of children's development or the ability of adults to manipulate children into consenting to things that benefit the adult alone.[47] The best that might be said is that a minority of children might be capable of exercising rights, but for the majority of children, giving them the same rights as adults would not lead to their liberation, but to their abuse.

A more moderate child liberationist claim, and one which would nowadays attract more support, would be that where children are as mature as an adult, we should treat the child in the same was as an adult. Further, that those areas where children are denied the rights that adults have, require a sufficient justification.

This leaves unanswered the question of how children's rights are to be understood. This is not the place to investigate that debate. But it is worth exploring one of the leading writers in this area: John Eekelaar. He argues that children have three types of interests: basic, developmental and autonomy interests. He explains that basic interests are children's claims concerning their physical, emotion and intellectual well-being. Developmental interests include children's claims to be able to maximise their potential, while an autonomy interest is 'the freedom to choose his own lifestyle and to enter social relations according to his own inclinations uncontrolled by the authority of the adult world, whether parents or institutions'[48] He explains that where there is a clash between these interests, basic and developmental should trump autonomy interests. There are two reasons for this ranking. First, he argues that we should consider how a child might retrospectively, as an adult, wish to be treated. He believes that most of us would not have wanted all our autonomy

---

[46] John Holt, *Escape from Childhood* (Pelican 1974).
[47] Jane Fortin, *Children's Rights and the Developing Law* (3rd ed Cambridge University Press 2009) 5.
[48] John Eekelaar, 'The Emergence of Children's Rights' (1986) 6 Oxford Journal of Legal Studies 161, 170-1.

wishes to be granted as we were growing up, certainly not those that
interfered with basic or developmental interests. Second, he argues that
the ideal which we should be striving for is that the child develops into an
18 year-old with maximum autonomy. They will, then, have the maximum
choice to decide for themselves how they wish to live their lives.

> [T]o bring a child to the threshold of adulthood with the maximum
> opportunities to form and pursue life goals which reflect as closely as
> possible an autonomous choice[49]

Eekelaar argues that to achieve this, we need to ensure that during a
childhood, the child's basic or developmental interests need to be
protected, even where the child's autonomy interests point in a different
direction. He argues, further, that enabling a child to have maximum
autonomy in adulthood requires restrictions on their childhood now. It also
requires that children be able to practice making decisions for themselves
as they grow up. Children therefore must exercise autonomy in order to be
able to have it later on. He also sees the exercise of autonomy by children
as a marker of an open society:

> A society can be imagined whose members consider that autonomous self-
> determination by children, and indeed by the succeeding adult generation,
> is deemed to be in no one's interests. But such a society would not be an
> open society. It is a precondition for an open society that the exercise of
> autonomy by an agent is assumed to be in that agent's interests. And it is a
> precondition of believing that people have rights to hold that they have a
> right to achieve competence and articulate their self-interests[50]

As Michael Freeman puts it:

> We would not be taking rights seriously if we only respected autonomy
> when we considered the agent was doing the right thing. But we also
> would be failing to recognise a child's integrity if we allowed him to
> choose an action, such as using heroin or choosing not to attend school,
> which could seriously and systematically impair the attainment of full
> personality and development subsequently.[51]

And it is worth adding, of course, that not only are there extremely serious

---

[49] John Eekelaar, 'The Interests of the Child and the Child's Wishes: The Role of
Dynamic Self-Determinism' (1994) 8 International Journal of Law Policy and the
Family 42.
[50] ibid 87.
[51] Michael Freeman, 'Taking Children's Rights More Seriously' (1992) 6
International Journal of Law Policy and the Family 42.

harms to adolescent sexual abuse, sexual penetrations carry risks even if consensual.

So, the position we have reached is this. If we accept a model of the kind promoted by John Eekelaar, there is an acceptance that some limitation can be imposed upon the autonomy of children, in the name of protecting their developmental or basic interests. These restrictions upon the autonomy of children are commonly justified in the name of promoting a child's autonomy later in life. The harms of non-consensual childhood sex are manifest. There are strong links between childhood sexual abuse and depression, eating disorders, emotional distress, self-harm, suicide attempts.[52] There are harms even where there is consent to sex.[53] Early sexual penetration is said to double the risk of developing cervical cancer.[54] Early pregnancy carries a high risk of physical, social and economic harms.[55] The argument of this chapter is that a restriction on a child's sexual autonomy is justified as necessary to protect the child's developmental or basic interests.

Capacity to Exercise Sexual Autonomy?

The next issue to consider is at what age children in fact have the capacity to exercise sexual autonomy. This requires us to consider a number of features: understanding; deciding; valuing; and the social context within which sexual choices are made.

(a) Capacity: Understanding

At what age, on average, do children understand the facts that they need to know in order to engage in sexual penetration? This depends in part on what it is that a child needs to understand. Section 2 of the Mental Capacity Act 2005[56] explains that a person lacks capacity if they are unable to make a decision for themselves. Section 3 states:

---

[52] Erica R Gold, 'Long-Term Effects of Sexual Victimization in Childhood: An Attributional Approach' (1986) 54 Journal of Consulting and Clinical Psychology 471.

[53] Michelle Madden Dempsey and Jonathan Herring, 'Why Sexual Penetration Requires Justification' (2007) 27 Oxford Journal of Legal Studies 467.

[54] NHS, 'Early sex cervical cancer link' (NHS 2009).

[55] Sarah Beresford, 'The Age of Consent and the Ending of Queer Theory' (2014) 4 Laws 759 sets out the research in detail.

[56] Technically the Act does not apply to children, only adults.

[A] person is unable to make a decision for himself if he is unable—
- (a) to understand the information relevant to the decision,
- (b) to retain that information,
- (c) to use or weigh that information as part of the process of making the decision, or
- (d) to communicate his decision (whether by talking, using sign language or any other means).

In *A Local Authority v H*,[57] Heldley J listed the following factors a person would need to understand and weigh up in order to be able to consent to sex:

- The 'mechanics of the physical acts'.
- 'That vaginal intercourse may lead to pregnancy'.
- 'Some grasp of sexual health', although that only need be rudimentary and it would 'suffice if a person understands that sexual relations may lead to significant ill-health and that those risks can be reduced by precautions like a condom'.
- Understanding that she does have a choice and that she can refuse.

In *R v GA*,[58] looking at when a person with learning difficulties had capacity to consent to sex it, was accepted that the law did not impose a high hurdle, but that is because even for people with capacity, the decision to have sex was 'largely visceral rather than cerebral, and owes more to instinct and emotion rather than to analysis'. It was not appropriate to require those with learning difficulties to make decisions about sex based on a sophisticated intellectual understanding of the issues, when people without capacity issues don't make decisions based on sex on that basis.

Adopting this approach, and given sex education in schools, we might assume that the rudimentary factors are known by the vast majority of children, even before the teenage years have been reached. But that may be too quick. Julie Jessop makes the following good point:

> Whilst the capacity for sexual arousal may be present from birth, and many young children may masturbate to orgasm, these experiences and sensations do not hold the same sexual connotations as they do for adults. Not until children learn the societal mores associated with adult sexuality can their behaviour be deemed to be sexual in the adult sense, and in

---

[57] *A Local Authority v H* [2012] EWHC 49 (COP).
[58] *R v GA* [2014] EWCA Crim 299.

attaching sexual significance to childhood activities adults can be seen to
[be] projecting their own motivations to those of children.[59]

As this quote indicates, it is easy to assume that actions that might appear
to indicate an understanding and appreciation of the sexual nature in the
act, may not involve a full understanding of the broader social
consequences of the act. Indeed evidence form the National Surveys of
Sexual Attitudes and Lifestyles, published in 2015, demonstrates that
70.6% of women reported not "knowing enough" at the time they felt
ready for their first sexual experience.[60] So while it might be assumed that
young people know far more about sex than they need, that is not the view
of young people.

(b) Capacity: Decision-Making

Having capacity is not simply about understanding facts. It is about being
able to use those facts to make a decision. Jennifer Drobac and Leslie
Hulvershorn have demonstrated that it is wrong to conclude that because
adolescents understand the facts about sex, they have capacity to consent
to sex:[61]

> Neurobiological studies suggest that assumptions concerning the
> distinction between adult and juvenile decision-making are likely accurate.
> However, a substantial amount of heterogeneity among youth creates a
> complex picture of juvenile decision-making. Scientists are just beginning
> to understand these cognitive processes. In particular, within the juvenile
> population, ten- to fourteen-year-old juveniles termed 'high-risk'
> demonstrate different neurobiological processes during risky decision-
> making than do 'healthy' comparison youth. Empirical findings suggest
> that high-risk youth are less able to engage regulatory brain regions than
> healthy comparison children during risky decisions. (…) Even though the
> neuroscience is new and the research ongoing, jurists can begin to consider
> whether juvenile sex crime statutes adequately protect our precious
> children.

---

[59] Julie Jessop, 'The Development of Sexuality' in Belinda Brooks-Gordon,
Loraine Gelsthorpe, Martin H Johnson, Andrew Bainham (eds), *Sexuality
Repositioned* (Hart 2004) 219.
[60] Clare Tanton et al 'Patterns and tends in sources of information about sex among
young people in Britain' (2015) 5 BMJ <*Open* e007834 doi:10.1136/bmjopen-
2015-007834> accessed 24th April 2016.
[61] Jennifer Drobac and Leslie Hulvershorn, 'The Neurobiology of Decision
Making in High-Risk Youth and the Law of Consent to Sex' (2014) New Criminal
Law Review 502.

There is, therefore, evidence that we cannot assume, even if adolescents know facts, that they are able to process them in a way which is appropriate for full autonomy.

(c) Capacity: Values

In order to exercise autonomy, it is not simply enough to know facts or to be able to apply them to issues to be decided. One must have values – values which one has adopted as one's own – and be able to apply the information one has to these values.[62] Catriona Makenzie and Wendy Rogers argue that in order to be able to exercise autonomy, we need to be:[63]

- Self-determining: being 'able to determine one's own beliefs, values, goals and wants, and to make choices regarding matters of practical import to one's life free from undue interference. The obverse of self-determination is determination by other persons, or by external forces or constraints'.[64]
- Self-governing: 'being be able to make choices and enact decisions that express, or are consistent with, one's values, beliefs and commitments. Whereas the threats to self-determination are typically external, the threats to self-governance are typically internal, and often involve volitional or cognitive failings. Weakness of will and failures of self-control are common volitional failings that interfere with self-governance'.[65]
  Having authenticity: 'a person's decisions, values, beliefs and commitments must be her "own" in some relevant sense; that is, she must identify herself with them and they must cohere with her "practical identity", her sense of who she is and what matters to her. Actions or decisions that a person feels were foisted on her, which do not cohere with her sense of herself, or from which she feels alienated, are not autonomous'.[66]

It may well be questioned whether in their early teens, young people acquire the maturity to take on values that are their own and adopt them in

---

[62] Jonathan Herring and Jesse Wall, 'Capacity to Consent to Sex' (2015) 22 Medical Law Review 620.

[63] Catriona Makenzie and Wendy Rogers, 'Autonomy, vulnerability and capacity: a philosophical appraisal of the Mental Capacity Act' (2013) 9 International Journal of the Law in Context 37.

[64] ibid.

[65] ibid.

[66] ibid.

the way Rogers and Makenzie talk about. Again this suggests keeping the age of consent at the higher end.

(d) Capacity: Social Context

There is a danger in discussing age of consent that the social reality is ignored. Even, assuming that I am wrong in all that has been argued so far, and that as a matter of theory, children can exercise sexual autonomy, can that be practically achieved in the real world?

Studies of sexual encounters involving under 16 year olds indicate that there are a host of factors that make girls particularly susceptible to coercion and abuse. These include: diminished self-esteem; uncertainty surrounding their changing bodies; reluctance to be assertive; fear and pressure; and a desire for male attention.[67] Michelle Oberman writes that:

> [T]he sexual bargains struck by girls often are so painfully one-sided that it is difficult for adults to understand what prompted the girl to consent. In this sense, the sexual bargains girls make are more like the commercial bargains they might make, were they permitted to act in the marketplace. The combination of girls' age-appropriate naïveté and insecurity and the norms of male sexual initiative make bad bargains inevitable.[68]

A particular theme in the lives of adolescent women is the impact of gender behaviour socialisation. Young women are taught that their success in the world and their personal sexual satisfaction is found in being sexually pleasing to men.[69] This message is reinforced by films, music, magazines aimed at teenagers, and 'romance fiction' in which popularity with men and sex are conjoined. This has reinforced disturbing evidence about the 'everyday' sexual harassment, bullying and aggression towards girls.[70] This ranges from casual sexual remarks and unwanted touching to serious sexual assault. An in-depth study of bullying and sexual bullying

---

[67] Michelle Oberman 'Regulating Consensual Sex with Minors: Defining a Role for Statutory Rape' (2000) 50 De Paul Law Review 799.

[68] ibid.

[69] Simone Buzwell & Doreen Rosenthal, 'Constructing a Sexual Self: Adolescents' Sexual Self Perceptions and Sexual Risk-Taking' (1996) 6 Journal of Research on Adolescence 489.

[70] Rosalyn Shute, Larry Owens and Phillip Slee, 'Everyday Victimization of Adolescent Girls by Boys: Sexual Harassment, Bullying or Aggression?' (2007) 57 Sex Roles 477.

in UK schools concluded that sexual bullying was widespread.[71] Grouping and sexual name calling are a normal part of school life. A recent study found that 73% of all children had reported sexual bullying in England.[72] A 2015 survey by Girl Guiding on the attitude of girls reported that 81% had experienced sexism in the week prior to the survey. 75% of girls say that they had been negatively affected by sexual harassment. 60% of girls had seen boys viewing pornography, with 15% saying that they saw this most days.[73]

This normalisation of sexual abuse is combined with messages that self-sacrifice, caretaking and obedience are seen as good female virtues.[74] Girls equate compliance and cooperation with 'niceness', and they perceive that being nice is central to being 'feminine'.[75] It is not surprising in the light of this that so many young women can become easy targets for unwanted sexual encounters.

Many of the factors mentioned are reflected in the following comments from Michelle Oberman:

> The stories girls tell about the 'consensual' sex in which they engage reflect a poignant subtext of hope and pain. Girls express longing for emotional attachment, romance and respect. At the same time, they suffer enormous insecurity and diminished self-image. (...) Teenage girls recognize that they are, or at least that they should be, objects of desire. (...) Girls want boyfriends, relationships, or somebody who will hold them and tell them that they are wanted. Girls negotiate access to the fulfilment of these emotional needs by way of sex.[76]

---

[71] Sian Williams, 'Sexual Bullying in one Local Authority' in Neil Duncan (ed), *Bullying* (Routledge 2013).

[72] Kate Milnes et al, *Sexual bullying in young people across five European countries* (Addressing Sexual Bullying Across Europe 2015) found at http://www.asbae.eu/ accessed 7th January 2015.

[73] Girl Guiding, *Girls Attitude Survey 2015* (Girl Guiding 2015) found at < http://new.girlguiding.org.uk/latest-updates/making-a-difference/girls-attitudes-survey-2015> accessed 7th January 2015.

[74] Kate Pierce, 'A Feminist Perspective on the Socialization of Teenage Girls through Seventeen Magazine' (1990) 23 Sex Roles 491, 495-500.

[75] Michelle Fine, 'Sexuality, Schooling, and Adolescent Females: The Missing Discourse of Desire' (1988) 58 Harvard Education Review 29.

[76] Michelle Oberman, 'Turning Girls into Women: Re-Evaluating Modern Statutory Rape Law' (1994) 85 Journal of Criminal Law and Criminology 15, 53, 65.

For young men too, having sex is seen as central to being regarded as a young man. Further, 'real men' are seen as being forward and even aggressive in his sexual proposition. This makes it harder for the woman to refuse as the man is seen as the decision maker and he will be disappointed if she were to say no. Julie Jessop's exploration of adolescent sexuality indicates that for young men, sexual activity focuses on the physical act and he regards his partner in a disembodied way.[77] This would reflect the widespread use of pornography among young men. She also reports sex being used as the basis for boasting to friends to maintain credibility among groups.[78] As Michael Kimmel notes:

> Boys are taught to try to get sex; girls are taught strategies to foil the boys' attempts. 'The whole game was to get a girl to give out', one man told sociologist Lillian Rubin: 'You expected her to resist (…) But you kept pushing. Part of it was the thrill of touching and being touched, but, I've got to admit, part of it was the conquest, too'. (…) 'I felt as if I should want to get it as often as possible', recalled another. 'I guess that's because if you're a guy, you're supposed to want it.'[79]

There are now ample statistics to show that these cause a social environment in which unwanted sexual encounters and intimate partner violence are very common and accepted.[80] A recent survey of young people in London found that 76% agreed that a woman encouraged violence from her partner if she did not treat a man with respect. Girls also reported as feeling they should put their boyfriend's "needs" above their own wishes.[81] A study by the NSPCC of teenage girls aged 13-17 found that a third had suffered sexual abuse in their relationship and that a quarter had experienced violence.[82] One sixth of those in relationships complained of being pressurised into have sexual intercourse. The Girl

---

[77] Julie Jessop, 'The Development of Sexuality' in Belinda Brooks-Gordon, Loraine Gelsthorpe, Martin H Johnson, Andrew Bainham (eds), *Sexuality Repositioned* (Hart 2004) 221.

[78] ibid.

[79] Michael Kimmel, *The Gender of Desires* (SUNY Press 2011) 5.

[80] Patrizia Romiot, *A Deafening Silence: Hidden Violence Against Women and Children* (Policy Press 2008); Janine Benedet, 'The Age of Innocence: A Cautious Defense of Raising the Age of Consent in Canadian Sexual Assault Law' (2010) 13 New Criminal Law Review 665.

[81] Anastasia Powell, '*Amor fati*? Gender habitus and young people's negotiation of (hetero) sexual consent' (2008) 44 Journal of Sociology 167.

[82] Teenage Research Unlimited, Teen Relationship Abuse Research 1 (Teenage Research Unlimited 2005).

Guiding survey found that 67% agreed that popular culture told boys they could coerce their girlfriends into doing what they want.[83] 13% reported being in a relationship where they felt frightened of their male partner.[84] A European-wide survey found that 41% of young women (aged 14 to 17) had experienced sexual violence, which was defined as being subject to pressure or force to engage in a sexual activity.[85]

There is a significant correlation between girls under the age of sixteen having sexual relations with their boyfriend and them being subject to violence.[86] In one study, 25% of women reported that first sexual intercourse was not wanted.[87] But it is clear these figures change when sexual experience starts at a young age. Another study found that 74% of those who had intercourse before the age of 14 and 60% of those who had sex before the age of 15 had suffered a forced sexual experience.[88] In one large U.S. survey, 22% of women whose first experience of sexual intercourse occurred before age 16 described that incident of intercourse as not voluntary, compared with 6.5% of women whose first sexual experience occurred at age 16 or older.[89] 42% of women but only 20% of men had regrets about their first sexual encounter, according to the British National Survey of Sexual Attitudes and Lifestyles.[90] Another study

---

[83] Girl Guiding, *Girls Attitude Survey* (n 73).

[84] ibid.

[85] Safeguarding Teenage Intimate Relationships (STIR) *Briefing Paper 2: Incidence Rates and Impact of Experiencing Interpersonal Violence and Abuse in Young People's Relationships* (STIR, 2015).

[86] Patrizia Romiot, *A Deafening Silence: Hidden Violence Against Women and Children* (Policy Press 2008).

[87] Joyce Abma et al, 'Young Women's Degree of Control Over First Intercourse: An Exploratory Analysis' (1998) 30 Family Planning Perspectives 12, 12-18.

[88] Patricia Donovan, Can Statutory Rape Laws Be Effective in Preventing Adolescent Pregnancy?' (1997) 29 Family Planning Perspectives 30, 34.

[89] Sharon G Elstein & Noy Davis, *Sexual Relationships between Adult Males and Young Teen Girls: Exploring the Legal and Social Responses* (American Bar Association 1997) iii.

[90] Welcome Trust, 'Survey examines changes in sexual behaviour and attitudes in Britain' (Welcome Trust 2013) can be found at <http://www.wellcome.ac.uk/News/Media-office/Press-releases/2013/Press-releases/WTP054816.htm> accessed 7th January 2015.

found that 70% of those who had had sex under the age of 16 in the UK believed that they should have waited longer.[91]

I suggest the picture is clear. There is considerable social pressure on young women to consent in circumstances in which sex is not fully wanted. There are clearly a large number of young women who are fearful of physical or emotional abuse if they do not agree to have sex with their boyfriends.

(e) Gender and Age of Capacity

Too often, the gendered aspect of the age of consent debated is not emphasised. The first point to make is that we have seen from the studies just discussed that societal and relational pressures within which autonomy is exercised are fundamentally different for boys and girls. Second, heterosexual intercourse carries with it far more risks for women than men, especially given the relatively low use of contraception typically use at first intercourse (around 10% of young people use no contraception when the parties have first had sex.[92] As Sarah Beresford points out:

> [T]he medical risks attendant for young teenage pregnancy includes low birth weight, premature labor, anemia, and pre-eclampsia. World Health Organization (WHO) research demonstrates that girls giving birth aged 14 or younger are five times as likely to die, and that stillbirths and new-born deaths are 50% higher among infants of adolescent mothers than among infants of women aged 20–29 years.[93]

Beresford also highlights the social and economic risks of early sexual pregnancy including impacts on education and socio-economic well-being.

Conclusion on the Age of Consent

I do not claim to have made a case for saying the age of consent should be 16. I have, however, made a case for the age being at the higher end of what reasonable people are likely to agree on. I have suggested that the

---

[91] Nigel Dickson, Charlotte Paul, Peter Herbison and Phil Silva, 'First sexual intercourse: age, coercion, and later regrets reported by a birth cohort' (1998) 316 British Medical Journal 29.

[92] Kate Wellings et al, 'Sexual behaviour in Britain: early heterosexual experience' (2001) 358 The Lancet 1843.

[93] Sarah Beresford, 'The Age of Consent and the Ending of Queer Theory' (2014) 4 Laws 759.

error in labelling the incompetent competent is far graver than labelling the competent incompetent, and so we should prefer a higher age. I have explained how a proper understanding of children's rights acknowledges the importance of giving them an environment in which they can develop their own values and autonomy, but that requires a degree of protection during childhood. I have also shown how capacity to consent is often exaggerated for children because the arguments fail to acknowledge the neuroscience on adolescent decision-making; the importance of acquiring values of one's own to autonomy; and the importance of the social context within which the decision is made.

Further Issues

This chapter has sketched out some of the arguments promoting an age of consent at the higher end of the scale. There are a number of issues which would also need to be considered, which I do not have space to cover in detail.

First, the alternative to relying on age of consent laws is to rely on the general law on rape. Clearly, a major issue is how well the law on rape and rape trials work in practice. There is extensive literature on the difficulties in the prosecution and conviction of rape. It is widely acknowledged that, for a wide range of reasons, it has proved enormously difficult to prosecute rape effectively. The experience of rape victims going through a rape trial is traumatic. Looking at the issue in terms of protecting girls from sexual abuse, a law which can be enforced without them needing give evidence at trial and which does not lead to use of rape myths to acquit defendants seems highly desirable. [94] This is particularly because child victims of sexual offences are notoriously reluctant, very understandably, to give evidence. When they do, their evidence is often not given the weight that it is properly owed.[95] Under the age of consent provisions, it must be established that the defendant sexually penetrated the victim and the victim was under the age, but that can be done without the witness having to give evidence.

---

[94] See Kim Stevenson, 'It Is What "Girls of Indifferent Character" Do', Complications concerning the Legal Age of Sexual Consent in the Light of R v C (2011)' (2012) 76 Journal of Criminal Law 130 for an excellent recent discussion of the problems in prosecuting rape involving young victims.
[95] Laura Hoyano and Caroline Keenan, *Child Abuse* (Oxford University Press 2010) ch 8.

Second, one of the most powerful arguments against setting an age of consent is that it will be assume that women above that age are able to consent. Catherine Mackinnon writes:

> The age line under which girls are presumed disabled from consenting to sex, whatever they say, rationalizes a condition of sexual coercion which women never outgrow. One day they cannot say yes, and the next day they cannot say no. The law takes the most aggravated case for female powerlessness based on gender and age combined and, by formally prohibiting all [underage] sex as rape, makes consent irrelevant on the basis of an assumption of powerlessness. This defines those above the age line as powerful, whether they actually have power to consent or not.[81]

Again, there is much that can be said about this issue, but I suggest that the better response is to develop a far more nuanced and sophisticated approach to determining what consent is generally, rather than abandoning the law on age of consent.[96]

Third, another strong argument against age of consent law is that it inhibits the sexual freedom of young people.[97] Professor Fran Olsen notes:

> On the one hand, [statutory rape laws] protect females; like laws against rape, incest, child molestation, and child marriage, statutory rape laws are a statement of social disapproval of certain forms of exploitation. . . . On the other hand, statutory rape laws restrict the sexual activity of young women and reinforce the double standard of sexual morality. On this account, statutory rape laws protect as they disempower.[98]

As argued earlier, this is not an 'either/or question'. It is not a matter of being either liberationist and respecting the rights of the autonomy of children or being paternalistic and imposing what is good for children on all. Whether one uses an age of consent or not, and what age one sets it at, will be a more effective protection for some people of that age, but will fail to protect the rights of others. It is a matter of striking the balance. Lowering the age of consent to 14, for example, will mean there will be

---

[96] Jonathan Herring, Herring, 'Consent in the Criminal Law: The Importance of Relationality and Responsibility' in Alan Reed and Michael Bohlander (ed), *General Defences in Criminal Law* (Ashgate 2014).

[97] Matthew Waites, 'The Age of Consent and Sexual Consent' in Mark Cowling and Paul Reynolds (eds), *Making Sense of Sexual Consent* (Ashgate 2004) 80.

[98] Frances Olsen, 'Statutory Rape: A Feminist Critique of Rights Analysis', 63 (1984) 64 Texas Law Review 387.

greater freedom (in terms of legal authorisation at least) to engage in sexual freedom for those able to exercise that freedom with capacity and in an autonomous way; but it will open others to being abused without their full autonomous consent, in a way which cannot be effectively responded to by the law. In balancing these competing claims, I have argued in favour of protecting the rights of those who would otherwise suffer abuse than the rights of those whose sexual freedom is imposed upon. This is not a matter of being paternalistic or not; it's a matter of determining which rights are more important.

Fourth, there is the issue of those who are close in age who may be prosecuted for 'sexual experimentation'. The current law deals with CPS guidelines which state 'Children of the same or similar age are highly unlikely to be prosecuted for engaging in sexual activity, where the activity is mutually agreed and there is no abuse or exploitation' and through sentencing where a similarity in age may well lead to a lower sentence.[99] It might be argued that these reveal that the current law is too broad. Worse, it can lead to so much prosecutorial discretion that race- and class-based discrimination can be revealed in how it is prosecuted.[100] That is a problem, but it exists for many crimes. The CPS guidance is tolerably clear and there is little reference in the media to cases where the offences have been improperly prosecuted.

Conclusion

This chapter has sought to argue in favour of a high age of consent, such as the current one set at sixteen. It has explained the theoretical justification for bright line drawing in the criminal law as being based on behaviour which has the potential to cause serious harm, but where the defendant is not well placed to determine whether his or her act will be safe. I have argued that a person wanting to have sex with an underage child is not well placed to know whether or not the child is sufficiently mature to consent. I have also argued that when fixing the age of consent, we need to balance the interests of children who will be treated as having capacity when they do not, with the interests of those who will be treated as lacking capacity when they do not. I have urged that the interests of the

---

[99] *R v Hines-Randle* [2012] 1 *Criminal Appeal* Reports (Sentencing) 375.
[100] Michelle Goodwin, 'Law's Limits: Regulating Statutory Rape Law' (2013) Wisconsin Law Review 418.

former group are far weightier than the younger group. The chapter has also explored how theories of children's rights generally do permit interferences in children's autonomy so as to maximise their opportunities to develop values of their own and exercise autonomy when they are older. The chapter has also explored the age at which we might expect children to be able to exercise sexual autonomy. When we look at current understandings of neuroscience; the need to have adopted values for yourself as central to autonomy; and the broader social context within which adolescent sexual autonomy is exercised, I have argued an age of around sixteen is appropriate. The chapter has acknowledged that this is a highly gendered question. Finally, the chapter has acknowledged the difficulties with setting a higher age of consent, but has sought to argue that they are outweighed by the advantages of this approach. Of course, in all these debates, perhaps all sides will agree that the role of the law is limited here. Changes in adolescent male societal attitudes about women and about sex will do far more to protect sexual autonomy than any change in the age of consent.

CHAPTER SIX

QUEERING CONSENT:
(RE)EVOLVING CONSTRUCTIONS OF
THE AGE OF CONSENT AND THE LAW

CHRIS ASHFORD

Introduction

In October 2012, the UK Labour MP Tom Watson[1] publicly asked the British Prime Minister, David Cameron, to investigate a 'powerful paedophile network that was linked to Parliament and Number 10 Downing Street.'[2] This Parliamentary question would spark a series of reports and investigations, including Operation Midland, that would engulf the British establishment. Together with the ongoing Goddard Inquiry – which includes thirteen sub-investigations[3] – debates would be re-opened about the historic links between paedophile groups and gay rights campaigners and organisations. Allegations about the late Prime Minister, Edward Heath and former Conservative MP Harvey Proctor[4] along with the celebrity Paul Gambaccini[5] would also conflate homosexual identities

---

[1] Elected Deputy Leader of the UK Labour Party in 2015.

[2] PMQs: Tom Watson on Paedophile Ring Links to Previous PM's Aide, BBC News, 24 October 2012, http://www.bbc.co.uk/news/uk-politics-20067409 (last accessed 22 April 2016).

[3] Independent Inquiry into Child Sexual Abuse,
https://www.iicsa.org.uk/investigations (last accessed 22 April 2016).

[4] See, Harvey Proctor, *Credible and True: The Political and Personal Memoir of K Harvey Proctor* (Biteback 2016).

[5] See, Paul Gambaccini, *Love, Paul Gambaccini: My Year Under the Yewtree* (Biteback 2015). Gambaccini had been investigated as part of Operation Yewtree which came in the wake of allegations of child abuse following the death of one-

with other sexual allegations.[6] Paedophilia and homosexuality would be
linked in such a way that had not been seen for at least two decades.

Two years after the Watson question, it was another Labour MP – the then
Deputy Leader of the Labour Party, Harriet Harman – who found herself
facing criticism for her historic links with the UK paedophile organisation,
Paedophile Information Exchange (PIE). The *Daily Mail* alleged[7] that
during her time as leader of the civil liberties campaigning group, the
National Council for Civil Liberties (NCCL)[8]in the late 1970s, the
organisation had supported PIE and thus Harman was at best 'soft' on
paedophiles, and at worst, a paedophile sympathiser.

The Harman controversy would eventually pass, but it brought into focus
the historic shift in attitudes towards group such as PIE and their
relationship with rights and liberation campaigners, particularly in the
1970s. The gay rights movement would go on to achieve a significant

---

time DJ and presenter Jimmy Savile. See more generally, Dan Davies, *In Plain
Sight: The Life and Lies of Jimmy Savile* (Quercus 2014).

[6] Heath didn't 'come out' as homosexual in his lifetime. In the midst of the slurs,
innuendo and allegations, former sex worker Myra Ling-Forde released a statement
indicating that she thought Heath was not a paedophile, he had simply been a 'old,
sad, gay man'. This was in contrast to allegations that in 1992, she had stated she
would expose Heath as a sex offender and it was alleged that she had escaped
prosecution as a brothel owner following the claims. See: Kunal Dutta, 'Ted Heath
Child Abuse Claims: Prime Minister was "Not a Paedophile…Just an Old, Sad,
Gay Man" Says Brothel Owner', *The Independent*, 10 August 2015,
http://www.independent.co.uk/news/uk/crime/ted-heath-child-abuse-claims-
former-prime-minister-was-not-a-paedophile-just-an-old-sad-gay-man-says-
10449259.html (last accessed 22 April 2016). Michael McManus, who had
worked for Heath and drafted his memoirs, wrote in 2011 that he was 'left in no
doubt whatsoever that Heath was a gay man who had sacrificed his personal life to
his political career, exercising iron self-control and living a celibate life.' See
Michael McManus, *Tory Pride and Prejudice: The Conservative Party and
Homosexual Law Reform* (Biteback Publishing 2011) 61.

[7] Martin Robinson, 'Letter from paedophile Group Links Harriet Harman and
Patricia Hewitt to it AFTER they said it had been Marginalised', *Daily Mail*, 7
March 2014, http://www.dailymail.co.uk/news/article-2575505/Letter-paedophile-
group-links-Harriet-Harman-Patricia-Hewitt-AFTER-said-marginalised.html (last
accessed 22 April 2016).

[8] The forerunner of today's civil liberties campaigning group, Liberty,
https://www.liberty-human-rights.org.uk (last accessed 22 April 2016).

transformation in their legal regulation with the introduction of employment protections, same-sex marriage, goods and services protections, adoption and fertility rights and hate crime protections. Yet, the gay men who were campaigning for more radical shifts in inter-generational relationships, the man/boy activists, and groups such as PIE, had been 'cast off' from this coalition of activists by the early 1980s.

Robinson had noted a number of years earlier the difficult relationship between the NCCL (which challenged the State's intervention in post-pubescent sex) and the PIE, but PIE's attempts as 'entryism' were ultimately unsuccessful when their membership application to the NCCL was turned down.[9] These attempts were founded on seeking to shape policy and political agendas, to access resource, and arguably to gain benefit from the credibility of groups such as NCCL.

For the media in 2014 and the years that followed, this historic relationship was one that appeared revelatory despite a number of scholarly sources discussing these links over the preceding decades. The Member of Parliament, and former Chair of the Inquiry into child sexual orientation in Rochdale,[10] observed that in the past 'a confusion between sexual liberation and sexual exploitation' had been used as a 'cover' by paedophiles.[11] Yet, this is just one of numerous narratives that have been forged to understand paedophilia and gay rights/the gay liberation movement.

As recently as 2016, the Labour Party was still dealing with fallout from this recent re-appraisal. In February 2016, Tom O'Carroll, the former chair of PIE, was suspended as a member after *The Times* revealed he had joined the party following the election of new leader, Jeremy Corbyn in 2015.[12] Over thirty years since PIE ceased to exist, it is still having a

---

[9] Lucy Robinson, *Gay Men and the Left in Post-War Britain: How the personal Got Political* (Manchester: Manchester University Press 2007).

[10] See http://www.gmpcc.org.uk/down-to-business/coffey-inquiry/ (last accessed 4 January 2016).

[11] Robert Booth, "Whitehall Study Wanted Age of Consent to Be 14." *The Guardian*, July 8, 2014.

[12] Ben Riley-Smith, 'Former Chairman of the Paedophile Information Exchange has Labour Party Membership Suspended', *The Telegraph*, 16 February 2016, http://www.telegraph.co.uk/news/politics/labour/12159428/Former-chairman-of-

political impact. Moreover, PIE and the North American Man Boy Love Association (NAMBLA) in the United States have arguably done much to influence the ways in which consent is regulated and the ways in which debates about consent continue to be framed.

Consent and Homosexuality

Homosexuality and paedophilia arguably have a long and contested relationship,[13] and whilst most would regard it as dubious at best that the two should be linked, hostility towards homosexuals – and arguably fear – has meant that the general public have historically been antipathetic about relationships between gay men and children, notably in relation to the employment of gay men as teachers, for example.[14] Paedophilia has been and continues to be utilized by anti-gay rights campaigners as an indication of gay behaviour[15].

By the 1950s, homosexuality was increasingly a source for social and moral concern, and growing cases of blackmail as depicted in the 1961 Dirk Bogarde film *Victim* were occupying police resources. The 1950s also saw the trial and conviction of journalist Peter Wildeblood, along with Lord Montagu of Beaulieu and Michael Pitt Rivers, for homosexual behaviour, revealing homosexuality at the heart of the establishment and serving in part to encourage the commissioning of the 1957 Wolfenden

---

the-Paedophile-Information-Exchange-has-Labour-Party-membership-suspended.html (last accessed 22 April 2016).

[13] See, for example: L. Eric Alcorn, 'A Critique of the Academic Process and Application of Evolutionary Theory in Pederasty: An Integration of Empirical, Historical, Sociological, Cross-Cultural, Cross-Species, and Evolutionary Perspectives by Dr Bruce Rind', in *Censoring Sex Research: The Debate over Male Intergenerational Relations*, (eds) Thomas K. Hubbard and Beert Verstraete, (Left Coast Press 2013) 145-159; and Bruce Rind, 'Pederasty: An Integration of Empirical, Historical, Sociological, Cross-Cultural, Cross-Species, and Evolutionary Perspectives', in Thomas K. Hubbard and Beert Verstraete (eds) *Censoring Sex Research: The Debate over Male Intergenerational Relations* (Left Coast Press 2013), 1-90.

[14] Dennis Howitt, *Paedophiles and Sexual Offences Against Children* (Chichester: Wiley 1995) 45.

[15] See, for example: Steve Baldwin, "Child molestation and the Homosexual Movement", *Regent University Law Review* 14 (2002) 267-282.

Report.[16] Wildeblood would go on to 'admit' his homosexuality and write a 1955 book which was to make the case for the decriminalisation of homosexuality. In this early political account, we see Wildeblood make the case that '[the homosexual] does not wish to seduce children, not only because it seems to him basically immoral to do so, but because he is not attracted towards them' and 'when all homosexual acts, whether between adult men or between men and boys, are treated by the law with equal severity, it is difficult for the general public to discriminate between them.'[17] That Wildeblood feels the need to make this point reflects the broader public anguish and fear about the 'seduction' of children, typified not only by the abuse of children but also their 'recruitment' to homosexuality and thus, their 'corruption.'

The 1957 Wolfenden Report – which would ultimately pave the way for the Sexual Offences Act 1967 and the effective decriminalisation of male homosexuality – had sought to strike a balance between protecting and criminalising youth when it came to the age of consent. Whilst recommending that the age of consent ought to be 21 for male homosexual acts, they also indicated that 'it is not, however, our intention to suggest that criminal proceedings ought to be taken in respect of any and every detected homosexual offence committed by a person under that age.' Leaving aside behaviour that has been accompanied by conduct that is criminal or vicious, the Committee argues that 'we hope that the responsible authorities, as well as parents or others under whose care the young men concerned might be living, would be ready to distinguish between conduct of this kind and behaviour which is often no more than the physical expression of a transient phase.'[18]

Here, at the effective birth of the contemporary legal landscape governing homosexual sexual relations under English law, we have concern about protecting children and also an assumption that homosexuality might be 'just a phase' whilst also seeming to place remarkable faith in the progressive and supportive instincts of parents and authorities towards a sexual practice that is at once constructed as potentially harmful, and thus

---

[16] Also see, John Wolfenden, *Turning Points: The Memoirs of Lord Wolfenden* (Bodley Head 1976) 131.
[17] Peter Wildeblood, *Against the Law* (Weidenfeld & Nicolson 1999) 6-7.
[18] Home Office/Scottish Home Department, *Report of the Committee on Homosexual Offences*, (HMSO 1957) 27-28.

to be protected from, and also as something innocuous, typically transient. At the very moment of seeking to extend the realms of consent, state control is also being delegated to the private home sphere and state agencies in order to regulate the operation of that consent.

Shifting Constructions of Consent

The age of 'heterosexual' consent has also been a subject of debate although it has been settled for considerably longer. In 1285, the age of consent was set at ten, rising to thirteen in 1875 and in 1885 it moved to sixteen, where it remains today. The Act that set the age of sixteen – the Criminal Law Amendment Act 1885 – also introduced the offence of gross indecency.[19] Lesbianism has been notable for its absence from this legal debate[20], as too has the heterosexual age of consent in recent decades.[21]

These historic understandings of consent have been predicated on the construction of consent within a heteronormative membrane. Until 1967, no other legal construction of consensual activity was possible and even after 1967, the law continued to be dominated by a heterosexual understanding of consent. Waites observed that this is further complicated by shifting and varying understandings of the term, but has come to refer 'to an age at which the law permits sexual behaviour without any straightforward assumption that this coincides with the law recognizing a young person's capacity to give consent, or that the law demands that consent be positively expressed.'[22]

---

[19] Jon Silverman and David Wilson, *Innocence Betrayed: Paedophilia, the Media and Society* (Cambridge: Polity Press, 2002), 14.

[20] See, Matthew Waites, 'Inventing a 'Lesbian Age of Consent'? The History of the Minimum Age for Sex between Women in the UK' [2002] 11(3) *Social & Legal Studies* 323-342.

[21] Rachel Thomson, '"An Adult Thing"? Young People's Perspectives on the Heterosexual Age of Consent' [2004] 7(2) *Sexualities* 133-149. It hasn't been entirely absent however, with some exceptions. See for example: Steve James, 'Romeo and Juliet were Sex Offenders: An Analysis of the Age of Consent and a Call for Reform' [2009-2010] 78 *UKMC Law Review* 241-262.

[22] Matthew Waites, The Age of Consent: Young People, Sexuality and Citizenship (Palgrave Macmillan 2005) 5.

The Sexual offences Act 1967 effectively decriminalised homosexuality for adult males aged twenty-one or over.[23] This was not, however, extended to Scottish law until 1980 and Northern Ireland until 1982.[24] The age was brought down to eighteen in all parts of the UK in 1994.[25] Attempts to equalize the age of consent stalled despite numerous efforts by the New Labour Government led by Tony Blair. Attempts to do so via the Crime and Disorder Bill of 1998 and the Sexual Offences (Amendment) Bill of the same year both failed with the age ultimately being lowered via the Sexual Offences Amendment Act 2000[26] with the Government also deploying the Parliament Act to force it through the House of Lords.[27]

Consent and power are key ideas that play out in this dynamic. For those who describe themselves as 'boy lovers' and as proponents of 'man-boy relationships', there is a noticeable lack of a symbiotic 'adult lovers' movement.[28] It is therefore perhaps inevitable that, as others have noted,

---

[23] Honore has noted, following Re Shurey [1918] 1 Ch. 263, that the age is obtained at the first moment of the day. The turning of the hand of a clock determines the line between legality and illegality; between consensual sexual activity and the activities of paedophile. See: Tony Honore, *Sex Law* (London: Duckworth 1978), 92. Public questioning that the age of twenty-one was too high was limited at the time the report was published. A notable exception can be found in Charles Berg, *Fear, Punishment, Anxiety and the Wolfenden Report* (George Allen & Unwin 1959).

[24] See Laurence R Helfer, 'Finding a Consensus on Equality: The Homosexual Age of Consent and the European Convention on Human Rights' [1990] 65 *New York University Law Review* 1044-1100

[25] Criminal Justice and Public Order Act 1994.

[26] In Northern Ireland, the age was lowered to 17 rather than 16 in line with the heterosexual age of consent.

[27] Jon Silverman and David Wilson, *Innocence Betrayed: Paedophilia, the Media and Society* (Polity Press 2002), 17. Also see, Debbie Epstein, Richard Johnson and Deborah Lynn Steinberg, 'Twice Told Tales: Transformation, Recuperation and Emergence in the Age of Consent Debates 1998' [2000] 3(1) *Sexualities* 5-30, and Matthew Waites, 'Equality at Last? Homosexuality, Heterosexuality and the Age of Consent in the United Kingdom [2003] 37(4) *Sociology* 637-655.

[28] This is a weakness apparent to the Man/Boy movement who have sought to marshal evidence to support their argument that a) children are sexually active and b) sexual relationships with adults can be positive. See Sarah D. Goode, *Paedophiles in Society: Reflecting on Sexuality, Abuse and Hope* (Palgrave Macmillan 2011, 132-143. DeYoung has more recently observed the use of accounts by NAMBLA, notably through their newsletter to members, as a way of 'normalising' paedophilia with letters apparently from boys, extoling the positive

the social sciences have almost exclusively studied such relationships as forms of sexual abuse.[29]

This is further complicated by the apparent historic viewing of homosexuality, as mentioned earlier, namely as a risk *to* children, both in terms of 'contamination' (the recruitment argument) and also in terms of 'exploitation' (the abuser argument).[30]   In the 1970s, for example, it was revealed that British Police kept 'secret dossiers' on those school teachers they believed to be 'corrupt'; that is to say, openly gay.[31]

Two decades earlier, at the time Wolfenden was published, many apparently seemed to believe that the report heralded a new threat to the moral fabric of the nation.   Chesser noted that this was all the more remarkable given that disarmament talks had just broken down and the USSR had just tested an inter-continental missile.[32]   In the face of

---

impact that their experience of 'boy love' has had on them. See: Mary DeYoung, 'The World According to NAMBLA: Accounting for Deviance' [2015] 16(1) *The Journal of Sociology & Social Welfare* 111-126.

[29] Theo Sandfort, Edward Brongersma, and Alex van Naerssen, 'Man-Boy Relationships: Different Concepts for a Diversity Phenomena' [1991] 1-2 *Journal of Homosexuality* 5-12.

[30] See for example W. Lindesay Neustatter, 'Homosexuality: The Medical Aspects' in J. Tudor Rees and Harley V Usill (eds), *They Stand Apart: A Critical Survey of the Problems of Homosexuality* (William Heinemann 1955) 108.   There were attempts to challenge these assumptions, even before the Wolfenden Committee reported.   Cory observed in 1953 that 'most homosexuals I have known, however, are little interested and hardly aroused in the presence of immature boys.   They were attracted to adolescents when they were in their teens, and the love-objects that seemed elderly when they were young appeared very attractive when they were somewhat older.' See: Donald Webster Cory, *The Homosexual Outlook: A Subjective* Approach (Peter Nevill, 1953) 66.   Westwood similarly recognised the widespread belief that people believed there was common ground between paedophilia and homosexuality, but argued there was no empirical basis for the claims.   See Gordon Westwood, *A Minority: Male Homosexuality in Great Britain* (Longmans 1960) 159.

[31] Don Milligan, *The Politics of* Homosexuality (Edinburgh Gay Activists Alliance Reprint 1978) 8.   In the United States, a number of cases exposed prejudicial attitudes to gay teachers. See: Joshua Dressler, 'Judicial Homophobia: Gay Rights Biggest Roadblock' [1979] *The Civil Liberties Review* 79-87.

[32] Eustace Chesser, *Live and Let Live: The Moral of the Wolfenden Report* (Heinemann 1958) 15.

Armageddon, the nation was more concerned about being buggered than nuked.

The decision to recommend twenty-one as the age of homosexual consent in the Wolfenden Report – an age ultimately enshrined in the Sexual Offences Act 1967 – was also significant. Suffee has argued[33] that the proposals created the sense that the law could continue to invade the private domain and render it public again at the whim of the government, not only in terms of a potential change to the age, but also, one might argue, in creating a situation in which the state, or its agents, might need to investigate the private realm where there was a reasonable belief that someone might be engaging in encounters with someone under twenty-one.

Roy Jenkins – the radical and reforming Home Secretary in the 1960s (and a second brief period in the 1970s) – instigated a review of sexual offences law, taking the Criminal Law Revision Committee to review the law alongside a new Policy Advisory Committee. Detailed discussion of this process can be found elsewhere,[34] but it is significant to note that whilst the Campaign for Homosexual Equality (CHE) argued that the age of consent should be equal, at 16, the National Council for Civil Liberties argued in its submission to the Criminal Law Revision Committee that there should be an equal age of consent at 14.[35]

Radicalism – and campaigners of the Left[36] – appeared to be struggling with a tension on these issues of consent. Thorstad noted that the Guardian newspaper had an internal discussion on the issue of so called 'man/boy love' and determined it as abusive behaviour, setting out their editorial position on the letters page. Thorstad described this position as a

---

[33] Reshad Suffee, 'Homosexuality and the Law: The Construction of Wolfenden Homonormativity in 1950s England' [2016] 63(2) *Journal of Homosexuality* 250-277.

[34] Matthew Waites, The Age of Consent: Young People, Sexuality and Citizenship (Palgrave Macmillan 2005) 133.

[35] Matthew Waites, The Age of Consent: Young People, Sexuality and Citizenship (Palgrave Macmillan 2005) 135.

[36] See more generally: Lucy Robinson, *Gay Men and the Left in Post-War Britain: How the personal Got Political* (Manchester: Manchester University Press 2007).

'surrender to bourgeois morality and antisex feminists'[37] but this argument fails to grapple with the issues of consent and capacity that add nuance to the sex radical tradition.

By the 1990s, campaigning and public debate resulted in what Waites has termed 'the hegemony of equality at 16'.[38] The Sexual Offences (Amendment) Act 2000 would finally enshrine this in law. By this point, a growing agenda of reform formed part of the broader sexual citizenship agenda,[39] but it was to be an agenda typically rooted in the homonormative.[40]

The unequal age of consent, recommended by Wolfenden and enshrined in the 1967 legislation, would create the circumstances in which organisations arguing for man/boy or inter-generational relationships could occupy the same political ground as gay rights activists in the decades that followed until the equalisation in consent laws in the year 2000. After all, when the age of consent is 21, arguing that an 18-year-old gay man can consent to sexual activity (a positon accepted without question today) renders one both a proponent of man/boy love and also a gay rights activist.

NAMBLA

One such organisation that would seek to argue for political and legal reform relating to the age of consent was the US group, the North American Man Boy Love Association (NAMBLA). Founded in 1978,[41]

---

[37] David Thorstad, 'Homosexuality and the American Left: The impact of Stonewall' [1995] 4 *Journal of Homosexuality* 319-350.

[38] Matthew Waites, "The Age of Consent and Sexual Consent," in Mark Cowling and Paul Reynolds (eds) *Making Sense of Sexual Consent* (Ashgate 2004) 73-92.

[39] Diane Richardson, 'Constructing Sexual Citizenship: Theorizing Sexual Rights' [2000] 20(1) *Critical Social Policy* 105-135.

[40] See, for example, Chris Ashford, '(Homo)normative Legal Discourses and the Queer Challenge' [2011] *Durham Law Review* 77-98, and Chris Ashford, 'Bareback Sex, Queer Legal Theory, and Evolving Socio-Legal Contexts' [2015] 18(1-2) *Sexualities* 195-209.

[41] Dennis Howitt, *Paedophiles and Sexual Offences Against Children* (Wiley 1995) 242. Also see the NABLA website: http://nambla.org/welcome.html (last accessed 22 April 2016).

the group sets itself the goal of challenging the age of consent laws in the United States.[42] It articulates this in terms of:

- building understanding and support for [man/boy] relationships;
- educating the general public on the benevolent nature of man/boy love;
- cooperating with lesbian, gay, feminist, and other liberation movements;
- supporting the liberation of persons of all ages from sexual prejudice and oppression.

NAMBLA and similar groups traditionally provided important hubs for contact and through which pederasty could be constructed, justified and normalized;[43] a role which has arguably been surpassed by the growing use of technology in recent decades, and online fora.[44]

NAMBLA has also existed in a popular cultural context, featuring for example in the American animated series, South Park. In an episode from Season 4 entitled 'Cartman Joins NAMBLA', first shown in 2000, we see one of the central characters (an 8 year old boy) advertise online for mature friends who like little boys, after deciding his own peers are too immature. He is inundated with interest and finds himself appearing as the 'poster child' for NAMBLA.[45]The episode sought to satirise the organisation and reflected a discourse that seeks to mock NAMBLA as much as, if not more than, it fears it. Such is this strong mocking discourse that NAMBLA has even been described as a 'universal whipping boy'.[46]

---

[42] For an overview of the US consent laws, see, Kate Sutherland, 'From Jailbird to Jailbait: Age of Consent Laws and the Construction of Teenage Sexualities' [2002-2003] 9 *William & Mary Journal of Women and the Law* 313-349.

[43] See, for a historical analysis of three US-based networks: the Rene Guyon Society, the Childhood Sensuality Circle and NAMBLA: N. De Young, 'The Indignant Page: Techniques of Neutralization in the Publications of Pedophile Organizations', Child Abuse and Neglect 12 (1988) 583-591.

[44] See for example: Keith F. Durkin and Clifton D. Bryant, [1999] 20(2) Deviant Behavior 103-127.

[45] Sarah D. Goode, *Paedophiles in Society: Reflecting on Sexuality, Abuse and Hope* (Basingstoke: Palgrave Macmillan, 2011), 63.

[46] Richard D. Mohr, "The Pedophilia of Everyday Life", in Steven Bruhm and Natasha Hurley (eds) *Curiouser: On the Queerness of Children* (University of Minnesota Press 2004) 20.

Kincaid has suggested that when NAMBLA speak of the 'rights of the child', 'we more than suspect that for them only the right of the adult to have sex with the child is at stake.'[47] Although largely viewed and positioned as a same-sex male organisation, NAMBLA have also acted as proponents of Woman/Girl love,[48] but this has not garnered the same public response.[49]

In the 1980s, NAMBLA would deepen its same-sex campaigning alliance by marching in gay pride parades. The one-time porn star, journalist and late queer commentator, Scott O'Hara, described the hissing and protesting that would accompany his marching through San Francisco Gay Day (Pride) parades under the NAMBLA banner. He describes the shouts of "we don't want you in our parade" and "you deserve to die". Perhaps, most significantly for this discussion, "you're not part of the gay community!"[50]

O'Hara carefully notes how was not – in his seven years marching with NAMBLA – someone who regarded himself as a lover of children (preferring older men) and was not himself a boy. Rather, he felt an affinity for the most stigmatized group at the parade. Moreover, he recalls fantasising about sex from the age of twelve and regarded himself a late bloomer for finally having sex at fifteen. When NAMBLA were eventually banned from the various pride marches across America, O'Hara also stepped away from the Pride events 'in disgust'.

---

[47] James R. Kincaid, *Child Loving: The Erotic Child and Victorian Culture* (Routledge 1992), 385. That Kincaid challenges this view was enough for his text to cause considerable controversy when published. He later noted that the book resulted in a high-profile negative review in the Sunday Times and calls from then Conservative MPs Dame Jill Knight and Ann Winterton for the book to be banned as they believed it encouraged paedophilia. See, also: James R. Kincaid, "Producing Erotic Children", in Steven Bruhm and Natasha Hurley (eds) *Curiouser: On the Queerness of Children* (University of Minnesota Press 2004), 3-16.

[48] Linda Frankel, 'Sappho Was a Right-On Girl Lover!', *NAMBLA Bulletin*, 4(3) (1983) 9.

[49] On sexual consent laws in the US context more generally, see: Carolyn E. Cocca, *Jailbait: The Politics of Statutory Rape Laws in the United States* (State University of New York Press 2004).

[50] Scott O'Hara, *Rarely Pure and Never Simple: Selected Essays of Scott O'Hara* (Harrington Park Press 1999) 51-54.

NAMBLA today finds itself in a paradoxical situation whereby to seek to understand the organisation is to raise suspicion and to become tainted by association and thus a rejection of NAMBLA and its agenda is now reflexive based not on an understanding of what the organisation does argue for, but on what people believe it argues for. Califia has noted that 'very few people who are not boy-lovers bother to read any NAMBLA literature before condemning it as worthless smut…simply possessing NAMBLA literature is often enough to make you look like a criminal in the eyes of the media or the cops.'[51]

As gay rights in the US moved from the radical liberation politics of the 1970s and seized the equality agenda which would manifest itself in the same-sex marriage movement of the 2010s, NAMBLA would find itself excluded. The few radicals such as O'Hara would be gone, faded from the political and activist scene, or through natural deaths, or as in O'Hara's case, as victims of HIV/AIDS.

The Paedophile Information Exchange (PIE)

The UK equivalent of NAMBLA was the Paedophile Information Exchange (PIE). The organisation came into existence in October 1974 with an early modest membership of around 250.[52] The group later merged with another pre-existing group known as Paedophile Action for Liberation[53] (PAL).[54]

O'Carroll – the controversial former leader of PIE – has suggested that at this point in the mid-1970s, the only people who seemed to be 'in the

---

[51] Patrick Califia, *Speaking Sex to Power: The Politics of Queer Sex* (Cleis Press 2002) 258.

[52] The Wilson and Cox survey which commenced in 1978 had a potential pool of around 180 members, suggesting a significant decline in membership in a relatively short period of time. Glenn D. Wilson and David N. Cox, *The Child-Lovers: A Study of Paedophiles in Society* (Peter Owen 1983), 12. Holmes and Holmes have suggested that 250 is the largest number of members the organisation achieved but don't provide any reference or evidence for this claim. See: Stephen T. Holmes and Ronald M. Holmes, *Sex Crimes: Patterns and Behaviour*, Second Edition (Sage 2002)

[53] PAL itself had formed as a 'breakaway' group from the South London Gay Liberation Front.

[54] Tom O'Carroll, *Paedophilia: The Radical Case* (Peter Owen 1980) 207.

know' about paedophile groups were 'readers of gay newspapers and magazines, and others in gay circles who had heard by word of mouth'.[55]

PIE was based in London and aimed to provide a network for paedophiles to share their concerns and provide support via their newsletter called *Magpie*.[56] Membership was open to any gender, but few women joined.[57]

PIE's first Chairperson, Michael Hanson, was a gay student living in Edinburgh. O'Carroll has stated that 'he wasn't even a paedophile',[58] as he had a relationship with someone he thought to be sixteen but who was actually fifteen. It was apparently this experience – the age of consent was 21 – that made Hanson identify with this group. As far as the law was concerned, he was a paedophile, and in 2015, remains so under the current legal framework. The group has its origins explicitly in the gay rights movement, forming as a special interest group within the Scottish Minorities Group, later known as the Scottish Homosexual Rights Group and later Outright Scotland.

Its second Chair, taking over a year later, reflected the group's shifting centre of gravity towards London. Keith Hose was twenty-three and was shaped by the GLF liberation ideas of the time, having previously been a member of South London GLF.[59]

PIE was indeed often to be found alongside broader gay campaigns and resources. For example, a 1978 text entitled *The Law and Sexuality: How*

---

[55] Tom O'Carroll, *Paedophilia: The Radical Case* (Peter Owen 1980), 207. O'Carroll was himself to alter and lead the organisation.

[56] The group also promoted an agenda that was and remains 'radical'. Inspired by the liberation movement, they advocated the abolition of the age of consent, suggesting instead that the law should be based around the communication of consent. It was on this basis that they suggested that consent was unlikely to be communicated below the age of four, but they also noted that there may be circumstances when sexual activity between an adult and a child below the age of four could be appropriate, even desirable. See: Tom O'Carroll, *Paedophilia: The Radical* Case (Peter Owen 1980), 112-117.

[57] Glenn D. Wilson and David N. Cox, *The Child-Lovers: A Study of Paedophiles in Society* (London: Peter Owen, 1983), 8.

[58] Tom O'Carroll, *Paedophilia: The Radical Case* (Peter Owen 1980), 209.

[59] Tom O'Carroll, *Paedophilia: The Radical Case* (Peter Owen 1980), 209.

to Cope with the Law if you're not 100% Conventional Heterosexual[60] was jointly published by Grass Roots Books and Manchester Law Centre. The Law Centre – now closed – provided free legal advice to the local community in Manchester whilst Grass Roots was a Newton Street based radical bookshop. The shop was run as a co-operative, founded in 1971 and continued until 1999, when it was forced to relocate and close soon afterwards. The store specialised in selling pamphlets and radical books.[61]

The book itself offers a comprehensive overview of the legal issues that one might have faced, from divorce and custody to censorship and the criminal law. The book also includes a chapter on the 'law's assumptions about sexuality' in which paedophilia – described as 'the love of children by adults'[62] is considered. The authors note that 'many young people take the initiative in their relationships with adults. The law, though, denies that this is possible, and there is not even a word equivalent to paedophilia to describe the feelings of a young person towards an older one.'[63] The guide goes on to provide the contact details for PIE and includes their contact details at the back of the book in their 'useful organisations and addresses' section under the heading 'counselling and befriending'.

Perhaps the moment that homosexuality and paedophilia was linked explicitly in the UK's public imagination as a unified political movement was following an intervention by the self-appointed moral custodian, Mary Whitehouse. Whitehouse sought to highlight the apparent connections between the more 'mainstream' and 'respectable' gay rights organisation, The Albany Trust and PIE. The Albany Trust was partially supported by grants from the UK government and thus she suggested, the Trust was supporting PIE, and so PIE was in part subsidized by taxpayers' money. This wasn't true, but the two groups had forged links, with the Trust

---

[60] Steve Cohen et al, *The Law and Sexuality: How to Cope with the Law if You're Not 100% Conventionally Heterosexual* (Grass Roots Books and Manchester Law Centre 1978)

[61] Out in the Past, 1980s, http://www.outinthepast.org.uk/timeline/1980 (last accessed 22 April 2016).

[62] Steve Cohen et al, *The Law and Sexuality: How to Cope with the Law if You're Not 100% Conventionally Heterosexual* (Grass Roots Books and Manchester Law Centre 1978) 150.

[63] Steve Cohen et al, *The Law and Sexuality: How to Cope with the Law if You're Not 100% Conventionally Heterosexual* (Grass Roots Books and Manchester Law Centre 1978) 151.

planning on publishing a Q&A booklet on paedophilia, following Keith Hose's meeting with some members of the trust at a MIND-organized Sexual Minorities Workshop.[64]

Former Albany Trust Director, Antony Grey, verifies this story but also commented that 'I never thought, and did not intend, that paedophilia should become a major focus of the Trust's work', and 'The Albany Trust's mistake was to be willing to behave as a rational, liberally-minded people towards PIE and PAL, and so to expose ourselves to violent attacks from the 'moral majority' upon the Trust's hard-won credibility.'[65]

The incident would damage the Albany Trust, but it would also convince PIE that its future lay outside the mainstream. PIE did, however, remain an important resource for researchers. Wilson and Cox targeted PIE in the late 1970s/early 1980s to study paedophile identities, agreeing with the PIE leadership on the questionnaire to be used.[66]

Gay News, which ultimately merged into the gay magazine *Gay Times* (GT) – a publication that continues in print and via digital delivery[67] – had emerged from the Gay Liberation Front (GLF) and permitted a voice to paedophiles.[68]

PIE is no more. Its one-time leader cannot even join a political party, such is his continued political 'radioactivity'. The group had been driven underground to secret meetings by 1977, and infiltration by journalists had

---

[64] Tom O'Carroll, *Paedophilia: The Radical Case* (Peter Owen 1980), 209.

[65] Antony Grey, *Quest for Justice: Towards Homosexual Emancipation* (Sinclair-Stevenson 1992) 209-210.

[66] An earlier survey design, using a 'Sex Fantasy Questionnaire' was rejected by PIE as they thought it was likely 'to produce results that could easily be misconstrued to the detriment of their members' public image'. See: Glenn D. Wilson and David N. Cox, *The Child-Lovers: A Study of Paedophiles in Society* (Peter Owen), 12.

[67] In 2015, GT stated that it had a print circulation of 65,000 with a readership of 170,000. There were an additional 10,096 digital editions and 626,520 unique users online and 1,165,981 page views https://www.gaytimes.co.uk/wp-content/uploads/2015/08/2015-MEDIAPACK.pdf (last accessed 4 January 2016).

[68] Matthew Waites, The Age of Consent: Young People, Sexuality and Citizenship (Palgrave Macmillan 2005) 131.

led to further public exposure which contributed to the collapse of the group following the O'Carroll trial.[69]

Conflation and Confusion

These historic 'overlaps' between the gay rights and liberation movements and man/boy activist networks inevitably have led to conflation and confusion in queer identities and have gone deep into the established fear discourse surrounding homosexuality; namely that homosexuals – principally gay men – will be coming after your children to 'recruit', to abuse.

The International Lesbian and Gay Association (ILGA) found itself at the heart of a global controversy surrounding the link between homosexuality and paedophilia, triggering what some have described as the 'the demise of gay liberation ideals'.[70]

In June 1993, the group was granted consultative (Roster) status with the United Nations Economic and Social Council (ECOSOC). It emerged that there was some membership of paedophile groups within ILGA and the US government subsequently indicated that they regretted voting for the ILGA's new status at the UN. The ILGA expelled their paedophile groups. This ultimately proved insufficient: following further US government interventions, the UN suspended ILGA's consultative status.[71] In 2011, the status was finally re-granted to ILGA with the United States joining those voting in favour.[72] This is the group that now effectively represents LGBTQ interests at the UN. It has only been able to do so when it has ensured – and convinced governments to this effect – that there are no paedophiles associated with the organisation. The practical effect of this is to create a situation where questioning, let alone re-framing or queering, age of consent laws is almost impossible.

---

[69] Paul Crane, *Gays and the Law* (Pluto Press 1983) 85.

[70] David Paternotte, 'The International (Lesbian and) Gay Association and the Question of Paedophilia: Tracking the Demise of Gay Liberation Ideals' [2014] 17(1-2) *Sexualities* 121-138.

[71] Helmut Graupner, 'Love Verses Abuse' [1999] 37(4) *Journal of Homosexuality* 23-56.

[72] http://ilga.org/ecosoc-lgbt-voices-at-the-united-nations-ecosoc-council-vote-grants-consultative-status-to-ilga/ (last accessed 22 April 2016)

Queer Radicals

Goode has argued that given the conflicting academic analyses of paedophilia, 'it is perhaps less surprising to find such a level of confusion within contemporary mainstream society'. Goode goes on to suggest that this confusion means paedophiles are cast as 'monsters', falling between the positions of sexual radicalism and normativity.[73] At a time of greater dominance by homonormative discourses, it is perhaps unsurprising that these more radical voices on consent should be silenced.

Waites has noted that although the paedophile 'movement' of the early 1980s found apparent support amongst a series of gay male liberationist writers and feminist sex radicals[74], the 'gay movement' moved over the following years to distance itself from these groups[75] as it sought to achieve practical political change. It remains to be seen whether a post-equality legal framework will lead to greater questioning of the boundaries of consent and age, but such a shift necessitates a debate which, as has been outlined in this chapter, is increasingly difficult to engage in.

Yuill and Durber[76] have noted the failure of queer theorists to mount a detailed querying of age boundaries, yet their continued framing of this issue as 'man-boy' sexual relationships crystallises the problem and perhaps the reluctance to query age boundaries.

To define this as a debate in terms of 'man-boy' love is to not only toxify it, with the political controversies outlined elsewhere in this chapter and the preceding Herring chapter, but it also imposes rigid structures of age and agency which serve as a prism through which consent is then constructed. The power of queer lies not only in disrupting traditional social and legal age constructions, but also in the identities that are then (re)constructed. Our contemporary understanding of 'boyhood' and

---

[73] Sarah D. Goode, *Paedophiles in Society: Reflecting on Sexuality, Abuse and Hope* (Basingstoke: Palgrave Macmillan, 2011), 84.

[74] Notably Tsang, Rubin, Sandfort and Weeks. See Matthew Waites, The Age of Consent: Young People, Sexuality and Citizenship (Palgrave Macmillan 2005) 25.

[75] Matthew Waites, The Age of Consent: Young People, Sexuality and Citizenship (Palgrave Macmillan 2005) 25

[76] Richard Yuill and Dean Durber, '"Querying" the Limits of Queering Boys Through the Contested Discourses on Sexuality' [2008] 12 *Sexuality & Culture* 257-274.

'manhood' are arguably abolished by queer, but these categories remain essential for those paedophiles who seek to mobilise and radicalize the age of consent agenda. These goals are incompatible with queer and thus queer has perhaps found an apparent limit to its use here[77].

Moreover, queer thus serves to underline that the agenda of paedophile activists – focusing upon a re-drawing of state power through legal constructions of consent and a shift in that power that sees greater sexual activity between those constructed as 'boys' and those constructed as 'men'.

In the 1970s and 1980s, radical writers and thinkers did undertake a critical engagement with the subject of inter-generational sex, although many of these writers have subsequently sought to clarify or evolve their positions in order to avoid being seen as supporters of paedophilia. The theorist Gayle Rubin wrote that 'we must not reject all sexual contact between adults and young people as inherently oppressive',[78] but she did so as part of a more general essay in which she explored 'the sexual fringe' challenging the law's interventions on sado-masochism, prostitution and anonymous blow jobs in public toilets.

Rubin later added that 'not all adults who do have sex with minors are harming them. All too often, homosexuals have defended themselves against the accusation of child stealing by joining with the general condemnation of all adult-youth sex and by perpetuating the myths about it.'[79]

Pat Califia, another radical writer, described how 'by abandoning boy-lovers to the police and gay kids to their homophobic families, we may hasten the day when adult lesbians and gay men have full civil right, but – will we ever be able to forgive ourselves?'[80]

---

[77] A limit that is not inherent in queer theory, but rather a limit given the intended narrow application of it.

[78] Gayle Rubin, 'The Sexual Fringe' in Daniel Tsang (ed) *The Age Taboo* (Gay Men's Press 1981) 115.

[79] Gayle Rubin, *Deviations: A Gayle Rubin* Reader (Duke University Press 2011) 113. This chapter was first published in 1981 and revised in 1982.

[80] Pat Califia, 'The Lesbian/Gay Movement', in Daniel Tsang (ed) *The Age Taboo* (Gay Men's Press 1981) 136

The day was arguably hastened and there has not yet been an outpouring of regret. Almost two decades later, Califia would announce that he no longer agreed with the NAMBLA political agenda but tempered this with the statement that 'I will still support the right of NAMBLA to march in gay events, publish their material, and debate these issues.'[81]

There has therefore long been recognition of separate identities between the gay rights movement and the man-boy movement. The question was ultimately one of whether there was a 'coalition' or 'alliance' of sex radicals that could be held together or whether the political objectives of gay rights necessitated a 'throwing off' of these other behaviours and identities including sex work and kink identities.

Recent years have seen the emergence of the homonormative law, and with this, there has been increased discussion about a 'post-Equality' landscape that recognises the new emergent non-binary discourse and diffuse activism supported by social media and technology.[82] This holds the potential to (re)evolve our constructions of consent and to deploy a resistance-based queer analysis that seeks to move beyond the traditional boundaries that have defined debates about the age of consent.

Conclusion

Kincaid has suggested that the Victorian approach to sexuality – arguably also reflected in their legislative approach – was one of silence. He noted that as late as 1921, Lord Desart, the then Director of Public Prosecutions, and Lord Birkenhead, the then Lord Chancellor, suggesting that if the word lesbian is not used, the activity shall not exist. This Victorian approach has arguably served to frame contemporary attitudes to sexuality.[83] When it comes to debates about the age of consent, the silencing of more radical voices arguably serves the same purpose. If we're not debating the behaviours, the behaviours are not happening.

---

[81] Pat Califia, *Public Sex: The Culture of Radical* Sex (Cleis Press 2000) 87.

[82] See Kelly Kollman and Matthew Waites, "United Kingdom: Changing political Opportunity Structures, Policy Success and Continuing Challenges for Lesbian, Gay and Bisexual Movements," in *The Lesbian and Gay Movement and the State: Comparative Insights into a Transformed Relationship*, eds. Manon Tremblay, David Paternotte, and Carol Johnson (Farnham: Ashgate, 2011) 181-195.

[83] James R. Kincaid, *Child Loving: The Erotic Child and Victorian Culture* (Routledge 1992) 36.

Whilst recent years have arguably seen greater prominence with regard to sex radicals and queer thinkers, and attempts to give voice to the silences about sexual behaviour, the age of consent remains a curious 'no go zone', a debate that is too controversial, too toxic for scholarly and political debate.

The paedophile that emerged in social and legal narratives in the late twentieth century[84] is one that appeared to increasingly sit ill at ease within the gay rights campaign organisation that had once included them. Paternotte has suggested[85] that this reflects a growing isolation for this discourse in groups such as the International Lesbian and Gay Association. The current social, legal and political landscape makes it hard to believe that we will again see a return of groups such as PIE or NAMBLA marching in high-profile Pride events as they once did. Queer theory does, however, hold the potential to move the debate on, to reformulate who is consenting and what they are consenting to. The debates about the age of consent are far from over.

---

[84] Steven Angelides, 'The Emergence of the Pedophile in the Late Twentieth Century' [2005] 36(126) *Australian Historical Studies* 272-295.
[85] David Paternotte, 'The International (Lesbian and) Gay Association and the Question of Pedophilia: Tracking the Demise of Gay Liberation Ideals' [2014] 17(1-2) *Sexualities* 121-138.

CHAPTER SEVEN

QUEERING FEARS:
PRO-LGBTI REFUGEE CASES

SENTHORUN RAJ

Introduction

Over the last three decades, an increasing number of jurisdictions have recognised asylum claims on the basis of sexual orientation and gender identity. Such 'pro-LGBTI cases'[1] have been heralded for 'progressing' queer rights by recognising the failure of states to protect individuals against homophobic and transphobic violence. Yet, the progressive promises of these cases have been limited. Typically considered under the rubric of a 'particular social group', the extent to which queer refugees have been granted protection has been contingent on whether they subscribe to (hetero)normative ideas of intimacy, identity, and injury. LGBTI[2] refugees must demonstrate that they have a 'well-founded fear of persecution' owing to their membership of a particular social group by

---

[1] While I use the term 'pro-LGBTI' to reflect the broader legal movements in which these cases have been situated and/or celebrated, it is important to note the lack of bisexual, transgender, and intersex discussion in the leading appellate jurisprudence.

[2] The term 'LGBTI' is an acronym to encompass lesbian, gay, bisexual, transgender, and intersex people. The acronym is contested and many queers who are grouped under this category do not identify with the label. I use the term here as a loose identity category to reflect the language adopted by international bodies such as the United Nations, but contest its normative implications throughout the paper. See Human Rights Council, 17th Session, Agenda Item 8, Human Rights, sexual orientation and gender identity, 15 June 2011, UN Doc. A/HRC/17/L.9/Rev.1
<http://ap.ohchr.org/documents/dpage_e.aspx?si=A/HRC/17/L.9/Rev.1> accessed 15 September 2012.

adhering to ethnocentric assumptions about popular culture consumption, public visibility, gender expressions, sexual practices, and social marginalisation. While the concept of fear has also been central to the granting of asylum under international law, it has also been mobilised in legal, political, and academic responses to the adjudication of it.

In this chapter, I query how fear acts in 'progressive' LGBTI refugee cases as a gesture to foreshadow danger or injury to the integrity of the refugee adjudication system. In discussing the affectivity of fear, Sara Ahmed argues that fear does not reside internally within a particular body.[3] Reading emotion as a gesture, then, I consider how fear is mobilised through both temporal and spatial enactments: it orients jurisprudence to the future (through the anticipation of injury) and locates threats (through the identification of risky places). Fear is sustained through a number of gestures that gather queer objects or bodies in order to reveal proximity to an overwhelming threat. Fear is not just confined to proximity to physical violence, but it also reveals our proximity to that which threatens the normative integrity of the refugee adjudication system itself.

Part I briefly outlines the disparate ways in which homophobic and transphobic violence have created a climate of fear for many LGBTI people.

Part II then maps out the ways that contemporary critical legal scholarship has responded to the limits of refugee law in granting protection to queer refugees. Specifically, I consider the way that much legal analysis has anchored around the need to both (de)construct and then represent queer intimacy, identity, and injury. However, I argue that the discursive emphasis on intimacy, identity, and injury within much of this scholarly literature has sidelined the gestures of fear that underpin the experience of both forced displacement and asylum adjudication.

Part III then offers a distinctive intervention into this existing legal scholarship. Using an emotional register, I track the so-called 'well-founded fear' in the Australian case *S395/2002 and S396/2002 v Minister*

---

[3] Sara Ahmed, *The Cultural Politics of Emotion* (Edinburgh 2004) 62-63; Sara Ahmed, 'Collective Feelings: Or, the Impressions Left by Others' (2004) 21(2) Theory, Culture & Society 25, 125.

for Immigration and Multicultural Affairs[4] and subsequent UK case *HJ &
HT v Secretary of State for the Home Department*[5] to examine how
demands for sexual discretion are both repudiated and reincarnated.

Part IV builds on legal scholarship that has mapped a shift in recognition:
from demanding discretion to a culture of disbelief about a claimant's
sexuality. By distinguishing an Australian and a UK judicial decision –
SZMDS v Minister for Immigration and Citizenship[6] and *SW v Secretary of
State for the Home Department*[7] – I introduce the concept of an 'anxious
adjudication' to capture the way a fear over allowing bogus asylum claims
results in an anxious scrutiny of (homo)sexuality.

Part V concludes the discussion by looking at two recent European Court
of Justice cases – *Cases X, Y, and Z* (2013) and *Cases A, B, and C* (2014)
– that have been celebrated for limiting assumptions about discretion and
the kinds of questions or evidence that can be used in asylum adjudication.
Despite the expanded recognition, these cases limit queerness: finding
visible acts of persecution (even when acknowledging it takes numerous
forms) and entrenching the legitimacy of scrutinising sexual identity (even
when circumscribing intrusive questions).

In bringing these cases together, I argue that fears manifest as gestures of
cover and containment – one that confines, constrains, or inhibits queer
subjects. Attending to these gestures is critical for courts navigating the
way fear circumscribes the scope of asylum when refugees make claims
for protection.

---

[4] *Appellant S395/2002 v Minister for Immigration and Multicultural Affairs,
Appellant S396/2002 v Minister for Immigration and Multicultural Affairs* [2003]
HCA 71 9 December 2003.
[5] *HJ (Iran) and HT (Cameroon) v Secretary of State for the Home Department*
[2010] UKSC 31.
[6] *Minister for Immigration and Citizenship v SZMDS & ANOR* [2010] 226 ALR
367.
[7] *SW (lesbians – HJ and HT applied) Jamaica v Secretary of State for the Home
Department, CG* [2011] UKUT 00251(IAC), United Kingdom: Upper Tribunal
(Immigration and Asylum Chamber), 24 June 2011, available at
<http://www.refworld.org/docid/4e0c3fae2.html> accessed 8 January 2016.

Part I – Contextualising LGBTI Asylum Jurisprudence

Under international law, refugees are entitled to seek asylum if they have a well-founded fear of persecution owing to race, nationality, religion, political opinion or membership of a particular social group.[8] Refugees must be outside their country of origin and unwilling or unable to seek protection from their country of residence. The Refugee Convention orients the legal analysis of a 'well-founded fear' by looking to the future: to assess whether there is a risk of persecution if a refugee is returned to their country of residence (irrespective of whether they have been persecuted in the past).[9] Persecution typically refers to sustained forms of serious discrimination or physical violence that are either directly perpetrated by the state or are condoned by it.[10]

Lesbian, gay, bisexual, transgender, and intersex people are subject to discrimination, violence, and harassment in all parts of the world. Whether in the developing or developed world, homophobia and transphobia remain pernicious and pervasive problems. In a legislative context, 76 countries criminalise consensual same-sex sexual activity and seven countries have capital punishment for such 'offences'.[11] Each year, many thousands of LGBTI asylum applications are made both to the United Nations High Commissioner for Refugees (UNHCR) and individual states.[12]

---

[8] Article 1A(2), *Convention Relating to the Status of Refugees 1951* (28 July 1951) available at <http://www2.ohchr.org/english/law/refugees.htm> accessed 6 August 2012.

[9] *Chan Yee Kin v Minister for Immigration and Ethnic Affairs* (1989) 169 CLR 379.

[10] Quoted in Kristen Walker, 'Sexuality and Refugee Status in Australia' (2000) 12(2) International Journal of Refugee Law 175, 177.

[11] ILGA, 'State Sponsored Homophobia – A world survey of laws: Criminalisation, protection and recognition of same-sex love' (May 2015) available at <http://old.ilga.org/Statehomophobia/ILGA_State_Sponsored_Homophobia_2015.pdf> accessed 15 June 2015.

[12] See Organization Refugee Asylum and Migration (ORAM), 'Opening Doors: A Survey of NGO Attitudes Towards LGBTI Refugees and Asylum Seekers' (June 2012) <http://www.oraminternational.org/images/stories/PDFs/oram-opening-doors.pdf> accessed 7 June 2013.

Statutory and procedural differences exist in the application of international refugee law in domestic contexts dealing with LGBTI asylum claims. Canada was the first Anglophone jurisdiction to extend protection to gay asylum seekers.[13] In Australia, protection is available to sexual minorities where a (homosexual) person 'belongs to or is identified with a recognisable or cognisable group within a society that shares some interest or experience in common'.[14] In the US, *Matter of Toboso-Alfonso* (1990) established the precedent that sexual orientation could constitute a valid social group.[15] The UK had a somewhat delayed response compared to Canada, US, and Australia when it came to recognising LGBTI claims.[16] In 2004, the European Union issued a Qualification Directive that extended protection specifically on the basis of sexual orientation.[17] Irrespective of these technical variations, administrative bodies continue to evaluate queer intimacy, identity, and injury by making (hetero)normative claims about what counts as 'proper' sexual expression or 'legitimate' sexual identities in order to authenticate queer asylum seekers from different cultural contexts.[18]

---

[13] See Nicole La Violette, 'Independent Human Rights Documentation and Sexual Minorities: An Ongoing Challenge for the Canadian Refugee Process' (2009) 13(2-3) The International Journal of Human Rights 437 and *Ward v Attorney-General (Canada)* (1993) 2 SCR 689, 739 (La Forest J).

[14] *Morato v Minister for Immigration, Local Government and Ethnic Affairs* (1992) 39 FCR 401, 404 (Toohey J).

[15] *Matter of Toboso-Alfonso* (1990) 20 I & N. Dec. 819 (BIA 1990). Transgender claims were recognised through an extension of sexual orientation in *Hernandez-Montiel v Immigration and Naturalization Service* (2000) 225 F.3d 10484.

[16] *Islam (A.P) v Secretary of State for the Home Department of Regina v Immigration Appeal Tribunal and Another Ex Parte Shah* (1999) 2 All ER 545, 452 (Steyn LJ).

[17] Sabine Jansen and Thomas Spijkerboer, 'Fleeing Homophobia' (September 2011) available at <https://www.rechten.vu.nl/en/Images/Fleeing%20Homophobia%20report%20EN _tcm23-232205.pdf>, 13 accessed 23rd May 2015.

[18] The Refugee Review Tribunal is an administrative body that reviews applications for refugee status in Australia. Similar bodies exist in the US (Bureau of Immigration Appeals) and the UK (Immigration and Asylum Tribunal).

Part II – Queering Asylum Scholarship

A: Intimacy, Identity, Injury, and Emotion

Recognition of decision-making limitations has precipitated ongoing scholarly debates that have focused on how to better address questions of intimacy, identity, and injury. It is beyond the scope of this chapter to detail them at any great length. Jenni Millbank's work, however, is worth noting, as she has been a leading voice in this field by interrogating the conceptual challenges that manifest from administrative decision-making through to judicial review.[19] Millbank has mapped out two key problems facing queer refugees when seeking protection: the notion of a 'well-founded fear of persecution' is highly gendered,[20] and subscribing to stereotypes remains a key basis on which (homo)sexuality is authenticated for the purposes of being considered part of a 'particular social group'.[21] Critical legal attempts to engage (and remedy) these conceptual problems

---

[19] See generally Jenni Millbank, 'Fear of Persecution or a Just a Queer Feeling?: Refugee Status and Sexual Orientation in Australia' (1995) 20(6) Alternative Law Journal 261; Jenni Millbank, 'Imagining Otherness: Refugee Claims on the Basis of Sexuality in Canada and Australia', (2002) 26(7) Melbourne University Law Review 144; Jenni Millbank, 'Gender, Sex and Visibility in Refugee Claims on the Basis of Sexual Orientation' (2003) 18 Georgetown Immigration Law Journal 71; Jenni Millbank, 'A Preoccupation with Perversion: The British Response to Sexual Orientation Refugee Claims, 1989-2003' (2005) 14(1) Social & Legal Studies 115; Jenni Millbank, 'The Ring of Truth: A Case Study of Credibility Assessment in Particular Social Group Refugee Determinations' (2009) 21(1) International Journal of Refugee Law 1; Jenni Millbank, 'From Discretion to Disbelief: Recent Trends in Refugee Determinations on the Basis of Sexual Orientation in Australia and the United Kingdom' (2009) 13(2-3) The International Journal of Human Rights 391; Jenni Millbank, 'The Right of Lesbians and Gay Men to Live Freely, Openly, and on Equal Terms is not Bad Law: A Reply to Hathaway and Pobjoy' (2012) 44 New York University Journal of International Law and Politics 497; Jenni Millbank, 'Sexual Orientation and Refugee Status Determination Over the Past 20 Years: Unsteady Progress Through Standard Sequences?' in Thomas Spijkerboer (ed) *Fleeing Homophobia: Sexual Orientation, Gender Identity and Asylum* (Routledge 2013).

[20] Millbank, 'Imagining Otherness', (n19) 172-174; Millbank, 'Gender, Sex and Visibility in Refugee Claims on the Basis of Sexual Orientation' (n19) 73-77; and Millbank, 'The Right of Lesbians and Gay Men to Live Freely, Openly, and on Equal Terms is not Bad Law' (n19) 516.

[21] Millbank, 'The Ring of Truth' (n19) 7-20; Millbank, 'From Discretion to Disbelief' (n19) 392-403.

in refugee law have brought to the fore the problem at the heart of positivist legal adjudication: representational fluidity often comes at the expense of certainty and closure.

Emotion and visibility within the bureaucratic context (both the decision-maker's and the refugee's) operate as a 'double bind' to erase queer refugee identity and injury. When it comes to visibility, those who do not experience discrete acts of violence are seen to lack a well-founded fear of persecution, while those who 'attract' homophobic violence in public are considered transgressive and should be discreet. When it comes to emotion, asylum seekers who are apathetic and fail to conform to sexual expectations are denied identity recognition, while those who perform sexual stereotypes too well are considered disingenuous and insincere. Hesitancy in oral testimony, for example, often undermines the credibility of the narrative, while a more apathetic recounting of experience is disbelieved for an alleged lack of emotional response.[22] Either refugees fail to provide a coherent and plausible narrative because of shame or trauma, or they respond in an unemotional manner, which makes the account of sexual persecution unbelievable.[23]

B: Making Queer Law

In bringing the recognition challenges to the fore, I want to consider a recent provocative critique of pro-LGBTI cases in this area: have pro-LGBTI asylum cases overreached insofar as they have altered the normative bases of refugee law?[24] In 'Queer Cases Make Bad Law', Hathaway and Pobjoy castigate pro-LGBTI appellate (*HJ & HT* discussed below in Part III) jurisprudence for failing to distinguish between 'exogenous' and 'endogenous' forms of sexuality expression and

---

[22] ibid.

[23] Louis Middelkoop, 'Normativity and Credibility of Sexual Orientation in Asylum Decision Making' in Thomas Spijkerboer (ed) *Fleeing Homophobia: Sexual Orientation, Gender Identity and Asylum* (Routledge 2013), 168; Eithne Lubheid, 'Afterword: Troubling identities and identifications' (2014) 17(8) Sexualities 1035, 1038; Toni Johnson, 'On Silence, Sexuality and Skeletons: Reconceptualizing Narrative in Asylum Hearings' (2011) 20(1) Social & Legal Studies 57, 58.

[24] James Hathaway and Jason Pobjoy 'Queer Cases Make Bad Law' (2012) 44 New York University Journal of International Law and Politics 315, 330-332.

behaviour in order to determine what counts as persecution.[25] Hathaway and Pobjoy are not unsympathetic to queer asylum claims. Yet, they suggest that by uncritically lauding this jurisprudence, we have abdicated an 'intellectual responsibility' to adjudicate claims within the ambit of asylum law.[26]

Much critical commentary has been generated in response to Hathaway and Pobjoy's argument.[27] I will pick this up in the following parts. For now, I want to probe the affective underpinnings of Hathaway and Pobjoy's critique. The idea of entrenching 'bad law' runs as an anxiety throughout their essay. In particular, asylum precedents that give greater accommodation to queer social expressions should be feared because they injure 'principled adjudication'.[28] By reading (homo)sexual identity in terms of an exogenous/endogenous binary, they attempt to attend to these fears by reasserting the normative bases of international refugee law that suggest definitions of persecution must be restrictive.

Writing more broadly about the evolution of refugee adjudication, Didier Faissin notes that the 'refugee question' has been tightly circumscribed by normative ideas of 'truth' (whether an asylum claim fits within the legal framework) and 'true' (the veracity of asylum experiences).[29] What was once an issue of 'humanitarian compassion' has now become a matter of 'anxious control'.[30] By tracing a broad historical shift, Faissin also reveals a shift in affective registers: seeking asylum is not a right born from the recognition that everyone is entitled to seek asylum but a matter of state discretion (or a 'gift') conferred once claims have been thoroughly scrutinised.[31] Faissin's argument gestures to the politics of anxiety that underpins adjudicating asylum claims: experiences must be interrogated to

---

[25] ibid 336.

[26] ibid 387.

[27] See Millbank, 'The Right of Lesbians and Gay Men to Live Freely, Openly, and on Equal Terms is not Bad Law' (n19); Ryan Goodman, 'Asylum and the Concealment of Sexual Orientation: Where not to Draw the Line' (2012) 44 New York University Journal of International Law and Politics 407.

[28] Hathaway and Pobjoy 'Queer Cases Make Bad Law' (n 24) 387.

[29] Didier Faissin, 'The Precarious Truth of Asylum' (2013) 25(1) Public Culture 39, 41.

[30] ibid 46-47; Ahmed (n 3) 79.

[31] ibid 55.

avoid 'bogus' claims succeeding. The hypermobility of bogus refugees is met with a need to contain them.[32]

Reading Faissin alongside Hathaway and Pobjoy reveals that anxiety about refugees' sincerity subtends both legal and scholarly interventions. Claims that are too queer, rather than being accommodated, become sites of anxious disavowal. Refugee adjudication becomes a site of vulnerability: vulnerable to disingenuous claims. Such vulnerability necessitates securing borders. [33] In adjudicating asylum claims, such normative legal or policy borders are reproduced through gestures that encourage decision-makers to thoroughly interrogate rather than merely evaluate or trust. This process generates a specific form of intimacy: decision-makers must attend to narrative closely in order to authenticate the sincerity (or otherwise) of a particular claim and the extent to which it falls into line with the circumscribed bases of existing refugee law.

C: Queer Interventions

Queer theory offers a way to respond to the normative investments in existing legal critique. Queer, broadly defined, is a theoretical term that refers to practices, pleasures, attachments, and identities that do not conform to normative ideas of heterosexuality, reproduction, and family.[34] While queer theory is closely aligned to deconstructing and challenging the marginalisation of homosexuality as an identity, it is more broadly used as an analytic gesture that points towards anti-normative movement. It exposes how objects, bodies, and identities that veer away from the norm are queer. To 'queer' is to 'twerk' or 'turn'.[35] Queerness, as it relates to subjectivity, is not ultimately confined to a discrete sexual identity or identification, but rather reveals our disparate sexual and cultural

---

[32] Ahmed makes a similar point in relation to terrorist bodies, Ahmed (n3) 73.

[33] ibid 70.

[34] David Bell and Jon Binnie, *The Sexual Citizen: Queer Politics and Beyond* (Wiley 2000) 13-15.

[35] Sara Ahmed, *Willful Subjects* (Duke University Press 2014) 8.

difference(s). [36] Queer is not a positive prescription but acts as a 'positionality'. [37]

Queer theory, then, cannot be confined to any single academic methodology. Queer theory takes up these positions to help us then 'move' beyond a liberal rhetoric of equality and inclusion. [38] That is, a queer political and academic project works by challenging that which is posited as the 'norm'. This chapter is an incitement for greater queer movement. There are enormously disparate theoretical departure points in queer theory, but this chapter takes up the theoretical emphasis on movement and orientation in purportedly progressive cases to 'queer' the way fear (as a gesture) and persecution (as a wound or harm) have been understood as subjects/objects to be remedied in the law.

The following sections queer fear.

Part III – Dismantling Discretion

As the aforementioned refugee scholarship attests, fear not only shrinks the space that people subject to systemic homophobic persecution can occupy, it also works to contain the horizons for understanding intimacy, identity, and injury that arise as a consequence of that persecution. Demands to cover, for instance, have limited the space of queer asylum claims. Refugees, who demonstrated that they were either 'voluntarily' discreet about their sexuality or could reasonably be expected to be less visible about their sexual identity, have had their claims rejected. In the Australian case *Gui*, for example, a Chinese man had his protection claim refused because his experience of injury – abuse from police after kissing his partner in public – was due to his 'conduct in public space' rather than

---

[36] Francisco Valdes, 'Queering Sexual Orientation: A Call for Theory as Praxis' in Martha Albertson Fineman, Jack E. Jackson and Adam P Romero (eds), *Feminist and Queer Legal Theory: Intimate Encounters, Uncomfortable Conversations* (2009) 107.

[37] Adam P Romero, 'Methodological Descriptions: "Feminist" and "Queer" Legal Theories' in Martha Albertson Fineman, Jack E Jackson and Adam P Romero (eds), *Feminist and Queer Legal Theory: Intimate Encounters, Uncomfortable Conversations* (Ashgate 2009) 192.

[38] Lisa Duggan, 'Queering the State' (1994) 39 Social Text 1, 5.

his sexual identity.[39] By distinguishing identity from conduct, the Court implied that homosexual expression could appropriately be regulated by criminal law. Yet, in doing so, the Court ignored the injurious impact such regulations have on the expression of queer identity and intimacy more generally.

This approach, colloquially described as the 'discretion test', formed the basis of an Australian High Court challenge in 2003. In *S395/2002 v MIMIA* (2003), a Bangladeshi same-sex couple, MD Jahangir Kabir (aged 28) and Syed Fazlur Rahman (aged 47), who had lived together for four years in Bangladesh sought asylum in Australia. Prior to coming to Australia, the couple claimed they had experienced a range of violent and harassing treatment: family ostracism, a fatwah, and physical and verbal assaults from local people.[40] Initially, their claims for protection were refused on the basis that the familial rejection they experienced did not amount to persecution and that they would not be at risk of persecution if returned because they would not be 'out' as a couple if sent back to Bangladesh.[41] Specifically, the RRT concluded that the couple had made a 'lifestyle choice' to live in a 'discreet manner'.[42] The Federal Court further endorsed the RRT's reasoning, stating that 'it is only if a homosexual couple force Bangladeshi society to confront their homosexual identity that they will encounter problems'.[43] Lindgren J's reference to 'force' in relation to homosexual identity implied that visibility marked the risks of persecution.

In responding to the earlier decisions, the majority of the High Court overruled the administrative use of discretion (the idea of managing sexual visibility to avoid persecution) in refugee decisions relating to sexual minorities. Firstly, the Court invalidated the tiered approach to recognising 'homosexuality' as a particular social group. That is, the distinction between 'open' and 'discreet' homosexuals for the purposes of the particular social group was erroneous.[44] Secondly, the court noted that the

---

[39] *Minister for Immigration and Multicultural Affairs v Guo Ping Gui* [1999] FCA 1496 at [28] (Heery Carr & Tamberlin J).

[40] *Kabir v Minister for Immigration & Multicultural Affairs* [2001] FCA 968, [9] (Lindgren J).

[41] ibid [12] (Lindgren J).

[42] ibid [14] (Lindgren J).

[43] ibid [17] (Lindgren J).

[44] *S395/2002 v MIMIA* (2003) 216 CLR 473, [40]-[44] (McHugh and Kirby JJ).

RRT had erred by failing to consider the future-focused question of persecution if the applicants were discovered to be gay.[45] Thirdly, it putatively suggested that the requirement to act discreetly to avoid the threat of serious harm amounted to persecution.[46] Taken together, the Court held that the previously unqualified administrative claim that asylum seekers should cooperate in their own protection by concealing their sexuality was misdirected and constituted an error of law.

Much of the jurisprudence in this case suggested that primary decision-makers should give careful consideration as to why a gay or lesbian refugee would be discreet (such as recognising the cultural context that necessitates sexual invisibility) and what would occur if the applicant was discovered to be non-heterosexual in their country of origin. For McHugh and Kirby JJ, the concern was fear:

> In such cases, the well-founded fear of persecution held by the applicant is the fear that, unless that person acts to avoid harmful conduct, he or she will suffer harm. It is the threat of serious harm with its menacing implications that constitutes the persecutory conduct.[47]

Here, the justices brought threat of injury and discretion into close proximity. By managing the public manifestations of their homosexual intimacy, the couple could avoid the harmful conduct. Yet, the compulsion to remain discreet – given the foreseeability of 'serious harm with its menacing implications' – was an act of persecution itself. In orienting their remarks around the RRT's misdirection on the issue of discretion, McHugh and Kirby JJ revealed their fears for the future safety of the couple with respect to the risk of physical abuse, employment discrimination, community expulsion, or police extortion.[48] They warned that where fear had resulted in people remaining discreet about their sexual orientation to avoid such risks, then decision-makers must probe whether such fears were well founded.[49]

Gummow and Hayne JJ expressed concern about the way discretion logic limited sexual identity:

---

[45] ibid [40]-[44] (McHugh and Kirby JJ).
[46] ibid [40]-[44] (McHugh and Kirby JJ).
[47] ibid [43] (McHugh and Kirby JJ).
[48] ibid [51] (McHugh and Kirby JJ).
[49] ibid [51] (McHugh and Kirby JJ).

Moreover, the use of such language will often reveal that consideration of the consequences of sexual identity has wrongly been confined to participation in sexual acts rather than that range of behaviour and activities of life which may be informed or affected by sexual identity.[50]

This analysis resisted conflating sexual identity with sexual acts. Moreover, the judges appeared to recognise that the logic of discretion overemphasised the sexual activities that a person may be 'discreet' about, while sidelining the ways homosexuality can be rendered visible (such as through physical comportment or bodily aesthetics) through non-sexual behaviours. By castigating discretion as a covering device – one that obscured the reasons why (homo)sexual visibility may be limited in the first place – Gummow and Hayne JJ opened up the adjudicative space for recognising how discretion can act as a marker of homophobic persecution.[51] Fear cannot be used to demand that sexual minorities cover who they are in order to avoid persecution.

S395/2002 has been heralded as a progressive moment in refugee decision-making because it marked the first time a supreme judicial body recognised that expecting sexual minorities to be discreet amounted to an unlawful limit on their claims for protection. By refusing a distinction between state violence encountered as a result of consensual private sexual acts and public manifestations of sexual identity, the case opened up the legal space for sexual minorities claiming asylum. Engaging with fear – in particular, the proximity of asylum seekers to state violence back in their country of origin – helped to broaden the definition of sexuality persecution. McHugh and Kirby JJ noted that living in a state of concealment regarding one's homosexuality could potentially be 'so oppressive' that it amounted to persecution.[52] Decision-makers were exhorted to focus on the *threat* of serious harm to determine if the conduct is persecutory.

The demand for discretion is not always expressed with such negativity. Privacy, for example, has been invoked alongside the logic of discretion as a way to contain queer asylum claims. Unlike Australia, the UK used the language of 'private life' rather than the concept of identity to recognise sexual minority refugee claims. In *Jain* (1999), the English Court of

---

[50] ibid [82] (Gummow and Hayne JJ).

[51] ibid [88] (Gummow and Hayne JJ).

[52] ibid [53] (McHugh and Kirby JJ).

Appeal held that the Refugee Convention provided protection to individuals (including, in this case a gay man from India) who were persecuted for 'private legitimate behaviour'.[53] However, the association between private life and discretion was sustained to refuse claims where an applicant claimed they could not be 'open' about their (homo)sexual identity. Millbank has referred to this adjudication trend in the UK as a 'preoccupation with perversion' where silence and containment were seen as preferable 'solutions' to the 'perversion' of homosexuality rather than recognising that the criminalisation of homosexuality was perverse.[54] In *XY*, the English Court of Appeal explicitly distinguished *S395/2002* and held that discretion necessarily prevented persecution. Specifically, homosexuals living discreetly would not attract 'adverse action' and could live without detriment to privacy.[55] Even if individuals wanted to live more openly, such a desire did not reach the level of 'seriousness' required to engender protection obligations.[56] Only activities confined to the bedroom should be free of criminal sanction – public expressions may be appropriately regulated.

The preoccupation with privacy and perversion subsisted in English law until the widely celebrated UK case of *HJ (Iran) and HT (Cameroon) v Secretary of State for the Home Department*. The case joined together two distinct asylum seekers – a gay Iranian man and a gay Cameroonian man – who at different times sought asylum within the UK. HJ was a 38-year-old man from Iran who had arrived in the UK in 2001 and claimed asylum due to a fear that if he returned, he would be persecuted for his homosexuality (including from his previous 'discreet' relationships with men during his military service).[57] HT was 35-year-old man from Cameroon who arrived in the UK in 2007 and claimed asylum, fearing his return back home would result in violence. He claimed, in one instance, a mob witnessed him kissing his partner in public and then assaulted him in an attempt to castrate him.[58] In both cases, protection was not granted as both

---

[53] *Sahm Sunder Jain v Secretary of State for the Home Department* (1999) WL 1071267.

[54] Millbank, 'A Preoccupation with Perversion' (n20) 128.

[55] *XY (Iran) v Secretary of State for the Home Department* (2008) EWCA Civ 911.

[56] ibid.

[57] *J v Secretary of State for the Home Department* (2006) EWCA Civ 1238, [2] (Maurice Kay LJ).

[58] *HT (Cameroon) v Secretary of State for the Home Department* (2008) EWCA Civ 1288, [3] (Rix LJ).

individuals lived discreet lives that (without any supervening public conduct) did not attract persecutory attention.

In hearing the claims together, the UK Supreme Court had to consider whether the expectation to live discreetly (or the decision to do so) amounted to an intolerable burden on fundamental human rights. Lord Hope opened the judgment by recognising the demeaning dimension of denying one's sexuality:

> To pretend that it does not exist, or that the behaviour by which it manifests itself can be suppressed, is to deny the members of this group their fundamental right to be who they are.[59]

Echoing *S395/2002*, Hope LJ brought to the fore the relationship between expression and identity. Rather than confine sexuality to 'private life', his judgment broadened the scope of identity to cover public associations. Concealment was positioned as antithetical to protection: recognising a sexual characteristic in order to keep it hidden from view was problematic.

Lord Rodger took up the analysis of intimate associations to consider how sexuality was more fluid than immutable. Specifically, he claimed that a gay asylum seeker from Iran did not need to demonstrate that:

> His homosexuality plays a particularly prominent part of his life. All that matters is that he has a well-founded fear that he will be persecuted because of that particular characteristic which he either cannot change or cannot be required to change.[60]

Rodger LJ reiterated that sexuality need not be individual, prominent or immutable in a biological sense. As Ryan Goodman suggests, by eschewing the language of whether an expression is 'fundamental' or not, the Court did not have to make subjective assessments about the 'inherent' value of particular sexual expressions and how essential they were to a particular emotional life.[61] While scholars like Hathaway and Pobjoy have questioned the legal correctness of such a holding, others like John Tobin and Millbank have welcomed the shift away from quarantining

---

[59] *HJ (Iran) and HT (Cameroon) v Secretary of State for the Home Department* (2010) UKSC 31, [11] (Hope LJ).
[60] ibid [61] (Rodger LJ).
[61] Goodman, 'Asylum and the Concealment of Sexual Orientation' (n22) 438.

homosexuality in the bedroom.[62] Given that what is 'fundamental' to refugee status is a person's right to express their sexual orientation, a person ought not to be required to forsake it or be discreet about it (in a general sense) to avoid persecution. Hathaway and Pobjoy condemn Rodger LJ's broad claim here as legally spurious because it failed to draw a distinction between 'endogenous' expressions and those that are 'exogenous'.[63] Such an 'over inclusive' reading of state persecution, Hathaway and Pobjoy claim, enables self-expression (such as drinking cocktails or gossiping about men) to be protected, regardless of how significant those expressions are to a person's sexual orientation.[64]

Yet, such an argument fails to appreciate what is at stake in limiting expression: dignity. In the judgment, the particularity of persecution is evinced through the applicant's fear. In rejecting the 'choice' assumption that underpins discretion logic, Rodger LJ recognised that unless HJ or HT were 'minded to swell the ranks of gay martyrs', the threats of violence vitiated their choices and compelled them to act discreetly.[65] Drawing upon McHugh and Kirby JJ's earlier judgment, Rodger LJ probed why HJ and HT were discreet in the first place.[66] In doing so, he concluded that the reason for the applicants' discretion was fear of persecution – not a matter of personal taste.

Freedom from fear became key for enabling full expression of, or lived experience of, sexual orientation. Rather than confine sexual identity to sexual activity, Rodger LJ recognised the need to locate sexuality in the context of non-sexual yet intimate associations:

> To illustrate the point with trivial stereotypical examples from British society: just as male heterosexuals are free to enjoy themselves playing rugby, drinking beer and talking about girls with their mates, so male homosexuals are free to enjoy themselves going to Kylie concerts, drinking exotically coloured cocktails and talking about boys with their straight

---

[62] John Tobin, 'Assessing GLBTI Refugee Claims: Using Human Rights to Shift the Narrative of Persecution Within Refugee Law' (2012) 44 New York University Journal of International Law and *Politics* 448, 468-472; Millbank, 'The Right of Lesbians and Gay Men to Live Freely, Openly, and on Equal Terms is not Bad Law' (n19) 516.

[63] Hathaway and Pobjoy 'Queer Cases Make Bad Law' (n24) 330-332.

[64] ibid 374-375.

[65] *HJ (Iran) and HT (Cameroon)* (n59) [78] (Rodger LJ).

[66] ibid [67] (Rodger LJ).

female mates. (…) In other words, gay men are to be as free as their
straight equivalents in the society concerned to live their lives in the way
that is natural to them as gay men, without the fear of persecution.[67]

Rodger LJ's listing of social activities here relied on, as he noted himself,
stereotypes about gay lifestyles. Despite the problematic nature of these
stereotypes, they are used in a way to broadly recognise the social
elements of gay life that exist in addition to its sexual manifestations. By
giving room to the former, Rodger LJ broadened the reach of asylum
protection for sexual minorities. It was not sufficient to say that privacy
affords gay men or lesbian women the ability to live together or engage in
sexual intercourse in the bedroom. Instead, dignity required that sexual
minorities be able to disclose their attraction, engage in conversation about
their personal lives, participate in events, and even consume pop culture.
The capacity for heterosexuals to engage in such activities became the
freedom benchmark against which (homo)sexual freedom was to be
measured. Deviations from the judicial benchmark – such as those that
require greater discretion of homosexuals as opposed to heterosexuals –
violated core human rights.

Fear of persecution, however, was distinguished from other emotional
pressures. In fact, Rodger LJ noted that people might choose to be discreet
for reasons not related to their fear of persecution:

> For example, he might not wish to upset his parents or his straight friends
> (…) he might worry that, if the fact that he was gay were known, he would
> become isolated from his friends and relatives, be the butt of jokes (…) or
> suffer other discrimination.[68]

Shame, upset, and worry are emotions that were distinguished from the
fear of persecution. Yet, by distinguishing such feelings from persecution,
Rodger LJ ignored the ways in which queers experience such isolation
quite distinctly from their heterosexual counterparts. Humiliation and
isolation can have debilitating impacts on physical and mental health.[69]
For the purpose of determining an asylum claim, fear must be isolated
from other emotions when determining the nature of sexual discretion, but,

---

[67] ibid [59] (Rodger LJ).

[68] ibid [61] (Rodger LJ).

[69] See generally Sharalyn Jordan, 'Un/Convention(al) Refugees: Contextualizing
the Accounts of Refugees Facing Homophobia or Transphobic Persecution' (2011)
26 Refuge 165.

by cleaving apart pressure from persecution, Rodger LJ constrained the recognition of fear.[70] Some queer refugee narratives are explicitly contained as both unexceptional and non-persecutory.

By emphasising that the Refugee Convention does not protect against 'social pressures', Roger LJ's judgment positioned some homophobic injuries outside the reach of protection obligations.[71] Jana Wessels argues that the judgment's refusal to demand concealment from refugees due to fear, as opposed to their indifference towards concealment attributable to pressure or worry, is emotionally difficult to grasp.[72] The line where worry ends and fear begins is porous. Moreover, in the same judgment that repudiated discretion, discretion was partially revived in relation to other feelings in order to limit the 'infinite' gradations of persecution definitions that may result.[73] Decision-makers must undertake an analysis as to why a person was discreet and discern whether it had been motivated by fear or pressure.

Hathaway and Pobjoy critique Rodger LJ's judgment as lacking necessary limits. However, the delineation between fear and pressure places a limit on what counts as persecution. In fact, I agree with Hathaway and Pobjoy's claim that the 'instinct to celebrate' should be met with caution.[74] Pushing farther, however, homophobic injury need not always be motivated by fear. Homophobia can engender shame, worry, humiliation, pity, and associated 'pressures' that limit the expression of queers in their country of origin.[75] Yet, by anticipating the way in which social pressures could shame and isolate queers into remaining discreet about sexuality, this case limited the circumstances where people enduring homophobic injury could seek surrogate state protection. *HJ & HT* and *S395/2002* pushed the borders of refugee law further with respect to the fear that 'closets' sexual minorities but simultaneously circumscribed those borders by refusing to grasp the forms of 'closeting' which are not necessarily

---

[70] See also Ahmed (n3) 69.

[71] *HJ (Iran) and HT (Cameroon)* (n 59) [61] (Rodger LJ).

[72] Janna Wessels, 'Discretion in Sexuality-Based Asylum Cases: An Adaptive Phenomenon' in Thomas Spijkerboer (ed) *Fleeing Homophobia: Sexual Orientation, Gender Identity and Asylum* (Routledge 2013), 73.

[73] *HJ (Iran) and HT (Cameroon)* (n59) [63] (Rodger LJ).

[74] Hathaway and Pobjoy 'Queer Cases Make Bad Law' (n24) 387.

[75] Tobin, 'Assessing GLBTI Refugee Claims' (n62) 459.

reducible to fear but are shamefully demeaning. Some queer claims were granted mobility while others were not.

Part IV – Anxious Adjudication

The move away from reliance on discretion marks a progressive moment in refugee law by broadening the contours of what counts as homophobic persecution. Cases like *S395/2002* and *HJ & HT* open up the space for queer asylum seekers by refusing to coerce sexual minorities into the proverbial closet in order to avoid (the threat of) serious harm. However, the interrogation of credibility – in relation to the veracity of an asylum seeker's sexual orientation – has reproduced ethnocentric ideas of both (homo)sexual identity and intimacy.

A: Reviewing Reasonability

In exploring the way anxiety manifests in adjudicating the veracity of sexual orientation and how such fears are shielded from review, I want to begin by navigating the Australian High Court judicial review case *SZMDS v Minister for Immigration & Citizenship* (2010). The case related to a 44-year-old Pakistani national who sought asylum in Australia on the basis of his homosexuality. In making his claim, the applicant noted that during his time working in the United Arab Emirates (UAE), he developed a same-sex attraction and had a relationship with an Indian man (Mr R).[76] Mr R was engaged in another same-sex relationship at the time (with Mr H) and all three were friends. However, upon discovering that Mr H was involved in bareback sex and illicit drug use, the applicant claimed he and Mr R left Mr H. At that time, the applicant feared that Mr H would disclose his homosexuality to the applicant's family. The applicant was married at the time. He feared that if he was 'outed', he would be subject to discrimination on his return and that his family would be shamed by the disclosure of his sexuality.[77] The applicant had also made visits to the United Kingdom during his work in the United Arab Emirates but did not seek asylum at that time because his relationship with Mr R and Mr H had not deteriorated. His application was refused on the basis that the RRT

---

[76] *SZMDS v Minister for Immigration & Anor* (2008) FMCA 1064, [2] (Scarlett FM).
[77] ibid [2] (Scarlett FM).

was not satisfied that he was a 'practising homosexual'.[78] On appeal, among other procedural issues, the Court had to consider whether the RRT had committed a jurisdictional error through its illogical or irrational reasoning by making findings about his (lack of) purported homosexuality with no evidentiary basis.[79] Despite some critique of the reasoning, the majority of the High Court held that no error had occurred.

The relationship between travel and fear of 'outing' sexual orientation was central to determining whether the applicant belonged to the particular social group of homosexual men in Pakistan. The RRT indicated that the applicant had not engaged in sexual activity with men since high school and determined that he had no desire to do so in the future.[80] Moreover, the RRT found the applicant's testimony that he feared being 'outed' incredible because he had returned to Pakistan for short trips on numerous occasions while working in the UAE.[81] The Federal Court critiqued the RRT's emphasis on the applicant's movements to determine the claim's veracity: there was nothing inconsistent about returning briefly to a place where you did not fear at the time that your sexual orientation would be known.[82]

Fear undercut the recognition of queer asylum claims through the containment of and turning away from embodied experience. Despite the Federal Court's critique, the High Court upheld the RRT's findings in respect to the applicant's credibility. For the majority, judicial review of administrative decisions was not an exercise in reviewing the preferrability of certain conclusions, but about determining whether any reasonable decision-maker could have made those conclusions.[83] Heydon J suggested that it was logical to disbelieve that an applicant would return to a place where he could face discrimination (even if he did not fear being outed at that point).[84] Here, the anticipation of injury – the fear of being found out as gay if visiting Pakistan – worked against the applicant's claim. Heydon J accepted that there was a logical basis to the finding that a homosexual man would not risk returning to a place where they would be outed. Fear

---

[78] ibid [2] (Scarlett FM).

[79] *SZMDS* (n 76) [13] (Gummow ACJ and Kiefel J).

[80] *SZMDS* (n76) [28] (Scarlett FM).

[81] *SZMDS v Minister for Immigration & Anor* (2009) FCA 210, [5] (Moore J).

[82] ibid [25] (Moore J).

[83] *SZMDS* (n76) [130] (Crennan and Bell JJ).

[84] ibid [86] (Heydon J).

was considered 'logically' to contain a genuine gay man's sense of movement. Yet, by pointing towards an abstract climate of homophobic fear, the Court worked to contain the applicant's own experience of fear. In light of the applicant's uncorroborated testimony and his marital history, the RRT's findings were deemed to have a logical foundation. However, the majority's reading of the applicant's situation evinced an act of covering and containment through differentiation of fears: the RRT's assumption that gay men from Pakistan would have an enduring fear about living in Pakistan (rather than contingent on circumstances) was used to cover over the asylum seeker's testimony that his fear manifested from the shift in his personal circumstances. Dismissing his narrative became a way for the Court to turn away.[85]

In *S395/2002*, the applicants' fear of violence for being 'out' was given prominence in the majority judgment in order to recognise the troubling impetus behind sexual discretion. Here, the emphasis on the applicant 'logically' fearing homophobic violence and shame worked as an abstract idea that undermined credibility and turned the decision-maker's attention away from the applicant's contingent experience of homophobic fear.

Fear of persecution and the fact that a risk of persecution existed, however, were distinguished in the dissenting judgment. Gummow ACJ and Kiefel J observed that there was no logical connection between being a homosexual man and assuming that – without more – such a man would be fearful of returning home.[86] Dismissing the testimony of the asylum seeker in respect to his failure to claim asylum in the UK and his return to Pakistan to visit his family without any evidence to contradict the testimony constituted a reviewable reasoning error.[87] Fear needed to be distinguished: the general fear of homophobic violence, from the specific fear of a refugee at risk of experiencing it.

B: Interrogating Identity and Intimacy

It is important to point out that *SZMDS* was circumscribed by a statutory context that shielded faulty and fearful logic from judicial review. In order to tease out how anxiety militates against recognition, we must also

---

[85] Ahmed, (n3) 67.
[86] *SZMDS* (n76) [51] (Gummow ACJ and Kiefel J).
[87] *SZMDS* (n76) [52] (Gummow ACJ and Kiefel J).

consider how intimacy and identity have been framed in decisions where the plausibility and consistency of refugee narrative has been questioned.

In the UK, following *HJ & HT*, the Asylum and Immigration Tribunal (AIT) had to consider how broadly the obligation for protection stretched in relation to discreet sexual minorities.[88] In *SW v The Secretary of State for the Home Department* (2011), a lesbian woman from Jamaica sought protection on the basis that she would face the risk of serious harm if she returned home. Specifically, the applicant had not experienced any direct incidents of harm due to her discreet sexual relationships with women but now feared that given her 'open' relationships with women in the UK, she was at greater risk of persecution.[89] Her claim was initially dismissed on the grounds that she had not sufficiently established her claim on the balance of probabilities, that Jamaica had sufficient state protection against homophobic violence, and that the applicant had not significantly changed her behaviour since living in the UK so as to risk persecution if she were to return.[90] On appeal to the AIT, her claim was successful. However, despite the effective implementation of the ruling in *HJ & HT*, the decision evinced how the anticipation of homophobic injury required a differentiation between visible/open queer bodies at risk of violence and those that can live without persecutory attention.

Much of the judicial reasoning in *SW* focused on the evidentiary basis of the appellant's claim about the nature of her 'open lesbian lifestyle'. The applicant's testimony began by outlining her life of secrecy in Jamaica: she had an ongoing sexual relationship with a married woman and participated in an anonymous online forum that catered for same-sex attracted women in Jamaica. Importantly, the applicant would not 'hold hands in public' with her then partner.[91] This life of discretion was then contrasted to her arrival in the UK that involved 'a freer atmosphere'.[92] In the UK, she had more public relationships with women, found a girlfriend,

---

[88] Unlike the Refugee Review Tribunal, the Asylum and Immigration Tribunal in the UK is a judicial body that makes decisions with precedential value/to which the doctrine of precedent applies.

[89] *SW (Jamaica) v Secretary for the Home Department* (2011) CG UKUT 00251, [27] (Gleeson J).

[90] ibid [12] – [14] (Gleeson J).

[91] ibid Appendix A.

[92] ibid Appendix A.

marched in a local pride parade, and signed up as a board member of a black lesbian organisation.[93] Gleeson J observed:

> She described herself firmly as an open lesbian and was not prepared to modify her behaviour on return: The Tribunal should find that honest and credible evidence.[94]

By framing her experience of 'living openly' as a process of moving from discretion to publicity, the applicant was not only able to demonstrate the authenticity of her sexuality but also its associated visibility. Honesty was tied to her willingness to 'own' her sexuality as a public expression. Specifically, Gleeson J made note that the applicant was not 'naturally discreet about her sexuality'.[95] Here, the participation in social events alongside having a public relationship with a woman rendered the applicant an 'open' lesbian whose earlier discretion was a feature of circumstance rather than choice. The applicant's desire to be 'out and proud' constituted a marker to measure the inhibiting nature of sexual invisibility in Jamaica. Gleeson J gave significant weight to the testimony of an academic who had documented the experience of homophobic violence in Jamaica (such as the presence of 'corrective' rape to 'cure' same-sex attracted women), the criminalisation of same-sex relationships more generally, the lack of protection afforded by public authorities to sexual minorities subject to abuse, and limits on human rights activism.[96]

Yet, by placing enormous emphasis on being 'open' as the panacea to discretion, Gleeson J obscured how sexual minorities that do not subscribe to a desire to live visibly are at risk of being disbelieved. By scripting a narrative of (homo)sexual development in terms of progressive linearity – moving from secrecy and shame to openness and pride – sexual minority refugee claims were rendered more plausible.[97] Evidence of active participation in social activities, sexual intimacy, and exhibiting public pride became the indexes to anchor an analysis of (homo)sexual authenticity. In *SZMDS*, the lack of 'openness' on the part of the Pakistani

---

[93] ibid [31] – [39] (Gleeson J).

[94] ibid [80] (Gleeson J).

[95] ibid [85] (Gleeson J).

[96] ibid [95] – [97] (Gleeson J).

[97] See also Laurie Berg and Jenni Millbank, 'Constructing the Personal Narratives of Lesbian, Gay and Bisexual Asylum Claimants' (2009) 22(1) Journal of Refugee Studies 1

asylum seeker who failed to eschew his family and country in favour of a more 'progressive' country undermined his credibility. Adverse credibility inferences were drawn because it was deemed implausible that a gay person would marry and/or want to visit their home country if they potentially could be persecuted there. Rather than open up a consideration of fear of persecution as a socially contingent emotion, both *SZMDS* and *SW* anticipated the likelihood of homophobic persecution by reading queer bodies along an ethnocentric axis of public visibility. Visibility can be a tool of containment rather than liberation. Associating sexual identity with public activity or demeanour risks dismissing claims for protection where sexual minorities do not make 'public' claims or 'flaunt' their sexuality.[98]

Part V – Fighting Fears

Recent cases from the European Court of Justice (ECJ) have pushed back against the intrusive questions and stereotypes used to determine asylum claims. Two cases from the ECJ adopted the positions in *S395/2002* and *HJ & HT* to overrule any residual use of 'discretion tests' and pornographic evidence for demonstrating the veracity of a person's sexual orientation. Yet, both decisions also denied that laws criminalising homosexuality constitute persecution per se and still permitted the use of some stereotypes to assess the credibility of an asylum seeker's self-identification about their sexuality.

A: Persecution Parameters

In *X, Y, and Z*, the Netherlands referred three asylum decisions to the ECJ to consider whether the criminalisation of homosexuality constituted persecution by itself or whether enforcement of the law needed to reach a particular level of severity.[99] X was a national of Sierra Leone, Y was from Uganda, and Z was Senegalese. In Sierra Leone and Uganda, homosexuality was punishable by up to life imprisonment.[100] Senegal had

---

[98] Venice Choi, 'Living Discreetly: A Catch-22 in Refugee Status Determinations on the Basis of Sexual Orientation' (2010) 36 Brooklyn Journal of International Law 241, 255; S Chelvan, 'From Silence to Safety: Protecting the Gay Refugee?' (2013) May 2013 Counsel 26, 27.
[99] Joined Cases C-199/12 to C-201/12 *X (C-199/12), Y (C-200/12), Z (C-201/12) v Minister voor Immigratie en Asiel* [2013] ECR I, Opinion of AG Sharpston, [12].
[100] ibid [15].

lower penalties: homosexual men could be jailed for up to five years and
fined.[101] Prior to the decision of the ECJ, Advocate General Sharpston
noted that while sexual minorities could constitute a particular social
group for the purposes of claiming asylum and should not have to be
discreet about their sexual identity, the question of persecution could not
be addressed without careful scrutiny.[102] She made note that refugee status
was necessarily 'restrictive' – it was confined to individuals exposed to
'serious denial or systemic infringement of their most fundamental
rights'. [103] In order for criminalisation to be considered persecutory,
adjudicators would need to consider the risk/frequency of prosecution,
severity of penalties, and associated social practices that an applicant may
'reasonably fear'.[104]

The ECJ accepted Sharpston's conclusions and held that specific
enforcement of criminal laws, not merely their general existence, must be
demonstrated to satisfy the threshold of persecution. Derogation from
protecting family life – in criminalising homosexuality – could not
constitute persecution in isolation of other acts (such as enforcement,
blackmail, etc.).[105] Drawing from Rodger LJ's reasoning in *HJ & HT*, the
Court observed that concealing sexual orientation to 'exercise reserve' in
its expression was not a reasonable expectation.[106] Protection was limited
to those who could demonstrate that their desire to avoid persecution was
annexed to a fear of specific enforcement rather than the shame or
humiliation experienced by the general existence of the law.

B: Credibility Challenges

In the following year, the ECJ was asked to consider the concept of
'family and private life' (in addition to human dignity) in a different
context of asylum adjudication: the assessment of sexual credibility. *A, B,
and C* involved three asylum seekers who were denied protection on the
basis that they had not been credible. In all three cases, applicants were
either willing to submit (or had already submitted) pornographic evidence

---

[101] ibid.
[102] ibid [63].
[103] Ibid [41].
[104] ibid [50].
[105] Joined Cases (n99) [55]-[61].
[106] ibid [76].

to 'prove' the veracity of their sexual orientation.[107] Each claim had initially been refused by the Netherlands (the receiving state) on the basis that the narratives were 'vague, perfunctory, and implausible'.[108]

Echoing her comments in *X, Y, and Z* in relation to assessing persecution, AG Sharpston argued that an assessment of sexual orientation began with self-identification which must be assessed in specific rather than general terms. After all, 'an averred sexual orientation cannot be objectively verified'.[109] In condemning current methods of sexual verification, AG Sharpston observed that medical exams, pornographic evidence, sexual stereotypes, and prurient questioning were inconsistent with the protection of privacy and dignity in the European Charter.[110] They were 'blacklisted'.[111] However, a number of methods of verification that exist on a 'grey list' were permissible in credibility assessment: including a failure to disclose sexual orientation at the earliest opportunity and a lack of 'general knowledge' about queer organisations in the applicant's home country.[112] Verification took on a 'public' rather than a 'private' dimension.

Even when moving away from stereotypes or invasive sexual questioning, AG Sharpston reiterated the need to authenticate the veracity of a person's sexual orientation. She not only condemned medical testing as problematic because homosexuality was not a disease, but also because sexual testing (like determining whether or not a person is physiologically aroused by gay pornography) failed to distinguish 'genuine applicants from bogus ones'.[113] Moreover, questions that relied on stereotypes were dangerous because 'bogus applicants' may have 'schooled themselves in preparing their application'.[114] Here, sincerity was an issue for adjudicators to probe but the current methods of credibility assessment militated against that. In fact, the anticipation of bogus claims worked – as a threat to the integrity

---

[107] Joined Cases C-148/13 to C-150/13 *A (C-148/13), B (C-149/13), C (C-150/13) v Staatssecretaris van Veiligheid en Justitie* [2014] ECR I, Opinion of AG Sharpston [22]–[29].
[108] ibid [26].
[109] ibid [43].
[110] ibid [52].
[111] ibid [54].
[112] ibid [54].
[113] ibid [62].
[114] ibid [65].

of asylum processing – to rethink methods of verification. Fear worked to reveal the proximity to threat: bogus claims were brought into circulation by stereotypes and assumptions that could be performed by anyone.

In reiterating the need for credibility assessment to respect dignity and privacy, the ECJ strengthened the need for assessment to ensure the veracity of queer claims. Self-identification was important, but it was not determinative of an applicant's sexual orientation. [115] The Court also returned to the use of stereotypes in a partial sense: they may be a 'useful element' in adjudication but they could not be the sole basis on which an asylum claim was determined (at the exclusion of personal circumstances). [116] The ECJ, however, repudiated the use of detailed questions about sexual experience, as it was contrary to respect for private life. In doing so, the Court suggested that even if applicants were willing to provide oral or visual evidence of their sexual activity, such evidence was to be refused on the basis that it has/had very limited probative value.[117] Dignity and privacy were invoked in this decision as both covers and containers – ones to shield sexual minority refugees from humiliating questions by containing the kinds of questions that may be asked of them. Containment here worked to shield queers from being forced to endure bureaucratic experiments to assess sexual orientation. The container worked to limit questions that affront personal dignity rather than to protect the (persecutory) administrative sensibilities that may be affronted by visible queerness.

Yet, these progressive gestures of containment also evince fear: encouraging stereotypes opened up the asylum process to abuse by 'bogus' claimants who threaten the integrity of adjudication. *A, B, and C* loosened the understanding of intimacy and expression to recognise the vulnerable position of queers in the status determination process.[118] Yet, gesturing to the performative dimensions of (homo)sexuality worked to expose the vulnerability of the determination process itself. Disingenuous applicants could 'game' the system by rehearsing the stereotypes used to measure (homo)sexual identity and intimacy. As a consequence, the Court found that a shift from demeaning sexual questions to ones that enable personal

---

[115] Joined Cases (n107) [52].
[116] ibid [62].
[117] ibid [65].
[118] ibid [70].

narrative would strengthen the quality of decision-making.[119] The act of eschewing prurient sexual questions and pornographic evidence became a means of protecting the adjudication process – containing the threat of insincerity. The demand for authenticity was reproduced rather than repudiated and the Court was able to pull away from facing the fact that all sexualities were performative.

Conclusion

Fear in pro-LGBTI asylum cases can be insidious. In tracing the gestures of containment, covering, and pulling away from anticipated threats, this chapter has argued that progressive decisions can contain queer experiences of identity, intimacy, and injury. Specifically, by taking up fear as a gesture – one that reveals proximity to threats – I examined how 'discretion' worked as a tactic of containment to deny protection. As I demonstrated, even the progressive impetus behind cases like *S395/2002* and *HJ & HT* that dismantled discretion, reproduced new demands to cover in circumstances where pressure, rather than fear, generated sexual invisibility.

The emphasis on visibility, moreover, generated new forms of 'anxious adjudication'. The scrutiny of sexual credibility reproduced new anxieties over accepting 'bogus' asylum claims and the need to guard against it by authenticating identity through visible rubrics of sexual activity, pop culture, political participation, and social scenes. Such gestures, like the ones pointing towards visibility, worked to cover over queer subjects that refused expression in public space.

Fear limits the recognition of queer subjects in asylum law. From contouring a well-founded fear of persecution to authenticating sexual credibility, the borders of asylum law are entrenched by fears in the same moments that they purport to stretch them further. We must queer these fears if we are to expand the horizons for queer refugees seeking protection.

---

[119] ibid [60]–[61].

CHAPTER EIGHT

SEX, LIES AND LAW:
RETHINKING RAPE-BY-FRAUD

VERA BERGELSON*

> Deceiver, dissembler
> Your trousers are alight
> From what pole or gallows
> Shall they dangle in the night?
>
> When I asked of your career
> Why did you have to kick my rear
> With that stinking lie of thine
> Proclaiming that you owned a mine?[1]

In November 2015, Gayle Newland was sentenced to eight years in prison after having been convicted by a British court of three counts of sexual assault for lying to her female sexual partner about her biological sex. Newland and her girlfriend of two years met on Facebook where Newland had posed as a man named Kye Fortune. A relationship developed and, after some time, became intimate. In the course of the trial, the court heard how the victim was persuaded to wear a blindfold whenever she and 'Kye' had sex. The victim said that she only discovered 'Kye's' true identity

---

* I am grateful to my research assistants Nicole Perez and Samuel Youssof for their help in researching and editing this paper. I would also like to thank Gyuora Binder, Michael Boucai, Luis Chiesa, Tony Diloff, Leo Zaibert, and other participants of Buffalo Criminal Law Theory seminar; Adil Haque, and other participants of Rutgers Law School faculty colloquia; and Larry Alexander, and other participants of the workshop The Ethics of Consent at the University of Zurich, for their generous and insightful comments.

[1] This excerpt (appropriately) comes from a fake—a poem, 'The Liar', falsely attributed to William Blake.
https://www.visualthesaurus.com/cm/dictionary/pants-on-fire/ accessed 23rd April 2016.

when she ripped off her blindfold during their last sexual encounter and saw Newland wearing a prosthetic penis.[2]

The sentencing judge thus addressed Newland and explained the sentence, 'These offences are so serious that only an immediate custodial sentence would in any way properly reflect the serious nature of your conduct. As an aspect of mercy, I do not increase the starting point beyond eight years.'[3]

Newland's conviction and harsh sentence have brought to public attention a difficult and largely unresolved question: in what circumstances should deception turn the apparently consensual sex into rape?[4] After all, people often lie in personal relationships about their age, weight, income, and accomplishments. Shall the state prosecute and punish those people too? And if not, is there a meaningful difference between their lies and Newland's?

Historical Approaches to Sex Procured by Lies

Historically, lies in the sexual context did not amount to rape. Rape was defined as sexual intercourse accomplished by force and without consent; and in the absence of force, the conviction could not be obtained. A judge in the first English prosecution of rape-by-fraud explained, while rejecting the charge, that there was a meaningful difference between compelling a

---

[2] Stephanie Linning, 'Woman, 25, who pretended she was a man to dupe female friend into sex is found GUILTY of three counts of sexual assault' *Daily Mail* (London, 15 September 2015) <www.dailymail.co.uk/news/article-3235421/Woman-pretended-man-dupe-female-friend-sex-GUILTY-sexual-assault.html> accessed 19 December 2015.

[3] 'Woman who pretended to be man to trick friend into sex jailed for eight years' *The Guardian* (London, 12 November 2015) <www.theguardian.com/uk-news/2015/nov/12/gayle-newland-sentenced-eight-years-prison-duping-friend-having-sex> accessed 19 December 2015.

[4] In this paper, the terms 'rape' and 'sexual assault' are used interchangeably since in many jurisdictions they mean the same offense, but the latter term has substituted the former in more recent legislation. In addition, the terms 'fraud' and 'deception', and 'rape-by-fraud' and 'rape-by-deception' are used interchangeably, just like in the majority of legal opinions involving consent to sex obtained by a false representation of fact or false promise. In addition, in this paper, when referring to the perpetrator or victim of an offense, I use the male and female pronouns interchangeably.

woman against her will when abhorrence would arise in her mind, and beguiling her into consent and co-operation.[5]

In the jurisdictions that still follow the traditional rule, the prevailing view is that consent to intercourse, even consent obtained by fraudulent representations, precludes conviction of rape.[6] Courts have opined that, where the statute requires an element of force, '[f]raud cannot be allowed to supply the place of the force,' and the 'essence of the crime [of rape] is not the fact of intercourse but the injury and outrage to the feelings of the woman by the forceful penetration of her person'.[7]

Jurisdictions with more modern statutes allow convictions of rape or other sexual crimes in cases of certain kinds of fraud, even in the absence of force. Courts in those jurisdictions usually distinguish between the deception that involves the nature of the act (fraud in the factum) and the deception that involves some collateral matter (fraud in the inducement). The former vitiates consent; the latter does not.[8]

The difference between the two kinds of fraud has been crucial in many cases, including *Boro v Superior Court*, in which the defendant lied to his victim that she had a life threatening disease, which could be cured by her having sexual intercourse with a donor who had been injected with a 'serum'. The victim consented under the mistaken belief that otherwise she would die, and the defendant had sex with her.[9] He was prosecuted on several charges, including rape. That charge failed, however, as the appellate court held that fraud in the inducement did not vitiate consent. The court characterized the defendant's lies as fraud in the inducement because the deception related not to the fact of the sexual intercourse but merely to the incentive for having that intercourse.[10]

In contrast, in *People v Minkowski*, in which the victims consented to a medical treatment but the doctor used the opportunity to sexually penetrate

---

[5] *R v Jackson*, (1822) 168 ER 911 (Dallas CJ).
[6] BK Carpenter, 'Rape by Fraud or Impersonation' (1963) 91 ALR 2d 591, s 2.
[7] *Commonwealth v Goldenberg* 155 NE 2d 187, 191-92 (Mass 1959).
[8] Ronald N Boyce, Donald A Dripps and Rollin M Perkins, *Criminal Law and Procedure* (12th edn, Foundation Press 2013) 1079.
[9] *Boro v Superior Court* 210 Cal Rptr 122 (1985).
[10] ibid.

them, the victims' consent was held to have been vitiated and the doctor was convicted of rape.[11] The *Boro* court explained the difference:

> The victims in *Minkowski* consented, not to sexual intercourse, but to an act of an altogether different nature, penetration by medical instrument. The consent was to a pathological, and not a carnal, act, and the mistake was, therefore, in the *factum* and not merely in the inducement.[12]

Another area of rape law in which the distinction between the fraud in the factum and fraud in the inducement could be quintessential to the defendant's conviction involved impersonation of a husband. In those cases, a woman (usually half-asleep and in the darkness of her room) would consent to sex mistakenly believing that the person in her bed was her husband. Jurisdictions have been split on how such impersonation should be characterized. A highly esteemed legal treatise explained:

> Some courts have taken the position that such a misdeed is fraud in the inducement on the theory that the woman consents to exactly what is done (sexual intercourse) and hence there is no rape; other courts, *with better reason it would seem*, hold such a misdeed to be rape on the theory that it involves fraud in the factum since the woman's consent is to an innocent act of marital intercourse while what is actually perpetrated upon her is an act of adultery. Her innocence seems never to have been questioned in such a case and the reason she is not guilty of adultery is because she did not consent to adulterous intercourse.[13]

In those latter jurisdictions, impersonation of a spouse was deemed to be rape because it changed the nature of the act, just like the physician's deception changed the nature of the act in *Minkowski*.

Other lies used for eliciting consent to sex usually did not vitiate consent and, even when punishable, did not result in the conviction of rape.[14]

---

[11] 23 Cal Rptr 92 (1962).

[12] Boyce et al (n 8).

[13] Rollin M Perkins and Ronald N. Boyce, *Criminal Law* (3rd edn, Foundation Press 1982) 1080-81 (emphasis added) (footnotes omitted). See also *Boro* (n 9).

[14] Model Penal Code (1980) s 213.1 cmt 7(b). The official commentary explains:
The situation with intercourse accomplished by contracting a void marriage was usually dealt with, if at all, under the law of bigamy. Penalties for that crime varied widely and were not integrated with the law of rape. [S]exual intimacy achieved by means of a sham marriage was generally held not to constitute rape and was therefore punishable only under special statutes dealing with seduction and the like.

Among those were lies about one's profession and personal life;[15] feigned
wedding ceremonies; false representations that the defendant and the
victim were legally married;[16] and nonpayment to a prostitute.[17] The
traditional explanation for the different treatment of those lies has been
that it is irrelevant for the law why a person gives consent to a certain act
as long as she gives that consent voluntarily and with the understanding of
the act she is consenting to.[18]

New Developments in the Law of Rape-by-Fraud

For many decades, the distinction between the fraud in the factum and
fraud in the inducement remained solid throughout the common law
world—up until recently. The growing consensus on the point that the
essence of rape is the violation of the victim's sexual inviolability has led
lawmakers, judges, and scholars to focus on the issue of consent and
reexamine the legal effect of obtaining consent by fraud.

Consent has been forcefully established as 'the main doctrinal category in
substantive criminal law that functions as a placeholder for considerations
of the victim's personhood, i.e., his capacity for autonomy'.[19]
Accordingly, it has been argued that the kind of fraud—in the factum or in
the inducement—should not make a difference for the validity of consent
if the victim's consent to sex was granted on the condition of certain
representations made by the defendant and if, but for those representations,
the victim would not have consented to sex with the defendant. Under this
view, any representations essential to the victim's consent are material,
and any material misrepresentations destroy consent.

---

[15] *People v Evans* 379 NYS 2d 912 (1975).

[16] *State v Murphy* 6 Ala 764 (1844); *Papadimitropoulos v R* (1958) 98 CLR 249
(Austl). The Model Penal Code has added two more kinds of deception to the list
of prohibited actions: one, inducing the victim to enter a void marriage by
deceiving her as to the defendant's eligibility to marry; and two, staging a mock
marriage to create the false supposition that the couple are man and wife. Model
Penal Code (1980) s 213.1 cmt 7(b). Under the Model Penal Code, the crime is not
rape but a gross sexual imposition, a felony of a lower degree.

[17] *R v Linekar* [1995] QB 250.

[18] 'It is not necessary that a woman know the true identity of her sexual partner or
know anything about him in order to consent, but she must be agreeable to the
penetration of her body by a particular "*membrum virile*".' *United States v Traylor*
40 MJ 248, 249 (1994) (footnote omitted).

[19] Markus Dirk Dubber, 'Toward a Constitutional Law of Crime and Punishment'
(2004) 55 Hastings LJ 509, 569.

The focus on consent (rather than force) in rape law has resulted in the expansion of the scope of the 'rape-by-fraud' doctrine in a number of jurisdictions. In Canada, a Supreme Court justice opined that rape is committed whenever sex is procured by dishonesty.[20]

In Israel, a number of courts convicted people for obtaining consent to sex by lying about their age, marital status, ethnicity, religion, employment, and personal connections.[21] In *State of Israel v Mehadakar*, for example, the defendant contacted young women through the internet presenting himself as a 17-22 year old man (while in reality he was 30 years old) and had intercourse with them. Based on his own admission, the defendant was convicted of rape in one of the cases and of fraudulently receiving a benefit in the other ones as a part of his plea bargain.[22] In *Denino v State of Israel*, a married man presented himself to the victim as divorced and waiting to receive the documents that would allow him to remarry. The appellate court affirmed his conviction of fraudulently receiving a benefit and opined:

> [A] woman deserves [to have the power] to decide whether she wants to have a relationship with a married man, a father, or whether she does not want to get impregnated by such a man; and the man does not have the power to determine whether to hide the facts from her that could influence her decision.[23]

In *Saliman v State*, the defendant pretended to be a senior government official. He told a woman that he would get her an apartment and increased social security payments if she slept with him; the woman agreed. The Supreme Court of Israel upheld Saliman's rape-by-fraud conviction. A Supreme Court Justice commented that a conviction of rape should be imposed any time a 'person does not tell the truth regarding critical matters to a reasonable woman, and as a result of misrepresentation she has sexual relations with him'.[24]

---

[20] *R v Cuerrier* [1998] 2 SCR 371, 374 (Can) (L'Heureux-Dube J).

[21] CrimA 2411/06 *Saliman v State* [2008] (Isr); *Denino v State of Israel*; *State of Israel v Mehadakar*; *State of Israel v Hen Alkobi*.

[22] Eugene Volokh, 'Israeli Rape by Fraud Cases' (*The Volokh Conspiracy*, 7 October 2010) <http://volokh.com/2010/10/07/israeli-rape-by-fraud-cases/> accessed 20 December 2015.

[23] ibid.

[24] Tomer Zarchin, 'Jurists Say Arab's Rape Conviction Sets Dangerous Precedent' *Haaretz* (Tel Aviv, 21 July 2010) <www.haaretz.com/jurists-say-arab-s-rape-conviction-sets-dangerous-precedent-1.303109> accessed 19 December 2015.

Yet another Israeli rape-by-fraud case, *Kashur v State*, involved a guilty plea in which the defendant admitted that he had lied to his victim about being a Jewish bachelor interested in a serious relationship whereas in fact he was a Muslim Arab, married, a father of two, and apparently not interested in any significant relationship.[25] The Supreme Court of Israel upheld Kashur's conviction on the basis of the facts admitted in his guilty plea, reasoning thus:

> The court is obliged to protect the public interest from sophisticated, smooth-tongued criminals who can deceive innocent victims at an unbearable price—the sanctity of their bodies and souls. When the very basis of trust between human beings drops, especially when the matters at hand are so intimate, sensitive and fateful, the court is required to stand firmly at the side of the victims—actual and potential—to protect their wellbeing.[26]

In the United Kingdom, only in the last few years, three young women were convicted of sexual assault for misrepresenting their biological sex.[27] In each case, there was evidence of gender ambiguity or confusion. Not surprisingly, their convictions raised concerns in the LGBT community. Professor Alex Sharpe, an LGBT rights advocate, has argued that 'prosecution, through singling out gender as the type of information that

---

[25] CrimA (Jer) 5734/10 *Kashur v State* [2010] (Isr). The details of the case, later declassified, revealed that the initial charge was of forcible rape but the prosecution agreed to the reduced charge of rape-by-deception because of the victim's confused account and concern at facing another court appearance. They also indicated that the woman was emotionally disturbed and had a history of sexual abuse. The court sent the victim to a mental hospital for treatment and convicted Kashur on the lesser charge. Rachel Shabi, 'Arab rape-by-deception charge "was result of plea bargain"' *The Guardian* (London, 8 September 2010) <www.theguardian.com/world/2010/sep/08/rape-by-deception-plea-israel> accessed 19 December 2015.

[26] Jo Adetunji and Harriet Sherwood, 'Arab guilty of rape after consensual sex with Jew' *The Guardian* (London, 20 July 2010) <www.theguardian.com/world/2010/jul/21/arab-guilty-rape-consensual-sex-jew> accessed 19 December 2015 (quoting Segal J).

[27] '"Not a flicker of remorse": Girl who disguised herself as a boy to trick female friends into sex jailed' *The Daily Mirror* (London, 5 March 2010) <www.mirror.co.uk/news/uk-news/girl-who-disguised-herself-as-a-boy-752004> accessed 19 December 2015; Steve Robson, 'Fake penis sex attack woman's 8-year sentence slammed as it emerges judge gave paedophile half the jail term' *The Daily Mirror* (London, 12 November 2015) <www.mirror.co.uk/uk-news/fake-penis-sex-attack-womans-6819911> accessed 19 December 2015.

demands disclosure, has fallen disproportionately, and so far, exclusively, on the LGBT community'.[28]

In Australia, a man was convicted of procuring sexual penetration by threats or fraud, a crime that could lead to ten years in prison, for lying on a dating website. Deepak Dhankar, a man of Indian descent and an average build, deceived a woman into believing that he was a muscular, blond-haired Caucasian named 'Jamie'. The woman kept her eyes closed throughout the sexual encounter but when she eventually opened her eyes, she discovered that Dhankar was not 'Jamie'.[29] The sentencing judge opined, 'It is a serious matter to obtain access to another person's body by deception.'[30]

In the United States, several jurisdictions have recently considered or adopted legislative proposals that would criminalize a broad range of situations in which consent to sex is obtained by deception.[31] An assemblyman for New Jersey has thus advocated the proposed bill, 'I truly believe that we have to look at the issue of rape as more than sexual

---

[28] Robson (n 27).

[29] 'Indian-born man who duped woman into sex by pretending he was Caucasian avoids jail' *news.com.au* (Surry Hills, 25 February 2015) <www.news.com.au/national/victoria/indianborn-man-who-duped-woman-into-sex-by-pretending-he-was-caucasian-avoids-jail/news-story/3defd87c9b97f40bf53dd789a8114570> accessed 19 December 2015. Dhankar was given a suspended sentence of two years and 200 hours of community service. ibid.

[30] ibid.

[31] Cal Penal Code § 261(a)(5) (West 2013) (foreclosing a loophole that permitted conviction for impersonation only in the case of spouse impersonation); Idaho Code Ann § 18-6101(7) (2015) (providing that a man is guilty of rape if his female victim believes he is someone else and that 'belief is induced by any artifice, pretense, or concealment by the accused to induce such belief'); Tenn Code Ann § 39-13-503(a)(4) (criminalizing 'sexual penetration . . . accomplished by fraud'). Massachusetts has recently considered and voted down a rape-by-fraud proposal. Joyce M. Short, 'Massachusetts missed the boat on defending women!' (*rapebyfraud.com*, 28 October 2014) <http://rapebyfraud.com/2014/10/28/massachusetts-missed-the-boat-on-defending-women> accessed 19 December 2015. In New Jersey, a bill was introduced in 2014, but no action has been since taken. Matt Friedman, 'Rape by fraud? N.J. lawmaker introduces bill to make it a crime' (*nj.com*, 24 November 2014) <www.nj.com/politics/index.ssf/2014/11/rape_by_fraud_nj_lawmaker_introduces_bill_to_make_it_a_crime.html> accessed 19 December 2015.

contact without consent. Fraud invalidates any semblance of consent just as forcible sexual contact does.'[32]

All in all, we have clearly reached the point when we need to determine and explain the reach and scope of rape-by-fraud law. The expansion of a criminal law doctrine always requires justification. This need is particularly acute in the climate of continuing overcriminalization of previously unpunished human behavior in the United States, the United Kingdom, and other countries. To provide the proper boundaries for the crime of rape-by-fraud, it is essential to determine the rationales for criminalizing certain kinds of deception used to procure sexual consent (sex-by-lies). We should look at the history of those rationales and, to the extent that some of them have become obsolete, rethink the meaning and scope of the law in today's world.

Traditional Rationales for Criminalizing Rape-by-Fraud

To construe the original meaning of rape-by-fraud, it is important to recall that, under the common law, a woman could not legally consent to sex with anyone but her husband. If she had consensual sex with someone else, she was guilty of a crime—fornication (if she was unmarried) or adultery (if she was married). If she took money for sex, she was guilty of prostitution. If she practiced a 'wrong' kind of sex, she could be guilty of sodomy. If she had sex with another woman, 'some kind of abomination took place, although authorities weren't exactly sure what'.[33] A woman was supposed to remain virginal until her wedding night and a man who lured her to bed by a promise of marriage was guilty of the crime of seduction. The only permissible sex was heterosexual, copulative, marital intercourse.[34] Anything different was an affront to the woman's chastity, and it was the duty of the state, as *parens patriae*, to protect the woman's chastity by all available means. As the court in the influential opinion of *Biggs v State* said, 'In what has society a deeper concern than in the protection of female purity, and the marriage relation?'[35]

---

[32] Ray Rossi, 'VOTE: Should there be a law making "rape by fraud" a crime?' (*New Jersey 101.5 FM (WKXW-FM)*, 24 November 2014) <http://nj1015.com/should-there-be-a-law-making-rape-by-fraud-a-crime> accessed 19 December 2015.

[33] Jud Rubenfeld, 'The Riddle of Rape by Deception and the Myth of Sexual Autonomy' (2013) 122 Yale LJ 1372, 1381 (citations omitted).

[34] ibid 1382.

[35] 29 Ga 723, 729 (1860).

The worst sexual transgression a woman could commit was marital infidelity: it breached not only her 'female purity' but also her husband's rights. In his *Commentaries on the Laws of England*, William Blackstone described adultery as a public crime and a civil injury of which 'surely there can be no greater'.[36] The origin of the offense of adultery lay in the property notions of the wife. Under the common law, 'the very being or legal existence of the woman [was] suspended during the marriage, or at least [was] incorporated and consolidated into that of the husband: under whose wing, protection and *cover*, she performe[d] everything'.[37] In return for support and protection, the wife owed her husband 'consortium' of legal obligations that included sexual intercourse.[38] Since adultery interfered with the husband's exclusive entitlements, it was perceived as 'the highest possible invasion of property,'[39] similar to theft. In fact, civil actions for adultery evolved from actions for enticing away a servant from a master and thus depriving the master of the quasi-proprietary interest in his services.[40]

The legal consequences of adultery were severe. In 1650, the Puritans of the Commonwealth enacted a statute that made adultery a capital offense punishable by death, and although this statute was nullified after the Restoration, the Puritans in the American colonies made adultery with a married woman a capital offense. Later, when the laws in most colonies were relaxed, death was replaced with a fine for men and flogging for women. Sometimes, adulterers were punished by life-long shaming. Like the heroine of the classic Hawthorne novel *The Scarlet Letter*, they could be forced to wear the embroidered letter 'A' (for adultery) on their garments or have the letter burned into their foreheads.[41]

Perception of adultery as a serious offense has determined its role as a legal defense for the deceived husband who discovered the adultery and killed the lover or (in later cases) the unfaithful wife. '[A] man cannot receive a higher provocation,' wrote Judge Holt in 1707.[42] He thought it to

---

[36] 3 Bl Comm 139.

[37] ibid 442.

[38] Dan B Dobbs, Robert E Keeton and David G Owen, *Prosser and Keeton on the Law of Torts* (5th edn, West Group 1984) 916.

[39] *R v Mawgridge* (1707) Kel 119, 137.

[40] Dobbs (n 36) 915-16.

[41] John D'Emilio and Estelle B Freedman, *Intimate Matters: A History of Sexuality in America* (2nd edn, University of Chicago Press 1997) 28.

[42] ibid.

be an anomaly of law that a husband who caught his wife in an act with another man and killed the offender was not entitled to complete justification.[43]

Until relatively recently, a few American states, by a statute or court decision, regarded killing in these circumstances as justifiable homicide.[44] For example, in Georgia, a person could be justified if he killed his spouse's lover in order to prevent the beginning or completion of an adulterous act.[45] The rule originated in *Biggs v State*, in which the court interpreted the justifiable homicide statute to include killing by a husband of his wife's paramour:

> The wife cannot surrender herself to another. It is treason against the conjugal rights (…) and if the wife is too weak to save herself, is it not the privilege of the jury to say whether the strong arm of the husband may not interpose, to shield and defend her from pollution?[46]

The woman's chastity and the man's marital entitlement to her exclusive sexual possession are the two common themes running from the cases and commentaries of the 18th century into recent modernity. The same two rationales have determined the traditional scope of the crime of 'rape-by-fraud'. The interests this crime sought to protect were the woman's chastity and the man's exclusive right to sexual possession of his wife. Thus, conviction could be obtained only when the woman was chaste—*she either did not consent to sex at all or consented to what she believed to be marital intercourse*—and when the husband was robbed of his exclusive entitlement.

In the last half-century, western society has undergone major social transformations—from the woman's role in the family and society to the public attitude toward marriage and sex. Fornication and adultery have

---

[43] ibid 138.

[44] NM Stat Ann s 40A-2-1 (1972); 1963 NM Laws ch 303, s 2–4 (justifying the use of 'deadly force upon another who was at the time of the homicide in the act of having sexual intercourse with the accused's wife'); repealed, 1973 NM Laws ch 241, s 6; 1876 Utah Laws 587; 1857 Tex Crim Stat 110, 1879 Tex Crim Stat 77, 1895 Tex Crim Stat 405, 1911 Tex Crim Stat 841 (justifying homicide 'when committed by the husband upon the person of any one taken in the act of adultery with the wife, provided the killing takes place before the parties to the act have separated'); repealed, 1973 Tex Gen Laws ch 399, s 3(a).

[45] *Campbell v State*, 49 SE 2d 867, 870 (Ga 1948).

[44] (n 35).

been largely decriminalized, and even where those laws still remain on the books, they are hardly ever enforced.[47] Similarly, seduction laws are long gone. Homosexual relationships are legal. And generally speaking, legislating morality is no longer perceived as legitimate state business.[48] At the same time, criminal law has eliminated the special entitlements of a man with respect to his wife. The traditional marital exemption from rape is no longer available; the justifiable homicide of a wife's lover has been abolished entirely; and at least one American jurisdiction explicitly eliminated the discovery of adultery as the grounds for mitigation from murder to manslaughter.[49] All in all, 'female purity' and the husband's marital 'entitlements' are no longer among the values which criminal law seeks (or may legitimately seek) to protect. Therefore, if we believe that sex-by-deception ought to be punished, we need to reject the historical rationales for rape-by-fraud and establish new rationales that reflect our current moral and political values.

Autonomy as the Modern Rationale for Rape-by-Fraud

The obvious candidate for the modern rationale for the rape-by-fraud law is autonomy, usually understood as an individual's capacity for self-determination and self-governance. The ability to give free, rational and informed consent is the ultimate manifestation of autonomy: by consenting to an act, a person waives a right he used to have and gives another person a certain privilege, power or immunity to do what he could not legitimately do before.[50] Deception interferes with personal autonomy because it distorts the choices open to the person and thus diminishes her ability to control her life. Even though her autonomy is not entirely destroyed (she is still free to make decisions about her life), she does not have a full opportunity to make the choices that reflect her goals and values.

---

[47] Martin J Siegel, 'For Better or for Worse: Adultery, Crime & the Constitution' (1991-92) 30 J Fam L 45. The Model Penal Code repealed adultery and fornication laws, the drafters calling them 'dead-letter statutes'. Model Penal Code pt II Commentaries, vol 1, 434-36 (Note following s 213).

[48] *Lawrence v Texas*, 539 US 558, 578 (2003).

[49] Md Code Ann, Crim Law s 2-207(b).

[50] See generally, Wesley Newcomb Hohfeld, *Fundamental Legal Conceptions* (Yale UP 1964).

Many courts have identified sexual autonomy as a *right* and the violation of this right as the essence of rape.[51] In the words of the U.S. Supreme Court, rape is a total contempt for the victim's sexual autonomy and her 'privilege of choosing those with whom intimate relationships are to be established. Short of homicide, it is the "ultimate violation of self"'.[52] Most scholars agree: the moral wrongness of rape lies in the violation of the victim's autonomy.[53]

A powerful dissenting view has been recently expressed by Jed Rubenfeld. He argues that the principle of autonomy cannot provide the foundation to the rape law:

---

[51] *Lawrence v Texas*, 539 US 558, 562 (2003) ('Liberty presumes an autonomy of self that includes (…) certain intimate conduct.'). See also *State ex rel MTS*, 609 A 2d 1266, 1278 (NJ 1992) (describing sexual autonomy as the 'right not only to decide whether to engage in sexual contact with another, but also to control the circumstances and character of that contact').

[52] *Coker v Georgia*, 433 US 584, 597 (1977) (plurality opinion).

[53] Susan Estrich, *Real Rape* (Harvard UP 1987) 102; Donald A Dripps, 'Beyond Rape: An Essay on the Difference between the Presence of Force and the Absence of Consent' (1992) 92 Colum L Rev 1780, 1785 (discussing sexual autonomy as 'the freedom to refuse to have sex with any one for any reason'); Dan Kahan, 'What Do Alternative Sanctions Mean?' (1996) 63 U Chi L Rev 591, 598 ('A rape, for example, is often more reprehensible than an ordinary assault – even if the assault results in greater physical injury – because the violation of a woman's sexual autonomy conveys greater disrespect for her worth than do most other violations of her person.'); Patricia J Falk, 'Rape By Drugs: A Statutory Overview and Proposals for Reform' (2002) 44 Ariz L Rev 131, 187 (the 'central value protected by sexual offense provisions is sexual autonomy (…), the violation of which represents a unique, not readily comparable, type of harm to the victim'). See also Stephen J Schulhofer, *Unwanted Sex: The Culture of Intimidation and the Failure of Law* (Harvard UP 1998) 16-17; Jonathan Herring, 'Mistaken Sex' [2005] Crim LR 511; Russell L Christopher and Kathryn H Christopher, 'Adult Impersonation: Rape-by-Fraud as a Defense to Statutory Rape' (2007) 101 NW U L Rev 75, 88. For a thoughtful discussion of autonomy as a 'bundle of rights,' see Stuart P. Green, "Lies, Rape, and Statutory Rape," in Austin Sarat (ed.), *Law and Lies: Deception and Truth-Telling in the American Legal System* (New York: Cambridge University Press, 2015), pp. 194-253, 206-207. I agree with Green when he writes:

> Sexual autonomy, similarly, can be thought of as a bundle of rights organized around the idea of securing for its possessor various forms of sexual self-determination. Sexual autonomy, on this view, is not a single, monolithic right to choose one's own sexual path, but rather a complex, multifarious collection of rights to engage in, or refrain from, various forms of sexual activity and sex-related conduct. ibid 207.

> If our criminal sex laws were really designed to recognize and vindicate a right of sexual autonomy, sex plus lies should equal jail time, whether the lie was a false claim of bachelorhood, 'I love you,' or any other material misrepresentation reasonably calculated to induce another person to have sex.[54]

Rubenfeld maintains that, as a general matter, sex-by-deception should not be criminalized: deception is part of life.[55] Few people know the whole truth about their sexual partners, at least at first; love is a 'vast engine of deception'; and most of us conceal some relevant information and even tacitly mislead others.[56] He writes:

> Clothing and underclothing can falsify. Make-up and hair dye can deceive. All cosmetics misrepresent. They can designedly and quite effectively convey false information concerning age, hair color, lost teeth, skin color or quality, bodily characteristics, genetic predispositions, ethnicity, and so on.[57]

Consequently, Rubenfeld insists that punishing sex-by-deception is untenable and undesirable, which leaves us no choice but to denounce sexual autonomy as the foundational principle of rape law. To replace autonomy, Rubenfeld proposes an alternative principle of self-possession. According to it, people possess their bodies; that is, people are in control of their bodies.[58] The evil of rape (like torture or slavery) consists of taking control of someone else's body. Sex-by-deception is outside of the reach of the rape law because a fraud victim does not lose his self-possession. 'He is manipulated, but his person – elementally, physically – remains his own. Fraud is an offense against autonomy, not self-possession.'[59]

Like some other scholars,[60] I do not find this self-possession argument particularly persuasive. It is not clear to me why criminal law ought to protect only the 'elemental, physical' control of one's body. Suppose a

---

[54] Rubenfeld (n 33) 1410.

[55] Rubenfeld would not object to a specific statute, for example, such that would criminalize lying about STDs. ibid 1416-17.

[56] ibid 1416.

[57] ibid.

[58] ibid 1426 ('Almost all of us enjoy a basic integration of mind and body that gives us an irreducible measure of physical governance over our bodies and makes our bodies our own.').

[59] ibid 1432.

[60] <www.yalelawjournal.org/forum> (vol 123) accessed 19 December 2015.

woman submits to the unwanted sex because she is threatened with imminent violence against her child. Her person remains her own, at least 'elementally, physically,' even though her apparent consent is clearly not free or voluntary. Shouldn't this violation of her autonomy be viewed as rape even though the woman maintains certain control of her body? Shouldn't the violations of the victims' autonomy in the sexual impersonation cases and cases like *Minkowski* be viewed as rape? The victims in those cases did not lose the 'elemental, physical' control of their bodies. And yet, their consent should hardly be considered valid. Finally, how would the self-possession rationale account for the cases in which the victims lacked the very capacity for consent, like in the situations of sex with a minor or sex with a mentally incompetence? Should a man who bought an 8-year old's 'consent' to sex using gifts or promises be relieved of criminal responsibility because the child did not lose the 'elemental, physical' control of her body? I doubt that Rubenfeld would hold so and I suggest that these lacunas are too big for a successful theory of rights.

Even though I reject Rubenfeld's self-possession argument, I completely share his line-drawing concern: if the basis for punishing rape is the violation of the victim's sexual autonomy, then, in theory, any act that violates the victim's sexual autonomy should be classified as rape. As one Israeli court acknowledged:

> [D]efining the offense ... is not simple ... and there is a danger of a slippery slope: Will it be considered rape every time a man lies to a woman concerning a detail which she considers of essence and because of it she decides to have intercourse with him? For example, a woman who does not wish to date any man older than 35 years old is approached on a dating site by a man who identifies himself as 32 years old. After she has intercourse with him, she incidentally finds out that he is 40 years old; is that rape? After all, this is an important detail in her eyes.[61]

It appears that, to maintain the autonomy rationale as the basis for rape law, we have two choices: one, to hold that, whenever consent to sex is obtained by a material lie (namely, the lie but for which such consent

---

[61] *Saliman* (n 19). The *Boro* court had a similar concern: 'It is not difficult to conceive of reasons why the Legislature may have consciously wished to leave the matter where it lies. Thus, as a matter of degree, where consent to intercourse is obtained by promises of travel, fame, celebrity and the like—ought the liar and seducer to be chargeable as a rapist? Where is the line to be drawn?' (n 8).

would not have been granted),[62] the deceiver commits a sexual offense; and two, to admit that sometimes the absence of consent does not result in a crime.

Tom Dougherty adopts the first choice, 'we should hold that there is a powerful case for rape law to consider sex-by-deception as a serious sexual crime whenever the deception is material to the victim's consent'.[63] Dougherty acknowledges the practical difficulties of establishing whether someone culpably deceived another into sex as well as the difficulties of framing a law that penalizes only seriously wrong misconduct.[64] Yet, he concludes that, assuming those worries could be assuaged, 'we should reluctantly accept that someone can be guilty of rape-by-deception by falsely saying he went to Yale'.[65]

To me, this result is unacceptable. As much as we value people's sexual autonomy, we have other values that we may want to protect too.

- The rights of due process and fair notice would be violated by the vague or overly broad laws attempting to punish sex procured by all sorts of lies.[66]
- Such laws would almost inevitably come into conflict with the freedom of speech and expression.
- They would equally inevitably infringe upon the people's right to privacy.
- Such laws would bring the state powerfully back into legislating morality.
- As a policy matter, a total ban on lying will negatively affect people's ability to reinvent themselves and have a 'fresh start'.
- The overbroad character of those laws would leave too much discretion to the prosecutors and could lead to selective prosecution and

---

[62] A material lie may come in the form of active deception or a failure to disclose, coupled with the knowledge that the undisclosed information is crucial for the other party's granting or denying consent. A case may be made that active deception is morally more reprehensible than the passive, and yet, as in many other areas of law (from medical law to real estate law), when the offender fails to disclose important information which, as he knows, may result in the other party's denying consent, the apparent consent is deemed invalid, and the offender is deemed as much at fault as in the case of active deception.

[63] Tom Dougherty, 'No Way Around Consent: A Reply to Rubenfeld on "Rape-by-Deception"' (2013) 123 Yale Law Journal 321, 331.

[64] ibid 332.

[65] ibid 333.

[66] This concern was the reason the legislative proposal in Massachusetts was voted down. Short, 'Massachusetts missed the boat on defending women!' (n 31).

discrimination of the less powerful political groups.
- Politically, turning a massive part of citizenry into potential criminals could generate distrust of the government and social order.

In short, the laws that criminalize *any* sex-by-deception would have enormous economic, political, and moral costs.

Furthermore, the 'all or nothing' approach to the protection of sexual autonomy is overbroad and untenable: we would have to find someone guilty of rape not only for falsely saying he went to Yale but also in any situation in which the actual sexual act differs from what the parties have agreed upon. Say, a man consents to sex on the (mistaken) assumption that his partner will not kiss him on the lips. If in fact she kisses him, has she committed a sexual offense? Or if a woman kisses her sleeping husband before going to work (a sleeping person obviously cannot give valid consent), has she become a criminal?

Even more dramatically, there will *always* be some unconsented-to component to the otherwise consensual sexual act. It will be there, without anyone's fault, simply because it is impossible to achieve full congruity between the parties' expectations (and even explicit agreement) and the actual encounter. A person may make a move that is not offensive in any sense, but it has not been agreed upon. In short, pursuant to Dougherty's logic, we would have to criminalize almost any sexual act. We may have to criminalize even those acts that are consensual in every single move if the *meaning* of the act is not the same for one party as it is for the other.[67] If one party would not have agreed to a sexual act but for the mistaken belief that it was the manifestation of 'happily ever after,' the other party could be guilty of violating that party's autonomy and, therefore, guilty of rape. This is obviously absurd.

In other words, Dougherty's reluctant choice in favor of *complete* sexual autonomy is unnecessary, undesirable, and unrealistic: even if we treat sexual autonomy very seriously, and sacrifice numerous other values for its

---

[67] The interesting observation about the meaning of the act was made by Jonathan Herring as one critique of the traditional distinction between fraud-in-the-factum and fraud-in-the-inducement. 'A prostitute may well regard sexual activities with her client as completely different from sexual relations with her partner. Similarly a religious person may regard marital intercourse as expression of spiritual union blessed by God, while an extra-marital union as an odious sin.' Herring, 'Mistaken Sex' (n 53) 514.

protection, we simply cannot protect *complete* sexual autonomy.

Could we perhaps soften the rule and say that the right to sexual autonomy is not absolute but instead is limited to the circumstances in which *a reasonable person* may legitimately expect the state to protect her interests? As a policy matter, or as a pragmatic and (relatively) easy to apply rule, this modification may help. After all, many criminal law doctrines use the 'reasonable person' standard, despite its many shortcomings. Under this standard, as applied to rape-by-fraud, the victim's consent would be vitiated *only* if the lie material to the actual victim would also be material to a reasonable person.

Should we adopt this approach, we would have to say one of two things. One would be that a person does not have the absolute right not to be subjected to nonconsensual sex; that right is limited to the standards of a 'reasonable person'. This approach, known as 'specification,' seems deeply flawed. Pursuant to it, a woman who realized her unreasonable mistake and pushed away her deceitful partner to stop the intercourse would be guilty of an assault. After all, she did not have the right not to be subjected to that intercourse (her mistake was unreasonable); thus she had no right to use force to stop it. And if at that moment her frustrated partner pulled out a knife, she would be powerless to defend herself lawfully because, under the specification theory, she would be deemed the initial aggressor, and the initial aggressor (at least in the majority of the U.S. jurisdictions) has no right to use deadly force in self-defense.[68] That outcome cannot be right.

The second thing we could say appears much more sensible. We could say that people have an *absolute* right to sexual inviolability, and any lie, material to the victim's consent, violates the victim's autonomy, regardless of how the same lie affects a reasonable person. And yet, as we saw before, it is impossible and undesirable to punish *any* violation of sexual autonomy. Therefore, as much as we take sexual autonomy seriously, we have to admit that certain violations of sexual autonomy are beyond the reach of criminal law: *nonconsensual sex always violates sexual autonomy but does not always deserve punishment*. This conclusion is much less radical than it may first appear.

---

[68] Sandford H Kadish et al, Criminal Law and Its Process 870 (ASPEN 9th ed). For more critique of the specification theory, see Vera Bergelson, *Victims' Rights and Victims' Wrongs: Comparative Liability in Criminal Law* (Stanford University Press 2009) 75-77.

Consider an analogy: I have the right to physical inviolability and this right is absolute.[69] However, this right of mine is violated practically every day. Sometimes, it is violated innocently as when a fellow subway rider falls onto me at an unexpected abrupt train stop. Sometimes, the violation is negligent as when the abrupt train stop is not so unexpected and a reasonable person would have held on to a rail. Moreover, sometimes the violation is even subjectively culpable (reckless) as when a person bumps into me while walking and texting. He has already bumped into several people earlier that day, so he is well aware of the substantial and unjustifiable risk of texting on the go. I would argue that I have the right that all those people (from the innocent to the reckless) not interfere with my physical inviolability, and yet it appears that those interferences are beyond the reach of criminal law.

In the same sense, a person has the absolute right not to be deceived about the matters that are material for his sexual consent. And yet, the violation of his right does not necessarily warrant criminal sanctions. What does this discussion establish? It establishes that we may have more choices than the ones presented by Rubenfeld and Dougherty.

We may persuasively maintain that the rationale behind protecting peoples' rights against rape (including rape-by-fraud) is *sexual autonomy.* Yet, while reinforcing sexual autonomy as the foundational principle of rape law, we do not need to fall into the extremes and prosecute someone who falsely claimed he had gone to Yale. What we need instead is a cohesive set of principles that would let us distinguish between the permissible and impermissible lies used to obtain sexual consent. In this paper, I will try to outline some of those principles.

Let's go back to my physical inviolability argument. I must confess that, to make my point, I chose easy examples. They were easy in two ways. One, in each scenario, the violation of my rights was unintentional, and generally speaking, we are much less likely to punish an unintentional violation than the one done purposely or knowingly. And two, the inflicted harm in each scenario was insignificant. Had the texting person accidentally pushed me in front of a running train, we would have treated his reckless violation of my rights quite differently. Thus, what I chose to do in my examples was to minimize (a) the actor's *culpability* and (b) the resulting *harm.* In the retributivist system of justice, these two variables usually control one's just

---

[69] Even when it is infringed upon by a non-culpable agent, I still retain my claim that it not be infringed upon. ibid.

deserts and determine the permissibility and the amount of punishment.[70] It would make sense, therefore, to explore their relationship in the context of sexual lies.

The underlying premise for this exploration is that violation of one's autonomy is not an all-or-nothing event; instead its magnitude may be graded: some violations are greater than other ones. The degree of the violation is determined by the interplay of the actor's culpability and the amount of harm suffered by the victim, which is determined by the importance of the welfare interest(s) set back by the violator and the seriousness of the injury to those welfare interest(s). Thus, a violation of one's autonomy would be more serious—and would justify a more serious punishment—if the perpetrator acted with a higher level of culpability (e.g., recklessly rather than negligently) and violated a more crucial right of the victim (e.g., the right not to be killed rather than the right not to be shoved).

The Interplay of the Actor's Culpability and the Resulting Harm in Cases of Sex-by Deception

(a) Innocent Actor. When the actor is not at fault at all (like when a fellow subway rider falls onto me at an unexpected abrupt train stop), *the amount of inflicted harm is irrelevant*: my fellow rider is not criminally liable. In the same sense, when a woman innocently misinforms her partner that she is free of HIV, she is not guilty of any crime even though that information was crucial for her partner's sexual consent. She is not guilty even if he contracts the HIV and later dies of AIDS. The outcome would be different, of course, had she misinformed her partner negligently or recklessly.

---

[70] Michael Moore, 'Victims and Retribution: A Reply to Professor Fletcher' (1999) 3 Buffalo Criminal Law Review 65, 86 ('it's not culpability alone that counts in determining desert (…) Rather, the amount of harm caused determines the seriousness of the wrong done, and the amount of wrong done does affect desert.'). I defended a similar view in Vera Bergelson 'Victims and Perpetrators: An Argument for Comparative Liability in Criminal Law' (2005) 8 Buffalo Criminal Law Review 385, 421-22. The opposing school of thought maintains that the amount of harm is irrelevant to the perpetrator's just deserts. See, for example, Herbert LA Hart, *Punishment and Responsibility* (Oxford University Press 1968) 131. ('Why should the accidental fact that an intended harmful outcome has not occurred be a ground for punishing less a criminal who may be equally dangerous and equally wicked?'). The debate over the moral and legal significance of the resulting harm has a long history and still continues.

(b) Negligent or Reckless Actor. When the perpetrator is at fault but does not act intentionally, the amount of the inflicted harm should determine whether he be held criminally liable. In a nutshell, it may be argued that, in our imperfect world, we may not legitimately expect everyone around us to be smart, thoughtful, and careful. We are doomed to come across some people who cannot help being dim, slow or clumsy. What we can expect though is that the people do their best not to set back our vital interests. The more serious is the interest (not being killed versus not being shoved), the stronger is our claim that others act reasonably.

Of course, determining the amount of harm is an issue of its own. How much shall the victim's view count in this determination? Say, Gayle Newland's girlfriend felt seriously violated—to her, the deception was worse than forcible rape. She told the court, 'People get raped by males and it sounds sick but I think I'd prefer it.' [71] Should the sentence reflect the victim's perception of harm?

Consider Leo Katz's illustrative hypotheticals. In one of them, a man is about to rape a woman. At the last moment, the woman pleads, 'I would rather die than be violated,' so he obligingly kills her. At his trial, the defense argues that, although the defendant is certainly guilty of a heinous crime, his punishment should be no more severe than punishment for rape. After all, the victim herself preferred murder to rape, i.e., regarded it as a lesser harm. In the opposite hypothetical, the perpetrator rapes the woman despite her desperate plea to take her life instead. At the trial, the prosecutor demands the death penalty for the defendant. He argues that,

---

[71] Stephanie Linning, 'I'd rather have been raped by a man, says woman "sexually assaulted by female friend who used bandages and a sex toy to pretend she was male"' *Daily Mail* (London, 8 September 2015) <www.dailymail.co.uk/news/article-3226030/Woman-posed-man-befriend-naive-25-year-old-Facebook-used-bandages-bind-chest-sex-toy-dupe-thinking-male.html> accessed 20 December 2015. It appears that the judge took the victim's view into account when deciding on the punishment: Newland's sentence is disproportionate to other sentences in similar cases. Gemma Barker was jailed for 30 months for tricking girls into sex by pretending to be a boy. '"Not a flicker of remorse": Girl who disguised herself as a boy to trick female friends into sex jailed' (n 27). And Justine McNally was sentenced to three years after admitting the same. She was freed after less than three months after the Court of Appeal ruled the sentence to be too harsh. Robson (n 27). I doubt Newland's sentence will survive the appeal.

although ordinarily the death penalty may not be imposed for rape, this case of rape is worse than murder: didn't the victim herself feel so?[72]

Obviously, neither argument should succeed. Partly, because the 'victim cares only about one dimension of the perpetrator's activities—the expected harm,'[73] whereas criminal law cares about harm as one of several criteria of a wrongdoing.[74] And partly, because the meaning of harm in criminal law is not limited to each victim's idiosyncratic perception of harm. Criminal law embodies a uniform hierarchical set of moral and legal principles, based on the values assigned by society to specific interests and the magnitude of a setback to those interests. For the purposes of punishment, the meaning of harm is objective and may not depend on the subjective perceptions of any constituency, be it the victim, the victim's family, the sentencing judge or a broader social group.

So, going back to balancing the considerations of harm and culpability, it seems fair to say that, *when the harm or risk of harm is to one's vital welfare interests (life; grave, long-lasting or irreversible physical harm), even a low level of culpability, such as negligence, should be punishable.* Say, negligently failing to inform a sexual partner about one's HIV infection warrants criminal punishment. On the other hand, negligently or even recklessly failing to provide accurate information about one's age should be outside of the criminal law jurisdiction, even though in each case, the deceived partner would not have consented to sex had she known the truth.

(c) Intentional Liar. The problem of intentionally lying for the sake of procuring a partner's consent to sex is of course at the crux of rape-by-fraud. In the paradigmatic rape-by-fraud case, the perpetrator knowingly deceives his victim about a material fact, with the purpose of having sex. The lies usually fall into the following categories:

1. A lie about the act itself (the victim believes she is undergoing a medical procedure);
2. A lie about the purpose of the act (the victim understands that the act is sexual but believes that it has a non-sexual meaning, e.g., medical treatment);

---

[72] Leo Katz, *Ill Gotten Gains: Evasion, Blackmail, Fraud and Kindred Puzzles of the Law* (University of Chicago Press 1996) 147.
[73] ibid 151.
[74] ibid.

3. Impersonation of a particular person with whom the victim has a
    relationship (spouse; boyfriend; girlfriend);
4. Misrepresentation of a fact or false promise related to the sexual act
    (lying about being free of STDs or falsely promising to wear a
    condom);
5. Misrepresentation of a fact about the sexual partner (one's age;
    biological sex; marital status; education);
6. False promises unrelated to the sexual act (of marriage; stardom;
    monetary compensation or procurement of benefits).

An intentional violation of one's rights is a serious wrongdoing, even
when the resulting harm is minimal. If a person has a legal right, others
have the legal duty not to infringe upon it.[75] When this duty is broken
intentionally, the wrongdoer deliberately disregards the rights of the victim
and the rules of the society. There are strong reasons to criminalize
intentional violations of legal rights even in the absence of any actual
harm. Say, if someone burglarizes my apartment but, not finding anything
of value, leaves it the way he found it and I never learn about this
intrusion, the burglar has nevertheless committed a crime and deserves
punishment. Even when the offender increases my wellbeing (say, because
the offender had kidnapped me, I missed my flight and avoided a deadly
plane crash), she still may be legitimately punished. In short, when the
culpability reaches the level of intent, the amount of harm plays no role in
framing a criminal prohibition.[76] *Any intentional violation of a right
recognized by criminal law may be punished.*[77]

Rights against Lies

The crucial question thus is: what are our legal rights with respect to
various lies used for securing sexual consent? Let's examine more closely
the categories listed above.

1. *A lie about the act itself.* We certainly have the right not to be deceived
    about the act itself. This right is recognized in all areas of law: consent
    to boxing is not consent to having an ear bitten off; consent to signing

---

[75] Hohfeld (n 48) 36-38; Judith Jarvis Thomson, *The Realm of Rights* (Harvard UP
1990) 348-53.
[76] The amount of harm would still be relevant of course for the grading of the
offense and for sentencing.
[77] I am not arguing that any intentional right violation should be punished. As a
policy matter, society may prefer to leave certain right violations (e.g. such that
caused little or no actual harm) unpunished.

a book is not consent to signing a royalty agreement; and so on. In the same sense, consent to a medical procedure is not consent to sex. Almost universally, deception about the very nature of the act eliminates consent.[78]

2. *A lie about the purpose of the act.* Understanding the purpose of an act is almost as essential as understanding its nature, and a person who was intentionally deceived about the purpose of an act, cannot be said to have given meaningful consent. Suppose, I was asked to push a button to light up a Christmas tree. I pushed the button. The Christmas tree did not light up; instead a building across the street blew into pieces. Can we fairly say that, by consenting to push the button, I automatically consented to blowing up the building? Of course not; I was misinformed about the true meaning of my act.

Similarly, in the sexual context, a person may consent to a physical act without comprehending its true meaning. In *R v Williams*,[79] for example, the defendant, a singing coach, had sexual intercourse with one of his pupils while telling her that he was performing the act in order to open her air passages to improve her singing. The court held the pupil's consent invalid and convicted the defendant of rape.

To sum up, consent to an act requires at least the basic understanding of its purpose, which is inconsistent with the deliberate deception. Since people have the right not to have nonconsensual sex, they have the legal right not to be lied to about the purpose of the act. Increasingly, jurisdictions move in the direction of recognizing that right. In the aftermath of *Boro*, California has revised its rape law.[80] Today, the definition of rape covers Boro's deception and includes 'fraudulent representation that the sexual penetration served a

---

[78] In the jurisdictions in which conviction of rape requires proof of force, lies about the nature of the act are still punishable—either as a lesser sexual offense (this is the approach taken by the Model Penal Code) or as battery.

[79] *Williams* [1923] 1 KB 340 (CCA).

[80] In 1987, Boro was apprehended again for the same scam and prosecuted under this new law that was inspired by him. Daniel J. Slomnicki, 'Rape by Fraud, Deception, or Impersonation – An Addition to New York's Penal Law: Rape in the First Degree Statute' (New York State Bar Association, 14 November 2013) <http://nysbar.com/blogs/lawstudentconnection/2013/11/rape_by_fraud_deception _or_imp.html> accessed 20 December 2015.

professional purpose when it served no professional purpose'.[81] Similarly, the Sexual Offenses Act adopted in the United Kingdom in 2003, added the words 'or purpose' to the definition of rape-by-fraud, so now it includes 'fraud as to the nature *or purpose* of the sexual act'.[82]

3. *Impersonation of a particular person with whom the victim has a relationship.* In most instances, consent is specific as to the person to whom it is granted.[83] So, logically, consent to sex with one partner should not be equal to consent to sex with a different partner. However, this logic is not universally shared. In the United States, the jurisdictions are split (with the significant majority rejecting sex-by-impersonation as a crime), and two very similar acts may lead to no punishment in one state and a lengthy sentence in another. In Massachusetts, for example, the court deemed the defendant not guilty in a case in which he disguised himself as his brother to have sex with the brother's girlfriend.[84] In contrast, in Tennessee, the perpetrator, dubbed by press as the 'Fantasy Man,' was found guilty of rape and sentenced to fifteen years in prison. He tricked numerous women into having sex with him blindfolded by pretending to be someone they knew and trusted.[85]

Punishing sexual impersonation appears warranted. Consider an analogy: suppose, a greedy surgeon has falsely promised several patients to operate on them on the same day. Yet, after each patient is sedated, the surgeon leaves the room, letting his assistants conduct the surgery. Few would disagree that the patients' legal rights were violated when the surgeon, personally known to the patient, was replaced by an assistant with whom the patient had no doctor-patient relationship. Similarly, the Massachusetts victim's rights were violated when a man with whom she had no relationship impersonated her boyfriend and had sex with her. And if the greedy surgeon deserves punishment, so does the boyfriend's brother. Perhaps even more so: because of the intimate nature of sex, sexual consent is even more

---

[81] Cal Penal Code s 261(a)(4)(D) (West 2013).

[82] Sexual Offenses Act 2003, s 76(2)(a).

[83] Not always, of course. I may leave some candies at my front door on Halloween night. By doing so, I consent to those candies being taken by various trick-or-treaters whose identity I don't know.

[84] *Suliveres v Commonwealth*, 865 NE 2d 1086 (Mass 2007).

[85] *Mitchell v Campbell*, 88 SW 3d 561, 563 (Tenn Ct App 2002).

person-specific than medical consent.

Partner impersonation, however, should be distinguished from the situation in which the victim is deceived merely about her partner's name or status. Say, at a party, a man lies to a woman that he is a famous producer in order to impress her and have sex with her. This is not impersonation in the strict sense, like in the examples above in which one body was effectively substituted for another. This kind of deception should be more properly viewed as misrepresentation of a fact about the sexual partner, which I will address shortly.

4. *Misrepresentation of a fact or false promise related to the sexual act.* Any sexual act inherently involves risks. It may be disappointing. It may be painful, physically or emotionally. It may result in an unwanted pregnancy or a disease. Should we hold that *any* lie about the sexual act violates a legal right?

As a general matter, I doubt that such a legal right exists (see discussion below). To the extent it does, it has to be derivative of some other legal right, e.g., the right not to be harmed physically. In its derivative form, then, the right not to be lied to about the sexual intercourse would be limited to the right not to be lied to about the facts relevant to the possibility of physical harm. This limited scope of the legal right intuitively makes sense—pursuant to it, a person lying about his enormous sexual prowess would not be criminally liable, but a person lying about being free of STDs or falsely promising to wear a condom would be guilty of a crime.[86] (I will discuss the nature of this crime later.) The higher is the probability that the risk of harm would materialize, and the more important is the jeopardized interest, the stronger is the legal right (claim) not to be lied to about it.

5. *Misrepresentation of a fact about the sexual partner.* Just like in the previous category, there does not seem to be an absolute right against lying. Clearly, lying for self-preferential reasons is morally wrong. But there is a strong autonomy-based argument that an individual should have the moral right to do what is morally wrong. For example, one should have the right to spend all the money won in a lottery to buy racehorses and champagne while refusing to donate any of it to a

---

[86] See, for example, *Assange v Swedish Prosecution Authority* [2011] EWHC 2849 (Admin), [2011] WLR (D) 315; *R v EB* [2006] EWCA Crim 2945, [2007] 1 WLR 1567.

desperately deserving charity.[87] The moral right to do what is morally wrong has been the subject of a fascinating philosophical debate to which I will not attempt to contribute.

Instead, I will stress a much less debatable point that, regardless of whether there is a moral right to do a morally wrong thing, in countless circumstances, there is a *legal* right to do what is morally wrong.[88] Jeremy Waldron maintains that this legal right may be construed either as a Hohfeldian privilege '(indicating merely the absence of a legal duty constraining the right-bearer with respect to the action specified)' or 'the stronger claim-right (indicating that others have certain duties to the right-bearer in respect to the action specified)'.[89] I suggest that, with respect to lying, this legal right can only be a privilege: I may not have a legal duty to tell my husband the real price of that Gucci bag I bought yesterday, but neither does my frenemy have a legal duty to keep her mouth shut about it.

So, since there is no general legal duty to tell the truth, then (like in the previous category) one's grievance relating to the sexual partner's lie may be only derivative. But is there a legal right that would support such a grievance? Misrepresentation of age, marital status or accomplishment cannot hurt the aggrieved party physically. It may of course lead to emotional distress (with further physical consequences) or financial or career disappointment, but such harms are not within the sphere of sex crimes law. Thus, those lies may not be criminally prosecuted. Naturally, by not prosecuting someone who falsely introduces himself as a famous producer, we as society do not condone his lie; we merely admit that we have no standing in this private matter.[90]

---

[87] Jeremy Waldron, 'A Right to Do Wrong' (Oct 1981) vol 92 Ethics No 1, 21.

[88] Ronald Dworkin, *Taking Rights Seriously* (Harvard UP 1977) 188 (suggesting that an individual may 'have the right to do something that is the wrong thing for him to do').

[89] ibid 23 Waldron ('I may be legally at liberty to perform a certain act even though that act is not permissible from the moral point of view; or, others may have a legal duty to me to refrain from interfering with my performance of a certain act, even though the act is morally wrong and their interference morally permissible.').

[90] R Anthony Duff, 'Harms and Wrongs' (2001) 5 Buffalo Criminal Law Review 13, 37. That does not of course preclude the deceived person from taking the liar to a civil court. If she successfully proves that the discovery of the defendant's lie about being a famous producer made her ill; that the defendant had acted at least

Accordingly, I disagree with the convictions in *State of Israel v Mehadakar*, in which the defendant lied about his age, and *Kashur v State*, to the extent the perpetrator's ethnic, religious and marital misrepresentations were held to be sufficient for the charge of rape.

I equally disagree with the conviction of Gayle Newland and other legal decisions involving misrepresentation of biological sex. One reason for the state to stay away from prosecuting those kinds of lies is compelling both morally and practically: there is more gray than black-and-white on the color spectrum of lies, half-lies, white lies, wishful thinking, and honest confusion about one's sexual identity.

Take Newland: she created the character of Kay Fortune at the age of 13 'because she found it difficult to speak to girls in real life'. By the age of 15 or 16, she had developed a Facebook profile of the young man. According to Newland, 'her accuser always knew she was pretending to be a man, and that her disguise was part of a sex game as they both struggled with being lesbians'.[91] Even if we disregard Newland's version of the story as far as her partner is concerned, we still have to face a person who was deeply ambivalent about her gender and sexual orientation.

Take a step further. Newland did not describe herself as transgender, but other people convicted for lying about their biological sex did. Consider Justine McNally.[92] Apparently, there was evidence that, prior to and at the time of the alleged offences (but not at the trial or thereafter), McNally identified as male: she lived, at least on a part-time basis, in the male gender role which made her 'feel more comfortable' and she stated her intention to undergo 'a sex change'.[93] Alex Sharpe persuasively argues that '[c]oupling transgender with

---

negligently with respect to the possibility of her developing the illness; and that her own fault was relatively insignificant, she may be entitled to a monetary compensation.

[91] Sophie Jane Evans and others, 'Ex-private schoolgirl who duped her friend into sex by pretending to be a man launches an appeal against her conviction' *Daily Mail* (London, 17 November 2015) <www.dailymail.co.uk/news/article-3322556/Ex-private-schoolgirl-duped-friend-sex-pretending-man-launches-appeal-against-conviction.html> accessed 20 December 2015.

[92] *McNally v R* [2013] EWCA Crim 1051, [2014] 1 QB 593.

[93] Alex Sharpe, 'Criminalising Sexual Intimacy: Transgender Defendants and the Legal Construction of Non-Consent' [2014] Criminal Law Review 207, 216.

impersonation, and therefore fraud, is to misunderstand the
phenomenon of transgender and its ontology'.[94]

In light of these concerns, I see the tendency of the U.K. courts to
analyze the misrepresentation of one's biological sex through the
theory of 'conditional consent' as highly disturbing and conceptually
flawed. The theory of 'conditional consent' used to be applied when
the perpetrator intentionally lied to the victim that he would wear a
condom[95] or withdraw before ejaculation.[96] Today, the Code for
Crown Prosecutors[97] puts the case of Justine McNally in the same
category as those lies. The *McNally* court used the theory of
'conditional consent' to hold that the defendant's deception destroyed
the victim's implicit condition: 'M chose to have sexual encounters
with a boy and her preference (her freedom to choose whether or not to
have a sexual encounter with a girl) was removed by the appellant's
deception.'[98]

Following the logic of this decision, almost any lie material to the
victim may be viewed as 'conditional consent' and result in the rape
conviction. The *McNally* court acknowledged that '[i]n reality, some
deceptions (such as, for example, in relation to wealth) will obviously

---

[94] ibid. But see Herring, 'Mistaken Sex' (n 53) 522-23 (arguing that a transgender
person is required to disclose her sexual history if this information is material for her
partner's sexual consent).
[95] *Assange* (n 86) (opining that defendant's 'conduct in having sexual intercourse
without a condom in circumstances where she had made clear she would only have
sexual intercourse if he used a condom would therefore amount to [a sexual]
offence').
[96] In *R (F) v DPP* [2013] EWHC 945 (Admin), the court stated:
  [S]he was deprived of choice relating to the crucial feature on which her
  original consent to sexual intercourse was based. Accordingly her consent
  was negated. Contrary to her wishes, and knowing that she would not have
  consented, and did not consent to penetration or the continuation of
  penetration if she had any inkling of his intention, he deliberately
  ejaculated within her vagina. In law, this combination of circumstances
  falls within the statutory definition of rape.
[97] The Code for Crown Prosecutors is described as 'a key document for the CPS
[The Crown Prosecutors Service]. It provides guidance to prosecutors on the
general principles they should apply when making decisions about prosecutions'.
<www.cps.gov.uk> accessed 20 December 2015.
[98] *McNally* (n 92) [26].

not be sufficient to vitiate consent,'[99] but there is no way to know where the court may draw the line in the next case, and the reality in which McNally is a convicted sexual predator is already disturbing enough.

6. *False promises unrelated to the sexual act itself.* The discussion of factual misrepresentations concerning the qualities of a sexual partner is equally applicable to the false promises of fame, marriage or monetary remuneration. As a general matter, giving a false promise is not a crime. To the extent that the state recognizes the contractual arrangement between the parties, it may be warranted to punish the perpetrator who has committed theft of services by fraudulently misleading the victim. So, in the legal regime, in which a contract for sexual services is legal, the state (arguably)[100] may punish fraudulent nonpayment to a prostitute the same way it punishes any fraudulent nonpayment; yet, this possibility has nothing to do with rape-by-fraud. Accordingly, I disapprove of the Australian court convicting a man of 'sexual intercourse without consent' for tricking a prostitute into providing services to him for free[101] as well as the Israeli court upholding conviction of rape-by-fraud on the basis of false promises of lodging and social security payments.[102]

I suggest that society should limit the reach of criminal law to regulating only those conflicts that jeopardize the most essential welfare interests of its citizens or endanger the public order.[103] Private conflicts should be resolved either without litigation or through private law suits. Thus, criminal law that respects sexual autonomy may and should punish the following as *some* crime:

* A lie about the act itself;
* A lie about the purpose of the act;

---

[99] ibid [25].

[100] The parenthetical reflects my skepticism about criminal punishment for any nonpayment.

[101] Megan Gorrey, 'Prostitute felt "violated" after man tricked her for free sex' *The Canberra Times* (Canberra, 6 February 2015) <www.canberratimes.com.au/act-news/prostitute-felt-violated-after-man-tricked-her-for-free-sex-20150206-137q6z.html> accessed 20 December 2015.

[102] *Saliman* (n 21).

[103] Herbert LA Hart, 'Immorality and Treason' (30 July 1959) 62 The Listener 162.

- Impersonation of a particular person with whom the victim has a relationship;
- Misrepresentation of a fact or a false promise related to the sexual act, to the extent that the lie violates or jeopardizes a welfare interest protected by criminal law;
- False promises unrelated to the sexual act, to the extent that the false promise is a part of an enforceable contract.[104]

Criminal law should not punish:

- Misrepresentation of a fact about the identified sexual partner;
- False promises unrelated to the sexual act (except as specified above).

What Crime Is It?

Deciding that certain deceptive and manipulative conduct deserves punishment still leaves open the question about the scope of rape-by-fraud. Which of the criminal transgressions should fairly be called 'rape'? Are all those transgressions equally bad? I suggest that they are not, and the wrongfulness of a transgression depends on the perpetrator's *culpability* and the victim's *harm*. That harm, in the context of sex-by-lies, depends on the magnitude of the violation of the victim's sexual autonomy. A lie about the act itself is intuitively the worst. The violation goes to the very core of sexual autonomy: the victim did not want to engage in a sexual act *at all*. This kind of deception is no better than any other nonviolent rape (e.g., sex with a person in a coma or sex with a minor).

Impersonation of another person with whom the victim has a relationship is a close second. Here too, the deception deprives the victim of his sexual autonomy. Consent to sex with a *different* person is essentially no consent at all. It is only fair to label and punish this wrongdoing as rape.[105]

Lying about the purpose or about another fact directly related to the sexual

---

[104] Once again, I take reservation on the issue of wisdom and justifiability of criminal punishment for any nonpayment.

[105] I agree with Sherry Colb who made a similar point. Sherry F Colb, 'Rape by Deception, Rape by Impersonation, and a New California Bill' (*Verdict*, 1 May 2013) <https://verdict.justia.com/2013/05/01/rape-by-deception-rape-by-impersonation-and-a-new-california-bill> accessed 20 December 2015 (observing that, 'at some level, she did not consent to have sex with this man. She consented to have sex with a different man, a distinct human being, who in fact was absent at the time.').

act, or giving a false promise directly related to the sexual act is a serious wrongdoing deserving of punishment. The victim's autonomy in these cases is certainly violated, but the degree of violation is not as high as in the first two categories. The victim at least has no objection to engaging in the sexual act with the particular person.

Thus, in the case of lying about the purpose of the act, the perpetrator may be convicted of a sexual offense but the offense must be of a lower degree than in the first two categories. It may be called sexual assault or gross sexual imposition or something else, and the punishment for it should be scaled down accordingly. The other two kinds of lies (false facts or promises directly related to the sexual act) should not vitiate the victim's sexual consent at all. To the extent those lies or omissions to tell the truth (intentional, reckless or negligent) cause or threaten physical harm (an STD or unwanted pregnancy), they may be punishable as a general assault or battery or criminal endangerment.[106]

Finally, a fraudulent promise unrelated to the sexual act only marginally violates the sexual autonomy of the victim. It may violate other rights though. Thus, a fraudulent promise to pay a prostitute may be punished as a form of theft in a society that recognizes prostitution as a legitimate business. Yet, such a false promise should not be classified as a sex crime.

Conclusion

In this paper, I examined the fascinating and disturbing legal developments in the area of rape-by-fraud. In the recent years, the doctrine of rape-by-fraud has been significantly expanded to provide grounds for criminal prosecution of the actors who lied to their partners to procure consent to sex. That expansion of the doctrine of rape-by-fraud has led to the overcriminalization of private conduct; inconsistent and conceptually flawed legal decisions; harsh verdicts; and public perception of discrimination against, and stigmatization of, certain social groups.

---

[106] I agree with the decision in *R v EB* [2006] EWCA Crim 2945, [2007] 1 WLR 1567. EB was HIV positive and failed to disclose this to his partner. The Court of Appeal held that a charge of rape could not lie in these circumstances. It opined, 'Where one party to sexual activity has a sexually transmissible disease which is not disclosed to the other party any consent that may have been given to that activity by the other party is not thereby vitiated. The act remains a consensual act.' [17].

Against this backdrop, I have tried to revisit the traditional doctrine of rape-by-fraud; questioned and rejected its historical rationales; argued in favor of an alternative rationale that better reflects our current moral and political values; and outlined new boundaries for rape-by-fraud laws.

I argued that the basis for punishing nonconsensual sex lies in the value we assign to sexual autonomy and that the right to sexual autonomy is absolute. I further argued that any lie material to the victim's consent violates that victim's autonomy. And yet, this autonomy violation and the resulting nonconsensual sex may not be punishable. Whether or not the perpetrator deserves punishment should be determined by the interplay of two essential criminal law categories—harm and culpability.

A nonculpable actor should not be punished, regardless of the amount of harm suffered by the victim. The punishment of a reckless or negligent actor should depend on the significance of the harm suffered by the victim. Finally, an actor who has intentionally violated any legal right of the victim deserves punishment, regardless of whether that violation has been accompanied by any actual harm.

To determine what legal rights a person may claim, I analyzed different categories of sexual lies. As a result of this analysis, I suggested that, when consent to sex is obtained by (a) lies about the nature of a sexual act or impersonation of a known sexual partner, the actor should be guilty of rape; (b) lies about the purpose of the sexual act, the actor should be guilty of a sexual crime of a lower degree; (c) lies about a fact related to the sexual act, the actor should be guilty of battery; (d) lies about the actor, which are unrelated to the sexual act, the actor should not be guilty of any offense; and (e) false promises unrelated to the sexual act, the actor should either not be guilty of any offense or be guilty of theft.

CHAPTER NINE

PERCEPTIONS OF CONSENT
IN ADULT MALE RAPE:
EVIDENCE-BASED AND INCLUSIVE
POLICY MAKING

NATALIA HANLEY AND PHILIP N.S. RUMNEY

Introduction

Interest in evidence-based policy making in the UK and elsewhere has been documented over many years.[1] There has also been much attention given to the issue of sexual violence from policy makers. Virtually all of this attention has been gendered in the sense that it has focused on female victims and male perpetrators. Given the gendered nature of rape, this is hardly surprising; however, to say that sexual violence and victimisation is a gendered phenomenon is not to suggest that males are invulnerable to sexual violation. Indeed, the empirical data makes clear that 'each and every body is permeable and appropriable'.[2] While the inclusion of males within the legal definition of rape under English law occurred more than twenty years ago,[3] policy development has not been similarly re-framed. It is the contention of this chapter that policy makers have failed to appropriately consider the experience of adult male victim-survivors as part of the UK government's Violence Against Women and Girls (VAWG) strategy and what is needed is an examination of female *and* male sexual victimisation at the policy level. This chapter will use findings from an empirical study of attitudes towards adult male rape, along with other data to examine the way in which myths and assumptions shape

---

[1] Ken Young et al, 'Social Science and the Evidence-based Policy Movement' [2002] 1 Social Policy and Society 215.

[2] Joanna Bourke, *Rape: A history from 1860 to the present* (Virago 2007) 247.

[3] Youth Justice and Criminal Evidence Act 1994, s142 amending s1 Sexual Offences Act 1956.

understandings of adult male rape and the credibility of complainants. It will be argued that given one of the objectives of the VAWG strategy is to change attitudes and behaviours in the context of female victim-survivors, a similar approach is needed for males. This chapter points to the various ways in which this neglect of male victim-survivors causes harm and why awareness raising and challenging problematic attitudes is important. It concludes by arguing for gender inclusive policy making in the context of sexual violence.

Evidence-based Policy Making and Male Sexual Victimisation

Interest in the use of evidence as an explicit element of policy making in the United Kingdom can be located within the context of a political commitment by successive governments to improve policy quality,[4] and help to 'better understand the problems we are trying to address.'[5] Such an approach places emphasis on the use of reliable, robust knowledge in making policy decisions, as opposed to relying on 'opinion-based policy' which may involve conjecture or ignorance.[6] Evidence-based policy making suggests a more careful approach to decision making compared with policy development driven by media pressure or public outrage – forces that are not uncommon in the context of sexual offending.[7] Evidence-based policy making requires careful and intelligent use of evidence, including a consideration of its strength and reliability.[8] This is particularly important for complex social and criminal justice issues which do not easily sit within a positivist approach to evidence production,

---

[4] Katherine E Smith and Kerry E Joyce, 'Capturing Complex Realities: Understanding efforts to achieve evidence based policy and practice in public health' (2012) 8 Evidence and Policy 57.

[5] Cabinet Office, *Modernising Government* Cm 4310 (1999) ch 2 [6].

[6] Marco Segone and Nicholas Pron, 'The Role of Statistics in Evidence-Based Policy Making' UNECEWork Session on Statistical Dissemination and Communication (2008)[3].

[7] See (n 17-18) and accompanying text.

[8] Paul Jensen, 'What is Evidence Based Policy?' Melbourne Institute Policy Brief No. 4/13 (2013). Available from
https://www.melbourneinstitute.com/downloads/policy_briefs_series/pb2013n04.pdf accessed 22nd April 2015.

typically regarded as the 'gold standard' of research evidence.[9] A wide variety of research methods are used to better understand the impact of policy/legal change,[10] but the lessons from this research may not be equally impactful on policy development.[11] There can be little doubt that policy makers 'need to be sophisticated in applying research',[12] but problems occur when policy makers ignore important evidence, rely on unreliable data or take account of a partial or selective reading of evidence.[13] The influence of civil servants, advisors, media, pressure groups and public opinion may also produce decisions that run counter to the best evidence available. Rosenstock and Lee have noted that evidence-based policy making can be deleteriously impacted by vested interests:

> A wide array of vested interests—and here we mean those who, for whatever reason, are committed to a predetermined outcome independent of the evidence ... These interests, which are often financial but may also be emotional, ideologic and political, may be acting alone or in combination.[14]

Domestic criminal justice policy makers have been criticised for being heavily influenced by political considerations at the cost of evidence-based perspectives.[15] This concern has been echoed by research participants working within and alongside law reform processes in Australia. Research has identified various barriers to making effective use of evidence in reforming responses to crime:

> Almost all of the participants highlighted the political nature of law reform as limiting the use and influence of social science research. In particular, it was noted that once election promises were made, reforms were often implemented regardless of expert advice or research-based evidence. Similarly, reforms responding to controversial or high-profile cases that

---

[9] Natalia Hanley et al, 'Improving the Law Reform Process: Opportunities for Empirical Qualitative Research' Australian and New Zealand Journal of Criminology [in press].

[10] Ian Sanderson, 'Evaluation, Policy Learning and Evidence-Based Policy Making Public' (2002) 80 Public Administration 1, 1.

[11] Natalia Hanley et al (n 9).

[12] National Audit Office, *Getting the Evidence: Using Research in Policy Making* (London: TSO, 2003) [4.1].

[13] ibid.

[14] Linda Rosenstock and Lore J Lee, 'Attacks on science: The risks to evidence-based policy' (2002) 92 American Journal of Public Health 14, 14

[15] Michael Tonry, *Punishment and Politics: Evidence and Emulation in the Making of English Crime Control Policy* (Willan 2004) 1.

sparked community outrage were cited as instances where empirical research could play little to no role in informing the expedited reform process.[16]

Indeed, in sexual offending policy making, high profile cases and external pressure on the political process undoubtedly influence policy development. Failures associated with high profile cases may, of course, point to problems that require intervention,[17] but politicians may advocate reforms that turn out to be either ineffective or counter-productive.[18] Further, where evidence does influence law and policy development, it will not necessarily address the institutional, social, and gendered factors that may impede progress in addressing the problem of sexual violence. Indeed, the limitations of criminal legal reform have long been recognised and has led to alternative interventions, including educational initiatives and professional training in order to address rape myths and stereotypes.[19]

Despite these limitations, the use of evidence in guiding state and agency responses to sexual violence can improve the quality of policy decisions in several ways. First, it provides a means of identifying data which serves to challenge misconceptions or ignorance. This is a relevant issue in the context of adult male rape because, as with rape generally, perceptions of victim-survivors can be influenced by a wide range of mistaken assumptions and beliefs.[20] Second, evidence-based policy making can assist in highlighting victim groups that have been previously neglected. Male victims-survivors undoubtedly fall within this category, as will be discussed below. Third, assuming that reliable data is identified and used in a responsible manner, then the use of evidence may lead to the avoidance of error, or negative unintended consequences upon policy implementation. Of course, such a rationalist approach to policy development can be seen as naïve in the face of forces that serve to

---

[16] Natalia Hanley et al (n 9).

[17] Kristine Coulter and David S Meyer, 'High profile rape trials and policy advocacy' (2015) 35 Journal of Public Policy 35.

[18] Of course, policy effect can only be accurately measured after implementation and disappointing or counter-productive results are an inherent part of the policy and law reform process. R. Corrigan, 'The New Trial by Ordeal: Rape Kits, Police Practices, and the Unintended Effects of Policy Innovation' (2013) 38 Law & Soc. Inquiry 920.

[19] Jennifer Temkin and Barbara Krahé, *Sexual Assault and the Justice Gap: A Question of Attitude* (Hart Publishing 2008).

[20] Noreen Abdullah-Khan, *Male Rape: The Emergence of a Social and Legal Issue* (Palgrave Macmillan 2008).

undermine a commitment to tackling problems in an informed way. But that does not undermine the utility of evidence; it re-emphasises the importance of sound policy making.

Tackling Problematic Attitudes towards Male Rape and the UK Government's VAWG Strategy

In the United Kingdom, successive governments have pursued a strategy to address the complex and important problem of violence against women and girls (VAWG) in its many forms. In November 2010, Home Secretary, Theresa May MP stated: 'The Government's ambition is nothing less than ending all forms of violence against women and girls'.[21] The strategy does not exclude male victim-survivors, but focuses most attention on where the problem is greatest – on male violence against women and girls. However, the policy has developed in a manner that focuses almost exclusively on women and girls, with little attention given to males[22] and the focus on VAWG has sometimes been used to explicitly justify the exclusion of males.[23] The VAWG strategy has influenced criminal justice

---

[21] The Rt. Hon Theresa May MP, 'Call to end violence against women and girls: strategic narrative' 25 November 2010.

[22] In a recent strategy document, for example, men and boys are repeatedly mentioned, but largely in the context of how they can help prevent VAWG. For example, 'Starting from the premise that men can be a powerful force in challenging negative behaviours, we will engage men and boys in challenging VAWG by working with organisations to support widespread awareness about VAWG and how men can be involved as an integral part of approaches to prevention': HM Government, *Ending Violence against Women and Girls: Strategy 2016-2020* (2016) 17. For similar comments, see: 25, 26, 52.

[23] For example, in a report on VAWG, the Department for International Development, states: 'DFID acknowledges the importance of preventing and responding to the sexual and gender-based violence suffered by women, men, boys and girls. *However, the focus of this How to Note is on women and girls, given that this is the focus of UK Government policy'* (emphasis added). Emma Bell and Kate Butcher, *Addressing Violence against Women and Girls in Health Programming* DFID Guidance Note: Part A Rationale and Approach (2015) 22 n 50 (emphasis added). The only other reference to men or boys in the report concerns working with males in order to address 'social norms that underpin violence' in the context of VAWG (at 13). See also: E. Bell and K. Butcher, *DFID Guidance Note: Part B: Practical Guidance (2015)* 13. A May 2014, *Addressing Violence against Women and Girls in Education Programming* DFID Guidance Note did give greater attention to boys as victims of abuse. This makes for a puzzling inconsistency between policy documents.

agencies and policy development in various government departments, resulting in the production of over 200 reports, updates, evidence summaries and strategy documents.[24] There is one specific aspect to the VAWG strategy that is of particular relevance to this chapter. The strategy includes a focus on attitudes towards sexual violence and awareness-raising. For example, one document discussing the VAWG prevention strategy set out a strategic vision, including: 'To prevent violence against women and girls from happening in the first place, by challenging the attitudes and behaviours which foster it and intervening early to prevent it'.[25] In its 2013 Action Plan, the government set out an objective for 2015 in which '[a] greater proportion of society believes violence against women and girls is unacceptable and is empowered to challenge violent behaviour'.[26] Other documents contain similar comments.[27] The most recent strategy document continues to emphasise the importance of changing attitudes towards VAWG,[28] with one objective to be pursued by the Foreign and Commonwealth Office: 'Challenge traditional attitudes to sexual violence in conflict and work to end the stigma suffered by many survivors, including men and boys, which leaves them ostracised from society'.[29] This objective is illustrative of a welcome, but rare reference to adult male victims in the voluminous VAWG documentation. It is also an indication of the strategy's poorly developed response to male victim-survivors that the issue of stigma is seen in the context of conflict, but is not mentioned in a domestic context or outside of conflict situations. This

---

[24] These can be found on the Home Office's VAWG policy web page: https://www.gov.uk/government/policies/violence-against-women-and-girls accessed 22nd April 2016.

[25] HM Government, *Call to End Violence Against Women and Girls* (2010) 5. See also: HM Government, *Violence Against Women and Girls Newsletter* Summer 2015.

[26] HM Government, *A Call to End Violence Against Women and Girls: Action Plan 2013* (2013) 13.

[27] An evidence digest made reference to measures that *inter alia* 'provided participants with tools to question and challenge negative behaviour and attitudes': *Violence against women and girls: Evidence digest* (2015) 1.

[28] The recent 2016-2020 strategy document refers to a number of strategic outcomes by 2020, including changing social norms, beliefs and attitudes. For example, 'Increased awareness across all sections of society that VAWG is unacceptable in all circumstances with individuals, communities and frontline agencies empowered to confidently challenge negative attitudes to VAWG': HM Government, *Ending Violence against Women and Girls: Strategy 2016-2020* (2016) 15.

[29] *Id.* 53.

lack of detailed thinking manifests itself in many ways, including the presentation of crime data by the Crown Prosecution Service (CPS).[30] Other CPS documents show some limited evidence of being more inclusive,[31] while others continue to refer to a number of criminal offences including rape as 'VAWG crimes'.[32] Implicitly including men and boys within the category of women and girls shows no understanding of why labeling males as females is problematic for male victim-survivors who

---

[30] In 2015, the Crown Prosecution Service published a crime data report on VAWG entitled: *Violence Against Women and Girls Crime Data 2014-15* (2015). The report did such a poor job of discussing male victim-survivors that it was removed from the CPS web pages and a revised version was published in September 2015. This followed public criticism of the way in which males were treated in the original report. See, for example, Ally Fogg, 'Why is the CPS erasing the experience of thousands of abuse victims?' (2015) <http://freethoughtblogs.com/hetpat/2015/06/26/why-is-the-cps-erasing-the-experience-of-thousands-of-abuse-victims/#ixzz3jIeRWX72> accessed 22nd April 2016. The retracted report makes reference to 16 case studies that illustrate the response of the CPS to rape, other sexual offences and child abuse. Of the 16, not a single one makes explicit reference to a male victim. 15 make explicit reference to a female victim or victims of various ages and one refers to 'children'. In this case study, the report states: 'A cancer treatment doctor in Cambridgeshire took advantage of 18 of his young patients who were battling serious illness by systematically sexually abusing them' (at 67). The consultant in question was Myles Bradbury who pleaded guilty to multiple sexual offences involving boys. The Crown Prosecution Service will have been well aware of the identity of his victims at the time the report was drafted. When Bradbury appealed against his sentence, the Court of Appeal made clear who they were: 'The offences charged against him on the indictment involved 18 boys who at the material time were aged between ten and 16': *R v Bradbury* [2015] EWCA Crim 1176 at [4]. The Director of Public Prosecutions, Alison Saunders denied males were being neglected by the CPS, but acknowledged: 'I fully accept the concerns raised by some, however, that we need to be clearer in our annual VAWG report about the inclusion of men and boys, which is why I have arranged for amendments to be made to the current, and all future, reports': Alison Saunders, 'Some violence is targeted at women and girls – we can't ignore that' *The Guardian* 28 July 2015. Despite the use of the VAWG tag, some other CPS documents are drafted in somewhat more inclusive language. See for example, CPS, Toolkit for Prosecutors on Violence Against Women and Girls: Cases Involving a Vulnerable Victim. <http://www.cps.gov.uk/publications/equality/vaw/toolkit_for_prosecutors_on_vawg_cases_involving_vulnerable_victims.pdf > accessed 22nd April 2016.
[31] CPS Toolkit *ibid.* (noting issues of sexuality).
[32] See: CPS, *Violence Against Women and Girls Crime Report 2014-15* Rev. version (September 2015).

may struggle with their own sense of self-image as men or boys, as well as their sense of masculinity and sexuality.

While the VAWG strategy neglects males, men and boys have often been neglected or treated as an afterthought in policy development.[33] This neglect allows problematic practices or beliefs to remain unchallenged and contributes to the failure of agencies to identify males as potential victims of sexual abuse.[34] Cohen has noted that policy documents, strategies and service provision often neglect male victim-survivors.[35] The lack of visibility of males and associated misconceptions may also impact the ability of victims to 'name' their experiences and identify pathways to reporting and support.[36] Mutchler argues: '[G]ay men are rarely thought to be the victims of date rape, for instance, and are scarcely ever prepared to deal with this situation as men in our society ... [with] few or no institutionalised ways of responding'.[37] While there are multiple reasons for such problems, one common element is poor understanding and negative attitudes towards male victim-survivors. Given that social attitudes are a specific target of the VAWG strategy, this chapter will explore some of the problematic attitudes that exist towards adult male victim-survivors and why these understandings should be included more explicitly within policy making.

A Brief Overview of Evidence on Attitudes towards Male Rape and Sexual Assault

Echoing the policy environment, the overwhelming majority of research literature on sexual violence and related-attitudes since the 1970s concerns

---

[33] A spokesman for a male victim support service made the point, thus: 'The Government still treats this as an add-on, and men and boys as secondary': Theo Merz, 'Male Victims of Sexual Abuse are Treated as Secondary' *The Telegraph* 24 March 2015.

[34] Children's Commissioner for England, *Protecting Children from Harm: A critical assessment of child sexual abuse in the family network in England and Priorities for Action* (2015) 48

[35] Claire Cohen, *Male Rape is a Feminist Issue: Feminism, Governmentality and Male Rape* (Palgrave Macmillan, 2014) 135.

[36] Philip Rumney, 'In Defence of Gender Neutrality within Rape' (2007) 6 *Seattle Journal for Social Justice* 481, 484-486; Michael Scarce, *Male on Male Rape: The Hidden Toll of Stigma and Shame* (Basic Books 1 1997).

[37] Matt G Mutchler, 'Young gay men's stories in the States: Scripts, sex and safety in the time of AIDS' (2000) 3 Sexualities 31.

female victim-survivors.[38] There also exists a significant body of work derived from mock juries,[39] focus groups and other techniques[40] which identifies the ways in which sexual encounters are 'scripted', the impact of these scripts on personal judgements and their possible role in sexual offending. In this context, scripting is used to refer to 'cognitive schema that instruct[s] people how to understand and act in sexual encounters'.[41] Scripts include elements that are descriptive and those that are normative, in the sense that they specify 'behaviours [that] are expected or accepted in the situation'.[42] Further, there are various levels at which scripts operate, and taken in combination, cultural, interpersonal and intrapsychic scripts shape an individual's beliefs about sexual behaviours and encounters.[43] It has been argued that in the absence of direct experience of sexual violence, people may draw on cultural level scripts[44] which can draw on common misconceptions and stereotypes. Alongside scripts of consensual sexual encounters are rape scripts. These scripts direct the 'nature and parameters of the sequences of events that are expected within a rape as well as the characteristics and conduct of the perpetrator and victim'.[45] Rape myths inform and become integrated within rape scripts,[46] and sexual scripts may also 'contribute to judgments of sexual intent'[47] that

---

[38] For discussion of some of this research, see: Liz Kelly, *Surviving Sexual Violence* (Polity Press 1988) 141. For a recent review of evidence, see: Nicole Westmarland, *Violence Against Women: Criminological perspectives on men's violences* (Routledge 2015).

[39] Louise Ellison and Vanessa E Munro, 'Of "Normal Sex" and "Real Rape": Exploring The Use of Socio-Sexual Scripts in (Mock) Jury Deliberation' (2009) 18 Legal & Social Studies 291.

[40] Barbara Krahé et al, 'The role of sexual scripts in sexual aggression and victimisation' (2007) 36 Archives of Sexual Behavior 687.

[41] Tatiana Masters et al, 'Sexual scripts among young heterosexually active men and women continuity and change' (2013) 50 Journal of Sex Research 409, 409. See also: John H Gagnon and William Simon, *Sexual Conduct: The Social Sources of Human Sexuality* (Aldine Publishing Company 1973) 19.

[42] Krahé et al (n 40) 687.

[43] Masters et al (n 41).

[44] M Diane Clark and Marjorie Carroll, 'Acquaintance Rape Scripts of Men and Women: Similarities and Differences' (2008) 58 Sex Roles 616, 617.

[45] Ibid citing: Sarah A. Crome and Marita. P. McCabe, 'Adult rape scripting within a victimological perspective' (2001) 6 Aggression and Violent Behavior 395.

[46] Katherine M Ryan, 'The relationship between rape myths and sexual scripts: the social construction of rape' (2011) 65 Sex Roles 774.

[47] Alison P Lenton and A. Bryan, 'An affair to remember: the role of sexual scripts in perceptions of sexual intent' (2005) 12 Personal Relationships 483, 484.

can be invoked when making decisions about whether a sexual encounter is within acceptable boundaries, which includes the issue of consent.[48]

There is only limited evidence examining scripts in the context of male rape[49] and a larger body of evidence that examines attitudes towards male sexual victimisation.[50] This empirical evidence demonstrates that adult male sexual victimisation is understood, in part at least, by reference to myths, stereotypes and other problematic attitudes. A number of myths[51] surrounding male rape have been identified by researchers. These include: that men cannot be raped because they are physically powerful, that men are able to resist or escape; that a man would not be affected by rape as significantly as a woman; that male victims of sexual violence must be gay and that a man would not be able to gain an erection or ejaculate while being raped or sexually assaulted.[52] The literature suggests that there are

---

[48] Heather L Littleton and Danny Axsom, 'Rape and Seduction Scripts of University Students: Implications for Rape Attributions and Unacknowledged Rape' (2003) 49 Sex Roles 465.

[49] Michelle Davies et al, 'The scripting of male and female rape' (2013) 5 Journal of Aggression, Conflict and Peace Research 68.

[50] See for example, Cindy Struckman-Johnson and David Struckman-Johnson. 'Acceptance of male rape myths among college men and women' (1992) 27 Sex Roles 85; Kristine M Chapleau et al, 'Male Rape Myths: The Role of Gender, Violence and Sexism', (2008) 23 Journal of Interpersonal Violence 600; Emma Sleath and Ray Bull (2010) 'Male Rape Victim and Perpetrator Blaming', (2010) 25 Journal of Interpersonal Violence 969.

[51] In this research, the authors tested *inter alia* whether three behaviour variables – lack of resistance, delay in reporting and the complainant experiencing an erection – would impact the perceptions of the complainant and alleged perpetrator in the vignettes. These behaviours are in fact, not unusual amongst male victim-survivors and the assumption that males do not behave in this way is clearly a myth in the sense that it is factually untrue:
Philip Rumney and Natalia Hanley, 'Gendering Rape: Social Attitudes Towards Male and Female Rape' in Jackie Jones et al, (eds.), *Gender, Sexualities and Law* (Routledge 2011); Philip Rumney and Natalia Hanley (2010) 'The Mythology of Male Rape' in Clare McGlynn and Vanessa Munro (eds.), *Rethinking Rape Law: International and Comparative Perspectives* (Routledge 2010). It is common for legal scholars to define 'myth' to mean any belief that they regard as problematic. However, in the context of the criminal justice system and related policy making, it is crucial to distinguish between true, factually untrue and claims based on assertion. No criminal justice system or policy initiative can operate effectively without such a distinction. .

[52] For a concise overview see: Kristine M Chapleau *et al*, 'Male Rape Myths: The Role of Gender, Violence and Sexism' (2008) 23 Journal of Interpersonal Violence 600.

some similarities[53] but also important distinctions in attitudes between male and female sexual victimisation.[54] For instance, Davies *et al* concluded that sexuality was important in scripting male rape but was not mentioned by any respondents in connection with female rape.[55] The acceptance of female rape myths has also been positively related to the acceptance of male rape myths[56] and thus the acceptance of any rape myth appears to increase the likelihood of further myth acceptance.[57]

Methodology

This research presents empirical data from seven focus groups investigating student attitudes towards four vignettes depicting an alleged male rape.[58] The vignette featured Ian, the complainant, and David, the alleged assailant. It describes a situation in which Ian meets David at a party and agrees to go back to his flat to watch football DVDs. Ian claims that when he decided to leave the flat David restrained and raped him. David claims that 'one thing led to another' and they had consensual sex. The vignette was modified to test the impact of four variables on student assessments of the allegation: lack of resistance, delayed reporting to the police, Ian's denial that he is gay and the complainant experiencing an erection during the alleged rape. The focus group research was conducted in a UK university over a 30-month period.[59] Convenience sampling[60] was utilised whereby undergraduate students from programmes including criminology and law were invited to participate in the research. A total of seven 50-minute focus group discussions were conducted, involving thirty

---

[53] Sleath and Bull (n 50).

[54] Davies et al (n 49). See also: Irina Anderson, 'What is typical rape? Effects of victim and participant gender in female and male rape perception' (2007) 46 British Journal of Social Psychology 225.

[55] Davies et al (n 49).

[56] Chapleau et al (n 52).

[57] Michelle Davies et al, 'Examining the relationship between male rape myth acceptance, female rape myth acceptance, victim blame, homophobia, gender roles and ambivalent sexism' (2012) 27 Journal of Interpersonal Violence 2807.

[58] The seven focus groups considered the three vignettes discussed earlier (n 51), plus a fourth variable, sexuality.

[59] There is no evidence of a significant difference of opinion between the earlier and later focus groups.

[60] Jane Ritchie et al, 'Designing and Selecting Samples' in Jane Ritchie and Jane Lewis (Eds), *Qualitative Research Practice: A Guide for Social Science Students and Researchers* (Sage 2003).

five participants with an average age of 21.4 years.[61] The groups consisted of male only, female only and mixed participants. Participants were presented with a fictional vignette, the legal definition of rape and whether the facts set out in the vignette suggested that a rape had occurred. There was no staff member present during the discussions and the research was conducted in compliance with institutional ethical standards and processes. The focus group transcripts were manually coded by the two researchers who then compared themes and any results that ran counter to those themes. Given the complexity of opinions and perceptions about sexual violence, and the contingent, context-driven nature around how and when particular attitudes are expressed, focus group discussions offer a useful window into the ways in which sexual violence is discussed, negotiated and understood in a group setting.[62] There are also important limitations to this method and the research design in general. As an exploratory study, this project had a small sample size, and the sampling technique and age of participants may mean that the findings are representative of broader social attitudes.[63] For this reason, it is important to contemplate these data alongside established research evidence. Drawing on these data and existing research literature, the next section examines our findings.

Consent and Credibility

One of the challenges of creating and implementing effective social or legal policy in this area is in understanding how people are informed by the various levels at which sexual scripts operate. Masters *et al*, for instance notes a distinction between participants' accounts of cultural norms in heterosexual sexual encounters and the participants' individual, and enacted desires.[64] Similarly, Krahé *et al* observes that 'the fact that people can state what the prevalent gender stereotypes are in their society does not allow one to infer what they personally hold to be the typical attributes of men and women'.[65] Indeed, the expression of problematic social attitudes towards male and female victims of sexual violence does not mean we can infer that they would apply these attitudes in social, criminal justice, policy or wider agency settings. However, given the risk

---

[61] Twenty-three of the thirty-five participants were female and twelve were male.

[62] Rumney and Hanley (n 51).

[63] Ritchie et al (n 60).

[64] N. Tatiana Masters et al, 'Sexual Scripts Among Young Heterosexually Active Men and Women: Continuity and Change', (2013) 50 The Journal of Sex Research 409.

[65] Krahé (n 40) 688.

of this it does indicate that greater attention to social attitudes towards female *and* male victims would be a positive policy step. The distinction between personally-held views and broader social interpretations of a sexual encounter was noted across several of our focus groups:

> It's certain things like what he was wearing and whether or not he went back to his house, I don't think should be relevant, but I think that I worry that they are. (Stephanie, FG 6)

> I don't think that he is in any way consenting to the intercourse. I don't think that, but that could be how it was interpreted, like the fact that he agreed to go to someone's house that he had just met that night after a party to talk about football. (Barbara, FG 5)

The focus group discussions indicated that group-based processes for working through an account of a sexual or sexually violent encounter represented a complex interplay between vignette characteristics and associated scripts. What is more, this interplay is a useful discursive device for contemplating the meaning of an encounter. Research which considers the content and outcome of group discussions is therefore well placed to offer evidence-based insight into the ways in which multi-level scripts play out in group settings. However, further evidence is needed to untangle how these scripts operate to inform the outcomes of discussion. Below, Phoebe and Morag move between discussion of the shared cultural meanings attached to an encounter and their own individual intentions and interpretations:

> Phoebe   As a woman, would you expect that would be expected of you? If you went back to, like, would you think 'if I go back to somebody's house, I am definitely going to have sex with them'?
>
> Morag   I wouldn't.
>
> Phoebe   *You* wouldn't, but ... (emphasis in original)
>
> Morag   If I went back to a guy's house, yeah I would think, yeah I'd think they were going to try it on.
>
> Phoebe   But would your intentions of going to the house be, 'I am going to be going back because I am probably going to be sleeping with him'?
>
> Morag   No, not always! (FG 6)

Although the vignette given to participants described an alleged sexually violent encounter between two men, the participants drew upon a heteronormative framing of the scenario in the first instance. This is perhaps unsurprising given that heterosexuality is culturally dominant and embedded in sexual scripts. Locating this in an historical context, Mutchler argues that the historic cultural scripting of sexual encounters and relationships is grounded in a heterosexual 'marriage for procreation' script.[66] In a contemporary context, however, Mutchler argues that this manifests itself as a 'romantic love' script for women and an 'adventure script' for men.[67] Perhaps reflecting this contemporary context, the overwhelming majority of participants in our research found the vignettes challenging to interpret because the characters were both male and therefore they did not have an immediately available alternative script through which to frame this scenario. Indeed, there was a general consensus in the groups that it would be unusual for a man to accept another man's invitation to watch football at home if they were previously unknown to each other,[68] as the two extracts below demonstrate:

> No, I don't know, it sounds a bit odd if two men who didn't know each other after drinking at a party...were going to one of their flats. Do you like, really talk about football, after a party? I think it's hard to believe that they probably both didn't think that something was going to happen when they went to the house. (Alan, FG 1)

> But that's the thing, you don't generally talk to other guys, you talk to girls. You wouldn't spend the whole night talking to one bloke would you? That seems a bit contributing [sic] to it. If Ian's not gay then I can't really see a straight person doing that, and then going back to their... [home]. (Mike, FG4)

---

[66] Mutchler argues that:

> [T]he traditional, 19th-century procreative scripts for sex mandates that sex be done for the purpose of procreation between one man and one woman who are married. Though this model presumes the heterosexuality of sexual actors (since lesbians and gay men cannot legally marry or procreate when engaging *solely* in same sex encounters), traditional scripts are available at the level of culture for heterosexuals and non-heterosexuals to draw upon' Mutchler (n 37) 35.

[67] ibid.

[68] Indeed, Ian's acceptance of an invitation to go to another man's flat was characterised pejoratively by some participants. See the 'Blaming the victim' section below.

At issue here was the 'real meaning' of Ian going from a party to the home of someone he had just met. Through the course of the group discussions (and at varying points), the participants applied a romantic script which was necessarily premised on the assumed homosexuality of one or both of the characters. Consequently, a significant part of all the group discussions involved participants reading the vignette as involving two gay men or as indicating that David was gay and Ian was interested in some kind of 'experimental' sexual encounter. In the words of one participant: 'I don't get this "one thing led to another" if they're not gay' (Laura, FG3). This latter view, which was expressed in several other groups, fails to acknowledge that when David claimed that 'one thing led to another' he could have been lying as part of a consent defence.

With the exception of one vignette where participants were told that Ian denied being gay, no further information was provided about the sexuality of Ian or David.[69] Research on sexually violent encounters has noted that in the absence of information, participants may be 'filling in the gaps' with scripts in order to better understand the vignette under consideration.[70] As noted above, participants were not able to easily read the scenario as one of platonic friendship, as the following exchange between Harry and Andy illustrates:

Harry   If, say, like, David was gay and Ian was straight, it could be that David had the wrong idea about Ian. And it might have been totally innocent on Ian's part that he just wanted to watch a DVD and talk about football.

Andy   The thing is if you were thinking that you've just met someone at a party and it was, say it was a girl, say she just came back to your house and you had been drinking, one thing led to another ... and I don't know it's kind of ... from David's point of view, he's consented already by just coming back to his house. From his point of view because he's drunk, well he's come back he's obviously willing. 'I'm in', basically. (FG 4)

Stuck on the application of heteronormative sexual/romantic scripts, participants initially and periodically compared the scenario to one in

---

[69] Ian's denial appeared to have had no impact on group discussions compared to the groups where the vignette made no explicit reference to sexuality.

[70] Emily Finch and Vanessa E Munro, 'Lifting the Veil: the Use of Focus Groups and Trial Simulations in Legal Research' (2008) 35 Journal of Law and Society 30, 51.

which a character was female, a point we have discussed in detail in previously published work.[71] The result of some discussions was a broad agreement that there would be at least some degree of implied consent by agreeing to return to a near-stranger's house after a party. However, these discussions did not reach full consensus with several focus groups containing one or more critical or challenging participant, as the exchange below indicates:

Fiona   I'd need hard evidence but I do think that Ian led him on, yeah; I
            do think Ian led him on.

Charlotte I think he's stupid for going back in the first place still, so
            therefore David felt Ian had half consented anyway.

Anna   Really?

Charlotte You just put yourself in a stupid position, to change your mind.
            (FG2)[72]

In another group discussion, participants also considered the vignettes through a heteronormative framework, assuming that Ian was heterosexual and therefore would not reasonably know nor would assume that David identified as gay. A minority of participants positioned themselves in the vignette suggesting that the invitation was not sexual in nature:

Des   But I wouldn't actually think this guy is going to try it on...you
            would have no idea.

Eric   If this guy invited you back, the first thing you wouldn't think of
            'is he gay? I shouldn't go back with him'. You would think
            'PlayStation.' (FG3)

Working with the idea that Ian and David were heterosexual precluded the possibility of rape for some participants. In this way, sexuality was constructed as binary and fixed at points in the focus group discussion. This can be contrasted with research evidence suggesting that sexual orientation and behaviour can, for at least some people, change over

---

[71] 'Gendering Rape' (n 51).

[72] This group also demonstrated another aspect to group discussions; that is, victim blaming by references to 'stupidity' and Ian 'leading on' David. This is an issue that will be discussed in the 'Blaming the victim' section below.

time.[73] This binary construction also warranted a search for an alternative plausible explanation for what was interpreted as Ian's false allegation of rape. Participants in one group imagined a revenge narrative based on an alleged argument between Ian and David: 'But that's only Ian's point of view. Ian could be lying, he could be trying to get David put away because they had an argument' (Shelly, FG3).

More commonly, group discussions canvassed the possibility that the complainant may have consented to a sexual encounter and the resultant embarrassment, shame or confusion led to feelings of anger. In this narrative, the rape allegation was understood as an act of revenge or a means to take control of the way the encounter was presented to others:

> There is no proof that David physically restrained him and used force on him. There is nothing. That is why he waited three days [to report to the police]. So, to be honest (...) I think he consented to it and he is just ashamed of it and just wanted to get payback somehow. Because maybe David is just a likeable (...) David could basically be someone that he has fancied for ages or had been in love with (Erin, FG7).

The revenge or false accusation narrative is in evidence within the female victim-survivor literature.[74] Most commonly, this takes the form of fear of reputational repercussions after a sexual encounter.[75] In our vignettes depicting a male complainant, reputational repercussions commonly featured and this involved issues of regret and sexuality. Here, the experimenting complainant struggling to come to terms with the implications of his sexual encounter with another man reacts by making an allegation of rape. As Cheryl suggested: 'I think, because he strongly denies he is gay, if he did consent to it he might feel ashamed and now he has decided "Oh my god, I am ashamed of what I have done. I am not

---

[73] See, for example, Ritch C Savin-Williams et al, 'Prevalence and Stability of Self-Reported Sexual Orientation Identity During Young Adulthood' (2012) 41 Archives of Sexual Behavior 103; Margaret Rosario et al, 'Sexual identity development among lesbian, gay, and bisexual youths: Consistency and change over time' (2006) 43 Journal of Sex Research 46.

[74] M. Diane Clark and Marjorie H. Carroll, 'Acquaintance Rape Scripts of Men and Women: Similarities and Differences' (2008) 58 Sex Roles 616: Clare Gunby et al, 'Regretting it after? Focus group perspectives on alcohol consumption, nonconsensual sex and false allegations of rape' (2012) 22 Social and Legal Studies 87, 96; Louise Ellison and Vanessa E Munro, 'A stranger in the bushes, or an elephant in the room? Critical reflections upon received rape myth wisdom in the context of a mock jury study' (2010) 13 New Criminal Law Review 781.

[75] Gunby et al, ibid.

gay, so it must have been like, rape'" (FG 5). This also points to a counter-
intuitive proposition that the strength of the complainant's denial about his
presumed homosexuality indicates the complainant's *lack* of credibility.
The denial/shame/revenge narrative was countered by a minority of
participants:

> Charlotte I reckon he is in denial. He's gay, and he had sex, and was like
> 'oh no, that shouldn't have happened'.
>
> Bella   But why does he go to the police and tell people?
>
> Charlotte Because he's mad at this man because he realises he is gay.
>
> Gill   Where have you got this from? Why? (FG2)

In the second exchange below, participants extend the vignette. For some
of the participants in group seven, after the encounter described in the
vignette, David continues to make unwelcome advances towards Ian
which limits his capacity to move on from the shame he is assumed to feel:

> Martin   [H]e could be ashamed that he gave in to gay sex, first time or
>   something, and now basically he feels ashamed that he has done
>   it, because maybe he has got a girlfriend, maybe he has got
>   family and he doesn't want anyone to find out.
>
> Erin   Actually that is a really good point. I didn't really think of that. It
>   could be that he wanted it.
>
> Martin   Yeah, and now he is ashamed of it basically, and maybe that
>   David just wants to tell people, he doesn't leave him [Ian] alone,
>   so he basically has to stop this, so he makes an allegation of rape.
>   (FG7)

For a minority of participants shame and embarrassment enhanced the
likelihood that the complainant was telling the truth, as Stephanie stated
'(…) but if you experiment, at the end of the day, and you don't like it,
you would kind of keep it a secret' (FG6). In this narrative, the
complainant's willingness to make public his shame becomes an indicator
of truth-telling:

> [I]f you were that ashamed of what you did though, and that is why he
> didn't want everyone to find out, why would he go and do that allegation?
> Because that is just going to blow that up … is obviously going to get more

talk about it and more attention about it, which obviously if he consented to it, he does not want that, does he? (Erin FG7).

The overwhelming majority of participants drew clear boundaries around the possibility of a rape occurring in the vignette and the sexuality of the complainant and defendant. With only an occasional exception all participants 'read' the vignette as involving one of two broad scripts: David was gay and had successfully enticed Ian, who was confused about his sexuality and possibly intoxicated, into a sexual encounter. Second, both men were gay and responsibility was largely attributed to Ian to clearly communicate non-consent through verbal or physical resistance. This expectation was reinforced by participants' use of the 'script' in a way that suggested to them that Ian was sexually interested and available to David. Both scripts involved an element in which Ian fabricated the allegation of rape and this involved various motives, including: revenge, embarrassment or shame for engaging in sexual activity with another male.

Blaming the Victim

There is a long history of placing blame on the victims of crime,[76] and debates over whether blaming or holding a victim partly or wholly responsible for rape are in essence the same thing have recently played out in the legal literature.[77] For the sake of simplicity, this chapter will make reference to blame. There is only limited evidence that has examined victim blame in the context of adult male rape, but the existing evidence suggests that factors including sexuality[78] and behaviour before, during

---

[76] There is voluminous literature in this area that has accrued over a number of decades. See, for example, Leo Montada and Malvin J Lerner (eds), *Responses to Victimization and Belief in a Just World* (Plenum Press, 2010). This literature makes clear that while victim blaming occurs in the context of rape, it also occurs in the context of many types of criminal victimisation and other life events.

[77] Helen Reece, 'Rape Myths: Is Elite Opinion Right and Popular Opinion Wrong?' (2013) 33 Oxford Journal of Legal Studies 445; Joanne Conaghan and Yvette Russell, 'Rape Myths, Law, and Feminist Research: "Myths about Myths?"' (2014) 22 Feminist Legal Studies 2; Helen Reece, 'Debating Rape Myths' LSE Law, Society and Economy Working Papers 21/2014.

[78] Edwin E Ayala et al, 'Blame Attributions of Victims and Perpetrators: Effects of Victim Gender, Perpetrator Gender, and Relationship' (2015) Journal of Interpersonal Violence 1; Michelle Davies and Samantha McCartney, 'Effects of gender and sexuality on judgements of victim blame and rape myth acceptance in a

and after an alleged rape, increase attributions of blame.[79] The role of Ian's behaviour as a way of explaining his own alleged victimisation was raised by participants in several ways. At its most crude, some participants, often with the agreement of other group members, commented negatively on Ian's decision to go to David's flat, thus: '[he's] very stupid or very innocent', '[Ian] could have led [David] on', 'I think he's stupid for going back [to the flat] in the first place', 'There is a lot of stupidity on Ian's part to go back', 'In a way, it's kind of like he led him on a bit by going back to his flat'. More common were somewhat subtler forms of victim blaming. There was some limited discussion within the focus group discussions regarding the steps David might have taken to ascertain Ian's consent. This is of course, an important element in the legal definition of rape,[80] with which all participants were provided.[81] Interestingly, while there was relatively little focus on David's efforts to actively seek consent, most, though not all, participants focused on the steps Ian took to communicate his *non*-consent, which is not legally required.[82] Alice and Matt illustrate this approach:

> If you put yourself into David's shoes and you liked Ian... they went to watch a DVD and talk and then when he was getting ready to leave, David restrained him, pulled down his trousers and anally penetrated him. But it does not say anything at any point that he said for him to stop. He doesn't, like, say that he struggled or anything, so from David's point of view, how did he know that he didn't consent if Ian didn't say any of this or struggle? (Alice, FG6).

> [I]f he's not putting up any sort of struggle against it, then you would assume that he's agreeing to it by choice, he's not voicing anything against it. (Matt, FG1)

In a number of the groups, a clear, verbal 'no' was deemed necessary for sex to be non-consensual. In focus group 1, Alan stated: 'Well, I don't

---

depicted male rape' (2003) 13 Journal of Community and Applied Social Psychology 391.

[79] Davies and McCartney ibid.

[80] Section 1(2) of the Sexual Offences Act 2003 provides that in determining whether or not the defendant possessed a reasonable belief in the complainant's consent, the jury can take into account *inter alia* 'any steps A has taken to ascertain whether B consents'.

[81] The vast majority of participants were law students or those who had done law as part of a joint honours degree. These students had studied the law of rape as part of a criminal law module.

[82] *R v H* [2007] EWCA Crim 2056 [31].

think he said "yes" I want to have sex, but I don't think he said "no". So by not saying "no", then I would have to say he did consent to having sex with David'. In focus group 7, Erin stated: 'If he had carried on with it, that was in my view consenting to it, because he didn't say he didn't want to do it'. A similar view was taken if Ian changed his mind and did not wish to have sex: 'Then he needs to say that though, doesn't he?' (Yvette, FG6)

In their research using focus group discussions, Gunby *et al* similarly noted an expectation that consent would be clearly and verbally communicated by the female victim.[83] Moreover, they noted that 'the dissonance between the law, which does not require consent to be verbally expressed ... and lay assumption is again apparent'.[84] In our own research the presumption that non-consent should involve a clear and verbally communicated 'no' was also questioned by some participants: In focus group 6, Alice stated: 'I am playing devil's advocate here: why should we wait to hear if somebody says "no" as opposed to waiting for him to say "yes"? Why is there a question?' One of the participants, Morag, responded to this question by focusing on naturalistic notions of victim physical and verbal resistance:

> [If] you take control of your life then, it is then you say 'No' I don't want this. Step away from me, it is you protecting yourself and that is a human instinct ... go along with it, stopping it is saying 'No'. It is everybody's instinct to say 'no' or to physically force.

In keeping with the way in which opinions expressed in focus groups can be quickly revised, Morag states: 'I don't necessarily believe that you would fight back'. Alice's 'devil's advocate' question also led to a response that re-emphasised the onus on Ian to communicate without reciprocal behaviour from David. Yvette stated: 'I think it is difficult but if Ian didn't shout, flinch away or try and get away or say 'No' or struggle, David couldn't have known without him saying anything. He couldn't have known that he didn't consent if he was not showing any resistance'.

Interestingly, however, in some discussions even when a 'yes' was seen as necessary it did not prevent sex from being viewed as consensual in the

---

[83] Gunby (n 74)100.
[84] ibid 94.

absence of a 'no' – a point noted by Alan above.[85] A similar point was noted by Clark and Carroll in their research comparing the rape scripts that male and female students drew upon. In that study, and consistent with the gendered 'romantic' and 'adventurous' contemporary sexual scripts noted earlier, participants drew upon a traditional sexual script in which women are the gatekeepers for sexual encounters and men the initiators.[86] When applying this sexual script to a vignette, some of Clark and Carroll's participants suggested that in a 'normal' sexual encounter, a woman would perform some resistance and therefore resistance could not be reliably understood as non-consent.[87] Instead, a woman was expected to escalate her resistance verbally or physically in order to unambiguously perform non-consent.[88]

While the question of consent represents one potential barrier to understanding male sexual coercion as rape, another barrier for men is physicality. In the focus groups, this was connected to Ian's ability to successfully resist an attacker. This represents both a point of similarity and departure from the ways in which female resistance was conceptualised. Davies *et al* found that there was some expectation of resistance in both male and female rape scripts, although depictions of male physical resistance was less than expected and inconsistent with previous studies.[89] While our research did not use a vignette involving a female victim, there was significant discussion of female rape which was used as a comparator. In our research, the threshold for female resistance was an *attempt* to resist an attacker. This can be contrasted with the tacit naturalistic assumption amongst our participants that a man *could* resist and explicitly *should* resist:

---

[85] Elsewhere, in focus group 2, some participants focused on a mixture of verbal communication and behaviour in order to determine the issue of consent:

   Fiona: I reckon not, I reckon...some may say, he could have said 'yes' then decided half way through 'no, shit, what am I doing?'
   Bella: But then he still should have been able to stop.
   Fiona: But it didn't say he said 'stop'.
   Gill: He tried to leave.

[86] Clark and Carroll (n 44) 623.

[87] ibid 624.

[88] In this research, the possibility of self-inflicted injury was occasionally raised. In group 2, Diane made reference to Ian's delay in reporting and went on to say: '[I]f he wanted it, make it up as something else, give yourself a whack'.

[89] Davies et al (n 49) 73.

Martin   Yeah. I mean some people's perception of like, especially men, it
           is like, and they should be able to, you know, defend themselves.

Erin   Yeah, exactly ... Ian should be like a man. (FG7)

Here, we see the cross-over of assumptions about men being strong and
invulnerable to harm and how male victim-survivors see themselves. In
her interviews with male victims, Allen found they were less likely to
blame themselves for the rape where 'excessive' force was used by the
perpetrator, [90] or where drugged or otherwise vulnerable males were
exploited.[91] In this way, males were able 'to justify to themselves and
others why they had failed to behave in an appropriate "masculine"
manner, and prevent the assault from occurring.'[92] In the focus group
discussions, intoxication was rarely seen as a potential source of Ian's
vulnerability, lessening his ability to give consent. Instead, it was seen
more as a source of potential memory failure;[93] a reason for engaging in
consensual sex, which Ian then regretted;[94] and a cause of unfairness to
David;[95] because he may not have been able to ascertain lack of consent
unless Ian was unconscious or unable to physically 'function'.[96]

---

[90] Stephanie Allen, 'Male Victims of Rape: Responses to a Perceived Threat to
Masculinity' in Carolyn Hoyle and Richard Young (eds.), *New Visions of Crime
Victims* (Hart Publishing 2002) 41.

[91] ibid 44.

[92] ibid 45.

[93] 'He could have consented and just forgot that he had consented, if he was
drinking, maybe' (Cheryl FG 5).

[94] In focus group 6, Yvette suggested consent on the basis that: 'Ian is drinking, he
has gone back to his flat (…)' But this was challenged by Alice: 'They are just
drinking, why does drinking mean that it is indicative to consenting?'

[95] In focus group 7, Erin stated: '[S]o maybe he was (…) really drunk in the mind,
but then I think to be fair it is not fair to blame David (…) If [Ian] obviously
consented, even if he was drunk, everyone does make mistakes when they are
drunk. They wake up the next day and "Oh, what did I do?"'.

[96] In focus group 7, Erin and Martin stated:

But it's not really fair on David, is it, because obviously David might have
thought he wasn't that drunk, it was just normal drunk because obviously
he has got enough to function during sex and obviously David thought that
he was not that too drunk.

I mean some people, you know drink a lot, but they are fine (…) they can
physically function (…).

In this sense, the potential target for sexual violence is required to actively resist an attacker and to be *seen* to be 'performing' non-consent, as one participant put it: '[Y]ou know women are seen to be physically inferior, so of course they can get raped by a man, but two men? Then surely he would fight it, wouldn't he?' (FG5). Such performances become written on the body through injury. While expectations of male resistance are relevant to understanding social constructions of male *and* female rape, they have a unique consequence for adult male victims whereby attaining victimhood denigrates hegemonic masculinity.[97] Yet, empirical evidence indicates that many male victim-survivors do not physically resist their assailant(s).[98] Indeed, the attribution of blame to male victims has been previously noted: 'Men are blamed more when they are judged not to have fought back sufficiently, or failed to escape'.[99] The existence of resistance and injury scripts in the context of rape are well supported by empirical studies of attitudes to female rape.[100] Physical injury, for many of the participants in the current research, represented a way to move beyond the vignette featuring 'one person's word against another' and in this way represented strong corroboration that a rape occurred.[101] However, counter-narratives were also posed in relation to evidence of physical injury. A minority of participants raised the issue that injury was suggestive, but not decisive evidence of non-consent,[102] and for others,

---

[97] Kathy Doherty and Irina Anderson, 'Making sense of male rape: Constructions of gender, sexuality and experience of rape victims' (2004) 14 Journal of Community & Applied Social Psychology 85.

[98] Adrian W Coxell and Michael B King, 'Adult male rape and sexual assault: prevalence, re-victimisation and the tonic immobility response' (2010) 25 Sexual and Relationship Therapy 372, 376.

[99] Davies et al (n 57) 2808.

[100] Louise Ellison and Vanessa E Munro, 'Turning Mirrors into Windows: Assessing the Impact of (Mock) Juror Education in Rape Trials' (2009) 49 British Journal of Criminology 363, 371-373.

[101] The assumption that injury would result from non-consensual sex is evident in the following examples: 'Surely there would be some physical [injury] (...) It was two men, men are quite strong anyway', 'There would have had to have been some sort of physical trauma to Ian's body', 'If someone was about to get raped, they [are] obviously not going to take it lightly as they are going to right back, and there would be some sort of marks whether it be scratches or bruises', 'Surely there would be some physical [injury]', 'Obviously if someone is physically restrained and held down, like they are going to have bruises on them', 'If it is like forced, it can, there are loads of signs that can be shown that he has been forced and his body would be bruised', 'Obviously there would be some bruising'.

[102] See, for example, 'I don't think it is indicative but I would certainly want to see whether or not he had any like bruises or anything on him'.

that injury might be unrelated to non-consensual sex but might be evidence of physicality and 'rough sex' which was consensual (Mike FG 4). In focus group 5, Barbara made similar comments: 'If Ian happens to be a gay man and he enjoys it quite rough, then you are not really going to see any marks from a new episode ... if someone is physically restrained and held down, like they are going to have bruises on them'. In this way, injury was a powerful, but problematic way of corroborating Ian's account – even when there was injury, it did not necessarily mean the sex was non-consensual as it could be explained by other means.

The attribution of blame in sexually violent encounters has been connected to hostile sexism towards both men and women. Hostile sexism is used to refer to negative and denigrating attitudes towards people who do not conform to anticipated gender roles.[103] For instance, women who are perceived as promiscuous may be more likely to be subject to hostile sexism, and, as a result be considered more blameworthy in their own sexual victimisation.[104] Hostile sexism can also operate alongside homophobic attitudes in the context of attitudes towards male rape.[105] Kassing *et al* have reported that the acceptance of male rape myths is positively correlated to negative attitudes towards gay men.[106] The view of a male who alleges rape as either experimenting, confused or gay (he was not raped, consented and is lying as a cover for his sexuality), or he resisted and is injured (he physically demonstrated his lack of consent and was raped) restricts the circumstances when rape can be perceived to have occurred.[107] The emergence of these limiting narratives perpetuate the

---

[103] Davies et al (n 57) 2809.

[104] Sabrian Koepke et al, '"She Deserved It": Effects of Sexism Norms, Type of Violence, and Victim's Pre-Assault Behavior on Blame Attributions Toward Female Victims and Approval of the Aggressor's Behavior' (2014) 20 Violence Against Women 446.

[105] Davies et al (n 57); Sandy White and Nikawo Yamawaki, 'The moderating influence of homophobia and gender-role traditionality on perceptions of male rape victims' (2009) 39 Journal of Applied Social Psychology 1116; Irina Anderson, 'What is typical rape? Effects of victim and participant gender in female and male rape perception' (2007) 46 British Journal of Social Psychology 225.

[106] Leslee R Kassing et al, 'Gender role conflict, Homophobia, Age and Education as Predictors of Male Rape Myth Acceptance' (2005) 27 Journal of Mental Health Counselling 311. For similar findings, see Davies et al (n 57) 2817.

[107] For discussion, see: Karen G. Weiss, 'Male Sexual Victimization: Examining Men's Experiences of Rape and Sexual Assault' (2010) 12 Men and Masculinities 275, 291-292.

constructed rarity of male victimhood and the notion that only certain kinds of males can be raped.[108]

Finally, while it is customary in attitudinal research for scholars to argue that discussion of injury or resistance involves an element of victim blame and the power of the so-called 'real rape' stereotype, [109] there is an alternative explanation. The study participants were searching for evidence in order to address the question of whether a rape had occurred. It is undoubtedly the case that signs of resistance and injury can provide corroborative evidence in support of an allegation of rape and may boost complainant credibility. This is not to doubt that judgements are also influenced by rape scripts pertaining to masculinity and an expectation that a raped adult male would be injured. However, scripts cannot be viewed as the *only* explanation for why participants viewed the vignettes in the way they did.[110]

Sexuality and Credibility

The perceived sexuality of Ian and David impacted on the ways in which participants made sense of the vignettes. After initially reading the scenario through a heteronormative lens which precluded rape, most participants questioned the complainant's claim in one vignette that he was heterosexual. In the remaining vignettes, the 'discovery' of Ian and David's sexuality was regarded as the most relevant piece of missing information.

Mike   Obviously I think that his sexual orientation would count a lot, would make things a lot easier to … get an answer out.

Andy   If Ian was gay and he's gone back to a guy's house, if they're both gay it might happen. (FG 4)

---

[108] ibid 291.

[109] 'Real rape' is the idea that rape commonly or normally involves characteristics such as injury, victim resistance or an attack by a stranger: Kimberley A Lonsway and Louise F Fitzgerald, 'Rape myths: In review' (1994) 18 Psychology of Women Quarterly 133. Janice Dumont et al, 'The Role of "Real Rape" and "Real Victim" Stereotypes in the Police Reporting Practices of Sexually Assaulted Women' (2003) 9 Violence Against Women 466.

[110] There is no doubt that data can be read in different ways and competing interpretations should be acknowledged: David Gurnham, 'Debating rape: to whom does the uncanny "myth" metaphor belong?' (2016) 43 Journal of Law and Society 1.

Alice   'One thing led to another', if he is straight, how did anything lead to anything?

Phoebe   Very unlikely that he would have consented if he is not gay, I would have thought. I don't know. (FG 6)

For some participants, Ian's behaviour, including going back to David's home, was suggestive that he consented to sex,[111] and this also led some participants to project upon him a gay identity, despite there being no direct evidence of this.[112] By the end of the group discussions, there was no agreement about how to make sense of sexuality in the vignettes. Indeed, the certainty that sexuality was relevant, but uncertainty about how to interpret it, was common across most of the group discussions. Here, Stephanie questions the connection between sexuality and consent that had been raised earlier in the discussion:

Stephanie Why is it more reasonable to assume he would consent, just on the basis that the person is of the same sexual orientation as you?

Stuart   If he was straight, he is more likely to say 'no, I'm sorry mate', whereas if he was gay then he might of being going along with the stuff.

Phoebe   You kind of assume where it would lead, if he did consent, whereas if he was straight (…) (FG 6)

Research on perceptions of male rape victims suggests that gay victims of rape are considered more blameworthy for their own victimisation than heterosexual victims and that all male victims are considered more blameworthy than female victims.[113] The greater attribution of blame noted for gay victims is echoed in the sexual victimisation of transgender men and women. Davies and Hudson found that heterosexual men in particular reported negative judgements about male or transgendered victims of rape, and these judgements resulted in greater victim-

---

[111] For example, in response to the vignette featuring Ian going to David's flat after the party, Anna stated: 'I don't see why you would leave a house party to watch a film' (FG 1).

[112] Sexuality was not mentioned except for one vignette in which David was explicitly described as heterosexual.

[113] White and Yamawaki (n 105) 1117.

blaming.[114] This lends further support to the argument that perceived deviation from hegemonic gender performances affects the availability of victimhood. After consideration of the impact of gender and sexuality on blame and rape myth acceptance, Davies and McCartney concluded that heterosexual men were most likely (compared to gay men and heterosexual women) to apply myths and attribute blame to gay male rape victims.[115] The prevalence of homophobic attitudes has been cited as one explanation for this observation. Alden and Parker, for instance, state that 'men who do not maintain the necessary gender performance to support the ideals of masculinity are stigmatized as not "real" men, or, even worse, as gay'.[116] The lack of attention given to the reality of sexual violence for diverse groups of people by policy makers enables such problematic attitudes to remain unchallenged.

Across the focus groups, discussion about consent centred on three key issues. First, participants drew on heteronormative sexual scripts to determine what the characters in our vignettes 'really meant' as the scenario unfolded. Second, the participants considered steps taken by the complainant to communicate *non*-consent. Here the discussion focussed on evidence of verbal and physical resistance, including signs of injury. Third, participants considered sexuality to make determinations about motivation for reporting and for the discrepancies in the conflicting accounts of Ian and David. In this way, credibility and truthfulness for both the complainant and defendant was tied to discussions about sexuality, although sexuality was not necessarily determinative, given the interaction of other script elements.

Implications for Policy Making

Simply acknowledging, as this study and wider research evidence suggests, that there are problematic attitudes towards adult male rape is not enough to facilitate recognition and improvement in the treatment of victim-survivors. That is why the inclusion of male sexual victimisation in the policy making process is important - the neglect of male victim-survivors will leave unchallenged the misunderstandings, myths and stereotypes discussed in this chapter. Addressing the problem of sexual

---

[114] Michelle Davies and Jennifer Hudson, 'Judgments towards Male and Transgendered Victims in a Depicted Stranger Rape' (2011) 58 Journal of Homosexuality 237, 243.

[115] Davies and McCartney (n 78).

[116] White and Yamawaki (n 105) 1119 (quoting Alden and Parker).

violence is a difficult task, not least because of the existence of these ill-informed attitudes.[117] It is evident that the rape scripts found in this study are problematic, not least because they are shaped by myths, stereotypes and assumptions about how an adult male-on-male rape should occur and how victims should behave in order to be seen as credible. The scripts contain elements that are gendered or counter-intuitive. This includes specific rape scripts relating to victim resistance or injury, false allegations, sexuality and blame which impact perceptions of complainant credibility.[118] Some of the assumptions underpinning these scripts have been recognised as impacting on criminal justice decision-making and are the subject of specific judicial directions which warn jurors in sexual offence cases about the danger of making assumptions.[119] These beliefs may be particularly problematic if they combine with other poorly informed attitudes and assumptions about victim credibility,[120] and may also impact on men's willingness to seek help,[121] along with limiting or misdirecting agency responses.[122]

---

[117] Temkin and Krahé (n 19).

[118] Some problematic attitudes identified in this research have been discussed elsewhere. This includes delayed reporting and involuntary physical reactions to rape. For discussion, see our work (n 51).

[119] Judicial College, The Crown Court Compendium (May 2016).ch 20.

[120] Victim Support, *At Risk, Yet Dismissed: The Criminal Victimisation of People with Mental Health Problems* (2013). This report found that male and female victims of crime who suffer serious mental health problems may not be seen as credible witnesses for a range of reasons, some of which pertain to negative attitudes and lack of awareness. The report also found that males who suffered from serious mental health problems were significantly more likely to be victims of sexual abuse compared to males who did not suffer severe mental illness.

[121] Weiss suggests that men's reluctance to report rape to the authorities 'may be exacerbated by a sense of shame for not fulfilling their masculine roles that dictate they be in control and take care of matters themselves': Weiss (n 107), 285; Siegmund F Fuchs, 'Male Sexual Assault: Issues of Arousal and Consent' (2004) 51 Cleveland State Law Review 93. In a recent report, the Children's Commissioner for England found a similar problem involving young males:

[B]oys and young men are less likely to tell someone that they have been sexually abused. Experts who participated in oral evidence sessions stated that there are additional pressures on boys not to tell, as male victims of sexual abuse may be stigmatised by the perceived impact of abuse on their masculinity. This has been noted particularly for some BME groups, and more generally. This is an issue that has been identified for all groups from all backgrounds (n 34) 48.

[122] Philip Rumney, 'Gay Victims of Male Rape: Law Enforcement, Social Attitudes and Barriers to Recognition,' (2009) 13 International Journal of Human

So how can policy making in the context of sexual offending be more inclusive? The gendered nature of rape[123] should not obscure the fact that any person can be sexually violated[124] and that negative social attitudes attach to and impact female *and* male rape. These basic insights are largely ignored in contemporary UK government policy making. One way of addressing the current neglect of male victim-survivors is to develop a parallel policy initiative alongside the VAWG strategy. Such a recommendation was recently made in a London Assembly Conservatives report, thus: 'The Mayor of London should develop a Sexual Offences Against Men and Boys strategy to specifically assist male victims of sexual offences'.[125] This, of course, requires a comprehensive approach, of which tackling problematic attitudes, raising awareness and changing practice is a part. Another means of developing an inclusive policy approach is to examine male victim-survivors as a vulnerable group. Fineman argues that: 'Vulnerability initially should be understood as arising from our embodiment, which carries with it the ever-present possibility of harm, injury ...'[126] This type of analysis is inclusive in that it recognises that any individual can be vulnerable without ignoring the specific disadvantages and vulnerabilities of particular groups. She goes on: 'Vulnerability analysis demands that the state give equal regard to the shared vulnerability of all individuals, transcending the old identity categories as a limitation on the recognition that the state has a vital role to play in protecting against discrimination.' [127] A focus on vulnerability requires the state to look beyond traditional victim or 'identity' categories

---

Rights 233. Research suggests that 'professionals have been said to have overlooked certain risky behaviours in boys that, it was argued, would have been more readily identified as child sexual exploitation-related in girls': Ella Cockbain et al, Not just a girl thing: A large-scale comparison of male and female users of child sexual exploitation services in the UK (2014) 26. This can be found at <http://assets.mesmac.co.uk/images/Not-just-a-girl-thing.pdf?mtime=20160108191711> accessed 22nd April 2016.

[123] While this notion can take many differing forms, for the purpose of this chapter, we simply mean that rape is a crime predominantly committed by males on females.

[124] Bourke (n 2) 247.

[125] Kemi Badenoch, *Silent Suffering: Supporting Male Survivors off Sexual Assault* (2015) 6. Can be found at <http://glaconservatives.co.uk/wp-content/uploads/2015/11/Silent-Suffering.pdf> accessed 22nd April 2016.

[126] Martha Fineman, 'The Vulnerable Subject: Anchoring Equality in the Human Condition' (2008) 20 Yale Journal of Law & Feminism 1, 20.

[127] ibid.

of male perpetrator/female victim[128] and requires the state and its policy makers to recognise a more nuanced understanding of sexual victimisation. This does not deny that most victim-survivors of sexual violence are female and that rape, as a social and legal phenomenon, is gendered. An inclusive approach is reflective of empirical reality and allows an acknowledgement that rape scripts and associated rape myths or victim blaming also transgress traditional victim categories.

Indeed, there are plenty of examples of inclusiveness outside of the VAWG strategy. In her review, Baroness Vivien Stern acknowledged vulnerability in an inclusive approach and discussed the experiences of young sex workers, including males who had 'fallen through the cracks' of the care system[129] and pointed to the importance of professionals being aware that males can be sexually victimised.[130] Similarly, a recent review of rape case treatment in London raised concerns regarding the treatment of male sex workers[131] and the treatment of male victims by the police.[132] Of particular relevance to this chapter is the way in which the VAWG strategy was seen in the review report as potentially having the 'unintended consequence' of adding to the 'further alienation of male victims who cannot relate to the justice system and feel their needs are not accommodated'.[133]

---

[128] Given the gendered nature of sexual offending, women and girls will be disproportionately represented in most vulnerability categories, but amongst males and females there are groups who appear to be particularly vulnerable to sexual violence, exploitation and abuse arising from such factors as age, mental health, status, homelessness and disability. See, for example (n 120).

[129] Home Office, *A report by Baroness Vivian Stern CBE of an independent review into how rape complaints are handled by Public Authorities in England and Wales* (2010) 113. The report also includes a number of other references to males: 12, 30-31, 35-36, 53, 56, 64, 66, 104, 128.

[130] ibid 113 'Those responsible for protecting the young need to be more aware than they sometimes are of the possibility of rape and sexual exploitation occurring, and need to form links with the police and local agencies to raise the level of protection that can be provided'.

[131] Rt. Hon Dame Elish Angiolini DBE QC, *Report of the Independent Review into the Investigation and Prosecution of Rape in London* (2015) [216].

[132] ibid [586]. The report author expressed concern about police specialist rape investigation units becoming 'unofficial specialist Violence against Women and Girls Units' and, given male and transgender underreporting, expressed 'serious concerns at the repositioning of the Units' and 'whether it is a helpful response to the need to improve rape prosecutions'.

[133] ibid [215].

A failure to formulate a comprehensive policy of action against male sexual victimisation will hinder the identification of vulnerable males and compound the reluctance of males to come forward, disclose what has happened, and engage with support services and the criminal justice system. This leaves some of the most prolific sex offenders free to victimise males *and* females of any age.[134] Indeed, a truly gendered response to rape does not simply reinforce existing gender binary stereotypes of female victims and male perpetrators. It reflects the true nature of sexual victimisation. Stemple has argued that 'female-specific approaches hinder[] advocacy for male victims and may also inhibit reporting because little effort is made to focus specifically on encouraging males to break their silence'.[135] She goes onto argue that:

> [T]o continue this approach to sexual violence in light of evidence that males constitute a small but sizable percentage of victims has problematic theoretical implications: it reifies hierarchies that treat some victims as more sympathetic than others, perpetuates norms that essentialize women as victims, and imposes unhealthy expectations about masculinity on men and boys.[136]

Indeed, the needs of male victim-survivors cannot be properly addressed as part of a policy agenda that neglects minority victim groups such as gay, heterosexual, bisexual and transgender males,[137] and women who have been sexually victimised by other women.[138] When relatively little

---

[134] Some research has suggested that it is category of offenders with a history of indecent assault against males which 'contains the most serious *sexual* predators of the four groups [featured in the research], who care little about either the gender or age of their victims or the nature of their offending behaviour': Keith Soothill et al, 'Sex Offenders: Specialists, Generalists-or Both?' (2000) 40 British Journal of Crime 56, 62-63. See also: Gene G. Abel et al, 'Multiple Paraphilic Diagnoses among Sex Offenders' (1988) 16 Bulletin American Academy Psychiatry Law 153, 158.

[135] Lara Stemple, 'Male Rape and Human Rights' (2009) 60 Hastings Law Journal 605, 637-639.

[136] ibid 606.

[137] Angiolini (n 131) [216].

[138] See for example, Lori B Girshick, *Woman-to-Woman Sexual Violence* (Northeastern University Press 2004) 57   Jessica Hatcher, 'Congo's Forgotten Curse: Epidemic of Female-on-Female Rape' *Time* 3 December 2013 Found at <http://world.time.com/2013/12/03/congos-forgotten-curse-epidemic-of-female-on-female-rape/> accessed 22nd April 2016; Miriam L Walters, *National Intimate Partner and Sexual Violence Survey (NISVS): 2010 Findings on Victimization by Sexual Orientation* (2013); Miriam Wijkman et al, 'Juvenile female sex offenders:

explicit attention is given to minority victim groups in policy development, it is simply naïve to think that their needs will be adequately addressed.

Conclusion

This chapter has examined findings from an empirical study of attitudes towards adult male rape, including assessments of victim-survivor credibility. We found that sexual scripts, including rape scripts, are used to make sense of sexual encounters. Our own research, as well as extant empirical research demonstrates that people draw upon myths and assumptions when making judgements about rape.[139] What is more, this study suggests that rape scripts incorporate myths and assumptions that are gendered. As such, this analysis, which draws on a wide body of evidence, has several implications for public policy making. First, neglecting the experiences of adult male victim-survivors in policy making is likely to result in strategies and actions that fail to grasp their needs. While the UK government's VAWG strategy includes occasional references to adult males or boys, there is little evidence of the kind of comprehensive multi-agency strategy that is required to address problematic attitudes as demonstrated in this, and other studies. These efforts need to be part of a comprehensive approach to addressing male, as well as female sexual victimisation.[140] This does not have to equate to equal resources or time given to the issue. Instead, a truly gendered response takes account of the prevalence and dynamics of differing types of victimisation, but is inclusive in the sense that the needs of minority victim groups are considered as part of the policy making process. Without such an approach, sexually victimised males of whatever age will continue to have their needs misunderstood and problematic attitudes will go unchallenged.

Offender and offence Characteristics' (2014) 11 European Journal of Criminology 23; Cambridge University Student Union, *Cambridge Speaks Out* (2014) 16.

[139] Michael W Wiederman, 'The gendered nature of sexual scripts' (2005) 13 Sex Therapy 496.

[140] For discussion, see: Badenoch (n 125).

CHAPTER TEN

#SPYCOPS:[1]
UNDERCOVER POLICING, INTIMATE
RELATIONSHIPS AND THE MANUFACTURE
OF CONSENT BY THE STATE

BEN FITZPATRICK

Introduction and the Context for Undercover Policing

This is a book about consent and control. Policing (or at least, the public policing with which this chapter is concerned) sits at a confluence of these two concepts: while much is made in the orthodox narrative of British policing of the importance of public consent to being policed,[2] policing also necessarily involves the authorisation of one group of citizens to exercise controlling and coercive powers on behalf of the State. The exercise of those powers – which are supported by the granting of legal privileges not possessed by other citizens – involves intrusions into people's lives, and restrictions on their liberty. In a liberal democracy – and indeed as a matter of fundamental justice – the exercise of these powers calls for special justification. Nonetheless, nobody can seriously dispute that policing modern society is challenging, and that certain intrusions and restrictions are politically and legally justifiable. A detailed account of the breadth of policing functions is beyond the scope of this

---

[1] '#spycops' is a common – and in some usages mildly pejorative – Twitter hashtag referring to undercover police.
[2] See, for example, Home Office, 'FOI release: Definition of policing by consent' (10 December 2012) <https://www.gov.uk/government/publications/policing-by-consent/definition-of-policing-by-consent> accessed 19 January 2016. For a critical engagement with the notion of policing by consent, see, for example, Robert Reiner, *The Politics of the Police* (4th edn, Oxford University Press 2010) 68-71.

chapter. Similarly, it is not necessary for present purposes to try to capture – even if it were possible – the incontrovertible nature and qualities of policing. Perhaps we can start from the position that among the purposes of policing should be the support, through law, of social conditions which enable citizens to pursue their own conceptions of the good life; to go about their business, without undue hindrance either from other citizens or from the State. Within that framework, when an individual violates the criminal law, they are acting against the interests of fellow citizens individually and collectively, and more broadly, against the interests of society and of the State. The roles of the police therefore include the pursuit of those who are thought to have broken the criminal law, the disruption of the activities of those who are about to do so, and the gathering of intelligence in relation to potential future law-breaking activity. In a liberal framework, the further away we get from a situation in which a citizen is *actually engaged* in criminal conduct, the more difficult it is to justify police engagement with or interference in the conduct of that citizen. That is not to say that those engagements or interferences cannot be justified, but it is to note that those justifications are not self-evident.

Now, a *visible*, overt police presence may be reassuring for citizens and may lead to successful apprehensions of offenders and effective deterrence of certain behaviours in certain contexts. However, visible policing may also have the effect, not so much of deterring criminal behaviour, but of merely displacing it to another time or place.[3] Moreover, there are people who and criminal behaviours which cannot effectively be countered merely by overt police activity. Consider, for example, those engaged in the supply of unlawful drugs, those engaged in people trafficking, or those planning terrorist activities. These behaviours may call for *covert* engagements with offenders, potential offenders and their associates, through, for example, the interception of communications, surveillance, or the infiltration of an offender's network.[4] These covert activities are also of a piece with the modern move to *intelligence-led* policing,[5] which seeks

---

[3] Or, it might not have this effect. See JM Hough and RVG Clarke, 'Introduction' in JM Hough and RVG Clarke (eds), *The Effectiveness of Policing* (Gower 1980) 4-5. On displacement generally, see Tim Newburn, *Criminology* (2nd edn, Routledge 2013) 597-598.

[4] By an undercover officer, or a tasked civilian informant.

[5] See, for example, Audit Commission, *Helping with Enquiries: Tackling Crime Effectively* (HMSO 1993). It is worth noting that intelligence-led policing is not a solely contemporary strategy: for discussion, see Cyrille Fijnaut and Gary T Marx

to target offenders by the systematic and proactive gathering of information – often by covert means – about their activities and intentions.

Society's delegation to the police of the function of dealing with criminality recognises that police may need to coerce and intrude, and must include an acknowledgement that some policing needs to be covert. That is not to say, however, that anything goes, or that the end always justifies the means: police powers must, in broad terms, be exercised in accordance with key principles such as legality, necessity and proportionality. Moreover, covert policing raises particular issues which might not be so evident in other contexts.[6]

Thus, Joe, a citizen, may encounter the coercive and intrusive aspects of policing in a variety of contexts. He may be suspected of involvement in a fight. He has an interest in not being unfairly coerced by the State in their investigation of him, and there are legal rules to protect that interest.[7] He may be suspected of supplying unlawful drugs. Perhaps a surveillance device has been placed in his car and his house is being 'staked out' from a neighbouring property. In this situation, Joe has a privacy interest with which the State may be interfering. It is perfectly conceivable that this interference can be justified, but a justification is called for.[8]

Now consider a scenario in which, rather than surveilling Joe's house from a neighbouring property, the police have tasked an acquaintance of his to come to his house and to ask if Joe has drugs which he is willing sell to

---

(eds), *Undercover: Police surveillance in comparative perspective* (Kluwer Law International 1995).

[6] For discussion of a range of issues in covert policing, see, for example, Simon McKay, *Covert Policing: Law and Practice* (Oxford University Press 2011); Clive Harfield and Karen Harfield, *Covert Investigation* (2nd edn, Oxford University Press 2008).

[7] Thus, the arrest and interviewing of suspects such as Joe are governed by the Police and Criminal Evidence Act 1984 and the associated Codes of Practice. For the Codes, see Home Office, 'Crime and policing – guidance: Police and Criminal Evidence Act 1984 (PACE) codes of practice' (26 March 2013) <https://www.gov.uk/guidance/police-and-criminal-evidence-act-1984-pace-codes-of-practice> accessed 19 January 2016.

[8] Surveillance activities are governed by the Regulation of Investigatory Powers Act 2000 and their accompanying Codes of Practice. For the Codes, see Home Office, 'Collection: RIPA Codes' (8 September 2010 – 24 December 2014) <https://www.gov.uk/government/collections/ripa-codes> accessed 19 January 2016.

him. The police have instructed the acquaintance to offer significantly above the market price to enhance any temptation that might exist, and to report back to them on their interaction. In this situation, Joe is being surveilled, and he is, in some respects, being deceived. The interaction with his acquaintance has been set up without his knowledge. It is not what he thinks it is. His relationship with the acquaintance has been manipulated and used for another purpose. Again, it is conceivable that this manipulation is justifiable, but, also again, a justification is called for.[9]

Covert policing may involve a range of interferences with citizen's interests, and those interferences may be evaluated for their efficacy in addressing criminality, for their ethical quality, and for their compliance with law. Where they are inefficacious, we might argue that policing resources are better deployed elsewhere; where they are unethical, we might argue against them and for a more principled approach; and where they are not compliant with the law, we might consider the possibility of repercussions for those responsible for the interference, or some kind of compensatory response for the wronged party. For the purposes of this chapter, I am especially interested in the legal and ethical quality of those interferences which, like the third of the scenarios involving Joe, appear to involve some type of manipulation or deception. More specifically, I will be focusing on the controversial practice of undercover police officers cultivating intimate, sexual relationships with members of a group against whom a policing operation is directed. In recent years, a series of high profile instances have come to light involving undercover officers who had infiltrated protest groups, and who had maintained their undercover status by cultivating such relationships. These cases and others have thrown light on a range of (at best) questionable policing tactics, and have led to a crisis of legitimacy around covert policing which has yet to be fully resolved.

The Criminal Law: On the Possibility that Intimate Relationships Undercover may involve the Commission of Sexual Offences

The most notorious of the cases have involved male undercover officers cultivating intimate relationships with female members or associates of targeted protest groups. I will argue that the nature of these relationships,

---

[9] ibid.

founded as they were on profound (and, indeed, hugely damaging)[10] deception, calls into question the consent given by the women in question to the sexual activity which took place in the course of those relationships. On that basis, I suggest that there is an arguable case that the relationships entailed the commission by the undercover officers of a range of non-consensual sexual offences. I suggest that a decision of the Crown Prosecution Service not to bring proceedings in relation to a number of allegations of behaviour which might have amounted to such offences was, though understandable, premature.[11] It would, I suggest, have been preferable if the relevant allegations had been tested in court. I also argue that even if the law were such that non-consensual sexual offences had not been committed on the facts, in some cases, prosecutions might have been brought for other sexual offences in relation to which it was not necessary to prove an absence of consent.

I suggest that the conduct of the police in these cases is, irrespective of its criminality or otherwise, damaging to the integrity of the criminal justice system.[12] I also argue that it speaks to failures which go deeper than shortcomings in formal regulation. Rather, there needs to be a fresh *cultural* settlement in covert policing, which acknowledges the wrongs

---

[10] For evidence of the damaging effects of the relationships, see the evidence given by some of the women involved to a Parliamentary Select Committee: House of Commons Home Affairs Committee, *Undercover Policing: Interim Report* (HC 2012-13, HC 837), Ev 1-Ev 8, and the statements appended to the letter submitted to the Select Committee by the solicitor acting for a number of the women, Harriet Wistrich: 'Letter from Harriet Wistrich, Solicitor, Birnberg Peirce & Partners, to the Chair of the Committee, 4 July 2013'.
<http://www.publications.parliament.uk/pa/cm201314/cmselect/cmhaff/557/557we 04.htm> accessed 18 February 2016.
[11] Crown Prosecution Service, 'Charging decision concerning MPS Special Demonstration Squad' (21 August 2014)
<http://www.cps.gov.uk/news/latest_news/charging_decision_concerning_mps_sp ecial_demonstration_squad/index.html> accessed 19 January 2016. I discuss this decision further below.
[12] In this context, integrity has at least two dimensions. The integrity of criminal justice is a good in itself, in that it is something which people deserve as a facet of a civilised society. It also has instrumental value in that it helps to confer legitimacy on criminal justice processes, and to encourage cooperation from citizens. For broader discussions of what is at stake when police use deception, see Andrew Ashworth, 'Should the police be allowed to use deceptive practices?' (1998) 114 Law Quarterly Review 108-140; Sissela Bok, *Secrets: On the Ethics of Concealment and Revelation* (Vintage Books 1989) ch XVII.

done and the harms caused in these relationships, which makes clear that the nature of the wrongs and harms is properly understood, and which entails a commitment that they will not be repeated.

Although a number of notorious instances are by now reasonably well-documented, involving, for example, undercover officers Bob Lambert and Mark Kennedy, it is not clear how widespread or routine the practice of officers engaging in intimate relationships undercover was.[13] The extent to which the officers' conduct was authorised or known about by those to whom the officers were reporting is also not clear.[14] However, it is clear that instances of relevant behaviour were taking place both before and after the coming into force of the Sexual Offences Act 2003 (which is significant for the purpose of determining which rules of criminal law apply to the conduct in question).[15] It is also not unreasonable to assume that those cases which have been brought to light and discussed in recent years in a range of public contexts are then, even if not merely the tip, also not the totality of the iceberg.

---

[13] See, for example, Rob Evans and Paul Lewis, *Undercover: The True Story of Britain's Secret Police* (Faber and Faber 2013). The nature of the behaviour in question is such that its true extent may never be fully known. It is also not clear whether or to what extent and under what circumstances the practice continues. Giving evidence to the Home Affairs Select Committee, Patricia Gallan, Deputy Assistant Commissioner, Metropolitan Police expressed disapproval of the practice, and suggested that it was the position of the Metropolitan Police that 'there could never be circumstances where it would [be] necessary and proportionate to authorise undercover officers, what we call CHISs, to engage in sexual activity' (House of Commons Home Affairs Committee (n 10), Q159, Ev 22-Ev 23). She went on to suggest that undercover officers are tasked with sufficient clarity that they know that intimate relationships undercover are not acceptable ((n 10) Q182, Ev 26-Ev 27) but when asked whether such behaviour could occur today, she conceded that she was not saying it could not happen ((n 8) Q183, Ev 27).

[14] Compare the evidence to the Home Affairs Committee given by Deputy Assistant Commissioner Patricia Gallan (House of Commons Home Affairs Committee (n 8) Ev 18-Ev 28) with that given by exposed undercover officer Mark Kennedy, who suggested, in the context of his own deployment, 'The circumstances were such that it would have been difficult to believe that they did not know that I was sleeping with somebody, albeit I did not tell them' ((n 8) Q199, Ev 29).

[15] The bulk of the 2003 Act came into force on 1 May 2004.

Now that the context for these deceptive intimate relationships has been explained a little more fully, I am going to consider the possibility that the sexual activity in these relationships might have given rise to the commission of a range of criminal offences.

The orthodox position is that a key purpose of sexual offences law is to protect sexual autonomy interests.[16] That is to say, in broad terms, the criminal law recognises the importance of people being able to choose freely whether and with whom to engage in sexual activity (subject, of course, to the free choice of the other person or persons). The importance of free choice shows that *consent* is at the heart of sexual offences law.

A range of sexual offences depend on there being an absence of consent on the part of the complainant. The most serious of these offences is rape,[17] and the Sexual Offences Act 2003 and the earlier law recognise and recognised a number of other non-consensual offences.[18] I am interested at this point in whether the deceptive nature of the undercover officer's conduct in these intimate relationships is such as to *vitiate* consent. That is to say, does it render the consent of the complainant ineffective as a matter of law?

For these purposes, I am going to focus on the male undercover officer who has vaginal sexual intercourse with the female complainant. As such, I will be focusing on the potential commission of the offence of rape, but the principles in relation to consent in the context of rape are, for present purposes, transferable to other offences, for example, indecent assault under the pre-2003 Act law,[19] or sexual assault under the 2003 Act.[20]

---

[16] The meaning of 'sexual autonomy' may of course be contested. Rogers argues, for example, that 'sexual autonomy' should refer to '(...) the willingness to be used for the sexual gratification of another in a way that shows regard to one's own sexual preferences'. Jonathan Rogers, 'The effect of "deception" in the Sexual Offences Act 2003' [2013] Archbold Review 7-9, 8. A counter-argument would be that this approach focuses unduly on the physical actions which comprise a sexual activity, with insufficient regard to the context in which those activities take place. In Rogers's view [2013] (Archbold Review 7-9, 9), the sexual autonomy of the complainants in the undercover cases had not been violated, notwithstanding that they would not have consented to the sexual activity had they known the true facts.

[17] The offence is currently defined in the Sexual Offences Act 2003, s 1.

[18] The principal other 'non-consensual' offences in the Sexual Offences Act 2003 are assault by penetration (s 2); sexual assault (s 3); and causing sexual activity without consent (s 4).

[19] Sexual Offences Act 1956, s 14 and s 15.

Given my focus on the issue of consent, it is important to remember that the absence of consent is only one of the elements of the offence of rape. So, under the current law, rape also requires the defendant's intentional penile penetration of the vagina, anus or mouth of another, and the absence, on the part of the defendant, of a reasonable belief that the other is consenting.

The Sexual Offences Act 2003 makes specific reference to the impact of deceptions on consent, for the purpose of specific offences, including rape. If it is proved that a defendant perpetrated one of the deceptions referred to in section 76 of the Act, it will be *conclusively presumed* that the complainant did not consent to the sexual activity in question, and that the defendant did not believe that the complainant was consenting. According to section 76, the conclusive presumptions operate when:

> *(2) The circumstances are that –*
> *(a) the defendant intentionally deceived the complainant as to the nature or purpose of the relevant act;*
> *(b) the defendant intentionally induced the complainant to consent to the relevant act by impersonating a person known personally to the complainant.*

So, the question is whether the behaviour of the undercover officers involved an intentional deception as to the nature or purpose of the sexual activity, or an impersonation of a person known personally to the complainant.

Let us take the impersonation point under section 76(2)(b) first: consider a situation in which David claims to be Tim, and has sexual intercourse with Christina. Let us say that the circumstances make David's false claim believable – the room in which the events take place is dark, and David and Tim are of similar build. Christina consents to the sex on the basis that she thinks that it is sex with Tim. Let us also say for the sake of argument that she would not have consented to sex with David had she known he was in fact David; that is to say, Tim's identity – the Tim-ness of Tim – is material to Christina's decision to consent. This is a paradigmatic case of impersonation for the purposes of section 76, and the conclusive presumptions of an absence of consent on the part of Christina, and of an absence of belief in consent on the part of David, would be triggered.

---

[20] See (n 18).

The undercover cases present a rather different form of impersonation. The law countenances a situation where David impersonates Tim, who is a real person. In the context of sexual relationships undercover, the undercover officer's impersonation would be of a fictitious character, constructed for the purposes of the operation. There is nothing in the concept of 'impersonation' in its regular usage which requires that the 'person' impersonated be a real, identifiable individual. Moreover, the magnitude and harmfulness of the deception experienced by Christina, and the culpability of (real) David do not depend materially on whether Tim is a real or non-real person. However, our normative judgements of harm and culpability may need, in this context, to give way to statutory language. Note that section 76(2)(b) of the Sexual Offences Act 2003 requires that the person impersonated be 'known personally to the complainant'.[21] Notwithstanding the potential breadth of the natural meaning of impersonation, and the fact that it is integral to the success of the undercover officer's 'legend' that the complainant feels that they are in the company of somebody they know personally, it seems inapt to describe a non-real person as 'known', still less 'known personally'. I suggest that a non-strained interpretation of section 76(2)(b) requires that it be confined to the impersonation of real persons.[22]

Moving to section 76(2)(a), does the undercover officer's behaviour entail a deception as to the *nature* or *purpose* of the sexual activity? Taking 'nature' first: a deception as to the nature of the activity would also vitiate consent at common law. What appears to be countenanced by 'nature' is rather functional: the type of deception which is required is as to the 'sexual activity-ness' of the sexual activity. Thus, where a defendant suggested that the sexual intercourse was a medical procedure, the consent of the complainant was vitiated.[23] In the undercover cases, there is no

---

[21] A deception by the defendant as to their identity could also be relevant under certain limited circumstances at common law. The 'known personally' qualifier in s 76(2)(b) illustrates that what Parliament had in mind was to (at least) reflect the rationale for the decision in *Elbekkay* [1995] Crim LR 163, [1994] EWCA Crim 1. That case established that a defendant impersonating a complainant's boyfriend could be guilty of rape, notwithstanding that the statutory definition of rape at the time made specific provision only for the impersonation of husbands.

[22] In the absence of an issue in relation to the nature or purpose of the sexual activity, which would be relevant to section 76(2)(a) of the Sexual Offences Act 2003, the impersonation of non-real persons would, in this view, go primarily to the issue of consent as partially defined in section 74, which is discussed below.

[23] *Flattery* (1877) 2 QBD 410.

suggestion that deceptions of this type took place. But that does not mean that the debate about nature is entirely closed off. The undercover cases raise the question as to whether one's acts of sexual intercourse are always of the same 'nature' as a matter of law, regardless of who one's partner is. Is sexual intercourse with Partner A inevitably the same in 'nature' as with Partner B?[24] For sure, the physical actions may be the same – but that seems to be a rather thin account of 'nature'. The terminology of 'nature' connotes objectivity and universality, but in practice, the 'nature' of an activity will be, in part, related to the meaning ascribed to it by those engaged in it.[25] On that basis, we should perhaps be cautious about suggestions that sexual intercourse (or any identified sexual activity) has a definitive, single 'nature'.[26] Of course, what we can say is that sexual intercourse is sexual intercourse, and it is not a medical procedure;[27] but whether we can describe the 'nature' of sexual intercourse in positive and substantive terms is more questionable. However, it may be that the thin, functional, formalistic account of nature is all that the law can realistically cope with. There is clearly a difference between sexual activity engaged in as part of an ongoing, intimate relationship, and sexual activity which takes place in the context of a duplicitous 'relationship' which has been established or facilitated on behalf of the State, which has been cultivated for the furtherance of State aims, and in which the complainant's partner holds themselves out as being a genuine sexual partner when in fact they are acting for the State. The question would be whether that difference is a difference in 'nature' which vitiates the consent of the complainant. The prevailing, thin account of 'nature' in the law suggests that it is not.

Perhaps there is a stronger argument that consent may have been vitiated by way of a deception as to the 'purpose' of the relevant act. The 'purpose' option under section 76(2)(a) was not available at common law, so this route is only open in principle in relation to conduct taking place after the coming into force of the 2003 Act. As Rook and Ward note, the drafting of the subsection appears to assume that an act has but a single

---

[24] Notwithstanding any attractiveness in principle, an argument that identity went to nature could, if accepted, undermine or render otiose the implicit reference to identity in s 76(2)(b), and would therefore be unlikely to succeed.

[25] An argument against this reading of 'nature' would be that it might in fact be better captured by 'purpose[s]'.

[26] For a discussion along similar lines, see Jonathan Herring, 'Mistaken sex' [2005] Criminal Law Review 511-524.

[27] See *Flattery* (n 23) and *Williams* [1923] 1 KB 340.

purpose.[28] That cannot be right as a matter of lived experience, nor as a matter of legal principle. Otherwise, the provision would only bite on situations where a defendant represented that the purpose of the act was *exclusively* one thing, when in fact, it was exclusively another.

In the undercover cases, the sexual intercourse in question forms part of a relationship which has been cultivated for the furtherance of a police operation, and there is therefore a strong argument that the sexual intercourse shares that purpose. Perhaps it could be suggested that the intercourse was in some way collateral to the relationship – that it was some kind of non-critical 'add-on' – and that it was *only* the relationship itself which was essential to the operation, and therefore only the relationship which was linked in purpose to it. However, this seems to risk drawing an artificial distinction: the sexual activity can be argued to form part of a package of conduct which is designed to further the operation by means of maintaining the covert persona of the undercover officer. That purpose can, in principle and in practice, coexist with other, less ignoble purposes. Thus, the officer may or may not also be genuinely committed to the relationship: we know that the psychology of undercover work is complex,[29] and that the motives of undercover officers may be or may become mixed. Nonetheless, in some cases, we might suggest that the *actual* primary purpose of the officer in engaging in sexual intercourse (the furtherance of the police operation) is materially different from what he *represents* as the primary purpose (an act of intimacy in the context of the 'real' relationship which the officer claimed existed, and which the complainant believed existed). The conceptual 'gap' between those purposes is broad and is material to the decision of the complainant to engage in sexual intercourse.[30] It is right in principle that conclusive presumptions which operate against a defendant, such as those envisaged

---

[28] Peter Rook and Robert Ward, *Rook and Ward on Sexual Offences Law and Practice* (4th edn, Sweet and Maxwell 2010) [1.194] 81.

[29] See e.g. Gary T Marx, *Undercover: Police Surveillance in America* (University of California Press 1988) ch 8.

[30] This kind of approach to purpose was countenanced in *Devonald* [2008] EWCA Crim 527. D was the father of a girl who wished to exact revenge on her former boyfriend, who had broken off their relationship. The father posed online as a woman and persuaded the ex-boyfriend to masturbate in front of a webcam. He was convicted of causing sexual activity without consent (under s 4 of the Sexual Offences Act 2003), based on a deception as to purpose. *Devonald* has been viewed with some scepticism by commentators (see e.g. Jonathan Rogers, 'Case Comment: Sexual offences: consent; "purpose" of defendant' (2008) 72 Journal of Criminal Law 280-282) and it has been doubted, albeit obiter, in *Bingham* [2013] EWCA Crim 823.

by section 76, are treated with caution and circumspection, and it may be that ultimately it is on that circumspection that this argument would founder.[31] However, I suggest that even if we concede that there is no difference in 'nature' between one act of sexual intercourse and another, there is a reasonable argument that in some of the undercover cases, a deception as to 'purpose' may have occurred, which would trigger the conclusive presumptions under section 76(2)(b).

Section 76 of the Sexual Offences Act 2003 deals with specific situations in which an absence of consent to sexual activity is to be presumed. Where the presumptions in section 76 do not apply, the basic position is that an absence of consent needs to be proved in the normal way, by the prosecution.[32] Prior to the 2003 Act, there was no statutory definition of

---

[31] The need for circumspection is noted in *Jheeta* [2007] EWCA Crim 1699, [2007] 2 Cr App R 34 (see at [23]: '(...) s.76 raises presumptions conclusive of the issue of consent, and thus where intercourse is proved, conclusive of guilt. They therefore require the most stringent scrutiny'), and is endorsed by commentators including Andrew Ashworth and Jeremy Horder, *Principles of Criminal Law,* (7th edn, Open University Press 2013) 347-348. They suggest that *Piper* [2007] EWCA Crim 2151, [2008] 1 Cr App R (S) 91 is a better potential illustration of a 'purpose' deception than *Devonald* (n 30) 347. *Piper* was a sexual assault sentencing case in which D had set up bogus modelling auditions during which he had sexually touched participants under the guise of taking measurements. The case arose from a guilty plea in the magistrates' court, so the extent of legal argument in the case is not clear. There is some ambiguity as to D's purpose. A pre-sentence report suggested that D's conduct was not sexually motivated, although D conceded that 'he had received at any rate a degree of sexual stimulation from his behaviour' *Devonald* (n 30) [20]. The court in *Jheeta* (n 31) [26] suggests that *Green* [2002] EWCA Crim 1501 is an example of a case which would now fall within the ambit of a deception as to purpose. In that case, D was a doctor who conducted bogus examinations on young patients which he claimed were testing, for example, for fertility issues, but were in fact for his sexual gratification.
One can agree with the tendency to interpret s 76 as narrowly as possible, while also noting that there is nothing on the face of the section to indicate that references to purpose cover only those situations where D represents that his purpose is something other than sexual gratification, when his actual purpose is in fact sexual gratification. In any event, even if in the *Devonald* approach to section 76(2)(a), deceptions as to purpose is rejected, it is clear that such deceptions may fall for consideration under the definition of consent in section 74, discussed below.
[32] Section 75 of the 2003 Act sets out a number of situations in which a complainant is taken not to consent, and a defendant is taken not to reasonably

consent. The key case was *Olugboja*,[33] which moved away from narrower historic approaches to consent by rejecting the idea that its absence needed to be grounded in a fear of force, or in the complainant's active resistance. The issue of consent was one to be considered by the jury 'applying their combined good sense, experience and knowledge of human nature and modern behaviour to all the relevant facts'.[34] Section 74 of the Sexual Offences Act 2003 was not intended to change the law,[35] but provides a short, partial definition of consent:

> [A] person consents if he agrees by choice, and has the freedom and capacity to make that choice.

The brevity of section 74 belies its complexity. It refers to a range of concepts – agreement, choice, freedom, capacity – which are all amenable to philosophical dissection.[36] In what ways might section 74 be relevant to the undercover cases? There has been some discussion of whether section 76 exhausts the situations in which a defendant's deception might be relevant to the issue of consent. That is to say, if a deception is not such as to trigger the conclusive presumptions – that is, if it is not about nature or purpose, and it does not involve a relevant impersonation – then we need not concern ourselves any further with the deception when we are considering whether consent is absent. However, there is nothing in the

---

believe that the complainant is consenting 'unless sufficient evidence is adduced to raise [the] issue' (s 75(1)). These situations therefore involve the application of non-conclusive, so-called 'evidential presumptions'. They apply where the defendant has done the 'relevant act' (s 77; for example, in rape, intentional penile penetration) and knows of a circumstance or circumstances specified in s 75(2). These circumstances, in broad terms, refer to situations in which the complainant's ability to give a free consent is hindered. They include: the use or threat of violence against the complainant or another person; the complainant's unconsciousness; the complainant's unlawful detention; a physical disability of the complainant hindering their ability to communicate consent or non-consent; the non-consensual administration to the complainant of a substance enabling them to be stupefied or overpowered.

[33] *Olugboja* [1982] QB 320, [1981] EWCA Crim 2.

[34] ibid [1982] QB 320, 332.

[35] See Home Office, *Setting the Boundaries: Reforming the law on sex offences: Volume I* (Home Office Communication Directorate 2000) [2.10.3]: 'In defining consent we are not seeking to *change* its meaning, rather to clarify the law so that it is clearly understood'.

[36] See, for example, Jennifer Temkin and Andrew Ashworth, 'The Sexual Offences Act 2003: (1) Rape, sexual assaults and the problems of consent' [2004] Criminal Law Review 328-346, 336.

language of section 74 which precludes the relevance of deceptions to the issue of consent. Moreover, when we read section 74 in conjunction with section 76, we can see that section 76 involves particular types of deception leading to particular (and severe) procedural consequences. It does not follow from that that a 'non-section 76' type deception cannot be relevant in other contexts: indeed, when we consider deceptions in the context of section 74, we are not necessarily interested in their 'deception-ness' in itself; rather we are interested in the extent to which the deception forms part of a package of circumstances which preclude the complainant's 'agree[ment] by choice' or their 'ha[ving] the freedom and capacity to make that choice'.[37]

So, is there anything about the circumstances in the undercover cases which engages section 74? The route in here might be through the reference to 'freedom' in section 74. 'Freedom' defies brief description, and it gets none in the Act itself.[38] Nonetheless, we should note that it may connote different things. First, it suggests an *absence* of relevant constraints. Thus, we could imagine threats and pressure on a complainant compromising their freedom. Second, 'freedom' – especially in the context of freedom to make a choice – suggests the *availability* of the tools necessary to make that choice genuine. The principal tool in this context is information. 'Freedom' speaks to the degree of 'informed-ness' which is required for consent to be real and valid. In the undercover cases, the issue is whether the deceptive behaviour of the undercover officer is such as to deny the complainant access to information of such materiality that her freedom to make the choice to engage in sexual activity with the undercover officer is compromised, thereby vitiating her consent to that activity.

Section 74, and the notion of consent, is sufficiently complex that it is difficult to articulate with precision the extent of correspondence between 'what the complainant believes she or he is agreeing to' and 'what actually happens', which is necessary for consent to be valid. It has been held that a

---

[37] See Karl Laird, 'Rapist or rogue? Deception, consent and the Sexual Offences Act 2003' [2014] Criminal Law Review 492-510. He alludes to this when he asks (at 500), 'So long as the Crown proves that D's deception had the effect of extinguishing C's freedom to choose whether to engage in intercourse, then should that not suffice for the purposes of s74?'

[38] Nor indeed in the Explanatory Notes: (Sexual Offences Act 2003: Explanatory Notes <http://www.legislation.gov.uk/ukpga/2003/42/notes> accessed 18 February 2016).

defendant's failure to disclose their HIV positive status to a complainant was not relevant to the issue of consent for the purpose of section 74 and the offence of rape.[39] On the other hand, where a defendant pressurised a complainant into sexual intercourse by way of an elaborate scheme which culminated in him sending her texts purporting to be from the police, instructing her that she should have sexual intercourse with him, and that she would be liable to a fine if she did not, then for the purpose of section 74, the complainant did not consent to at least some of the instances of intercourse in question.[40] It has been suggested that where a defendant does not use a condom in sexual intercourse with a complainant, without the complainant's knowledge, and knowing that the use of a condom was a condition of the complainant's agreement to intercourse, that can be relevant to the issue of consent under section 74.[41] Similarly, should a defendant intentionally ejaculate in the body of the complainant, knowing that consent to intercourse has been granted on the basis that the defendant will withdraw before ejaculation, the validity of the complainant's consent under section 74 might be in question.[42] In these cases, the issue is that the behaviour of the defendant may have compromised the ability of the complainant to agree freely, as required by section 74, to what was happening. The Court of Appeal reached a similar conclusion in the context of offences of assault by penetration in relation to a defendant who deceived the complainant as to their gender.[43] Given that section 74 was designed to clarify rather than substantively change the law, although these cases post-date the coming into force of the 2003 Act, they are also useful for interpreting consent in the context of pre-Act conduct.

In the undercover cases, the complainant is under the impression that the sexual intercourse is taking place in the context of whatever relationship she believes she is having with the undercover officer. The officer is presumably aware that this is the complainant's position, and his behaviour may be taken to represent to the complainant that he is aware that this is her position. For the purpose of determining the validity of a

---

[39] *B* [2006] EWCA Crim 2945, [2007] 1 Cr App R 29. The failure to disclose could, however, be relevant to the commission of the offence of malicious infliction of grievous bodily harm under s 20 of the Offences against the Person Act 1861. See *Dica* [2004] EWCA Crim 1103, [2004] QB 1257; *Konzani* [2005] EWCA Crim 706, [2005] 2 Cr App R 14; *Golding* [2014] EWCA Crim 889.

[40] *Jheeta* [2007] EWCA Crim 1699, [2007] 2 Cr App R 34.

[41] *Assange v Swedish Prosecution Authority* [2011] EWHC 2849 (Admin).

[42] *R(F) v DPP* [2013] EWHC 945 (Admin), [2014] QB 581.

[43] *McNally* [2013] EWCA Crim 1051, [2014] QB 593.

complainant's consent to sexual intercourse, the law tolerates certain lies and a certain lack of candour, notwithstanding that they may be material to the complainant's agreement. The difficulty is in determining the scope of tolerance.[44] So, the defendant who makes exaggerated claims about his wealth or social status will not be guilty of the offence of rape where these blandishments lead to the complaint's consent to sexual intercourse. In such a case, the law fails to vindicate the complainant's autonomy, but the argument goes that this is the price to be paid to avoid overcriminalisation.[45] Let us concede for the sake of argument that certain situations in which a defendant knowingly takes advantage of another's misunderstanding, or certain types of lie, or certain types of deceptive conduct, are not the proper concern of the offence of rape. Notwithstanding that concession, an undercover officer's representation (by words, other conduct or both) that the sexual intercourse in question forms part of a relationship with the complainant which has a particular (and apparently mutually understood) status, when in fact he is using the relationship to gather intelligence for the State is not (and I ask for tolerance of the double negative) self-evidently *not* the concern of the criminal law. It does not of course follow from the suggestion that the behaviour may be the proper concern of the criminal law that the mechanism for expressing such proper concern is the offence of rape. However, there is a respectable argument that the complainant does not have sufficient information about the situation to give free agreement and that they therefore do not give a valid consent to the sexual intercourse for the purpose of section 74, or, in relation to conduct taking place before the coming into force of the 2003 Act, for the purpose of the common law.

Under section 3 of the Sexual Offences Act 1956, the law recognised the criminality of procuring sexual intercourse by way of false pretences – that is to say, deception – even where that deception was not of such a kind as

---

[44] For discussions, see Laird (n 37); Rebecca Williams, 'Deception, mistake and vitiation of the victim's consent' (2008) 124 Law Quarterly Review 132-159.

[45] Although not everybody would accept that argument. Herring argues for an approach to consent which gives significant weight to autonomy; in his argument, consent would be vitiated whenever a person was mistaken as to a fact material to their consent (i.e. they would not have consented had they known the truth): Jonathan Herring, 'Mistaken sex' [2005] Criminal Law Review 511-524, 517. Herring's approach has been criticized, for example, by Hyman Gross, 'Rape, moralism, and human rights' [2007] Criminal Law Review 220-227; and Michael Bohlander, 'Mistaken consent to sex, political correctness and correct policy' (2007) 71 Journal of Criminal Law 412-426.

to vitiate consent. Section 3 was abolished without replacement in the Sexual Offences Act 2003 and it is not entirely clear why this is.[46] A similar offence was recommended in the consultation exercise leading to the 2003 Act,[47] but by the time of the White Paper preceding the Act, the issue seems to have become bound up exclusively with the specific (entirely proper) concern with affording special protections to complainants with mental impairments which made them especially vulnerable.[48] Thus, there is no longer an offence of general application relating to procuring sexual intercourse through a non-consent-vitiating deception. Section 3 of the 1956 Act might, however, be relevant to undercover cases pre-dating the coming into force of the 2003 Act. The key legal concept in the offence is 'procur[ation]'. It has been suggested that the meaning of 'procure' is a matter of common sense for a jury,[49] although this might be an optimistic suggestion given the rarity of its usage in everyday contexts. Courts have suggested that procure means 'to produce by endeavour',[50] and that the concept might involve bringing about behaviour in another, which that other would not have undertaken 'spontaneously of [their] own volition'.[51]

It is reasonable to assume that the complainants in the undercover cases would not have acted as they did but for the false pretences of the officers. There could be some arguments relating to some kind of concept of remoteness. So, the deceptive conduct of the officers was not necessarily directed principally towards acts of sexual intercourse, but at the establishment and maintenance of the relationships with the complainants more broadly. This might call into question the issue of whether the *intercourse* itself was 'procured', or 'just' the relationships. On the other hand, drawing a distinction in this way, in this context, between the relationships and the intercourse might be artificial: the latter was closely connected with the former, and, indeed, that connection might be so integral that the former *depended* on the latter. If that is the case, it does not seem inapt to speak of procuring the sexual intercourse, notwithstanding that the intercourse was one component of the broader relationships, which were the principal concern of the officers. There is, it

---

[46] Laird (n 37) 499.

[47] Home Office (n 35) Recommendation 14, 30.

[48] Home Office, *Protecting the Public: Strengthening protection against sex offenders and reforming the law on sexual offences* (CM 5668, 2002) [63].

[49] *Broadfoot* (1977) 64 Cr App R 71, 74.

[50] *Attorney General's Reference (No 1 of 1975)* [1975] QB 773, 779.

[51] *Broadfoot* (n 49) 74.

seems, a reasonable argument to be had about whether the undercover cases involve the commission of offences under section 3 of the Sexual Offences Act 1956.

Of course, even if a prosecution was brought in any of the undercover cases, and even if the court was of the view that the elements of the offence in question had been made out, the officer facing prosecution might seek to avoid criminal liability by raising a defence. What shape would such a defence take? If one were to seek a defence in the general criminal law, it would presumably be grounded in the 'positive' motives underlying the conduct in question. The argument would be that, although the elements of the offence of, for example, rape, were admitted, the motives of the officer – in relation to the furtherance of the undercover operation and the ultimate frustration of criminal purposes – would provide a defence to a charge. An attempt might be made to base such a defence in *necessity*, although this seems to be far-fetched. There is longstanding judicial resistance to the development of such a defence, and it would be a bold claim on the facts to suggest that there was no way of realising the aims of the undercover operation other than by engaging in sexual activity with the complainants. Insofar as there may be a defence of necessity, its requirement that the harm to be avoided by the otherwise criminal activity outweighs the harm caused by it would also be difficult to meet in these cases. Moreover, a key mischief which the law on necessity seeks to avoid is starkly present in the undercover cases: just as it was said to be inappropriate for Dudley and Stephens to make the decision to kill the cabin boy Richard Parker in the lifeboat of the Mignonette, even where this was with a view to their own survival,[52] so, the argument would go, it is not for the police officer himself to arrogate the interests of the police operation above the sexual autonomy interests of the complainant.

An alternative route to a defence might be by reading across from the law on accessoryship the suggestion that there *may be* a limited defence available to those who participate in an offence with a view to frustrating its ultimate purpose. Such a defence might be available for example to the participant in the burglary who drives with the proceeds of the burglary to a pre-arranged meeting with police in order to return the goods and to provide evidence in relation to other offenders. The key case, *Birtles*,[53] involved the conduct of an accessory, but it is not clear that other cases are

---

[52] *Dudley and Stephens* (1884) 14 QBD 273.

[53] *Birtles* (1969) 53 Cr App R 469.

restricted to such parties;[54] nor is there any compelling non-legal reason for such a restriction.[55] However, insofar as there might be a defence for accessories, or indeed, for anybody, it may well be restricted to participating in those offences which are going to take place anyway – to use the phrase from the cases, those offences which are already 'laid on'.[56] An appeal to a defence based on the frustration of the purpose of a criminal offence will not succeed for a defendant who encouraged or assisted that offence, when it would not otherwise have been committed; 'crime creation' is not tolerated. If in the undercover cases the elements of say, rape, are made out, that would appear to be an offence which would not otherwise have taken place, and the availability of the defence by virtue of the analogy with accessoryship appears to be unlikely. The 'frustration of criminal purpose' defence also suffers from the deficiency identified above in relation to necessity: it is not clear why the police officer himself should be entitled to judge that the sexual autonomy of the complainant should be subservient to the interests of the police operation.

An undercover officer seeking a substantive defence in relation to conduct taking place prior to the coming into force of the Regulation of Investigatory Powers Act (RIPA) 2000 would need to seek that defence in the general criminal law. There may be another option available in relation to post-RIPA conduct. This option would be based on the undercover officer being 'authorised' as a Covert Human Intelligence Source ('CHIS').[57] Because there was no clear statutory authority for authorisations pre-RIPA, those authorisations could not meet the requirement of Article 8 of the European Convention on Human Rights that interference with privacy rights be 'in accordance with law'.[58] RIPA was intended to remedy this deficiency. Section 27(1) of RIPA states that the conduct of a CHIS in accordance with the authorisation will be 'lawful for all purposes'. While this is principally intended to meet the requirements of the European Convention – 'lawful' meaning 'in accordance with law' – there is an ambivalence in the meaning of 'lawful'

---

[54] *Clarke* (1985) 80 Cr App R 344.

[55] In simple terms, accessorial behaviour is not always less blameworthy than that of the relevant principal offender. So, if a defence is in theory available to an accessory, then the mere fact that a particular defendant is a principal offender should not, of itself, preclude the availability of the defence to that defendant.

[56] *Birtles* (n 53) 472; *Clarke* (n 54) 348.

[57] Regulation of Investigatory Powers Act 2000, ss 26, 29.

[58] See, for example, *Khan v UK* (2001) 31 EHRR 45; *PG v UK* (2008) 46 EHRR 51.

which is compounded by the words 'for all purposes'. The question here is whether section 27(1) confers some kind of immunity from criminal liability for the CHIS who acts in accordance with the authorisation. On this interpretation, 'lawful', in section 27(1) refers not merely to the principle of legality, but also to compliance with the demands of the criminal law; in effect to the existence of a substantive defence, based on 'authorisation', which allows the officer to avoid criminal liability. The CHIS Code of Practice is, to use McKay's term, more circumspect.[59] It suggests that '[n]either Part II of the 2000 Act nor this code of practice is intended to affect the existing practices and procedures surrounding criminal participation of CHIS'.[60]

If there are some situations in which a valid CHIS authorisation can serve to confer some kind of immunity on an officer's otherwise criminal conduct, while they may may defy comprehensive or precise definition, they must presumably be framed narrowly in order that citizens' rights can be adequately respected, and to comply with the basic political and constitutional principles of a liberal society. Only in the rarest of instances – if at all – could it be realistically suggested that the State-sanctioned violation of the sexual autonomy of citizens would comply with these principles.

---

[59] McKay (n 6)[7.69] 209.

[60] Home Office, *Covert Human Intelligence Sources: Code of Practice* (2014) <https://www.gov.uk/government/uploads/system/uploads/attachment_data/file/38 4976/Covert_Human_Intelligence_web.pdf> accessed 22 February 2016, [1.9]. Writing about an earlier version of the Code, Whitaker had suggested a narrow reading of section 27(1), claiming that it 'is intended to provide a lawful basis for activity previously lacking statutory regulation, rather than to confer immunity from [sic] otherwise illegal criminal activity by making such activity lawful'; Quincy Whitaker, 'Surveillance and Covert Human Intelligence Sources under the Regulation of Investigatory Powers Act 2000', in Keir Starmer, Michelle Strange and Quincy Whitaker (with Anthony Jennings and Tim Owen), *Criminal Justice, Police Powers and Human Rights* (Blackstone 2001) 63-73, 71). By contrast, an earlier version of the Code of Practice stated: 'In a very limited range of circumstances an authorisation under Part II [of RIPA] may (...) render lawful conduct which would otherwise be criminal', Home Office, *Covert Human Intelligence Sources: Code of Practice* (undated) <http://webarchive.nationalarchives.gov.uk/20130128103514/http://homeoffice.go v.uk/crimpol/crimreduc/regulation/codeofpractice/humanintell/part2.html> accessed 22 February 2016, [2.10].

To be valid under RIPA, a CHIS authorisation must satisfy a number of substantive and procedural requirements.[61] Should any of those not be met, the authorisation will be deficient, and incapable, of itself, of supporting a claim for immunity from criminal liability. In the context of the undercover cases, the question has also been considered of whether there is any conduct which is incapable of being the subject of a valid authorisation. In *AKJ and others v Commissioner of Police for the Metropolis and others*,[62] a case brought, *inter alia*, by some of the women with whom undercover officers had entered into intimate relationships, Tugendhat J differentiated between undercover conduct which would violate a complainant's right to be free from degrading treatment, which could not be authorised under RIPA, and conduct which violated a complainant's right to privacy, which could. In his view, a sexual relationship founded on deception would not *necessarily* violate a complainant's right to be free from degrading treatment; it was therefore not possible to conclude that *all* such relationships were incapable of authorisation under RIPA.[63]

Perhaps a *substantive* defence is not the most legally appropriate response to an allegation of sexual offending in an undercover case. So, where an officer has been *authorised to* form, or even *tasked with* the development of an intimate relationship as part of an undercover operation, that authorisation or tasking comes, in effect from the State. Assuming that the officer acts in good faith, he may suggest that it is unfair for the State which authorised or encouraged his behaviour, to then prosecute him for that same behaviour. This would in effect be a claim that to prosecute him would be an abuse of process.[64] This claim does not contest that the elements of the offence of rape are made out; nor does it seek directly to diminish the agency of the officer by appealing to a blameworthiness-

---

[61] These relate, for example, to the purpose for which the authorisation is granted; to the status of the party granting the authorisation; and to the arrangements in place for monitoring the CHIS. See Regulation of Investigatory Powers Act 2000, s 29; *CHIS Code of Practice* (n 60).

[62] *AKJ and others v Commissioner of Police for the Metropolis and others* [2013] EWHC 32.

[63] ibid [156]-[161].

[64] See, for example, Andrew L-T Choo, *Abuse of Process and Judicial Stays of Criminal Proceedings* (2nd edn, Oxford University Press 2008). The argument against abuse of process would be that while the doctrine is used against improper executive conduct, in the intimate relationships cases, the officers are themselves also engaged in improper conduct.

reducing defence. Rather, it suggests that to go ahead with a trial would be improper.

I suggest that the above discussion shows that there is, at a minimum, sufficient ambiguity in the law, both prior to and since the coming into force of the Sexual Offences Act 2003, to suggest that the undercover cases *may* involve the commission of offences of rape and (in the case of pre-2003 Act conduct) procuring intercourse by false pretences. I put it no higher than *may*, and it may be that such an argument would fail, or that a prosecution would founder, for a range of reasons. These include (i) the narrow approach at common law to the 'nature' of an act; (ii) the limited relevance at common law of the 'identity' of an actor; (iii) strict construction of the conclusive presumptions in relation to consent under the 2003 Act; (iv) a restrictive approach to the meaning of consent at common law and in section 74 of the 2003 Act; (v) a finding of too great a degree of remoteness between the relevant false pretences and the sexual intercourse, for the purpose of section 3 of the Sexual Offences Act 1956; (vi) a successful argument in relation to a substantive defence, rooted in the general criminal law or in a RIPA authorisation; or (vii) a successful abuse of process argument.

The Crown Prosecution Service has made one decision not to proceed with prosecutions in relation to pre-2003 Act alleged undercover sexual conduct by members of the Special Demonstration Squad.[65] I suggest that this decision, while not irrational, may be viewed as premature. The basis for the decision is a lack of sufficient evidence for a realistic prospect of conviction.[66] This conclusion would be stronger if the principal facts were seriously in issue, but there is no indication that that is the case: nobody appears to be claiming that the relevant instances of sexual intercourse did not take place, nor that the women were not under the misapprehensions as to who their sexual partners actually were. Rather, the decision of the CPS appears to rest on particular interpretations of the law, and on the implication that a court would interpret the law in the same way. I have suggested that that is not certain. I also suggest that, all else equal, it would have been defensible with reference to the Code for Crown

---

[65] Crown Prosecution Service, 'Charging decision concerning MPS Special Demonstration Squad' (21 August 2014) <http://www.cps.gov.uk/news/latest_news/charging_decision_concerning_mps_sp ecial_demonstration_squad/index.html> accessed 19 January 2016.
[66] ibid.

Prosecutors[67] for the prosecutions in question to proceed, and that there
would have been ancillary advantages in having the legal arguments
judicially resolved either way. It remains to be seen whether further
complaints of criminal behaviour are made in respect of the undercover
cases. The CPS may have to address different issues from those it
considered in the SDS decision where conduct relates to conduct taking
place after the coming into force of the 2003 Act. Moreover, even in
relation to pre-2003 Act conduct, the legal arguments have not gone away,
albeit that the SDS decision might act as a deterrent to prosecution.

The Future for Undercover Policing
and the Implications for Intimate Relationships

From the point at which undercover officer Mark Kennedy's identity was
exposed, leading to the collapse of trials and the quashing of convictions
of environmental activists in relation to planned protest activity at
Ratcliffe-on-Soar power station,[68] there has been a spectacular unravelling
of the fabric of undercover policing. A combination of official scrutiny[69]
and investigative journalism[70] has cast serious doubt on the legitimacy of a
number of aspects of undercover activity by bringing to light a range of
troubling practices and allegations, including: the systematic use of the
identities of dead children to bolster and secure undercover 'legends';[71] the

---

[67] Before a prosecution proceeds, two tests under the Code for Crown Prosecutors
need to be satisfied. The first test relates to evidential sufficiency, and it is at this
hurdle which the potential SDS prosecutions fell. The second test relates to the
public interest. Thus, if there is sufficient evidence for a realistic prospect of
conviction, a prosecution will still only go ahead if it is in the public interest for it
to do so. I would suggest that had the evidential sufficiency test been satisfied,
there would have been a plausible case that the public interest test would also have
been satisfied. See Crown Prosecution Service, *The Code for Crown Prosecutors*
(2013)
<http://www.cps.gov.uk/publications/docs/code_2013_accessible_english.pdf>
accessed 22 February 2016, 6-10.
[68] *Barkshire and others* [2011] EWCA Crim 1885. For discussion, see, for
example, Evans and Lewis (n 13) 3-8, chs 14-18; Kingsley Hyland and Clive
Walker, 'Undercover policing and underwhelming laws' [2014] Criminal Law
Review 555-574, 565-570.
[69] See the various reports documented by Hyland and Walker (n 68) at 567-570.
[70] See, for example, Evans and Lewis (n 13).
[71] See, for example, House of Commons Home Affairs Committee (n 10); Mick
Creedon, *Operation Herne Report 1: Use of covert identities* (2013)
<http://content.met.police.uk/cs/Satellite?blobcol=urldata&blobheadername1=Con

deployment of an undercover officer into an activist group associated with the campaign for justice for Stephen Lawrence, the victim of a racist murder, at the time of a public inquiry into his killing;[72] reports that undercover officers had testified in cases under their assumed personas, thereby deceiving the court itself.[73] The deep sense of disquiet has been compounded by the intimate relationships cases. The distressing nature of the women's stories[74] presents a compelling narrative of individual lives turned upside down for the apparent benefit of the State.[75] This has reinforced the point that when undercover policing is in some way out of control, the consequences may not be limited to mere 'roguery' or the 'technical' subversion of legal processes.

The recent and sustained public scrutiny has brought undercover policing to something of a watershed moment, which has been reached independently of whether the behaviour of the undercover officers in the intimate relationships cases was actually criminal. The situation may not be of quite the same order as that which followed the murder of Stephen Lawrence and the subsequent MacPherson Inquiry and Report.[76] That,

tent-Type&blobheadername2=Content-
Disposition&blobheadervalue1=application%2Fpdf&blobheadervalue2=inline%3
B+filename%3D%22480%2F119%2FCO634-
12OpHernereport.pdf%22&blobkey=id&blobtable=MungoBlobs&blobwhere=128
3637911711&ssbinary=true> accessed February 22 2016.
[72] Mark Ellison QC, *The Stephen Lawrence Independent Review: Possible corruption and the role of undercover policing in the Stephen Lawrence case: Summary of Findings* (2014, HC 1094)
<https://www.gov.uk/government/uploads/system/uploads/attachment_data/file/28
7030/stephen_lawrence_review_summary.pdf> accessed February 22 2016.
[73] House of Commons Home Affairs Committee (n 10).
[74] ibid. See also Police Spies Out of Lives: Support group for women's legal action against undercover policing, *Our Stories* <https://policespiesoutoflives.org.uk/our-stories/> accessed 22 February 2016.
[75] See, for example, Carole McCartney and Natalie Wortley, 'Raped by the state' (2014) 78 Journal of Criminal Law 1-3. The title of McCartney and Wortley's article is taken from a phrase used by a woman with whom Bob Lambert had an undercover intimate relationship, which led to the birth of a child. See Paul Lewis, Rob Evans and Sorcha Pollak, 'Trauma of spy's girlfriend: "like being raped by the state"' (24 June 2013) <http://www.theguardian.com/uk/2013/jun/24/undercover-police-spy-girlfriend-child> accessed 22 February 2016.
[76] William MacPherson, *The Stephen Lawrence Inquiry: Report of an Inquiry by Sir William MacPherson of Cluny, Volume I* (1999, Cm 4262-I)
<https://www.gov.uk/government/uploads/system/uploads/attachment_data/file/27
7111/4262.pdf> accessed 23 February 2016.

after all, could have been taken to represent a judgement on the racial inequities of *all* policing practice. What faces us in relation to undercover policing is a collapse of trust in *particular* aspects of police work; but those aspects are of especial significance in the broader context of smart, targeted, intelligence-led policing activity. To respond to this problem, the Home Secretary announced in 2015 that there would be an Inquiry[77] into undercover policing.[78] The Inquiry is being chaired by Lord Justice Pitchford and it is hoped that it will report in Summer 2018.[79] The terms of reference of the Inquiry[80] suggest that it could involve a root and branch review of undercover policing, from first principles.[81] While the Inquiry reaches far wider than the intimate relationships cases, it is to be hoped that it will consider, for example the ethicality, legality and efficacy of the cultivation of intimate relationships as a means to achieving otherwise

---

[77] Home Office, *Written Statement made by: The Secretary of State for the Home Department (Mrs Theresa May) on 12 Mar 2015: Undercover policing*, (12 March 2015, House of Commons: Written Statement (HCWS381)) <http://www.parliament.uk/documents/commons-vote-office/March%202015/12%20March%202015/31.HOME-Undercover-policing.pdf> accessed 23 February 2016.
[78] See Undercover Policing Inquiry <https://www.ucpi.org.uk> accessed 23 February 2016. The Inquiry is governed by the Inquiries Act 2005.
[79] Undercover Policing Inquiry, 'About the Inquiry' <https://www.ucpi.org.uk/about-the-inquiry/> accessed 23 February 2016.
[80] ibid.
[81] According to the Terms of Reference, see (n 79), the purpose of the Inquiry is: 'To inquire into and report on undercover police operations conducted by English and Welsh police forces in England and Wales since 1968 and, in particular, to:
- investigate the role and the contribution made by undercover policing towards the prevention and detection of crime;
- examine the motivation for, and the scope of, undercover police operations in practice and their effect upon individuals in particular and the public in general;
- ascertain the state of awareness of undercover police operations of Her Majesty's Government;
- identify and assess the adequacy of the:
  o justification, authorisation, operational governance and oversight of undercover policing;
  o selection, training, management and care of undercover police officers;
- identify and assess the adequacy of the statutory, policy and judicial regulation of undercover policing.'

desirable policing outcomes.[82] The terms of reference give some hope for
cautious optimism in this regard.[83]

Questions remain as to what will follow from the Inquiry. In 2013, the
Home Affairs Committee envisaged a 'fundamental review of the
legislative framework governing undercover policing, including the
Regulation of Investigatory Powers Act 2000',[84] and that is written into
the Inquiry terms of reference.[85] In simple terms, however, one does not
change behaviour in any organisation – including the police – *simply* by
changing the laws and formal rules which apply to that organisation. If we
are to avoid repetition of the devastating and unjustified damage caused by
the intimate relationships cases, the *culture* which allowed them to be
viewed as tolerable needs to be acknowledged and addressed. Again, there

---

[82] Any observations made by the Inquiry in relation to the legality or otherwise of
intimate relationships undercover will not necessarily lead to prosecutions. To
facilitate cooperation with the Inquiry, the Attorney General may give an
undertaking that evidence given by a witness to the Inquiry will not be used in
criminal proceedings against that witness. See *Undercover Policing Inquiry:
Counsel to the Inquiry's Note on Undertakings* (8 January 2016)
<https://www.ucpi.org.uk/wp-content/uploads/2016/01/160108-undertakings-
note.pdf> accessed 3 March 2016.

[83] See (n 81), especially the second bullet point in the Terms of Reference
concerning the purpose of the Inquiry, particularly the reference to '[the] effect [of
undercover operations] upon individuals in particular and the public in general'.
Also relevant here is the suggestion in the Terms of Reference (n 81) regarding the
scope of the Inquiry that '[t]he inquiry's investigation will include, but not be
limited to, whether and to what purpose, extent and effect undercover police
operations have targeted political and social justice campaigners.' The intimate
relationships cases have taken place in the context of targeting such groups.
In the context of the proceedings of the Inquiry, there are ongoing arguments in
relation to the extent to which evidence will be given in open session. There have
been police representations regarding the desirability of taking some evidence in
closed sessions, given the sensitivity of the issues (see, for example, Metropolitan
Police Service, *In the Undercover Policing Inquiry: Submissions on Restriction
Orders* (12 February 2016) <https://www.ucpi.org.uk/wp-content/uploads/
2016/02/160212-submissions-on-the-legal-approach-to-restriction-orders-Met-
Police.pdf> accessed 3 March 2016). This suggestion, as one would expect, has
met with some controversy (see, for example, Rob Evans, 'Police to request
secrecy for parts of undercover officers inquiry' (21 February 2016)
<http://www.theguardian.com/uk-news/2016/feb/21/police-request-secrecy-
undercover-officers-inquiry> accessed 3 March 2016).

[84] House of Commons Home Affairs Committee (n 10) [15] and Conclusions and
recommendations [2].

[85] See (n 79), (n 81).

are some grounds for cautious optimism, although we will not be in a
position to judge properly for some time. The apology to the women in
question and and the acknowledgement by the Metropolitan Police that a
number of undercover intimate relationships were 'abusive, deceitful,
manipulative and wrong',[86] given as part of a broader settlement, suggests
at least that the magnitude of the situation is recognised by those in
authority.[87] The development by the College of Policing of a Code of
Ethics,[88] as part of a broader workstream on police integrity, might also be
seen to be an indication of organisational commitment to good practice.[89]
The CHIS Code of Practice has been developed to differentiate between
civilian informants and undercover officers, the latter now being subject to

---

[86] Metropolitan Police, 'Claimants in civil cases receive MPS apology' (20
November 2015) <http://news.met.police.uk/news/claimants-in-civil-cases-
receive-mps-apology-138574> accessed 26 February 2016.
[87] That the gravity of a situation is recognised in one constituent group of an
organisation does not guarantee that that position is shared across the organisation
as a whole. That the cultures and priorities of different constituencies within the
police may be at odds has been acknowledged by commentators. See, for example,
Bethan Loftus, *Police Culture in a Changing World* (Oxford University Press
2009) 93; Roger Graef, *Talking Blues: The Police in their Own Words* (Fontana
1990). Accordingly, it would be possible for managers and leaders to acknowledge
the wrongness of undercover intimate relationships, while that acknowledgement
was not shared, and indeed could be undermined, by those more directly involved
with undercover activity.
[88] College of Policing, *Code of Ethics: A Code of Practice for the Principles and
Standards of Professional Behaviour for the Policing Profession of England and
Wales* (2014) <http://www.college.police.uk/What-we-do/Ethics/Documents/Code
_of_Ethics.pdf> accessed February 27 2016.
[89] Although the extent of its applicability to undercover intimate relationships
cases may be not absolutely clear. The Code refers to covert policing in the context
of the 'Honesty and integrity' 'Standard of Professional Behaviour' (*Code of
Ethics* (n 88) 5, [1.4-1.7]; there is a general prohibition on 'sexual conduct or other
inappropriate behaviour when on duty' in the 'Authority, respect and courtesy'
standard (*Code of Ethics* (n 88) 6, [2.3]. A rather unresolved exchange between
Alex Marshall, Chief Executive Officer of the College of Policing, and the Home
Affairs Select Committee suggests that whether the Code precludes undercover
intimate relationships under all circumstances is not clear (see House of Commons
Home Affairs Committee, *Leadership and standards in the police: follow-up;
Minutes of Evidence* (29 October 2013, HC 2013-14, HC 756-ii),
<http://www.publications.parliament.uk/pa/cm201314/cmselect/cmhaff/756/13102
9.htm> accessed 27 February 2016, Q540-Q550. And of course, the question of
what the impact of the Code will be on actual policing behaviours remains (see (n
88) Q539 for a note of caution).

an enhanced regime of authorisation and oversight.[90] More generally, the normalisation of 'rights' in the orientation of contemporary policing is a useful counter to the default utilitarianism of aspects of historic undercover activity:[91] the idea that the ends do not always justify the means is now fairly conventional. Although policing cultures are complex and can be (in this context, small-c) conservative, moments of public crisis such as that currently facing undercover activity can catalyse reflection and lead to change.[92] A key question will be whether the Pitchford Inquiry is sufficiently external to the police to garner public legitimacy, while also demonstrating sufficient practical and cultural knowledge and understanding of policing to gain traction with police leaders and individual officers.

It is unlikely that any legal changes which flow from Pitchford will *directly* affect the content of sexual offences law. Indeed, if the current CPS position is followed,[93] sexual offences law is a substantive non-issue. Even if that view is challenged, which I have suggested it should be, the relevance of sexual offences law to intimate undercover relationships will be via the issues of what CHIS behaviours can be authorised, and the extent to which authorisation provides a substantive defence or the basis for an abuse of process argument. There is no doubt that crafting a post-Pitchford RIPA-replacement which addresses the intimate relationships issue will be challenging, and there might be some questions over whether such a law would need to refer explicitly to such relationships, or whether

---

[90] Previously, whether a CHIS was a civilian or was an undercover officer, the legal regime for dealing with them was, in essence, the same. Now, an undercover officer is, for the purposes of RIPA and the Code of Practice, a 'relevant source', to whom the new arrangements apply (see *CHIS Code of Practice*, (n 60) Annex B).

[91] See, for example, Peter Neyroud and Alan Beckley, *Policing, Ethics and Human Rights* (Willan 2001). It has been suggested that the move towards due acknowledgement of rights has not gone far enough (see, for example, Hyland and Walker (n 68)). On the matter of historic utilitarianism, an unofficial (and utilitarian) motto used by members of the Special Demonstration Squad was 'By Any Means Necessary' (see Evans and Lewis (n 13) 17).

[92] See Janet BL Chan, *Changing Police Culture: Policing in a Multicultural Society* (Cambridge University Press 1997). Chan's work refers to the impact of a damning TV documentary throwing light on the responsibility of police in a district of Sydney, Australia for their abject relations with the Aboriginal community. The documentary, entitled *Cop it Sweet*, can be viewed online: <https://www.youtube.com/watch?v=Nft5cn7EHvQ> accessed 1 March 2016.

[93] See (n 65).

they are adequately addressed through consideration of the underlying issues of whether the relationships were necessary and proportionate.[94] The failings involved in the intimate relationships cases suggest that whatever the law ultimately looks like, there is value in attention being drawn in some way[95] specifically to the issues which are particularly relevant in such situations.

Gardner and Shute memorably described the wrongness of rape as the 'sheer use of a person'.[96] Intimate relationships undercover may or may not amount to rape, but the 'sheer use' label seems apt nonetheless. It is presumptively wrong for one person to use another, and it is presumptively wrong for the State to use citizens in the manner suggested by such relationships.[97]

Writing in the context of police malpractice more broadly, Sanders, Young and Burton allude to the possibility of 'encourag[ing] a frank debate in which the police are open about what they do, lawfully and unlawfully, and what they can deliver without rule-breaking.'[98] Pitchford provides an opportunity for this, and let us hope that it is taken. In the general context of undercover policing, rule-breaking should in broad terms be a last resort. As to the particular issue of the cultivation of intimate relationships undercover, the rules and the relevant organisational culture should reflect the fact that our tolerance should be given on an exceptional basis, if at all.

---

[94] Necessity and proportionality would presumably remain as aspects of the statutory requirements for authorisation.

[95] For example, it may be that the intimate relationships issue might be usefully written into the Code of Practice as a matter for consideration (and of which consideration should be evidenced) in relevant cases.

[96] John Gardner and Stephen Shute, 'The Wrongness of Rape' in Jeremy Horder (ed), *Oxford Essays in Jurisprudence* (Fourth Series, Oxford University Press 2000) 193-217, 205.

[97] It has been suggested that specific issues may arise when the State is the 'user' which may not arise when the use is 'merely' by one person of another. Marx points to the position of the State as the 'symbolic repository of societal values' and its attendant 'need to avoid setting bad examples' (Gary T Marx, 'Under-the-Covers Undercover Investigations: Some Reflections on the State's Use of Sex and Deception in Law Enforcement' (1992) 11 Criminal Justice Ethics 13-24, 13).

[98] Andrew Sanders, Richard Young and Mandy Burton, *Criminal Justice* (4th edn, Oxford University Press 2010) 716.

CHAPTER ELEVEN

CRIMINALISATION OF HIV TRANSMISSION: ANGLO-NORTH-AMERICAN COMPARATIVE PERSPECTIVES AND OPTIMAL REFORMS TO FAILURE OF PROOF DEFENCES

DAVID HUGHES AND ALAN REED

Introduction

The Law Commission have recently considered the broader ambit of reform of offences against the person precepts.[1] This important review has directly examined whether, under a revised statute in this arena, bespoke criminal liability should apply to the transmission of disease, particularly in the context of the reckless transmission of HIV or sexually transmissible infections through consensual sexual intercourse.[2] The recommendation promulgated is that the creation of any individuated offence attached to the transmission of HIV ought to be delayed pending a wider review of substantive principles, but that disease may fall within the wider definition of 'serious injury', under more general statutory reform proposals that can propitiously be advanced immediately.[3]

A fundamentally different perspective to the criminalisation of transmission of HIV is advanced in this chapter. It is asserted that a de novo legislative response is urgently needed to specifically address thresholds of culpability and blameworthiness to 'legitimate' any potential inculpation, and to provide much needed clarity and certainty that there is a troubling lack of predictability in an area of the law that cries out for

---

[1] Law Commission, *Reform of the Offences Against the Person* (Law Com No 361, 2015).
[2] ibid [6.1 - 6.146].
[3] ibid [6.143 - 6.146].

certainty.. There is an egregious failure under extant law to distinguish
between levels of culpability and levels of (risk) of harm, and to
consequentially avoid the danger of over-criminalisation for consensual
sexual activity.[4] In this context our focus is to consider a spectrum of
legislative defences that ought to apply as failure of proof factorisations,
and are individually exculpatory.[5] The parameters of these failure of proof
defences are examined against three posited questions: (1) If D1 uses a
condom, is it imperative still to disclose their HIV status?; (2) If D1 has a
non-detectable or a very low viral load, can non-disclosure still result in
criminal liability?; and (3) Can a failure of proof defence apply if the
sexual activity that D1 is engaging in is viewed as low risk? These
postulations are extirpated in a comparative sense, reviewing extant
English law in juxtaposition with Canadian precepts, and set against a
myriad of beguilingly inconsistent current principles adopted across a
panoply of US states. The aim is to charter a pathway towards a novel
optimal reform model for statutory defences applicable to the transmission
of HIV. Moreover, it is contended whether if D1 was justified in exposing
V to the risk of infection without disclosing the condition should be a
question for the jury in each particular case.[6] The evaluation by jurors, as
moral arbiters, should be with an awareness that the evaluation of
recklessness or otherwise on the part of D1 may apply in certain defined
situations at an earlier temporal individuation than consent.[7]

A cogent rationale exists for autonomous individual determination to
consent to the risk of becoming infected with HIV via consensual
intercourse. This is not, nor should it be, the end of potential defences for
D1and there are a number of other circumstances whereby it can be argued
that an actor has behaved in a responsible manner to sexual activity, and
no criminal liability should apply.[8] If a defendant uses condoms, or is
aware of the level of their low viral load, or knows that certain sexual
activities pose less of a risk of transmission, then they should be able to
utilise these defences, either disjunctively or conjunctively, to avoid

---

[4] See generally, Jonathan Rogers, 'Criminal Liability for the Transmission of HIV'
(2005) 64(1) Cambridge law Journal 20.
[5] See generally, Matthew Weait, *Intimacy and Responsibility: The Criminalisation
of the Transmission of HIV* (Routledge-Cavendish, Abingdon 2007).
[6] See generally James Chalmers, *Legal Response to HIV and AIDS* (Hart
Publishing, Oxford, 2008).
[7] Udo Schuklenk, ' Should We Use Criminal Law to Punish HIV Transmission'
(2008) International Journal of Law in Context 277.
[8] Law Commission (No 361) (n 1) [6.19].

criminal sanctions. Medical and scientific advances in our understanding of the disease, and effective prevention, should prompt a wider recategorisation of harm/risk of harm.

The statistical probability attached to no transmission through safe sex, the advancement of anti-retroviral medication, and that certain types of sexual activity pose less of a risk of transmission, signify that there are more extenuating circumstances where the defendant should not be criminally responsible for his actions. Condom use, viral load, and certain types of sexual activity should be considered to be defences of 'reasonable precautions',[9] where the defendant has attempted to reduce the risk of the virus being transmitted, and the risk was a reasonable one to take in that the risk of transmission is very small. The concomitant is that the issue of recklessness, and conscious advertence to the risk of harm on the part of the defendant, is presented at an earlier temporal individuation, prior to the consent question.[10] Recklessness, or otherwise, may, thus, arguably be viewed through a legal prism where it is supererogatory with consent not affected by non-disclosure. These defences can be categorised as 'failure of proof' defences,[11] in that condom use, viral load, and low risk sexual activities negate definitional elements of the offence (recklessness), and with an affirmative evidentiary onus on D1. The defendant as a practical matter may have to act affirmatively to present evidence on the issue of a given element of the offense; he may have certain evidentiary burdens. Robinson has categorised the ambit of such defences in the following broad terms:

> Failure of proof defenses consist of instances in which, because of the conditions that are the basis for the 'defense', all elements of the offense charged cannot be proven. They are in essence no more than the negation of an element required by the definition of the offense.[12]

The focal inquiry should be whether a defendant, who uses a condom, has awareness of low viral load from a practitioner, or engages in low risk sexual activity, is reckless ab initio, in light of medical and scientific

---

[9] Keith JM Smith, 'Sexual Etiquette, Public Interest and the Criminal Law' (1991) 42 Northern Ireland Law Quarterly 309, 328.
[10] See generally, Sun Goo Lee, 'Criminal Law and HIV Testing: Empirical Analysis of How at Risk Individuals Respond to the Law' (2015) 14 Yale Journal of Health Policy Law and Ethics 194.
[11] Paul H. Robinson, 'Criminal Law Defenses: A Systematic Analysis' (1982) 82 Columbia law Review 199, 204.
[12] ibid 204.

developmental awareness. As previously stated, recklessness embodies not only that the individual actor knowingly adverts to and takes a risk, but also that the conduct was 'unjustified' in the circumstances that D knows or believes it to be. This factorisation should involve a wider pantheon of legitimate inculcations that extend to the social value of the activity in question (freedom to pursue sexual relationships), the level of harm risked, and probability of actual harm or consequential harm reduction.[13]

The corollary is that awareness of one's undetectable viral load per se may denote that an individual is not being reckless or acting intentionally as to harm through transmission, encompassing situations where a medical practitioner has confirmed that the actor was not infectious at the time of the sexual contact. It has been recently submitted that the risk in such circumstances is de minimis, practically non-existent in practice, with a study of 44,000 unprotected sex acts involving an HIV positive partner, but with an undetectable viral load due to treatment, revealing no cases at all of actual transmission;[14] a stark iteration of positive scientific developments impacting on harm reduction.

Furthermore, condom use per se as a defence is in line with public health initiatives, and utilising such precautions should be encouraged, given that they can significantly decrease the risk of transmission of the virus, and thereby encourage safe sex practices. It is proposed that if condom use can be a defence, then viral load, and certain types of sexual activity, should also be permitted as failure of proof categorisation defences, and all constitutively *ejusdem generis*. The defences share particulated commonalities in that the statistical probability of transmission through protected intercourse can be the same as, or more risky than, a low or undetectable viral load, and can be akin to certain types of sexual activity. Systematic review and meta-analysis have indicated, for instance, that the risk of transmission in vaginal sex decreases to 1 in 10,000 for the woman and 1 in 20,000 for the man.[15]

The subsequent parts of this chapter are split into four sections, examining in turn the current relevance of condom use, low or undetectable viral

---

[13] See generally, Scott Burris, 'Do Criminal Laws Influence HIV Risk Behaviour? An Empirical Trial' (2007) 39 Arizona State Law Journal 467.
[14] Law Commission No 361 (n 1) at [6.19].
[15] Isabel Grant, 'The Prosecution of Non-disclosure of HIV in Canada: Time to Rethink *Cuerrier*' (2011) McGill Journal of Law and Health 7; and see generally Sun Goo Lee (n 10).

load, and types of sexual activity as a probative defence, or otherwise, within England, Canada and identified U.S. states. Extirpation of the individuated legal systems is conducted in a comparative review framework in order to promulgate an optimal statutory defence template for universal adoption and holistic incorporation: our new template reconceptualises individuated legislative responses that have been beneficially adopted in Iowa, Illinois and California. The aim is to present a cathartic panacea to incremental ad hocery and uncertainties that obfuscate extant law in terms of fault (recklessness) conjoined with appropriate defence parameters. It will also assist jurors as moral arbiters in terms of the determination of questions of fact, invoking systematic medical and scientific guidance appurtenant to probative exculpatory conduct.

Failure of Proof Defences: English Law

Condom Use as a Potential Defence to the Reckless Transmission of HIV

Neither the common law of England, nor specific legislation, has determinatively stipulated that any defence, other than informed consent, can be raised in a sexual transmission of HIV case.[16] Under extant precepts, as determined in *Dica* and *Konzani*, liability prevails for the infliction of grievous bodily harm (HIV) where four offence-definitional constructs apply: (i) transmission of the disease occurs, and exposure to the risk of infection is insufficient; (ii) D intends to inflict some harm upon V or consciously adverted (recklessly) to that risk; (iii) there was no prevailing consent on the part of V to the risk of infection; and (iv) a lack of honest belief on D's part that V consented to such a risk. In *Dica*,[17] Judge LJ stated obiter that levels of precaution 'may' lead to a defence, and that it could be left for the jury to assess whether such protection would be sufficient:

> If protective measures had been taken by the appellant that would have provided material relevant to the jury's decision whether, in all the circumstances, recklessness was proved.[18]

---

[16] The Law Commission has recently considered the relevance of condom use in cases of HIV Transmission: Law Commission, *Reform of Offences against the Person A Scoping Consultation Paper* (Law Com SP no217, 2014).

[17] *Dica* (n 17) [11].

[18] ibid [11].

Further comments by Judge LJ in *Dica* seemed to indirectly indicate that other circumstances, including potentially the use of condoms, could present a defence: illustratively, consent to running the risk of becoming infected should not be invalidated where[19] a Catholic couple,[20] because of religious beliefs, are unable to use protective precautions, even though one may become infected by the other, and there is prior awareness that one partner is HIV+. The inference, albeit disjunctive, is that condom use may be utilised as a defence in other cases as the risk of transmission is significantly reduced, and the use of precautions in such circumstances would demonstrate that a defendant was acting responsibly. Emphasis was also made of condom use when referring to casual encounters.[21] Additional support for this proposition can be found in the Crown Prosecution Service (CPS) guidelines,[22] where it is acknowledged that prophylactic measures may implicate that no prosecution should ensue: it would be problematic to establish that the person using the precautions was acting recklessly.[23] The CPS appears to concede that a defendant's actions demonstrate responsible behaviour, the apotheosis of recklessness. It was, however, emphasised that it is the responsibility of the infected person to ensure that precautions are taken. The CPS guidelines also indicate that public policy rationalisations implicate that prosecutions will not take place when precautions have been used.[24] The statement of Judge LJ in *Dica* and the CPS guidelines are rational proposals: an individual should be viewed in such circumstances as acting responsibly, and by acting responsibly D's conduct may be justified. If the infected person is practising safe sex, then it would be extremely difficult for the prosecution to prove that he acted recklessly or intentionally. The counterpoise is that use of condoms is more effective in restricting the spread of the virus than informed consent: consenting to running the risk of infection offers no protection.

---

[19] ibid [49].

[20] ibid [48].

[21] *Dica* (n 17) [47].

[22] Crown Prosecution Service (CPS), 'Intentional or Reckless Sexual Transmission of Infection'
<http://www.cps.gov.uk/legal/h_to_k/intentional_or_reckless_sexual_transmission_of_infection_guidance/index.html#Safe> accessed 18th April 2015.

[23] ibid.

[24] ibid.

Further support for this proposition has emanated from a number of academicians.[25] As early as 1991, it was advocated that condom use could be a defence in these types of cases: it is 'a proper and necessary concession to human nature'.[26] To restrict an individual from becoming intimate with another person as a result of their condition, and allowing consent as the only means to circumvent liability, is a threshold that is set too high. There should be a different inculpatory-exculpatory gradation whereby an individual can still maintain intimate sexual relationships, particularly as stigma is still attached to those who are carrying the virus.[27] It is paradoxical to allow consent to act as a defence, but not the use of condoms. It is conceded that consent gives a person the opportunity to make an informed decision, and this is not an attempt to exclude consent as a defence, but consent does not reduce the risk as significantly as precautions. In concurrence with this proposition, it has been suggested by a number of commentators that precautions should be demarcated as higher than informed consent via disclosure, and that even attempted use of protective measures should be sufficient as a defence to transmission.[28] The effective use of protection should be a defence, but attempted use should not, as it is the equivalent to unprotected intercourse. In such circumstances, disclosure of HIV status should be a requirement to ensure that the party who is unaware has the opportunity to make an informed decision. A distinction must also be drawn, as Chalmers has articulated, between a moral duty and a legal duty, when referring to the use of precautions,[29] and the disclosing of HIV status. Indeed, an individual has a moral duty to inform all of their prospective sexual partners, even when he is using protection, but a moral duty does not necessarily equate to a legal duty, a proposition that has been helpfully advanced by Bergelson in the wider context of the overarching parameters of consent.

---

[25] Matthew Weait, 'Criminal Liability for Sexually Transmitted Infections' (2009) 173 Justice of the Peace 45; Samantha Ryan, 'Risk-Taking, Recklessness and HIV Transmission: Accommodating the Reality of Sexual Transmission of HIV within a Justifiable Approach to Criminal Liability' (2007) 28 Liverpool Law Review, 215.

[26] Smith (n 9) 328.

[27] Emily Mackinnon and Constance Crompton, 'The Gender of Lying: Feminist Perspectives on the Non-Disclosure of HIV Status' (2012) 45 University of British Columbia Law Review 407, 425.

[28] Dennis Baker, 'The Moral Limits of Consent as a Defence in the Criminal Law' (2009) 12 New Criminal Law Review 93, 114.

[29] James Chalmers, 'The Criminalisation of HIV Transmission' (2002) 28 Journal of Medical Ethics 160, 162.

If a defendant uses a condom, does that mean that he is being reckless or otherwise? It is arguable that even if the defendant used precautions, the Crown, in contrast to the CPS guidelines, may still establish that the defendant foresaw harm, and still took an unjustified risk.[30] This, we contend, is unsustainable, as the use of condoms demonstrates that the user is seeking to alleviate the risk of transmission: responsibility rather than recklessness is the apposite standardisation.[31] Recklessness is best defined as unjustifiable risk taking,[32] and Judge LJ stated in *Dica* that recklessness is established, 'if he knew or foresaw that the complainant might suffer bodily harm and chose the risk that she would'.[33] The use of a condom establishes that the defendant is conscious that he may infect another, and as he has used precautions, it can be persuasively asserted that he has endeavoured to eradicate the risk of transmitting the virus, to a reducibly justifiable threshold. It is worth re-emphasising that statistical data, in reference to protected receptive vaginal intercourse, set the approximate risk in such a situation as extremely remote at one in ten thousand for the woman, and one in twenty thousand for the man. A failure of proof defence predicated on lack of mens rea is consequently adumbrated. The use of prophylactics indicates that the threshold for reckless behaviour has not been met: the risk has been so significantly reduced that D1's actions should not establish culpability.

English Law and the Relevance of an Individual's Viral Load

A number of proponents have suggested that actors with an undetectable viral load would not be considered reckless for transmission of HIV within the purview of English law,[34] but strikingly, there is no judicial clarity on the matter.[35] Confusion reigns supreme as to whether a low or undetectable viral load can act as a defence, or whether it ought to be exculpatory, as this has not been an issue that has been directly raised within our courts. The guiding appellate decisions in *Dica* and *Konzani*[36]

---

[30] Simon H. Bronitt, 'Spreading Disease and the Criminal Law' (1994) Criminal Law Review 21.

[31] Ryan (n 25) 234.

[32] *R v G* [2003] UKHL 50.

[33] *R v Konzani* [2005] EWCA Crim 706 [2005] 2 Cr. App. (Judge LJ) [37].

[34] James Chalmers (n 6) 146.

[35] The Law Commission has recently considered the relevance of viral load in cases of HIV transmission: Law Commission, *Reform of Offences against the Person A Scoping Consultation Paper* (Law Com SP no 217, 2014).

[36] *R v Konzani* (n 33) 14.

were concerned with unprotected intercourse, and the issue of consent. Probatively, a defendant who has a low or undetectable viral load would need to be fully aware of the level in order to raise it evidentially as a failure of proof defence. Support for this proposition has been cogently advanced by Smith, who submits that relying on medical advice should enable the defendant to evade responsibility.[37] This would be achieved by regular testing of the level of the viral load. The World Health Organisation endorses such proposals by suggesting that the level of an individual's viral load is one of the greatest risks in transmitting the virus to another person, and that reducing the viral load can be one of the most effective ways of diminishing the possibility of HIV transmission.[38] The level of an individual's viral load can be a deciding factor as to whether the virus will be transmitted: the lower the load, the less likely is the possibility of infecting another person.[39] The viral load is reduced by taking antiretroviral treatment (HAART), and consistent use of the medication can decrease the load to an amount where it will be undetectable.[40] A further, and more radical, endorsement has emanated from the Swiss Federal Commission for HIV/AIDS vis-à-vis the use of HAART, and the transmission of HIV. It was announced that if an individual does not have another sexually transmitted disease, complies with their HAART, and has had an undetectable load for at least six months, they will be unable to transmit the virus.[41] In light of this factorisation, the CPS have acknowledged that the risk may be significantly reduced, and that it can be argued that the level of the viral load can be just as effective as condom use.[42] This may denote that an individual's viral load might need to be taken into practical consideration when deciding whether to prosecute an individual. If the accuracy of the

---

[37] Smith (n 9) 328.

[38] World Health Organisation 'Antiretroviral Treatment as Prevention (TasP) of HIV and TB: 2012 update
WHO/HIV/2012.12' (June 2012)
<www.who.int/hiv/pub/mtct/programmatic_update_tasp/en/index.html> accessed 20 April 2015.

[39] ibid.

[40] ibid.

[41] Pietro Vernazza and others, 'HIV-positive individuals not suffering from any other STD and adhering to an effective anti-retroviral treatment do not transmit HIV sexually' (January 2008)
http://www.edwinjbernard.com/pdfs/Swiss%20Commission%20statement_May%202008_translation%20EN.pdf accessed 20 April 2015

[42] Crown Prosecution Service (n 22).

Swiss statement is to be assumed, then an undetectable viral load is even more effective than condom use in terms of effective harm diminution.

England: The Transmission of HIV and the Type of Sexual Activity

Although experts have recognised the complexity of providing a precise assessment of the risk of sexually transmitting HIV, it is accepted that some activities carry less of a risk than others.[43] Statistical and meta-data analysis have revealed, for instance, that risk of infection from oral intercourse is extremely low, and risk of infection from unprotected anal intercourse is higher with a dissonance between whether the HIV partner is receptive / insertive. Where the HIV partner is the receptive participant, risk has been assessed at 4 in 10,000 for each act of unprotected intercourse. Even though there is no prescriptive formula for assessing the risk, it is evident that certain types of sexual activity can reduce the risk of transmitting the virus. As the risk of transmission fluctuates between the types of conduct, Bennett *et al*,[44] propose that if an individual participates in low risk activities, these do not require a duty to inform the other person of one's HIV status as the risk is reduced, and they are therefore acting in 'a responsible and morally justifiable way'.[45] Thus, it is suggested that the type of activity in which the defendant partakes may signify that he has been acting in a responsible manner if he is aware that this would reduce the risk of infecting another person. The type of activity is important in assessing the probability of transmission. Although, as stated, it is recognised that unprotected anal intercourse, where the insertive partner is HIV+, is the most precarious activity,[46] the risk of transmitting the virus becomes far more attenuated when assessing other types of interaction. Unprotected vaginal intercourse poses less of a risk[47] when it involves male to female transmission. The risk is even more diminished when it encompasses potential transmission from unprotected female to male

---

[43] Eric Mykhalovskiy, Glenn Betteridge and David McLay, 'HIV Non-Disclosure and the Criminal Law: Establishing Policy Options for Ontario' (August 25, 2010) http://www.catie.ca/pdf/Brochures/HIV-non-disclosure-criminal-law.pdf accessed 20 April 2015.

[44] Rebecca Bennett, Heather Draper and Lucy Frith, 'Duties to Forewarn Ignorance is Bliss? HIV and Moral Duties and Legal' (2000) 26 Journal of Medical Ethics 9.

[45] ibid 12.

[46] Carol Galletly and Steven D Pinkerton 'Toward Rational Criminal HIV Exposure Laws' 2004 32 Journal of Law Medicine and Ethics 327, 328.

[47] ibid.

through vaginal intercourse. What ought to make the type of sexual activity a defence is that when the HIV+ partner is the receptive partner, the statistical probably of transmission through protected intercourse is thought to be the equivalent of female to male unprotected vaginal intercourse.[48] If condom use is to be a defence, particularly as public health initiatives encourage their use, then certain types of sexual activity should also be included within our range of failure of proof bespoke defences.

It is incongruous to homogenise different types of sexual activity, each carrying the same penalty, particularly when disparate types are clearly less likely to transmit the virus. Under extant law, the particular type of sexual activity is treated as irrelevant where transmission occurs, and where the complainant has not consented to running the risk of infection. The failure to evaluate perspicuitous consideration of sexual risk by D1 is counterfactual, and treating all types of sexual activity in the same manner in terms of thresholds of hard gradations, 'would be irrational and unfair'.[49] An individual who deliberately takes part in low risk activities ought not, and should not be, as culpable as a person who only partakes in high risk activities. There are suggestions that the type of sexual activity should not be taken into account, because someone involved in sexual intimacy that is a low risk may, on that particular occasion, be as likely to have transmitted the virus as someone taking part in high risk activity.[50] This is indefensible as it inappropriately blends together different levels of risk. This cannot be the case; if they were, then they would both pose the same level of risk on each occasion. It is the equivalent of stating that someone who has placed a bet on a 2000 to 1 horse winning a race is just as likely to win as someone who has put wager on the favourite on that occasion. The level of risk is calculated for a reason: the more remote the risk of transmission, the less likely that an individual will transmit the virus, and this factorisation needs remedial legislation to reflect effective due process, responsibility, and blameworthiness.

---

[48] ibid.
[49] Ryan (n 25) 229.
[50] Matthew Weait (n 5) 176.

Canada: The Defences of Condom Use, Viral Load and the Type of Sexual Activity

The Canadian position is that a defendant can be prosecuted for a variety of substantive criminal law offences[51] if he does not disclose his HIV status to sexual partners. It is irrelevant whether the virus is transmitted. Some find it problematic to comprehend how there are a number of different charges that can be brought for the same conduct as a defendant never really knows what offence they can potentially commit.[52] This invariably conflicts with the law being certain. The first case that was heard in the Supreme Court was *Cuerrier*,[53] where the defendant was prosecuted under the aggravated assault provisions of the Canadian Criminal Code.[54] Cuerrier engaged in unprotected intercourse with two women, and did not disclose that he was HIV+; this was despite the fact that he had been told, on a number of occasions, by health officials that he must use condoms, and disclose that he was carrying the virus. It was held that consensual intercourse without disclosure of HIV status was fraud if there is 'a significant risk of serious harm', and thus vitiated consent.[55] The majority judgment stated that fraud vitiating consent embraced not simply deceptions as to the nature and quality of the act itself, and the identity of the person, but that it extended to circumstances where there was a significant risk of serious harm. It was felt that a broader view of fraud was justified at common law: a particularised definition of fraud had been removed from the Canadian Criminal Code.[56]

Cory J[57] asserted in *Cuerrier* that the 'proper use of condoms' might reduce the risk so that it would no longer be considered 'significant'. The utilisation of condoms could provide a defence to any charge that could be put before the courts, but emphasis was provided that each case should be dealt with incrementally on its own specific facts, and subsequent precedents have revealed a lack of clarity as to the parameters of this failure of proof defence. Prosecutors in Canada, at least prior to *Mabior*, seemed willing to provide specificity and lucidity, endorsing the use of

---

[51] For example common nuisance: *R v Summer* 1989 98 A.R. 191, A.J. No. 78 to Murder: R v Aziga 2011 ONSC 4592, 2011.

[52] Isabel Grant (n 15) 9.

[53] *Cuerrier* [1998] 2 S.C.R. 371.

[54] Criminal Code, RSC 1985, c C-46, s. 268.

[55] *Cuerrier* (n 53) [128].

[56] ibid [105].

[57] ibid [129].

condoms as an affirmative defence, and prepared to distinguish between protected and unprotected intercourse.[58]

Their Lordships have subsequently adopted a straitened conjunctive dual threshold standardisation for exculpatory defences attached to HIV transmission/exposure in Canada. The Supreme Court decision in *Mabior*[59] provided explicit guidance on condom use, and the duty to disclose: condom use will only provide a defence where the defendant in juxtaposition has a low viral load. A combination of dual bifurcatory factors are essential, with a higher defence threshold standardisation in non-disclosure cases, notwithstanding that the Supreme Court in *Mabior* concluded that further medical advancements and other matters could be taken into account. The decision sends out an inappropriate message, and can be seen as discriminatory to women as the odds of transmission from the recipient are greater than from the insertive partner. Furthermore, it is detrimental to public health initiatives, as the defendant who has used protection will still be susceptible to criminal sanctions. This now means that there is no overarching incentive for using a condom, and could increase reckless behaviour. Even more perplexing is the rather contradictory manner of the court in acknowledging that proper use of good quality condoms would mean that the virus will not be transmitted to another individual.[60] If this is the case, then why criminalise protective consensual sexual intercourse? The judgment has raised more questions than answers vis-à-vis exculpatory-inculpatory standardisations: it confuses the culpability/blameworthiness contextualisation in terms of genuine risk of harm, obfuscates legitimate fault principles, and unduly widens the net of liability. It seems that unprotected or protected intercourse *per se* is now unimportant in Canada: it is no longer considered to be the demarcation line for prosecutions.[61]

Prior to the decision in *Mabior*, condom use as an affirmative defence had received significant academic approval. It had legitimately been suggested that allowing condom use is a more effective way of reducing transmissions than relying on disclosure.[62] There is also a consensus of

---

[58] *McGregor* 2008 ONCA 831, 240 CCC (3d) 102 [7]; *R v Wilcox* 2011 QCCQ 11007 (available on CanLII).

[59] *Mabior* [2012] SCC 47.

[60] ibid [98]

[61] This has been affirmed in a number of cases for an example see *R. v. Felix*, 2013 ONCA 415 [48].

[62] Grant (n 52) 19.

opinion that it is generally accepted that condom use is one of the most widely recognised ways to prevent transmission.[63] The promotion of condom use as a failure of proof defence is particularly relevant when a significant number of infections take place before the actor is aware that they are carrying the virus.[64] As previously stated, consent will not protect an individual from the risk of infection, but condom use can be an effective way of protecting against infection. An individual who uses condoms is being conscious of his own, and others', sexual health. By using such protection, it can be seen that there is a genuine attempt at reducing the risk of not only HIV, but a number of other sexually transmissible infections. If criminalisation of sexual exposure to HIV does not act as a deterrent, then allowing the use of condoms at least sends a message that is consistent with health policies,[65] and as a matter of policy, using protection should be encouraged under the auspices of legislative policy inculcations.

Moreover, the Supreme Court has clarified that a low viral load per se will not present an affirmative defence in non-disclosure cases.[66] It has been determined that the ambit of any failure of proof defence, predicated on low/non-detectable viral load, poses probative evidential difficulties.[67] If this is correct, then why conjunctively enable a low viral load conjoined with condom use to be a supererogatory defence?[68] The outcome in *Mabior* demonstrates that a low viral load in isolation is irrelevant, but the Supreme Court appears to indicate that, solipsistically, an undetectable load may still be relevant in other factual circumstances.[69] However, in *D.C.* the Supreme Court affirmed that an undetectable viral load could not present a bespoke defence.[70] Lower courts, however, have not strictly applied the test that was set out in *Mabior*. In the recent case, for example, of *R. v J.T.C.*,[71] the Provincial Court of Nova Scotia has affirmed that, providing there is cogent expert evidence of the remoteness of the possibility of infection, a defendant will not be considered to have

---

[63] Isabel Grant 'Rethinking Risk: The Relevance of Condoms and Viral Load in HIV Nondisclosure Prosecutions' (2009) 54 McGill Law Journal 389, 398.
[64] Grant (n 52) 19.
[65] Grant (n 63) 400.
[66] *Mabior* (n 59) [101].
[67] ibid [102].
[68] ibid [102].
[69] ibid [102].
[70] *D.C.*, 2012 SCC 48 {29}.
[71] *J.T.C.*, 2013 NSPC 105.

'criminally exposed' another through unprotected intercourse. Judge Campbell stated that 'the Supreme Court of Canada did not intend in *R. v. Mabior* and *R. v. D.C.* to impose evidentiary findings on trial courts that are incompatible with the evidence actually before those courts'.[72] Dr Schlech, the expert in the case, proposed that the odds could be one million to one of the virus being transmitted with an undetectable viral load.[73] It was accepted by Judge Campbell that his decision was specific to that case, and there was no realistic possibility of the virus being transmitted by the defendant. Significantly, there was disregard for the binary defence standardisation established in *Mabior*, and in *R. v J.T.C.*, Judge Campbell clearly preferred scientific estimations and guidance to judicial precedent.

It is evident that the lower courts within Canada, adopting and adapting more nuanced perspectives to failure of proof defences, are recognising that understanding of viral loads has developed to such an extent that the viral load needs to be taken into consideration when assessing the risk that is posed.[74] When there is an undetectable viral load, it is arguable that harm is not foreseeable,[75] and there should be no prosecutions when a load is at that level.[76] It is inexplicable to contemplate that the defendant with a low or undetectable viral load would need to disclose their status when the risk of transmission is negligible or non-existent in such circumstances.[77] The real issue with low/non-detectable viral load is that not everyone is able to take the appropriate medication, but this does not justify disavowing it as a defence. When the viral load is at an undetectable or low level, any non-disclosure requirement ought not to be affected.

Concerns have been raised about the accuracy of viral loads, and what is not detectable one day does not mean it will remain the same the next.[78] This was addressed by the Supreme Court in *Mabior* when deciding that viral load could not be used in isolation,[79] but developments within the lower courts appear to indicate otherwise.[80] A further issue that has been

---

[72] ibid [99].

[73] ibid [55].

[74] Grant (n 52) 20.

[75] ibid [25].

[76] ibid [11].

[77] Something that was confirmed in *J.T.C.* (n 71) 105.

[78] Grant (n 63) 401.

[79] *Mabior* (n 59) [02].

[80] *J.T.C.* (n 71) 105.

identified is that defendants may begin to make their own 'risk assessments',[81] but to do this, the defendant would need to know the level of their viral load. To be able to know that level would require the appropriate test and medical advice. Grant has stated that the viral load factorisation can lead to problems regarding the burden of proof.[82] Canadian courts, before the Supreme Court decision in *Mabior*, had been using their good sense by looking at average viral loads, and stating that it is an evidential rather than legal burden when raising the issue of viral loads.[83] When precise information was unavailable, the courts had been willing to accept average viral loads for determining whether there was a significant risk, and in such circumstances, it would be an evidential burden of showing that they had a low or undetectable viral load over that period of time.[84] The position has been clarified by the Supreme Court in *Mabior* to the extent that it is an evidential burden that also conjunctively requires condom use.[85]

A further Canadian development can be seen in *R. v J.A.T.*,[86] where statistics regarding the type of sexual activity were utilised in order to acquit the defendant. It was proposed that whether the defendant's conduct means there is a significant risk of harm, needs to be assessed by the type of sexual activity, and the statistical probably of transmitting the virus. In that case, the receptive partner was HIV+, and in such circumstances it was accepted that the risk was insufficient to be considered a serious risk of harm.[87] Their Lordships also heard expert opinion that stated that this type of sexual activity was equal to protected intercourse where the insertive partner had the virus.[88] This case embodies the fundamental issues attached to any inculpatory-exculpatory threshold gradation: it indicates that a defendant may still have a defence when he participates in certain sexual activities. A pressing need exists for clarity on where the demarcation point lies. The type of sexual activity can no longer be used in isolation; it may, however, be utilised with either protected intercourse or viral load. There is no guidance on these matters: clear unequivocal direction is required, and this was not achieved by the Supreme Court in

---

[81] Grant (n 63) 402.
[82] ibid [402]
[83] *Wright* 2009 BCCA 514 [32] [33]
[84] ibid.
[85] *Mabior* (n 59) [105].
[86] *J.A.T.* 2010 BCSC 766.
[87] ibid [88].
[88] ibid [31].

Mabior.[89] Courts have subsequently addressed the relevance of low risk sexual activities and a defendant's viral load. In *McKonnen*,[90] for instance, the Court of Appeal in Nova Scotia seemed to accept that oral intercourse and a low viral load would not pose a realistic possibility of the virus being transmitted. There has also been an acceptance of a defence based upon oral intercourse and an undetectable viral load before the Superior Court of Justice in Ontario.[91] In this latter case, there was confirmation that a defence based upon low viral load and oral intercourse did not pose a realistic possibility of the virus being transmitted. Expert evidence presented in *Murphy*[92] was to the effect that the odds of becoming infected could be as high as one hundred thousand to one.[93] It seems that there is an acceptance of oral intercourse and a low or undetectable viral load acting as a defence, but there is no clarity as to whether low risk sexual activities can be used disjunctively, beyond the conjunctive requirements of condom use/low viral load.

Grant has submitted that if condom use and viral load are to be conjunctive defences, then why not the type of sexual activity as a bifurcated stand-alone failure of proof type defence?[94] The type of sexual activity may also play a pivotal role in ascertaining whether disclosure is required, and each case is dealt with in an ad hoc manner by lower courts, rather than on evolving common law precepts as declared by the Supreme Court.[95] This means that any combination of the three suggested defences may be used to lower the realistic risk of transmission. Such a proposition may lead to further unpredictability as cases will still be relying heavily on expert evidence to ascertain whether there is realistic possibility of transmission.[96] *Mabior* left the door open for individuated solipsistic determinations, stating that medical advancements and 'other risk factors' may mean that there is no 'realistic' possibility of transmission.[97] Issues

---

[89] Alison Symington, 'R v Mabior and R v DC: Sex, Lies, and HIV: Injustice Amplified by HIV Non-Disclosure Ruling' (2013) 63 University of Toronto Law Journal 485.

[90] *Mekonnen*, 2013 ONCA 414.

[91] *Murphy* 2013 Can LII 54139 (ON SC).

[92] ibid.

[93] ibid [82].

[94] Grant (n 52) 27.

[95] *Mabior* (n 59) [81].

[96] Grant (n 52) 44.

[97] *Mabior* (n 59) [95].

remain to be addressed over the accuracy of expert evidence,[98] and it is still questionable whether expert opinion becomes a 'numbers game'.

Canadian law, in truth, remains inherently uncertain in a variety of dissonant respects in terms of gradation of harms that are viewed as sufficient to negate consent and endanger life. Recent lower court decisions, beyond earlier Supreme Court analysis in *Cuerrier* and *Mabior*, reveal individuated and solipsistic determinations related to types of sexual activity interdependent on conflicting expert evidence and individual risk assessment. The dual threshold criterion of condom use, conjunctively aligned with low viral load, has become attenuated, and appellate courts have recently been predisposed to leave matters to jurors, as moral arbiters, to evaluate the significance and level of risk attached to individual conduct.

U.S. State Law Perspectives: The Failure of Proof Defences of Condom Use, Viral Load and Type of Sexual Activity

The United States: Condom Use as a Defence

The U.S. Presidential Commission recognised that the use of precautions ought to be promoted and adapted as a defence: the recommendation presented was that condom use should correlate to a complainant consenting to protected intercourse with an HIV+ individual.[99] The response at state level, however, to this directed recommendation has proved eclectic, and diversely nuanced perspectives are currently in operation. Our research indicates that dissonant approaches can be compartmentalised into three classifications: (1) a limited number of U.S. states have legislatively enacted the recommendations of the Commission and facilitated the use of precautions as a defence, but only conjunctively when their use is aligned with the informed consent of the complainant; (2) other statutes have exceeded the recommendations of the Presidential Commission and approved condom use disjunctively and singularly as the basis of a defence against criminalisation; and (3) finally, there are a limited number of states that reject condom use as a defence to any specific criminal sanction. The allowance of condom use as a defence

---

[98]Grant (n 52) 27.
[99] The Presidential Commission on the Human Immunodeficiency Virus Epidemic Report (1988) 131.

corresponds to public health initiatives within the United States, and accedes to the harm principle by recognising the relevance of the probability of the risk of serious harm.[100] The facilitation of the defence is further cemented by various studies that denote that using such measures reduces the risk of the virus being transmitted by 95%, in comparison to unprotected intercourse: utilisation significantly reduces the risk of infection.[101] A defence of this type also achieves a legitimate equipoise in terms of balancing rights/responsibilities attached to sexual intercourse, constitutively 'minimising legislative intrusion into intimate sexual activity.'

Missouri is the only U.S. state that has expressly disavowed the Commission's recommendations: a legislative framework has been assimilated that explicitly stipulates the exclusion of condom use as a defence.[102] Certainty is promulgated within the constrained Missourian framework, but their deontological and mechanistic bright line exclusionary provision disregards any theoretical foundation or policy basis for the disaggregation of condom use as an affirmative defence. No consideration is given to the probability of harm occurrence or culpability thresholds of the 'criminal' actor, and the framework is contrary to, and out with, beneficial public health initiatives.[103] The Missourian legislative offence is centred on an exposure to the virus definitional construct, but it is evident that the legislators did not perceive the importance of balancing the social utility of sexual interaction, the magnitude of harm and the probability of harm. The exclusion of condom use as a defence conveys an egregious message that their utilisation is immaterial to individuals who are already infected with the virus.

Generally, in the absence of an explicit legislative inclusion of condom use as a bespoke failure of proof defence, it will not be accessible to a defendant at common law.[104] The assertion by a defendant that he has utilised protective measures, and that an affirmative defence ought to apply, have been disregarded by a number of appellate courts. By way of

---

[100] See <http://www.cdc.gov/hiv/prevention/programs/condoms/> accessed 20 April 2015.
[101] Steven D. Pinkerton and Paul R. Abramson, 'Effectiveness of Condoms in Preventing HIV Transmission' (1997) 44 Social Science and Medicine 1303, 1310.
[102] Mo. Rev. Stat § 191.677 (2016).
[103] See (n 100) accessed 20 April 2015.
[104] However, see *State v Rhoades,* 848 N.W.2d 22, 27-28 (Iowa 2014).

illustration, in *State v White*,[105] the Supreme Court of Arkansas refused to countenance the defendant's contention in relation to condom use, irrespective any legislative response to the issue, and it was determined that sufficiency of probative evidence favoured the State for inculpation.[106] The Supreme Court of Arkansas affirmed that the offence was committed once a defendant had sexual intercourse with an unsuspecting complainant, and with liability predicated on non-disclosure:[107] statutory liability extended to unprotected and protected intercourse. The failure to facilitate condom use as an affirmative defence is detrimental to public health awareness and conscious advertence to risk:[108] Perone has cogently argued that U.S. states that are stultifying the defence of condom use are 'indirectly' suggesting that protective measures are ineffective in preventing the virus being transmitted.

Appellate courts in other U.S. states have expressly declined the opportunity to consider and deliberate the potentiality of condom use as a defence, and disavowed the import of scientific and medical data analysis in terms of genuine risk. In *State v Gamberella*,[109] a case heard in the Court of Appeal of Louisiana, the court categorically refused to explore the defence, and the judiciary were hostile to the defendant's submissions in relation to the probative evidentiary relevance of 'intentional' utilisation of protective measures. This disavowal in Louisiana of any proof of fault defence is counterintuitive and counterfactual, especially as the extant legislative provision places primordial offence-definitional construction on the fault element: a defendant must act with 'intention' in relation to harm, and correspondingly, the use of condoms may have negated that intent.

The judiciary took a contrary position in *State v Gamberella*, and determined that the intent of the defendant was established at a rudimental level when he knew that he was HIV+, and that he could transmit the virus to another, without elaboration of the temporal individuation of fault occurrence or harm negation. Even where the defence has been presumptively denied as an evidentiary predicate, the analysis provided has been confused, convoluted and, on occasions, Janus-facing: the

---

[105] *State v White* 370 Ark. 284 (2007).

[106] ibid 289.

[107] ibid 290.

[108] Angela Perone, 'From Punitive to Proactive: An Alternative Approach for Responding to HIV Criminalization that Departs from Penalizing Marginalized Communities' (2013) 24 Hastings Women's Law Journal 363.

[109] *State v Gamberella*, 633 So.2d 595 (La. Ct. App. 1993).

Criminal Appeals Court of Tennessee, for instance, in *State v Bonds*[110] refused to countenance the defence, but in an opaque and skewed delineation made implicit reference to the relevance of harm gradations:

> [T]he majority of the convictions were upheld without evidence of an "exchange" of bodily fluids. Indeed, our prior case law's emphasis on "unprotected" sex supports the conclusion that "exposure" means simply to submit to a risk of contact with bodily fluids, such a risk being substantially more prevalent in unprotected sex than when some form of prophylactic is utilized.[111]

The availability of condom use as a defence, or otherwise, within Tennessee may require further reconsideration following the recent Supreme Court of Tennessee's decision in *State v Hogg*.[112] The case did not directly concern condom use *per se*, but it was stated therein that the risk of transmission must be 'more definite than a faint, speculative risk',[113] and it may subsequently be argued that the risk of infection can be speculative if protective measures have been used.

A number of U.S. commentators have rejected condom use as an affirmative defence, and it is instructive to evaluate the perspectives advanced. Markus[114] has propounded that condom use does not conclusively prevent impeding transmission, and should, therefore, not act as an evidentiary defence.[115] Schulman has specified that because of the deficiencies that are intrinsically linked to condom prevention, these protective measures should not be considered to be an alternative defence.[116] Deficiencies can be identified with condom use, but this should not superimpose a conclusive rationale for excluding their use as an affirmative defence. There has been no case before the U.S. state courts where the virus has been transmitted when the defendant intentionally and reasonably used a condom. Studies also demonstrate the effectiveness of condom use when they are correctly and consistently used as a protective

---

[110] *State v Bonds,* 189 S.W.3d 249 (Tenn. Ct. App. 2005).

[111] ibid.

[112] *State v Hogg* 448 S.W.3d 877; 2014 Tenn. LEXIS 668.

[113] ibid 889.

[114] Mona Markus, 'A Treatment for the Disease: Criminal HJV Transmission/ Exposure Laws' (1999) 23 Nova Law Review 847.

[115] ibid 870 -871.

[116] Eric L. Schulman, 'Sleeping with the Enemy: Combating the Sexual Spread of HIV-AIDs through a Heightened Legal Duty' (1996) 29 John Marshall Law Review 957, 986.

measure.[117] Under those conditions, they significantly reduce the risk of the virus being transmitted. Criminalisation should not include those who have used condoms, and it is unrealistic to assume that there are activities where it is certain that transmission cannot transpire, something that other states appear to have accepted.

The use of protection forms the basis of an individuated statutory defence within a minority of U.S. states.[118] Illinois has accommodated condom use in a bespoke affirmative provision that may be beneficially adopted within other criminal justice systems:

> (a) A person commits criminal transmission of HIV when he or she, with the specific intent to commit the offense:
>
> (1) engages in sexual activity with another without the **use of a condom** knowing that he or she is infected with HIV (emphasis added).

Condom use has been prescriptively incorporated as a defence within the legislative framework of Illinois, and this response has been replicated in California, Iowa and Minnesota. An appropriately worded statutory schema has been adopted in this panoply of jurisdictions, establishing a definite and translucent defence, consequently providing certainty and an effectual safeguarding of interests. It represents the obverse of the delimiting strictures inappropriately applied in Louisiana and Tennessee.

Interestingly, the appellate courts in a number of other U.S. states have determined that the use of protective measures can negate the *mens rea* of the offence to provide a failure of proof defence: in effect, 'judicial' legislation has been interposed as a remedial panacea where statutory response is silent or deficient. In *State v Richardson*,[119] a case heard in the Supreme Court of Kansas, it was asserted that use of condoms may be relevant when considering whether the defendant had formed an 'intention' to expose the complainant to the virus:[120]

> [Kansas' Statute] not only requires proof that the defendant knowingly engaged in sexual intercourse, but it also requires evidence of a specific intent to expose the defendant's sexual partner to a life-threatening

---

[117] Steven D. Pinkerton and Paul R. Abramson (n 101).

[118] Cal. Health & Safety Code § 120291 (2016); Minn. Stat. § 609.2241(2015); 720 Ill. Comp. Stat. § 5/12-5.01; Iowa Code § 709D.2.

[119] *State v Richardson* 289 Kan. 118; 209 P.3d 696; 2009 Kan. LEXIS 180.

[120] ibid 128.

communicable disease. Thus, under our statute, condom use can be germane to the defendant's specific intent.[121]

The use of condoms ought to exculpate a defendant when inculpation is based upon a fault element of intention (or recklessness). Their use is indicative in ascertaining whether the defendant intended to transmit the virus.[122] A defendant who has used protective measures has endeavoured to remove/reduce the risk of the complainant becoming infected with the virus. Minahan, however, contrary to our standpoint, iterates that defence enablement may, 'create a false sense of security' on the part of that complainant, as the expectation is upon the infected party to reduce the risk.[123] This is counterintuitive and does not accord with the realities of sexual intimacies. Moreover, it is irrational for an infected individual not to use a condom if he knew that their use may form the basis of a defence or negate the *mens rea* of the criminal sanction.

A distinctive cadre of U.S. states have conjunctively facilitated the use of condoms as a defence, aligned with disclosure of their sero-status to a prospective sexual partner. In North Carolina and North Dakota, the legislative framework explicitly stipulates words to that effect, thereby connoting condom use, in isolation, to be irrelevant.[124] It seems that the provisions within these states are following the recommendations of the Commission, but are placing an undue burden upon a defendant to disclose their status, even when the risk of transmission is significantly reduced. There are suggestions that disclosure and condom use serves the purpose of protecting those who are unsure as to what they have consented.[125] This concern would be eradicated if a fully informed consent was expected, as a potential sexual partner needs to be fully aware of the risks associated with having unprotected intercourse with an infected defendant.[126]

---

[121] ibid 128 -129.

[122] Margo Kaplan, 'Rethinking HIV-Exposure Laws' (2012) 87 Indiana Law Journal 1517, 1545.

[123] W Thomas Minahan, 'Disclosure before Exposure: A Review of Ohio's HIV Criminalization Statutes' (2009) 35 Ohio Northern University Law Review 83, 106.

[124] 10A N.C. Admin. Code 41A.0202(2015); N.D. CENT. CODE § 12.1-20-17 (2015).

[125] Kathleen M Sullivan and Martha A. Field, 'Aids and the Coercive Power of the State' (1988) 23 Harvard Civil Rights-Civil Liberties Law Review 139, 182.

[126] ibid.

The combined statutory defences of condom use and disclosure have proponents: Sullivan and Field advocate the use of precautions and disclosure in the following terms:

> It more clearly imposes on persons with AIDS and AIDS carriers affirmative duties, as a condition of engaging in sexual intercourse, to disclose their condition to their sexual partners, to obtain their partners' knowing consent, and to use precautions such as condoms. Such a statute has a more realistic chance of influencing behavior, because it permits a person to pursue a sexual relationship if he complies with these affirmative duties.[127]

Sullivan and Field do not consider our preferred optionality, whereby in specific circumstance an individual should be given the opportunity to consent to unprotected intercourse, even when that would increase the risk of transmission. The facilitation of a hard paternalistic approach to unprotected sexual liaisons precludes any right to intimate connection, procreation, and the autonomy of the prospective partner. The allowance of a defence of condom use in isolation would also allow individuals to pursue sexual relationships, and would act as a greater incentive to individuals to use protective measures. Newman legitimately recommends a defence that is based upon protective measures as their use is an important factor that assists in reducing the risk of infection, even if it has an impact upon the frequency of a defendant disclosing their status.[128] The defence of condom use ought to be an alternative to, but not a replacement of, disclosure. If the ultimate aim is to encourage condom use, then indubitably a defence of protective measures affords a more solid foundation that encourages individuals to be proactive in their use. By allowing condom use in isolation would provide a further juncture for a defendant to act responsibly. If every individual who has contracted the virus used a condom, under the principle of unity, the virus would eventually be eradicated.[129] Therefore, consent and condom use should be distinctive defences, as should an undetectable viral load.

---

[127] Sullivan and Field (n 125) 186.

[128] Sarah J Newman, 'Prevention, Not Prejudice: The Role of Federal Guidelines in HIV-Criminalization Reform' (2013) 107 North Western University Law Review 1403, 1422.

[129] Steven D. Pinkerton and Paul R. Abramson (n 101).

U.S. State Law and the Risk of Transmission:
The Relevance of Viral Load

The U.S. Presidential Commission proposed that states enact legislation that would criminalise conduct that, '(…) according to scientific research, is [sic] likely to result in transmission of HIV'.[130] The level of a defendant's viral load may be relevant to the likelihood of risk of the virus being transmitted, and may form the basis of another defence. Statistical studies have revealed that if the defendant's viral load is consistently undetectable for a period of six months, then the virus cannot be transmitted.[131] A low viral load also significantly reduces the risk of the virus being transmitted.[132] The majority of U.S. states, however, have not considered, or continue to disregard, the relevance of a defendant's viral load. Only two states have promulgated statutory responses to the criminalisation of HIV transmission that potentially allow examination of probative relevance of a defendant's viral load, although this has also occurred on a limited number of occasions at common law.[133] By way of contrast, the preponderance of state legislators have taken an alternative stance, disregarding the probability of harm, and with a primary focus upon magnitude of harm precepts.

Idaho's statutory response provides a rare exception in crystallising the potential for an affirmative defence of an undetectable viral load.[134] The Idaho provision states that:

(3) Defenses:

… (b) Medical advice. It is an affirmative defense that the transfer of body fluid, body tissue, or organs occurred after advice from a licensed physician that the accused was non-infectious.[135]

The statute clearly enables a defence to apply when the virus cannot be transmitted as the actor was non-infectious; however, no specification or delineation applies to the actual contours of undetectable viral load. Any potential defence is heavily reliant upon a medical professional confirming

---

[130] The Presidential Commission (n 99) 131.

[131] Pietro Vernazza et al (n 41).

[132] World Health Organisation (n 38).

[133] Idaho Code Ann. § 39-608 (2015); Iowa Code § 709D.2 (2015).

[134] Idaho Code Ann. § 39-608 (2015).

[135] ibid (3)(b).

that the defendant cannot transmit the virus. Disappointingly, trial courts in Idaho have adopted a particularised reading of the ambit of any defence, disregarding section import, by allowing a defendant with an undetectable viral load to simply plead guilty.[136] The provision, therefore, appears to be devoid of any substance. This disregard of probative evidence is particularly disappointing when the wording of the statute is clear and self-evident. Criminalising a low or undetectable viral load, Waldman denotes, is 'an incident of the accident fallacy'.[137] The generalisation of the law is failing to take into consideration the specifics of an individual case and, therefore, the law is being 'inappropriately applied'.[138] This is at its most evident in Idaho,.

Recent common law developments in Iowa have indicated that the defendant's viral load will be a relevant factor in ascertaining whether there is a risk of the virus being transmitted. Judicial legislation has triumphed in this regard over antediluvian state legislation: the former legislative framework of Iowa was to the following effect:

1. A person commits criminal transmission of the human immunodeficiency virus if the person, knowing that the person's human immunodeficiency virus status is positive, does any of the following:
    a. Engages in intimate contact with another person.

---

[136] See *State v Thomas* 154 Idaho 305 (Ct. App. 2013): the defendant had pleaded guilty even though he had an undetectable viral load. The Court denied the defendant the motion to withdraw his guilty plea as he stated that he was not forewarned about the severity of the custodial sentence. There was no discussion of his viral load within the judgment as the appeal was not based upon this issue. <http://www.washingtonblade.com/2014/06/13/iowa-high-court-reverses-conviction-hiv-criminalization-case/> accessed 23 April 2015; also see Perone (n 108) 381.

[137] Ari Ezra Waldman, 'Exceptions: The Criminal Law's Illogical Approach to HIV-Related Aggravated Assaults' (2011) 18 Virginia Journal of Social Policy and Law 550, 561: 'The Accident Fallacy occurs when a general rule is applied to a specific situation in which the rule – because of unique individual facts, or "accidents" – is inapplicable. The mistake occurs when the general rule is applied inappropriately so it misses salient differences in a heterogeneous population and fails to recognize exceptions where they should exist or when a rule of thumb is used to come to over-inclusive conclusions. It has two steps: (1) generalize about a population, and (2) incorrectly use that generalization to describe a unique subset of that population.'

[138] ibid 564.

b. "Intimate contact" means the intentional exposure of the body of one person to a bodily fluid of another person in a manner that could result in the transmission of the human immunodeficiency virus.[139]

The lack of an appropriately worded legislative framework in Iowa, beyond the rigid schema above, was highlighted in a number of important judicial pronouncements. In *State v Rhoades*,[140] a case heard in the Supreme Court of Iowa, it was stressed that the judiciary could no longer take judicial notice of the defendant having the potential to transmit the virus when he in fact had an undetectable viral load:

With the advancements in medicine regarding HIV between 2003 and 2008, we are unable to take judicial notice of the fact that HIV may be transmitted through contact with an infected individual's blood, semen or vaginal fluid, and that sexual intercourse is one of the most common methods of passing the virus to fill in the gaps to find a factual basis for Rhoades's guilty plea.141

The court in *State v Rhoades*[142] acknowledged that the level of risk may become so insignificant that it no longer poses a likelihood of the virus being transmitted. The appeal was upheld, and it was clear that there was no longer an acceptance, by the judiciary in Iowa, that sexual contact can potentially transfer the virus to another when the defendant has a low or undetectable viral load and this is replicated within their new statutory provision:

'Practical means to prevent transmission' means substantial good faith compliance with a treatment regimen prescribed by the person's health care provider, if applicable, and with behavioral recommendations of the person's health care provider or public health officials, which may include but are not limited to the use of a medically indicated respiratory mask or a prophylactic device, to measurably limit the risk of transmission of the contagious or infectious disease.[143]

The decision in *Rhoades*,[144] and the new legislative framework in Iowa, represents an extremely positive incremental development for failure of

---

[139] Iowa Code § 709C.1.

[140] *State v Rhoades* (n 104).

[141] ibid 33.

[142] ibid.

[143] Iowa Code § 709D.2 (2015).

[144] *State v Rhoades* (n 104).

proof defences, but it stands in stark contrast to other U.S. jurisdictions where reform is still urgently needed. No allowance has been generally attributed to the defendant's viral load. In Nevada, for instance, a defendant with an undetectable viral load has very recently pleaded guilty to the statutory offence of exposing another to the virus on the basis that he would be convicted of a lesser charge.[145] There was no consideration of the probative relevance of a defendant's viral load. Similarly, in *State v Richardson*,[146] a case heard in the Supreme Court of Kansas, although there was superficial discourse of the viral load issue, ultimately the defendant's undetectable viral load was not fully considered in any real sense.[147]

The majority of U.S. state statutes are 'overbroad' in that the law does not compartmentalise defendants into those who act in a culpable manner or otherwise, or reflect lack of blameworthiness on the part of individuals who act responsibly by ensuring that they have consistently had an undetectable viral load.[148] Enactments are not accounting for advancements in preventative measures within the medical sphere. Newman has expressed the importance of new medication within the penumbra of the inculpation-exculpation equation by stipulating that the use of antiretroviral therapy has changed HIV from a 'death sentence', and it is unfortunate that the law has not kept up with medical advancements.[149] The advancement in preventative medicine should, but has not, lead to detailed statutory amendments.[150] The construction of a legislative framework that takes into account the concentration of the virus within the defendant's blood would denote that an undetectable and possibly low viral load could form the basis for an affirmative failure of proof defence.

What is apparent from our exposition of the current position in the U.S., with the notable exception of Iowa, is that the relevance of an undetectable viral load should not be left to the judiciary to consider in isolation, and

---

[145] Rashida Richardson, Shoshana Golden and Catherine Hanssens, 'Ending & Defending against HIV Criminalization a Manual for Advocates: Volume 1 State and Federal Laws and Prosecutions' 149. <http://www.hivlawandpolicy.org/sites/www.hivlawandpolicy.org/files/HIV%20C rim%20Manual%20%28updated%204-3-15%29.pdf> accessed 21 April 2015.

[146] *State v Richardson* (n 119).

[147] ibid.

[148] Perone (n 108) 400.

[149] Newman (n 128) 1410.

[150] Kaplan (n 122) 1566

that it necessitates an expressly stated statutory footing. Perone has cogently identified the deficiencies within the U.S. standardisations of criminalisation for HIV transmission/exposure and submits that such statutory provisions:

> (…) produce contrary results and actually increase misconceptions about HIV transmission by criminalizing people with HIV regardless of a person's likelihood of transmitting HIV because of condom usage, viral load, and/or engaging in activity with a very low or non-existent likelihood of transmission.[151]

The United States and the Criminalisation and Decriminalisation of Sexual Activity

The U.S. Presidential Commission specified that HIV+ individuals whose conduct posed a 'significant risk' of harm should be accountable for their actions.[152] The risk of the virus being transmitted depends upon a number of factors including the type of sexual activity, and this has been confirmed by empirical studies that specify that certain types of intimacy pose less of a risk of transmission than other intimate acts.

The reality is that a significant majority of U.S. states do not consider the likelihood of the virus being transmitted, and the preponderance of statutory provisions do not define the type of sexual activity that is to be prohibited.[153] Thus, there is a diverse legislative framework within the United States on the criminalisation of HIV, and the type of prohibited sexual activity. For current purposes, our focus will be on two main categorisations: (1) states that ensure that all types of sexual activity[154] are encapsulated by the legislation; and (2) states that have restricted, or have attempted to restrict, prosecutions relating to specific sexual acts.[155]

There are a number of U.S. states that have expressly stipulated an extensive list of prohibited sexual activities.[156] Wolf suggests that the

---

[151] Perone (n 108) 379.

[152] The Presidential Commission (n 99) 130 -131.

[153] For example: Wash Rev Code § 9A.36.011 (2015); Iowa Code § 709C.1(2)(b) (2011); La. Rev. Stat. Ann. § 14:43.5 (2016).

[154] Ark Code § 5-14-123 (2015); Mich. Comp. Laws Ann. § 333.5210 (2016).

[155] Cal. Health & Safety Code § 120291 (2016); 720 Ill. Comp. Stat. § 5/12- 5.01; Kan. Stat. Ann. § 21-5424 (2015).

[156] Ark Code § 5-14-123 (2015) ; Mich. Comp. Laws Ann. § 333.5210 (2016).

criminalisation of activities that pose no risk emanates from the legislators' utilisation of the wording of other criminal offences: 'it seems likely that this result is the unintentional effect of adopting definitions from sexual assault or rape statutes'.[157] It may also have been the outcomes of the legislator drafting individuated statutes in a manner that requires a defendant to always disclose their sero-status to prospective partners. Whatever the motive, these provisions have been vituperatively criticised for failing to take into account the risk of harm,[158] and they are, 'all consistent in one way: they do little to link the actual risk of infection with violation of the law.'[159] These wide-ranging statutes can be surveyed throughout a number of states.[160] Two of these states are Arkansas[161] and Michigan,[162] where the bespoke statutes, holistically drawn, encompass wide categorisations of potentially criminal conduct:

> (…) sexual intercourse, cunnilingus, fellatio, anal intercourse, or any other intrusion, however slight, of any part of a person's body or of any object into a genital or anal opening of another person's body.[163]

The statutory frameworks within Arkansas and Michigan engage a number of activities that pose virtually no risk of the virus being transmitted. The provisions extend culpability to conduct where an HIV+ individual may not have physically come into contact with the sexual organs of the complainant. Evidently, emphasis is placed upon the seriousness of infection with no consideration of the 'actual' risk of the virus being transmitted or foresight of harm occurrence. This is an affront to contemporary scientific literature that has reviewed the type of sexual

---

[157] Leslie E. Wolf and Richard Vezina, 'Crime and Punishment: Is There a Role for Criminal Law in HIV Prevention Policy?' (2004) 25 Whittier Law Review 821, 851.

[158] Christina M Shriver, 'State Approaches to Criminalizing the Exposure of HIV: Problems in Statutory Construction, Constitutionality and Implications' (2001) 21 Northern Illinois University Law Review 319, 326.

[159] James B. McArthur, 'As the Tide Turns: The Changing HIV/AIDS Epidemic and the Criminalization of HIV Exposure' (2009) 94 Cornell Law Review 707, At 719.

[160] For example see: MINN. STAT. § 609.2241 (2015) ;OHIO REV. CODE ANN. § 2903.11 (E) (4)(2016).

[161] Ark Code (n 154).

[162] Mich. Comp. Laws Ann. § 333.5210 (2016).

[163] ibid (2).

activity, and the possibility of the virus actually being transmitted.[164] There is a chasm between real and imagined risks, and Galletly and Pinkerton have proposed that, 'it is unacceptable for statutes to include activities that pose no risk of transmission.'[165] A 'knee-jerk' reaction to criminalise the transmission or exposure to the risk of HIV infection has occurred, unfortunately reinforcing the paradigm presumption that sexual activity with an HIV+ individual is itself a harm.

In *State v Flynn*,[166] by way of illustration, the inculpatory breadth of Michigan's statutory provisions was unsuccessfully challenged. The case involved allegations of exposure due to unprotected intercourse, and the Court of Appeals in Michigan rejected the defendant's contention that the statute was 'too broad', defining sexual penetration to include the use of 'objects'. The challenge was disregarded, as the activities that Flynn had partaken in were not those that he was challenging. Markman J stated that:

> This case, which does not involve a charge that defendant used an object to commit sexual penetration of the victim, requires the same conclusion. Defendant cannot challenge the scope of M.C.L. § 333.5210; MSA 14.15(5210) as overbroad where his charged conduct is encompassed by the language of the statute.[167]

Flynn was unable to dispute the validity of the statute, as he had been convicted of exposure due to unprotected intercourse, and this did not include the use of objects.[168] The judgment has not assisted in determining whether the wording of the Michigan statute is appropriate. Currently, there have been no further appeals on the matter; it seems that any type of sexual exposure is within the 'umbrella' of potential criminalisation.

A few states have adopted a more enlightened review of the harm/risk of harm kaleidoscopic legal prism, notably contained within the purview of California and Illinois perspectives. It is only the most high-risk types of sexual conduct that are criminalised in California and Illinois. This corresponds with scientific literature that acknowledges that unprotected sexual intercourse is most likely to transmit the virus. It also denotes a

---

[164] Matthew Cornett, 'Criminalization of the Intended Transmission or Knowing Non-disclosure of HIV in Canada' (2011) 5 McGill Journal of Law and Health 61, 95.

[165] Galletly and Pinkerton (n 46) 335.

[166] *State v Flynn* 1998 WL 1989782 (Mich. App.).

[167] ibid.

[168] *People v Jensen*, 586 N.W.2d 748, 751-52 (Mich. Ct. App. 1998).

reflective equipoise attached to the contemplation of harm principle.[169] The express stipulation of types of prohibited activity creates certainty, and enables individuals to tailor their conduct in order to engage in a responsible manner.

The legislative responses to HIV criminalisation within California and Illinois propose that exposing an unsuspecting complainant to the virus through unprotected sexual activity may lead to a successful prosecution.[170] In both statutory provisions, sexual activity is defined as unprotected anal or vaginal intercourse; clearly the conduct that is prohibited must pose a significant risk of harm. The restriction of prosecutions to unprotected activity may be seen to strike the appropriate balance between social utility, the probable risk of serious harm and the magnitude of any harm. None of these determinants appear to operate in a supererogatory manner as the statutory definitions afford an effective acknowledgement of dissonant factors. Wolf and Vezina are strong proponents of the Californian legislation, contending that it has struck the 'correct balance' in the context of failure of proof defences.[171]

Proponents of the Californian approach to criminalisation of HIV have suggested their statutory reforms present the 'model' code to follow in light of precision.[172] This clarity of drafting is evident throughout the Californian statute as it is specific in restricting the types of exposure that are criminalised. It is apparent that the legislators have balanced the risk of harm and the magnitude of harm, and only prohibited conduct that poses a significant risk of harm is criminalised.[173] It is for this reason that Klemm opines that the provision is 'instructive' for other state legislators.[174]

A vignette of the prevailing uncertainty attached to sexual activity as an affirmative failure of proof defence is constitutively highlighted by recent volte-faces within the Floridian criminal justice system. The Floridian

---

[169] Joel Feinberg, *Harm to Others: The Moral Limits of Criminal Law* (Oxford University Press 1984).

[170] Cal. Health & Safety Code § 120291 (2016); 720 Ill. Comp. Stat. § 5/12- 5.01; Kan. Stat. Ann. § 21-5424 (2015).

[171] Wolfe and Vezina (n 157) 879.

[172] Jaclyn Schmitt Hermes, 'The Criminal Transmission of HIV: A Proposal to Eliminate Iowa's Statute' (2002) The Journal of Gender, Race & Justice 473, 479.

[173] Sara Klemm, 'Keeping Prevention in the Crosshairs: A Better HIV Exposure Law for Maryland' (2010) 13 Journal of Health Care Law and Policy 495, 523.

[174] ibid 523.

legislative schema presumptively prohibits exposure through sexual intercourse, but recent judicial precepts from this jurisdiction have struggled to appropriately identify criminally restricted activities.[175] The provision has received extensive judicial scrutiny, and sexual intercourse has been interpreted to be exclusive to vaginal penetration by the penis, but, disingenuously, to also encompass other 'types of sexual activity'.[176] No consideration has been made to statistical probability of transmission within any of the conflicted state judgments. In *State v L.A.P.*,[177] a case where the defendant exposed the unsuspecting complainant to the virus through oral intercourse and digital penetration, the Court of Appeal in Florida held that sexual intercourse was exclusive to vaginal penetration by the penis.[178] Two further appellate decisions have since extended the definition of sexual intercourse to include anal, vaginal and oral intercourse. In *State v D.C.*,[179] the appellate court interpreted the statute so that it included all of the aforementioned activities. The definition from *D.C.* was affirmed by the majority in *State v Debaun*,[180] but Shepherd C.J., in a powerful dissenting judgment, suggested that the majority had mistakenly neglected to consider previous decisions, and inaptly utilised a dictionary definition of sexual intercourse.

Judicial conflict in determining the applicable definition of sexual intercourse within Florida signifies again the requirement of any legislative framework to provide interpretative precision and certainty, and that this must also correlate with the probability of the risk occurring.[181] An appropriately worded statute should clarify the parameters of criminal activity, with no attendant ambiguity as to what will be considered to be culpable conduct, as we set out subsequently. Culpability should only be based upon activities that, 'reach a certain threshold',[182] and that 'threshold', in cases of exposure, should only be the riskiest activities; there have been no reported cases of the virus being transmitted through

---

[175] Fla. Stat. Ann. § 775.0877 (2015) 384.24.
[176] *State v LAP* 62 So. 3d 693; 2011 Fla. App. LEXIS 8462; *State v Debaun* 129 So. 3d 1089; 2013 Fla. App. LEXIS 17224; *State v D.C.* 114 So. 3d 440; 2013 Fla. App. LEXIS 8595.
[177] *State v LAP* ibid.
[178] ibid.
[179] *State v D.C.* (n 176).
[180] *State v Debaun* (n 176).
[181] Markus (n 114) 867 -869
[182] Kaplan (n 122) 1540.

oral intercourse.[183] The demarcation line must be unprotected anal and vaginal intercourse, even though there are permutations depending upon who is the receptive or insertive partner.

There are substantial variations as to what will equate to culpable sexual activity within the differentiated legal state jurisdictions of the United States. Provisions that have facilitated all types of sexual activity within the penumbra of potential criminalisation may be described as 'too broad', and as there is no consideration of statistical probability of the virus being transmitted. While it is conceded that HIV can be a life-debilitating virus, and therefore the magnitude of harm is particularly relevant, it must be offset with the probability/risk of harm factorisation. At some point, the risk of transmission must be considered immaterial for criminalisation purposes, as acknowledged in California.

Conclusions

The issue of condom use, viral loads and type of sexual activity have not been directly raised as failure of proof defences before the English courts, but have been addressed within the Canadian and American legal systems. The distinction may be attributed to the fact that all cases within England have involved transmission of the virus, whilst in Canada and the United States, transmission is not a requirement for criminalisation. It is regrettable that the majority of those jurisdictions have not enacted legislation that would facilitate the defence of condom use and viral load, or would restrict culpability to certain types of sexual activity, and a new statutory pathway is urgently needed to reflect altered societal expectations, and appropriate thresholds of blameworthiness, fault and risk of harm temporal individuation.

Legislation is the appropriate rectification as a cathartic panacea for current problems, consequently eliminating the uncertainty that is evident within England and Canada, and avoiding retrospectivity challenges. Extant common law in both countries demonstrates that the use of non-specific HIV precepts attached to criminalisation simply promotes ad hoc interpretative measures with the unfortunate need to seek recourse in judicial divining rods; hardly a satisfactory response to significant criminal law/public health arguments. Legislative initiatives per se, however, have

---

[183] See <http://www.cdc.gov/hiv/risk/behavior/oralsex.html> accessed 24 April 2014.

not provided logical consistency or clarity within the U.S. state laws, and a multiplicity of definitional constructs of liability are contained in the divergent provisions, but no structured template as to offence-definition modification. The multi-faceted provisions, as stated herein, provide an important comparative contextualisation for the review and optimisation of approach: Illinois for accommodating condom use in a bespoke affirmative provision; Iowa for statutory promulgation of viral load considerations; and California for sexual activity standardisations. In general, however, specific U.S. state legislators have omitted to consider important scientific data; any new legislation needs to develop with this contemporary awareness.[184] Any proposed legislation needs to specify that factorisations of condom use, viral load or type of sexual activity within defined circumstances and parameters could be utilised as a defence.[185] This would enable HIV+ individuals to continue to engage in sexual activity without the fear of prosecution or rejection, and they would not generally be required to disclose their status within the boundaries of a new offence-definition modification.

It is unfortunate that the English courts have not taken the opportunity to clarify their position, although it is conceded that some of the issues were not identified or raised at the time of *Dica* or *Konzani*. It is suggested that the orthodoxy adopted in Canada, before the Supreme Court decision in *Mabior*, represents a preferred approach to the criminalisation of the sexual exposure/transmission to HIV. Allowing these defences would promote safe sexual practices and be in line with public health policies initiatives,[186] the ultimate goal being to reduce transmission of the virus.

Our proposed legislative failure of proof response to criminalisation of HIV constitutively promotes condom use and low viral load defences, and considers that certain types of sexual activity should be precluded from criminal sanctions. De novo legislation in relation to viral load must be constructed in a manner that promotes the administration of anti-retroviral medication. The benefits of this are twofold: it will encourage individuals to get tested; and encourage defendants to achieve an undetectable viral load. An optimal reform model for failure of proof defences may be stated in the following definitive terms:

---

[184] As was suggested *Mabior* (n 59).

[185] An evidential burden rather than legal.

[186] See generally Kate Harker and Ellen Wright, 'The HIV Stigma: Duty or Defence?' (2015) 4 UCL Journal of Law and Jurisprudence 55.

The offences:
A person will have committed an offence under this statute if he:

(1) Intentionally or recklessly transmits HIV to another by having unprotected vaginal or anal intercourse; or,
(2) Intentionally exposes another to HIV by having unprotected vaginal or anal intercourse

Defences

Protective Measures: Condom Use

Only the correct and consistent use of condoms (protective measures) will form the basis of a defence to the criminal acts of intentional exposure and reckless transmission of HIV.

Viral Load

An accused will not be considered to have exposed/transmitted the virus to another if he had a non-infectious viral load at the time of the sexual act.

In order to establish that the accused had a non-infectious viral load, the sexual act must have transpired after advice from a medical professional that he was non-infectious.

The wording of the suggested legislative defence of condom use ensures that a defendant can rely upon the exculpatory nature, but may still be held accountable if they are not used correctly or consistently. This would ensure that defendants are aware that their use may exonerate them from criminal sanctions, and encourage the correct use of these protective measures. It is also an acceptance that there may be a chance of the virus being transmitted; in practical terms this is unlikely to transpire, but the mechanism is in place if transmission occurs. This may also indirectly encourage disclosure by the defendant.

The preponderance of medical studies encourages the exclusion of a non-infectious viral load from the ambit of criminal sanctions. The first subsection articulates that the defendant can assert that he had a low or undetectable viral load at the time of the sexual contact. This avoids any ambiguity in relation to the defence. It also anticipates that the defendant has an evidentiary burden to establish that he had a low or undetectable viral load. This will be a relatively undemanding burden to discharge as the defendants' medical records will confirm their viral load at that time, and will not contravene the defendant's presumption of innocence. The second element of the suggested statutory provision relies upon Idaho's recognition that the advice must emanate from a legal professional, ensuring that there is a formal requirement to the defence, and much needed consistency and certainty. Contrary to recent Law Commission perspectives, a bespoke legislative response is needed to address the overbroad criminalisation of HIV transmission, and to propagate appropriate failure of proof defences.

CHAPTER TWELVE

A SPECIAL CASE FOR PERSONALITY DISORDER: ARE THE DISTINCTIONS BETWEEN PERSONALITY DISORDER AND MENTAL ILLNESS IN CLINICAL AND LEGAL PRACTICE JUSTIFIED?

RAJAN NATHAN AND KEITH RIX

'How do we preserve the dignity of those found to lack adequate behavioural controls?'

David L. Bazelon[1]

Introduction

Personality disorder is diagnostic rubric used to describe a group of psychiatric conditions in which there are disturbances of thinking, feeling, and behaving that arise during the developmental period, persist over the life course, are evident across a range of domains, and are associated with significant distress to the individual and/or to others.[2] Distinctions between personality disorder and mental illness have been made in clinical, legal and policy contexts. In this chapter, we explore the development of the

---

1 David L Bazelon, 'The morality of the criminal law' (1976) 49 Southern California Law Review 385 (Chief Judge, United States Court of Appeals for the District of Columbia Circuit).

[2] A more detailed examination of the personality disorder construct can be found in Rajan Nathan, H Wood, 'Forensic Psychiatry and Forensic Psychology: Personality Disorder' in Jason Payne-James and Roger Byard (eds) *Encyclopaedia of Forensic and Legal Medicine Volume 2* (2nd edn, Elsevier 2016).

personality disorder construct and how it has been distinguished in legal and clinical principle and practice from other recognised forms of mental disorder. The basis of these distinctions and legitimacy for maintaining them will be examined.

The current use of the term 'personality disorder' as a broad concept arching over a series of specific diagnostic categories can be traced back to Schneider. In 1923, he presented a taxonomy of 'psychopathic personalities'.[3] Although he identified ten categories, his approach was in effect a statistical or dimensional one: these were abnormal personalities because they deviated statistically from the norm. His categories continue to be reflected in some of the current personality disorder diagnoses. For example, in DSM 5, Schneider's 'insecure, anankastic' personality persists as obsessive-compulsive personality disorder, his 'emotionally unstable' as borderline personality disorder, his 'insecure, sensitive' as avoidant personality disorder and his 'callous' personality as antisocial personality disorder.

The boundaries of the term 'mental illness' are not universally agreed. In the USA, mental illness has encompassed 'collectively all diagnosable mental disorders'[4] including personality disorder.[5] In the UK, the use of the term mental illness is often confined to conditions which are considered to represent a qualitative deviation from the individual's premorbid psychological functioning (e.g. mood disorders, anxiety disorder, schizophrenia spectrum disorders). This definition, therefore, excludes conditions that become apparent at an early age and continue through adulthood with little variation (e.g. developmental disorders and personality disorders). Whatever the interpretation of the term mental illness, the tendency to distinguish personality disorder from other forms of mental disorder (such as depressive illness, mania and schizophrenia) occurs across geographical boundaries.

---

[3] Kurt Schneider, *Psychopathic Personalities*, Hamilton M (trans) (Cassell 1958).

[4] US Department of Health and Human Services. *Mental Health: A Report of the Surgeon General*. Rockville, MD: US Department of Health and Human Services: Substance Abuse and Mental Health Services Administration, Centre for Mental Health Services, National Institutes of Health, National Institute of Mental Health, 1999.

[5] Sally C Johnson and Eric B Elbogen, 'Personality disorders at the interface of psychiatry and the law: legal use and clinical classification' (2013) 15 Dialogues in Clinical Neuroscience 203.

Clinical Approaches to Personality Disorder

Documented intellectual interest in the notion of personality disturbance appears as early as 400 BC in Hippocrates's application of the humours to medical enquiry. [6] Personality disorder, and specifically psychopathic personality disorder, as a clinical concept in modern medical history, has its origins in Pinel's concept of *manie sans délire*.[7] However, it is regarded by many, but probably somewhat mistakenly, as having taken shape in the form of 'moral insanity', which was defined by the English physician Prichard, in 1842, as 'morbid perversion of the natural feelings, affections, inclinations, temper, habits, moral dispositions and natural impulses, without any remarkable disorder or defect of the intellect or knowing and reasoning faculties and particularly without any insane illusion [8] or hallucination'.[9] There has been debate about whether Prichard's cases, when seen through present day diagnostic lenses, may have been suffering from mental illness[10]; his illustrative cases are middle-aged, they showed no previous evidence of antisocial behaviour and some recovered. [11] Furthermore, Prichard referred to 'a state of mind strikingly different from the previous, and habitual or natural character'. Therefore, not surprisingly, a careful review of his work led Bowden[12] to side with what he regarded as the more discriminating authorities and 'see little to support the notion that the psychopath is a descendant of the morally insane'. Nevertheless, within the definition, we can see a distinction between character flaws on the one hand, and intellectual impairment and positive psychotic symptoms on the other. The German psychiatrist Koch, in his

---

[6] Frederick L Coolidge, Daniel L Segal, 'Evolution of the personality disorder diagnosis in the Diagnostic and Statistical Manual of Mental Disorders' (1998) 18 Clinical Psychology Review 585.

[7] Philippe H Pinel (1806) *A Treatise on Insanity*. Reissued trans. D Davis (New York Academy of Medicine, Hafner Publishing 1962).

[8] Prichard's 'Illusion' equates to the present day 'Delusion'.

[9] James Cowles Prichard, *Forms of Insanity* (Hippolyte Baillière 1842); Aubrey Lewis, Psychopathic personality: a most elusive category' (1974) 4 Psychological Medicine 133.

[10] Frances Anthony Whitlock, *Criminal Responsibility and Mental Illness* (Butterworths 1963) 78.

[11] Frances Anthony Whitlock, 'Prichard and the concept of moral insanity' (1967) 1 Australian and New Zealand Journal of Psychiatry 72.

[12] Paul Bowden, 'Pioneers in forensic psychiatry. James Cowles Prichard: moral insanity and the myth of psychopathic disorder' (1992) 3 Journal of Forensic Psychiatry 113.

1891 text 'Psychopathic Inferiorities', refers to a clinical condition which 'comprises all abnormalities – either hereditary or acquired – which influence a human's personal life, but which do not constitute – even in the worst cases – mental illnesses, although the person suffering from them does not seem to be of sound mind and sound physical capabilities'. [13] Likewise, Kraepelin, whose use of the term 'moral insanity' evolved between 1883 and 1904, used the term to refer to 'moral atrophy in its most severe form (…) characteristic of the born criminal who chooses and follows his course in life because moral considerations have no power over him', also adopted the term 'psychopathic inferiority' and finally wrote of 'psychopathic personalities' which included born criminals, liars and swindlers, the unstable and pseudoquerulants. [14] So, again and again, the fault line between a concept considered to be a forerunner of 'personality disorder' and mental illness is described.

A significant influence on the conceptual separation of mental illness and personality disorder in clinical practice was the introduction in 1980 of the multiaxial system of diagnosis by the 3rd edition of the American Psychiatric Association's official system of diagnosis (DSM III). [15] This approach encouraged the simultaneous exploration of a wide range of problems that were grouped along separate axes. The first axis, labelled 'clinical syndromes' described 'distinct clinical states'. [16] Axis I included psychiatric conditions, such as schizophrenia and manic-depressive illness, that were considered to be mental illnesses. Personality disorder, by contrast, was located on Axis II. The intention was to ensure that in addition to the assessment of discrete symptoms states (i.e. mental illnesses), the clinician explored more enduring patterns of personality functioning. [17] The multiaxial system was retained in subsequent iterations of DSM, until the most recent version (see below).

---

[13] Philipp Gutmann, 'Julius Ludwig August Koch (1841–1908): Christian, philosopher and psychiatrist (2008) 19 History of Psychiatry 202.

[14] Paul Bowden, 'Pioneers in forensic psychiatry, James Cowles Prichard: moral insanity and the myth of psychopathic disorder' (1992) 3 Journal of Forensic Psychiatry 113.

[15] American Psychiatric Association, *Diagnostic and statistical manual of mental disorders* (3rd edn Psychiatric Association 1980).

[16] Theodore Millon, 'The DSM-III: An insider's perspective' (1983) 38 American Psychologist 804.

[17] ibid.

Although the distinction between personality disorder and mental illness therefore has a long and now respectable history, it is a distinction which has been challenged. A significant challenge came from Kendell,[18] an internationally recognised authority on the nature of mental disorder. In 2002, he concluded that the distinction was being undermined by both clinical and genetic evidence. The clinical evidence to which he referred was the similarity in the time course of personality disorders and mental illness, the significance of this being that the conditions had hitherto been distinguished on the basis that personality disorders were considered to be part of the normal spectrum of personality variation and stable through adult life whereas mental illnesses were held to be the result of some sort of morbid process and to have a recognisable onset and time course. He noted, for example, that schizophrenic illnesses have the same time course as a personality disorder. He referred to research showing that the genetic bases of affective personality disorders and mood disorders and of schizotypal personality and schizophrenia have much in common. He was most disconcerted to note that avoidant personality disorder has so much in common with the mental illness known as generalised social phobia that the American Psychiatric Association had expressed the suspicion that they might be alternative conceptualisations of the same or similar conditions.

Since 2002, there has been further research which has cast doubt on the validity of the distinction. Tyrer, for example, has shown that borderline personality disorder is more properly regarded as a condition of unstable mood and behaviour – what he terms 'fluxithymia' – and is more appropriately classified as a form of mood disorder than personality disorder.[19] It has been found that, far from being a life-long condition, at least 50 per cent of its sufferers improve sufficiently so as not to meet the diagnostic criteria 5–10 years after first diagnosis, this probably being a spontaneous development or associated with increased maturity and self-reflection, so that only a minority have symptoms that persist into late life.[20]

---

[18] Robert E Kendell, 'The distinction between personality disorder and mental illness' (2002) 180 British Journal of Psychiatry 110.

[19] Peter Tyrer, 'Why borderline personality disorder is neither borderline nor a personality disorder' (2009) 3 Personality and Mental Health 86.

[20] Mary C Zanarini, Frances R Frankenberg, John Hennen et al, 'The longitudinal course of borderline psychopathology: 6-year prospective follow up of the

Albeit setting out the issue in a slightly different way, and considering whether personality disorders are a form of mental illness, the debate in the 1990s in Australia illustrates the difficulties which psychiatrists have brought upon themselves in arguing for personality disorder to be treated differently. Neal called for clear criteria upon which to conclude, as the Royal Australian and New Zealand College of Psychiatry did, that neuroses and psychoses were to be included within the concept of mental illness but not personality disorder. [21] He is critical of the College's reasoning. It laid a great deal of stress on *treatability* as a criterion of illness, but he listed a number of illnesses that do not respond to treatment and asked if, for example, certain forms of cancer that did not respond to treatment were any the less illnesses. He noted the claim that personality disorders are *permanent* conditions whereas illnesses are temporary, but observed that 'the notion of illness as a short-term phenomenon belies a great deal of the practice in psychiatric hospitals where a sizeable proportion of the patient population is there on a very long-term basis'. The third set of arguments which he identified had to do with questions which were not really germane to the issue of personality disorder being a form of mental illness, but they illustrate how psychiatrists were prepared to discriminate against people with personality disorder. It was argued that, as psychiatry could do so little for people with personality disorder, it was a more rational use of resources to devote them to people who could be helped. As Neal observed, this is not an argument about mental illness and personality disorder, but an argument that people with personality disorder are less deserving of treatment than other people. So, as Kendell was later to observe:

> [I]t is commonplace for a diagnosis of personality disorder to be used to justify a decision not to admit someone to a psychiatric ward, or even to accept them for treatment – a practice that understandably puzzles and irritates the staff of accident and emergency departments, general practitioners and probation officers, who find themselves left to cope as best they can with extremely difficult, frustrating people without any psychiatric assistance.

---

phenomenology of borderline personality disorder' (2003) 160 American Journal of Psychiatry 274.

[21] David Neal, 'Personality disorder, the criminal justice system and the mental health system' in Sally-Anne Gerull and William Lucas (eds), *Serious Violent Offenders: Sentencing, Psychiatry and Law Reform* (Australian Institute of Criminology 1993) 1.

The weight of evidence in favour of removing the distinction between mental illness and personality disorder is confirmed by the publication in 2013 of DSM-5 which discards the axial approach and lists all mental disorders, including mental illnesses and personality disorder, together.[22] Additionally, DSM-5's acceptance of the legitimacy of a dimensional approach to assessing personality disorder (as an alternative to, rather than a replacement for, the traditional categorical typology of diagnosing mental disorder) is in line with the evidence base. The distinction between personality disorder and mental illness has been justified on the basis that it has been difficult to 'establish' that personality disorder involves dysfunction, in the sense of 'failure of a mental mechanism to perform a natural function for which it was designed by evolution'.[23]

This difficulty has been resolved by the sizeable empirically-based literature which has identified an array of psychological and neurobiological disturbances underpinning personality disorder traits. A review of the range of different processes examined is beyond the scope of this chapter, but replicated findings support the presence of specific disturbances of mental mechanisms in personality disorder.

For example, borderline personality disorder is associated with impaired facial affect recognition. Patients with this condition are more liable to negatively misinterpret ambiguous or neutral facial expressions.[24] Such misinterpretation of non-verbal cues is likely to be an important contributory factor to the characteristic disturbances of oversensitivity and relationship problems. The psychological processes involved in in-the-moment recognition of the affect state of others are automatic and implicit. They are instantly activated without effortful attention. Implicit processes, which are constantly running, are essential for the rapid appraisal of an ever changing social environment. The presence of implicit mechanisms does not mean that the individual is unaware of his or her behaviour. Rather, this dual process model of understanding human behaviour recognises that for all of us, as well as conscious (explicit and effortful)

---

[22] American Psychiatric Association, 'Diagnostic and statistical manual of mental disorders' (5th edn, American Psychiatric Publishing 2013).

[23] Kendell (n 18).

[24] Alexander R Daros, Konstantine K Zakzanis, Anthony C Ruocco, 'Facial emotion recognition in borderline personality disorder' (2013) 43 Psychological Medicine 1953.

influences on behaviour, there are also 'subconscious' (implicit) ones.[25] The point in relation to understanding the challenging behaviour sometimes displayed by patients with borderline personality disorder is that disturbances at the level of implicit processing are critical. Adopting a developmental approach to examining process disturbances offers extra insight into the nature of the personality disorder. Neuronal pathway malleability, which is an evolutionary advantage in positive rearing environments, may allow changes to adverse childhood experiences that are associated with the long-term problems seen in borderline personality disorder. Whilst the recalibration of threat detection mechanisms to more readily identify threat may be seen as adaption to actual danger, repeated exposure to danger during the developmental period may lead to intractable and generalised biases to attribute malevolent intent to the actions of others including in situations where there is no real risk of harm. Evidence for many different mental mechanism aberrations have been found in borderline personality disorder and in other personality disorder categories, particularly antisocial personality disorder and psychopathy.

In summary, there is not an evidence-based case to differentiate personality disorder categorically from other forms of mental disorders with regard to the clinical attention or resource allocation.

Jurisprudential Approaches to Personality Disorder

Since the Middle Ages, a variety of terms have been used in the criminal law to describe the mentally abnormal.[26] The major distinction which developed was between those who lacked something in their mental make-up and whose deficiency existed from birth (the mentally deficient) and those who possessed a disorder of the mind (the lunatics). However, Coke included in his category of '*non compos mentis*' the person 'that by his own vicious act depriveth himself of his memory and his understanding, as that he is drunken'.[27]

In the early years of the last century, when the distinction between idiocy and lunacy still persisted, personality disorder was regarded as a form of

---

[25] Daniel Kahneman, *Thinking, fast and slow* (Allen Lane 2011).
[26] Homer D Crotty, 'History of insanity as a defence to crime in English Criminal law' (1924) 12 California Law Review 105.
[27] ibid.

idiocy or mental deficiency. The Mental Deficiency Act 1913 recognised four classes of 'defectives': idiots, imbeciles, the feeble-minded, and moral imbeciles. The last were 'persons who from an early age display some permanent defect coupled with strong vicious or criminal propensities on which punishment has had little or no effect'. Scotland adopted the same definition in its Mental Deficiency and Lunacy (Scotland) Act 1913. The Mental Deficiency Act 1927 replaced the term 'moral imbecile' with the term 'moral defective', but Scotland retained the term until the Mental Health (Scotland) Act 1960.

Civil Commitment

With regard to psychiatric disorder for which involuntary hospital treatment could be considered, in England and Wales, the 1959 Mental Health Act (at section 4(1)) disaggregated '*mental disorder*' into four categories '*mental illness, arrested or incomplete development of mind, psychopathic disorder, and any other disorder or disability of mind*'. If compulsory admission was being considered for a patient with personality disorder, the Mental Health Act category of psychopathic disorder was invoked. Psychopathic disorder had a specific meaning ('*a persistent disorder or disability of mind (whether or not including subnormality of intelligence) which results in abnormally aggressive or seriously irresponsible conduct on the part of the patient*', section 4(4)), which is not equivalent to the clinical construct of personality disorder. As an aside, there was sometimes confusion in the use of '*psychopathic*', which as well as a Mental Health Act category, is used as an adjectival descriptor of individuals who clinically are considered to meet the criteria for psychopathy. In some respects, the Mental Health Act psychopathic disorder, with its focus on aggressive and irresponsible behaviour, was more restrictive than clinically defined personality disorder, which includes problem behaviours other than antisocial ones. In other respects, the Mental Health Act psychopathic disorder was broader since it could be used for intellectually unimpaired individuals with autism spectrum disorder who were violent.[28]

---

[28] Val Hawes, 'Treating high risk mentally disordered offenders; the dangerous and severe personality disorder initiative' in Annie Bartlett and Gill McGauley (eds) *Forensic Mental Health: Concepts, systems, and practices* (Oxford University Press 2009).

Differences in the law relating to involuntary hospital admission for mental illness and psychopathic disorder were enacted in the Mental Health Act 1959. The definition of psychopathic disorder included the caveat '*and requires or is susceptible to medical treatment*', which was not a requirement for mental illness to be considered within the ambit of the Act. Moreover, whereas compulsory admission to hospital for mental illness could take place '*in the case of a patient of any age*', for psychopathic disorder, this could only occur '*in the case of a patient under the age of 21 years of age*'.[29] This reflected the position at the time that the effectiveness of intervention for personality disorder was dependent on the age of the patient.[30]

The Mental Health Act 1983 retained the term '*psychopathic disorder*' within the four categories of mental disorder and the same definition of this term (although '*subnormality of intelligence*' was replaced by '*impairment of intelligence*'). The definition did not include a caveat relating to medical treatment and there was no reference to age. However, what came to be known as the 'treatability test' was applied to compulsory admission for treatment of psychopathic disorder ('*in the case of psychopathic disorder or mental impairment, such treatment is likely to alleviate or prevent a deterioration of his condition*').[31]

As a consequence of the amendments introduced by the Mental Health Act 2007, the categories of mental disorder, including psychopathic disorder, and the 'treatability test' were removed. A wide-ranging definition of mental disorder was introduced ('any disorder or disability of mind').[32] An appropriate treatment clause ('appropriate treatment is available for him')[33] was also introduced, but this applies to the broad category of mental disorder and so is not applied differentially to personality disorder.

In Ireland, s 8(2)(a) of the Mental Health Act 2001 excludes personality disorder from the provisions for compulsory powers. There is a similar provision in Northern Ireland where s 3(2) of the Mental Health (Northern

---

[29] Mental Health Act 1959 s 26.

[30] Phillip Fennell, 'Radical risk management, mental health and criminal justice' in Nicola S Gray, Judith M Laing and Lesley Noaks (eds) *Criminal Justice, mental health and the politics of risk* (Cavendish Publishing 2002).

[31] Mental Health Act 1983 s 3(2)(b).

[32] Mental Health Act 2007 s 1(2).

[33] Mental Health Act 2007 s 4(2)(b).

Ireland) Order 1986 states that no person shall be treated under the order by reason only of personality disorder. In Scotland, s 328(1) of the Mental Health (Care and Treatment) (Scotland) Act 2003 includes personality disorder in the definition of mental disorder. The Mental Health (Jersey) Law 1969 and the Mental Health (Bailiwick of Guernsey) Law 2010 do not distinguish personality disorder specifically or by implication and so personality disorder could be regarded as subsumed under their categories of disability or disorder of mind.

In the USA, two states deserve mention.[34] Arizona excludes personality disorders from its definition of mental illness for the purposes of civil commitment. Florida specifically excludes antisocial personality disorder.

In summary, in many, but not all, jurisdictions, there has been a higher bar for compulsory admission for the treatment of patients with personality disorder. Of note, in England and Wales, the difference in the Mental Health Act criteria between patients with personality disorder and mental illness has been removed.

Criminal Proceedings

In a number of jurisdictions, personality disorder – particularly and sometimes specifically antisocial personality disorder – is excluded from mental condition defences and partial defences, and from consideration at the mitigation stage.

In the USA, a number of states have adopted the American Law Institute Model Penal Code[35] which excludes from its definition of mental disease or defect, for the purposes of its test of reduced criminal responsibility, 'an abnormality manifested only by repeated criminal or otherwise antisocial conduct'. The federal standard for insanity[36] which requires 'a severe mental disease or defect' is most often interpreted as excluding personality disorders as the sole diagnoses of concern.[37] California and Oregon specifically exclude all personality disorders from the insanity defence,[38]

---

[34] Johnson and Elbogen (n5).

[35] American Law Institute Model Penal Code s 4.01 (2).

[36] 18 United States Code, s 17.

[37] Johnson and Elbogen (n5).

[38] Richard J Bonnie Should a personality disorder qualify as a mental disease in insanity adjudication? (2010) 38 Journal of Law and Medical Ethics 760.

and in Arizona, statute excludes 'character defects' from the insanity defence [39] and its Supreme Court has refused to allow character or personality disorder as a mitigating factor in capital cases.[40] However, there are exceptions. In *State v Galloway*,[41] the New Jersey Supreme Court held that a defendant's borderline personality disorder was capable of affecting cognitive functioning, such that the essential ingredient for the crime of murder of purposeful action could not be met. In New York, it is permissible to take into account 'underlying personality disorders' when the defence of extreme emotional disturbance is raised.[42]

In Australia, it is also a mixed picture. Under the common law, personality disorder, in the form of antisocial personality disorder, is not sufficient for a defence of insanity. [43] However, both the Commonwealth *Criminal Code*[44] and the Australian Capital Territory *Criminal Code*[45] recognise severe personality disorder as evidence for the purpose of the mental impairment defence.

In Scotland, where the defence of not being criminally responsible has replaced the insanity defence, s 51A of the Criminal Procedure (Scotland) Act 1995, as amended by the Criminal Justice and Licensing (Scotland) Act 2010, people with personality disorder cannot qualify for the defence if their personality disorder 'is characterised solely or principally by abnormally aggressive or seriously irresponsible conduct'. It has been observed that, in practice, it is highly unlikely that any personality disorder could qualify under this section because it would be unlikely to meet the test in s 51A(1) that the person was 'unable by reason of mental disorder to appreciate the wrongfulness of the conduct'.[46]

---

[39] Arizona Revised Statutes 13-502A (2007).

[40] *State v Richmond* 560 P. 2d 41 (1976).

[41] *State v Galloway* 133 NJ 631, 628A.2d 735 1993.

[42] Bonnie (n 38).

[43] *Willgoss v R* (1960) 105 CLR 295; *Jeffrey v R* [1982] Tas R 199; *Hodges v R* (1985) 19 A Crim R 129.

[44] Criminal Code (Cth) s 7.3(8).

[45] Criminal Code (ACT) s 27(1).

[46] Rajan Darjee and Louise Roninson, 'Psychiatric defences' in Lindsey Thomson & Joanna Cherry (eds) *Mental Health & Scots Law in Practice,* (2nd edn, Thomson Reuters/W Green 2014) 327.

In England and Wales, personality disorder is not excluded as a qualifying condition for diminished responsibility. This partial defence to the offence of murder, codified by the Coroners and Justice Act 2009, is dependent on a finding that the defendant was suffering from an abnormality of mental functioning arising from a recognised medical condition which substantially impaired the defendant's ability to do one or more of three things (to understand the nature of his conduct, form a rational judgement or exercise self-control) and which provides an explanation for his acts and omissions in doing or being a party to the killing. A medical condition is 'recognised' if it appears within a widely accepted system of psychiatric classification (e.g. ICD,[47] DSM[48] or other authoritative approach). Thus, if the criteria are met for a personality disorder diagnosis according to such a system, then this element of the defence may be satisfied.[49]

In general, personality disorder is not afforded a status equivalent to mental illness within legal systems. Johnson and Elbogen have listed factors that may contribute to the persistence of this lack of equivalence. (Box 1)[50]

Factors influencing differences in legal approaches to personality disorder from other mental disorders (based on Johnson and Elbogen)	
1	The prevalence of personality disorder in the relevant populations (e.g. among offender groups) is high
2	The common occurrence of personality disorder as a comorbid condition makes apportionment of responsibility more confusing in the legal arena
3	Diagnostic categories of personality disorder are not clearly or exclusively defined
4	A perception of overlap between personality disorder traits and the limits of normal functioning
5	Difficulty setting thresholds on a continuum between normality and disorder

---

[47] International Statistical Classification of Diseases and Related Health Problems.

[48] Diagnostic and Statistical Manual (n22).

[49] Rajan Nathan and Simon Medland, 'Psychiatric evidence and the new defences of diminished responsibility and loss of control' (2016) 22 BJPsych Advances 277. Although cf Dowds [2012] EWCA Crim 281.

[50] Johnson and Elbogen (n5).

6	Inferences about personality disorder traits being under voluntary control
7	Individuals with personality disorder often not defining their own problems in terms of mental disorder
8	Perceptions of personality disorder as untreatable
9	The similarity between a common personality disorder diagnosis in forensic settings (i.e. antisocial personality disorder) and general concepts of criminality
10	Perceptions that personality disorder does not significantly impair an individual's capacity to make choices

Public Policy Approaches to Personality Disorder

Alongside the conceptual separation in clinical practice of personality disorder from mental illness, there was a perception that personality disorder was not responsive to interventions and patients with this condition did not merit the input of mental health services.[51] Negative attitudes toward patients with personality disorder were common.[52] Against this pessimistic backdrop, in the early 1990s, there were pleas to bring personality disorder in from the fringes of psychiatry.[53] Furthermore, academic inquiry began to be focused on the evidence for the effectiveness of interventions for personality disorder.[54]

In the late 1990s, there was a niche policy development focused on a very small number of patient/offenders that had far reaching consequences for approaches to, and services for, personality disorder. The policy proposal published by the Home Office and the Department of Health in 1999 was *'designed to achieve the objective of providing better protection for the public from dangerous severely personality disordered people'*, a group

---

[51] Martyn Pickersgill, 'How personality disorder became treatable: The mutual constitution of clinical knowledge and mental health law' (2013) 43 Social Studies of Science 30.

[52] Glyn Lewis, Louis Appleby, 'Personality Disorder: the patients psychiatrists dislike' (1988) 153 British Journal of Psychiatry 44.

[53] Tyrer (n19).

[54] Bridget Dolan and Jeremy Coid, *'Psychopathic and antisocial personality disorders: treatment and research issues'* (Gaskell 1993).

that was '*estimated to be just over 2000 people*' in England and Wales.[55] The two central elements of the proposed change were 'ensuring that dangerous severely personality disordered people are kept in detention for as long as they pose a high risk' and 'managing them in a way that provides better opportunities to deal with the consequence of their disorder'.

The narrative of what came to be known as the Dangerous and Severe Personality Disorder (DSPD) services often starts in 1996 with an account of the brutal killings of Lin Russell and her daughter, Megan, and the serious attack on Megan's sister, Josie Russell. Michael Stone, who was convicted of these crimes, not only had a history of serious offending, but also had been diagnosed with personality disorder and was subject to psychiatric treatment and supervision. The purported mismanagement of Michael Stone by the mental health services within the popular portrayal of this crime was illustrative, according to the government, of the problems inherent in the contemporary psychiatric approach to this group of patients.[56] The context that provided the momentum for a different approach to high risk offenders with personality disorder was more complex than a single high profile case. The focus of a second major inquiry in a decade at Ashworth Hospital was on the practices on the personality disorder service in this high secure hospital.[57] As well as confirming serious cultural problems in the service, having undertaken a review of forensic mental health models for the management of personality disorder, the inquiry team recommended hospital and prison placements for a 'severely personality disordered group'. The political motivation to address the problem of high risk personality disordered offenders was also driven by a wider climate of reduced tolerance for risk.[58] More clinically grounded contextual factors included the use of

---

[55] Home Office and Department of Health, '*Managing Dangerous People with Severe Personality Disorder: Proposals for Policy Development*' (1999).

[56] Max Rutherford, 'Imprisonment for public protection: genesis and mental health implications' (2008) 13 Mental Health Review Journal 47.

[57] Philip Fallon, Robert Bluglass, Brian Edwards, Granville Daniels, '*Report of the Committee of Inquiry into the Personality Disorder Unit, Ashworth Special Hospital*' (The Stationery Office, 1999).

[58] Anthony Maden, 'Dangerous and severe personality disorder: antecedents and origins' (2007) 190 British Journal of Psychiatry 8.

more refined approaches to the assessment and management of risk and offending.[59]

The DSPD programme invested heavily in specialist assessment and treatment units in the high secure prison and hospital estate. In HMP Whitemoor, an existing wing was converted to accept admissions of DSPD prisoners from 2000.[60] New build facilities opened in HMP Frankland and Rampton Hospital in 2004 and in Broadmoor Hospital in 2005. In 2006, a DSPD unit for women was opened in HMP Low Newton. The final total capacity of the five high secure DSPD services was 286. Additionally, there were 52 placements in three medium secure hospitals and community based services in two localities. Treatment periods within prison-based units could not extend beyond the point at which the offender's sentence expired. For those sentenced offenders transferred to hospital-units, the default Mental Health Act process results in the continued involuntary detention of the 'patient' after the sentence expiry date. There were substantial misgivings about the detention of offenders in hospital without good clinical rationale for a period longer than the Court had determined was appropriate for the offence(s) of which they had been convicted.[61]

Although, the DSPD initiative was influential in the development of clinical and academic interest in personality disorder in forensic settings, the service model proved to be relatively short-lived. Despite the over threefold greater cost of a bed in a hospital unit in comparison to a prison unit, departmental evaluation of the services concluded that prisons were better able to provide the required context for successful treatment.[62] The merits of directing extensive resources to the management of such a small number of the most seriously disordered individuals were also questioned.

The manifest policy shift for personality disordered offenders was formally marked in 2011 with the publication of the Consultation on the Offender Personality Disorder Pathway Implementation Plan by the

---

[59] ibid.
[60] Nick Joseph, Nick Benefield 'The development of an offender personality disorder strategy' (2010) 15 Mental Health Journal 10.
[61] Stuart M White, 'Preventive detention must be resisted by the medical profession' 28 Journal of Medical Ethics (2002) 95.
[62] Department of Health, 'Personality disorder pathway implementation plan' (2011).

Department of Health and Ministry of Justice.[63] Funding for services for a larger number of offenders than offered by DSPD services relied on a policy of decommissioning the costly hospital DSPD units. The central component of the new model is the pathway through the criminal justice system involving (i) screening and early identification, (ii) assessment, case formulation, sentence and intervention planning, (iii) community provision and case management, and (iv) residential treatment units predominantly within the prison estate.

The more widespread problem of people with personality disorder being excluded from secondary mental health services led to the publication in 2003 of the landmark policy directive, Personality Disorder: No Longer a Diagnosis of Exclusion by the National Institute for Mental Health in England (NIMHE).[64] Clear intentions for the development of personality disorder services in general and forensic mental health settings were laid out. The call for specialist services (e.g. 'a specialist multi-disciplinary personality disorder team' and 'specialist day patient services' in general mental health; and 'personality disorder services nationally within regional forensic services') pointed to new services parallel to the provision that existed for mentally ill patients, rather than a more integrated model.

Of interest to the conceptual debate, this publication seemed to be attempting to combine the personality disorder and mental illness constructs with the opening statement: 'The National Service Framework for adult mental health sets out responsibilities to provide evidence based, effective services for all those with severe mental illness, including people with personality disorder who experience significant distress and difficulty'. Further to the welcome stimulus for the development of personality disorders provided by the 2003 NIMHE document, a more standardised and evidence-based approach by general mental health services to patients with diagnoses of borderline and antisocial personality disorder was encouraged by the publication in 2009 of the NICE guidelines for borderline and antisocial personality disorders.[65]

---

[63] ibid.

[64] National Institute for Mental Health in England (NIMHE) available at <https://www.nimh.nih.gov/index.shtml> accessed 7th January 2016.

[65] NICE 'Borderline personality disorder: treatment and management, NICE clinical guideline 78' (2009); NICE 'Antisocial personality disorder: treatment, prevention and management NICE clinical guideline 77 (2009).

This section illustrates, with reference to developments in England and Wales over the past two and a half decades, how policy directives informed by clinical insights can drive positive changes in mental health services. There remain lessons to be learned about how health service policy designed primarily to deal with topical political imperatives may produce poorly designed service models. Policies specifically addressing personality disorder in forensic settings may be especially vulnerable to political pressures because of associations with risk of harm.

Why do the Distinctions Persist?

There have been positive developments in relation to personality disorder over recent decades, notably in the form of amendments to the Mental Health Act and the development of specialist services and expertise with the intention of reducing the disparity of mental health service provision between personality disordered and mentally ill patients. Despite the lack of a compelling clinical case for a qualitatively different approach to personality disorder from mental illness, the evidence suggests that, outwith specialist personality disorder services, there has not been an appreciable change in clinicians' negative attitudes towards personality disorder. [66] Why have these attitudes proved so resistant to change? Interestingly, analyses of problematic beliefs held by clinicians about personality disordered patients reveals some themes in common with the rationale for different approaches within the law between personality disorder and mental illness.

The use of the terms 'attention-seeking' and 'manipulative' by clinicians to explain disturbed behaviour by patients diagnosed with personality disorder[67] implies the behaviour is considered to be the result of conscious deliberation and awareness. Take, for example, the scenario in which a patient with a diagnosis of borderline personality disorder on an inpatient unit who, following the refusal by nursing staff to agree to the patient's

---

[66] Dominic Markham, Peter E Trower, 'The effects of the psychiatric label "borderline personality disorder" on nursing staff's perceptions and causal attributions for challenging behaviours' (2010) 42 British Journal of Clinical Psychology 243; Gemma King, 'Staff attitudes towards people with borderline personality disorder' (2014) 17 Mental health Practice 30.
[67] Ruth Gallop, William J Lancee, Paul Garfinkel, 'How nursing staff respond to the label "borderline personality disorder"' (1989) 40 Hospital Community Psychiatry 815.

request for medication to ease distress, returns shortly thereafter to ask for treatment for self-inflicted cuts to his arm. One explanation, which not uncommonly would be offered by clinicians, is that annoyed by the nurse's refusal to administer the medication, the patient decides to engineer a situation that makes it difficult for the nurse to ignore him.

This explanatory account relies on assumptions about the patient knowingly acting in a way as to influence others for his own purpose (i.e. 'manipulation'), including to secure the attention of others (i.e. attention-seeking). The attribution by observers of such deliberate and malign motives to the actions of the subject is likely to be associated with negative feelings towards the subject. If, in a clinical setting, these feelings are unchecked, then clinicians' willingness to maintain a therapeutic stance may be tested. Consider the alternative scenario of a patient, with a diagnosis of acute schizophrenia manifest in the experience of alien voices issuing commands to harm herself, who presents to nurses in an acutely psychotic state with lacerations on her arm. Attending clinicians are more likely to explain the self-harm behaviour in terms of the triggers for the behaviour (i.e. symptoms of mental illness) rather than the function of the behaviour (i.e. motives) and they are less likely to infer malign motives which would provoke negative attitudes.

It may run counter to common clinical narratives, but the evidence would suggest that the explanation above of the personality disorder scenario may be reasonable if it were not for the presence of personality disorder. Reference to the psychological and neuroscientific evidence base for processes underpinning disturbed behaviour in borderline personality disorder (including self-harm) would lead to very different conclusions about triggers and motives.

For example, emotional dysregulation and impaired self-soothing capacities are characteristic of borderline personality disorder [68] and therefore complaints of distress without objective triggers should not be unexpected. A particular readiness of patients with borderline personality disorder to approach others for support at times of subjective distress is considered to be associated with difficulties tolerating being alone. As a

---

[68] Amy E Hughes, Sheila E Crowell, Lauren Uyeji, James A Coan, 'A developmental neuroscience of borderline pathology; emotional regulation and social baseline theory' 40 Journal of Abnormal Psychology (2012) 21.

consequence of an over-reliance on actions rather than stated intentions to understand the mental state of others, patients with borderline personality disorder are more likely to demand a physical response by others (in this case, offering medication) as a demonstration of concern and to be soothed less by verbal utterances of concern.[69] Moreover, rejection (in this case, conveyed by the refusal of the request for medication) is a cue to which patients with borderline personality disorder are particular sensitive.[70] The tendency to direct the negative affect, arising from a discordant exchange, towards the self (in the form of self-harm urges) is often influenced by a vulnerability to low self-regard and blameworthiness that many patients with borderline personality disorder possess.[71] The relief provided by the act of cutting or by the sight of blood is another example of the reliance on physical representations of mental states (teleological stance).[72] The persistence, even in clinical settings, of 'lay formulations' of the sort initially described above to explain disturbed behaviour in personality disorder, despite the evidence base in favour of process disturbances, is likely to be related, in part, to the complexity of the alternative evidence-based explanatory approach.

A wide range of process disturbances (often involving complex models) have been identified and the selection of the relevant mechanisms to explain a particular type of behaviour requires familiarity with a significant body of literature and an opportunity to undertake a detailed analysis with the patient of the psychopathology associated with the behaviour.[73] In contrast, the explanation of the self-harm in the mental illness scenario involves a straightforward analysis of data more immediately available (i.e. self-harm in response to imperative voices instructing self-harm). Secondly, the 'lay formulation' would be a

---

[69] Anthony Bateman, Peter Fonagy, '*Psychotherapy for borderline personality disorder, mentalization-based treatment*' (Oxford University Press 2004).

[70] Melanie Bungert et al, 'Rejection sensitivity and symptoms severity in patients with borderline personality disorder: effects of childhood maltreatment and self-esteem' 2 Biomed Central (2015).

[71] ibid.

[72] Peter Fonagy, 'The mentionalization-focused approach to social development' in Jon G Allen and Peter Fonagy (eds) *Handbook of mentalization-based treatment* (John Wiley and Sons 2006).

[73] Rajan Nathan and Keith JB Rix, 'Suicide: Self-harm' in Jason Payne-James and Roger Byard (eds) *Encyclopaedia of Forensic and Legal Medicine, volume 2* (2nd edn, Elsevier 2016) 622.

reasonable and intuitive explanation in a non-clinical setting for a train of events involving the escalation of demands following initial refusal. Therefore, to hold in mind the process disturbance approach to explaining disturbed behaviour in personality disorder requires not only a level of expertise, but also a confidence to resist more automatic and intuitive ways of making sense of the actions of others that generally suffice in every day interactions.

Given the difficulty that clinical services have in maintaining a more informed and therapeutic stance to personality disorder, it should not come as a surprise that legal deliberations are heavily influenced by 'lay' explanations for disturbed behaviour. Furthermore, whilst the evidence-base for disturbed mental mechanisms in personality disorder relies on group-level data, the legal analysis of responsibility occurs at the level of the individual. Consider the case of a patient who has an established diagnosis of borderline personality disorder who accepts that he fatally stabbed his partner and reports that her rejecting overtures led him to become increasingly annoyed and to enter a subjective state of unreality and reduced awareness in which he impulsively attacked her. Although the evidence may suggest, in general, that patients with borderline personality disorder are more likely to experience intense negative emotions and anger dyscontrol, particularly in discordant attachment-based interactions, and to be prone to impulsiveness and dissociative states, there are no agreed standardised tests of process disturbances that an expert could administer retrospectively to determine that at a specific time, the individual in question was impaired by particular process disturbances. To the contrary, the account of a patient with an agreed diagnosis of a psychotic mental illness who explains homicidal violence as a response to bizarre delusions seems more testable with reference to objective evidence such as previously recorded bizarre behaviour of a similar sort and witness descriptions of odd behaviour around the time of the alleged offence.

The 'lay' explanations for disturbed behaviour, which emphasise premeditation and conscious control and seem superficially plausible, feed into observers' judgements about responsibility. Informal clinical dialogue about self-harm or aggression by patients with personality disorder often includes statements about the patient being responsible for his or her actions. Responsibility is also at the root of legal analysis of an individual's actions. A fundamental tenet of criminal law is that a person must be responsible for his or her actions to be culpable and liable for punishment[74]. A person may be considered not responsible in a criminal sense if he committed the criminal act because he had no real choice.[75] This choice theory explanation of responsibility[76] depends on the notion of freedom of choice not to commit the act. A conscious, rational decision to act in a particular way to achieve a desired goal points to freedom of choice and therefore unimpaired responsibility. Bizarre beliefs arising from a psychotic mental illness that are held to have driven a defendant's actions at the material time are more likely to be accepted as undermining freedom to choose and therefore as the basis for the defendant's responsibility being attenuated. Two questions arise. Firstly, does this acceptance in the case of mental illness stand up to scrutiny? Secondly, what is the relevance of the alternative evidence-based approach to explaining disturbed behaviour in personality disorder to questions of legal responsibility?

The first step in answering both questions is to understand in what way, if it all, the legal and medical interpretations of the responsibility construct are aligned. Current legal thinking accepts that 'a person is not to be held responsible for an act or omission where, for reasons beyond his or her control, he or she lacked the capacity to control his or her conduct'.[77] An abnormal mental state, not knowingly brought on, associated with a lack of self-control may be worthy of consideration. The medical abnormality (psychopathology), in the case of a defendant who acts violently in response to bizarre delusions, is the presence of abnormal beliefs that are held with absolute conviction despite strong evidence to the contrary (i.e. delusions). Such beliefs may influence the patient's decisions about a preferred course of action, but delusions per se are not characterised by a loss of self-control. Similarly, loss of self-control is not a necessary facet of other psychotic symptoms, such as hallucinations or thought disorder.[78] However, delusions, which represent a disturbance of rational thought,

---

[74] Law Commission, Criminal liability: insanity and automatism, a discussion paper (2013) available at <http://www.lawcom.gov.uk/wp-content/uploads/2015/06/insanity_discussion.p> accessed 7th January 2016.

[75] Herbert Hart, *Punishment and Responsibility* (Clarendon Press 1968).

[76] Michael Moore, 'Choice, character and excuse' in Paul Fred Miller and Jeffrey Paul (eds) *Crime, culpability and remedy* (Blackwell 1990).

[77] Law Commission (n74).

[78] There is a specific sort of delusion, passivity, in which an action is experienced as outside the patient's control.

may reach an alternative legal threshold for lack of responsibility, i.e. an inability to think rationally.[79] Mental illness may lead to a state of mind that is accepted for legal purposes to be lacking responsibility. It is important to note that this conclusion is based on an examination of psychopathology and could not be reached by merely identifying the presence of a mental illness. Lack of responsibility, whether defined by inability to control one's actions or to exercise rational thought, is not inherent to a mental illness diagnosis. Rather, it depends on the effects of the manifestations of that illness on internal processes.

There is strong evidence that personality disorder is associated with internal process disturbances that have a bearing on self-control and decision-making. Drawing again on the example described above of the homicidal attack by an individual with borderline personality disorder on his partner, it should be noted that the stated dysfunctions (e.g. abnormal propensities to negative affect including anger, emotional dysregulation, impulsiveness and depersonalisation), which influence self-control and rational decision-making, are not consciously acquired or activated. However, the state of mind caused by these dysfunctions does not negate the capacity to control, or to be consciously aware of, the criminal behaviour. Current understanding of the psychological mechanisms influencing behaviour (and their dysfunction in personality disorder) would support the proposition that in such a case, there may have been pathological processes, which (i) were not consciously generated, (ii) are associated with a recognised mental disorder, and (iii) are likely to have caused a relative impairment of self-control and rational thinking. As highlighted by Peay, [80] there is a disjunction between this type of continuum approach (involving varying degrees of impairment) and the dichotomous model which the law is required to adopt in deciding whether a capacity threshold is reached or not. However, for the purposes of examining the distinction between mental illness and personality disorder, the explanatory proposition above would equally apply to the defendant whose lethally violent actions were linked to bizarre delusions. The pathological processes (bizarre delusions) were not consciously generated and are associated with the psychotic mental illness diagnosis (e.g. schizophrenia). Unless the delusional thinking extends to all inferences

---

[79] Law Commission (n74).

[80] Jill Peay, 'Personality disorder and the law: some awkward questions' 18 Philosophy, psychiatry and psychology (2011) 231.

about external reality, which would be unlikely, then the impairment of rational thinking is relative. Thus, explanations of disturbed behaviour in personality disorder informed by the scientific evidence base allow legal questions of responsibility to be addressed on an equal footing to mental illness.

Conclusions

Against the tide of the theoretical and empirical evidence, a special (and mostly disadvantageous) case is made for legal and clinical approaches to personality disorder in comparison to mental illness. The singling out of people with personality disorder for special treatment, whether it is preventive detention, criteria for detention that do not apply to others ('the treatability criterion'), or exclusion from particular defences or pleas in mitigation, may reassure society that it is protecting itself from a group of people who might otherwise escape their just desserts for their offending, obtain what is often perceived as the soft option of hospitalisation instead of imprisonment, or cause chaos and violent disorder, but it has the effect of being unfair and discriminatory.

The perpetuation of the differences in approach can be explained in large part by the popular models of understanding behaviour in personality disorder.

In clinical arenas, these models influence counter-transference dynamics and opinions about whether an individual (or a subset of individuals) is deserving of finite resources. Legal approaches to disassembling the actions of a personality disordered individual bear upon judgements about responsibility.

In both contexts, diagnosis-level analysis of mental disorder is necessary (e.g. for clinical decisions about treatment options, or for legal decisions about whether or not there is formal abnormality). However, understanding at the level of diagnosis does not explain behaviour sufficiently to ensure that clinicians maintain an objective therapeutic stance, or to allow proper exploration of responsibility in a legal sense. The alternative dimensional approach is psychometrically more acceptable, but concern has been raised about the potential for diminution of the relative importance of personality disorder when viewed as being on a continuum with normality. [81] More importantly, the dimensional approach in itself does not enhance our understanding of behaviour.

Analysis at the level of identified mental mechanisms (especially where there is neurobiological support) is primarily concerned with understanding behaviour and is likely to lead to clinical and legal paradigms that are more valid and that do not discriminate on the basis of broad diagnostic categories such as mental illness and personality disorder. However, as yet, there is no agreed framework to structure the continually growing neuroscientific evidence-base relating to the psychic correlates of complex behaviour. The challenge for mental health clinicians and academics is to develop such a framework, without which it will be difficult to develop usable models of understanding personality disordered behaviour for clinical practice and legal analysis, and to preserve the dignity of those who lack adequate controls.

---

[81] Johnson and Elbogen (n5).

CHAPTER THIRTEEN

DIVERSION OF INDIVIDUALS WITH DISABILITY FROM THE CRIMINAL JUSTICE SYSTEM: CONTROL INSIDE OR OUTSIDE CRIMINAL LAW? [1]

LINDA STEELE

The past two decades have witnessed across Anglo-American jurisdictions increased scholarly,[2] government[3] and disability rights advocacy[4] interest

---

[1] Thank you to Arlie Loughnan, Leanne Dowse and Kristin Savell for their feedback on earlier versions of this chapter. Thank you to Evan Salmon and Russell Steele for their ongoing support.

[2] See, for example, Eileen Baldry, Leanne Dowse and Melissa Clarence, *People with Intellectual and Other Cognitive Disability in the Criminal Justice System* (Family & Community Services: Ageing, Disability & Home Care 2012); Leanne Dowse et al, *People with Mental Health Disorders and Cognitive Disabilities in the Criminal Justice System: Impact of Acquired Brain Injury* (Brain Injury Association of New South Wales and Brain Injury Australia 2011); Jenny Green, 'Experiences of Inmates with an Intellectual Disability' in David Brown and Meredith Wilkie (eds), *Prisoners as Citizens: Human Rights in Australian Prisons* (Federation Press 2002) 49; Susan C Hayes et al, 'The Prevalence of Intellectual Disability in a Major UK Prison' (2007) 35(3) British Journal of Learning Disabilities 162; Anthony J Holland, 'Criminal Behaviour and Developmental Disability: An Epidemiological Perspective' in William R Lindsay, John L Taylor and Peter Sturmey (eds), *Offenders with Developmental Disabilities* (John Wiley & Sons 2004) 23; Jessica Jones, 'Persons with Intellectual Disabilities in the Criminal Justice System: Review of Issues' (2007) 51(6) International Journal of Offender Therapy and Comparative Criminology 723; Kathleen Kendall, 'Female Offenders or Alleged Offenders with Developmental Disabilities: A Critical Overview' in William L Lindsay, John L Taylor and Peter Sturmey (eds), *Offenders with Developmental Disabilities* (John Wiley & Sons 2004) 265;

Kathryn A Vanny et al, 'Mental Illness and Intellectual Disability in Magistrates Courts in New South Wales in Australia' (2009) 53(3) Journal of Intellectual Disability Research 289.

[3] In the Australian context, see Australian Human Rights Commission, *Access to Justice in the Criminal Justice System for People with Disability: Issues Paper* (Australian Human Rights Commission 2013); Australian Human Rights Commission, *Equal before the Law: Towards Disability Justice Strategies* (Australian Human Rights Commission 2014); Australian Law Reform Commission, *Equality, Capacity and Disability in Commonwealth Laws* (Report No 124, 2014); Tom Calma, P*reventing Crime and Promoting Rights for Indigenous Young People with Cognitive Disabilities and Mental Health Issues* (Australian Human Rights Commission 2008); DLA Piper, *Background Paper on Access to Justice for People with Disability in the Criminal Justice System* (Australian Human Rights Commission 2013); Abigail Gray, Suzi Forell and Sophie Clarke, *Cognitive Impairment, Legal Need and Access to Justice* (Justice Issues Paper No 10, Law and Justice Foundation of New South Wales 2009); New South Wales Law Reform Commission, *People with Cognitive and Mental Health Impairments in the Criminal Justice System: An Overview*, (Consultation Paper No 5 2010); New South Wales Law Reform Commission, *People with Cognitive and Mental Health Impairments in the Criminal Justice System: Diversion* (Report No 135, 2012); Victoria, *Inquiry into Access to and Interaction with the Justice System by People with an Intellectual Disability and their Families and Carers: Final Report* (Parl Paper No 216, 2013). For examples from overseas jurisdictions, see Keith Bradley, *The Bradley Report: Lord Bradley's Review of People with Mental Health Problems or Learning Disabilities in the Criminal Justice System* (Department of Health (UK) 2009).

[4] In the Australian context, see Phillip French, *Disabled Justice: The Barriers to Justice for Persons with Disability in Queensland* (Queensland Advocacy 2007); Intellectual Disability Rights Service, Coalition on Intellectual Disability and Criminal Justice and NSW Council for Intellectual Disability, *Enabling Justice: A Report on Problems and Solutions in Relation to Diversion of Alleged Offenders with Intellectual Disability from the New South Wales Local Courts System: With Particular Reference to the Practical Operation of s 32 of the* Mental Health (Criminal Procedure Act 1990 *(NSW)* (Intellectual Disability Rights Service, Coalition on Intellectual Disability and Criminal Justice & NSW Council for Intellectual Disability 2008); Mary Langdon, *Acquired Brain Injury and the Criminal Justice System: Tasmanian Issues* (Brain Injury Association of Tasmania 2007); Mental Health Law Centre (WA), *Interaction with the Western Australian Criminal Justice System by People Affected by Mental Illness or Impairment* (Mental Health Law Centre (WA) 2013); Nick Rushworth, *Out of Sight, Out of Mind: People with an Acquired Brain Injury and the Criminal Justice System* (Brain Injury Australia 2011); Mindy Sotiri, Patrick McGee and Eileen Baldry, *No End in Sight: The Imprisonment, and Indefinite Detention of Indigenous*

in issues relating to individuals with cognitive impairment and mental illness ('individuals with disability') in the criminal justice system. These issues include the over-representation in the criminal justice system (including police contact, courts and prisons) and the difficulties encountered in participating in court proceedings, the vulnerability in prison, the lack of appropriate mental health and disability support services in the community and in prison, and the overuse of remand and non-custodial orders. Diversion from the criminal justice system into disability and mental health services has been identified in a number of Anglo-American jurisdictions as a strategy for addressing the issues facing individuals with disability in the criminal justice system.[5] Diversion of individuals with disability from the criminal justice system involves redirecting an individual *off* the assumed criminal justice trajectory of charge, trial, conviction and punishment and *out* of criminal justice spaces

---

Australians with a Cognitive Impairment (Aboriginal Disability Justice Campaign 2012). For examples from overseas jurisdictions, see American Civil Liberties Union, *Mental Illness and the Death Penalty* (American Civil Liberties Union 2009); Canadian Mental Health Association and Public Interest Law Centre, *Equality, Dignity and Inclusion: Legislation that Enhances Human Rights for People Living with Mental Illness: Final Report* (Canadian Mental Health Association & Public Interest Law Centre 2011); Graham Durcan et al, *The Bradley Report Five Years On: An Independent Review of Progress to Date and Priorities for Further Development* (Centre for Mental Health 2014); Kimmett Edgar and Dora Rickford, *Too Little Too Late: An Independent Review of Unmet Mental Health Need in Prison* (Prison Reform Trust 2009); National Federation of Women's Institutes and Prison Reform Trust, *Care Not Custody Action Pack* (National Federation of Women's Institutes & Prison Reform Trust, undated);Yvonne Peters, *Federally Sentenced Women with Mental Disabilities: A Dark Corner in Canadian Human Rights* (DisAbled Women's Action Network (DAWN) Canada, 2003); Jenny Talbot, *No One Knows* (Report and Final Recommendations, Prison Reform Trust 2008).

[5]   Susanna Every-Palmer et al, 'Review of Psychiatric Services to Mentally Disordered Offenders Around the Pacific Rim' (2014) 6 Asia-Pacific Psychiatry 1; David V James, 'Diversion of Mentally Disordered People from the Criminal Justice System in England and Wales: An Overview' (2010) 33(4) International Journal of Law and Psychiatry 241; Michael Parsonage, *Diversion: A Better Way for Criminal Justice and Mental Health* (Sainsbury Centre for Mental Health 2009); Elizabeth Richardson and Bernadette McSherry, 'Diversion Down Under – Programs for Offenders with Mental Illnesses in Australia' (2010) 33(4) International Journal of Law and Psychiatry 249; Richard D Schneider, 'Mental Health Courts and Diversion Programs: A Global Survey' (2010) 33 International Journal of Law and Psychiatry 201.

such as court and prison, and *onto* an alternative trajectory of individual therapeutic interventions aimed at addressing matters at the nexus of an individual's disability and offending and *into* alternative spaces of community-based mental health and disability services.

To date, diversion has received support from law reform organisations, disability advocacy organisations and criminal justice and forensic mental health and disability service providers which are increasingly contemplating and recommending the introduction, improvement and expansion of diversionary schemes for people with disability in the criminal justice system.[6] This support is paralleled by a body of scholarship on diversion, generally written by legal scholars and forensic mental health and disability scholars.[7] In this scholarship, diversion is

---

[6] In the Australian context, see Intellectual Disability Rights Service, Coalition on Intellectual Disability and Criminal Justice and New South Wales Council for Intellectual Disability, *Enabling Justice: A Report on Problems and Solutions in Relation to Diversion of Alleged Offenders with Intellectual Disability from the New South Wales Local Courts System: With Particular Reference to the Practical Operation of s 32 of the* Mental Health (Criminal Procedure Act 1990 *(NSW)* (Intellectual Disability Rights Service, Coalition on Intellectual Disability and Criminal Justice & NSW Council for Intellectual Disability, 2008); New South Wales Law Reform Commission, *People with Cognitive and Mental Health Impairments in the Criminal Justice System: Diversion* (n 3); Julian Elliott Thomas, *Diversion and Support of Offenders with a Mental Illness: Guidelines for Best Practice* (Justice Health, Victorian Government Department of Justice & National Justice Chief Executive Officers' Group 2010). For examples from overseas jurisdictions, see Keith Bradley, *The Bradley Report* (n 3); Law Commission, *Criminal Liability: Insanity and Automatism: A Discussion Paper* (Discussion Paper, Law Commission 2013); Law Commission, *Unfitness to Plead: An Issues Paper* (Issues Paper, Law Commission 2014); National Federation of Women's Institutes and Prison Reform Trust, *Care Not Custody Action Pack* (n 4).
[7] See, for example, Alison Evans Cuellar, Larkin S McReynolds and Gail Wasserman, 'A Cure for Crime: Can Mental Health Treatment Diversion Reduce Crime Among Youth?' (2006) 25(1) Journal of Policy Analysis and Management 197; David De Matteo, 'Community-Based Alternatives for Justice-Involved Individuals with Severe Mental Illness: Diversion, Problem-Solving Courts, and Reentry' (2013) 41 Journal of Criminal Justice 64; Wendy Dyer, 'Criminal Justice Diversion and Liaison Services: A Path to Success?' (2013) 12(1) Social Policy & Society 31; Susanna Every-Palmer and others, 'Review of Psychiatric Services to Mentally Disordered Offenders Around the Pacific Rim' (2014) 6 Asia-Pacific Psychiatry 1; Lee-Ann Fenga et al, 'Mental Health and the Criminal Justice System: The Role of Interagency Training to Promote Practitioner Understanding

characterised as a beneficial and humane mechanism because it avoids the negative effects of the criminal justice system and links up individuals with much needed services and treatments designed to address the disability-related causes of their offending and to enable their integration into the community.[8] The scholarship focuses on describing particular diversionary schemes and/or making suggestions for the fine-tuning of such schemes to enhance the scope and efficacy of their operation. It is suggested that the scholarly support for diversion might in part be explained by the focus directed by scholars to the *material* and *administrative* spaces of diversion – criminal justice system space and community disability and mental health service system space. It seems to follow from this spatialisation of diversion that individuals are not 'controlled' by criminal law because once they are diverted they are no longer within the space of the criminal justice system. This spatialisation of diversion obfuscates the more abstract *legal* dimensions that order

of the Diversion Agenda' (2014) 36(1) Journal of Social Welfare & Family Law 36; David V James, 'Court Diversion in Perspective' (2006) 40(6–7) Australian and New Zealand Journal of Psychiatry 529; David V James, 'Diversion of Mentally Disordered People from the Criminal Justice System in England and Wales: An Overview' (n 5); Loraine Lim and Andrew Day, 'Mental Health Diversion Courts: A Two Year Recidivism Study of a South Australian Mental Health Court Program' (2014) 32 Behavioural Sciences and the Law 539; Loraine Lim and Andrew Day, 'Mental Health Diversion Courts: Some Directions for Further Development' (2013) 20(1) Psychiatry, Psychology and Law 36; Allison D Redlich et al, 'Is Diversion Swift? Comparing Mental Health Court and Traditional Criminal Justice Processing' (2012) 39(4) Criminal Justice and Behaviour 420; Elizabeth Richardson and Bernadette McSherry (n 5) 249; Richard D Schneider, 'Mental Health Courts and Diversion Programs (n 5); Richard D Schneider, Hy Bloom and Mark Heerema, *Mental Health Courts: Decriminalizing the Mentally Ill* (Irwin Law 2007); David A Scott et al, 'Effectiveness of Criminal Justice Liaison and Diversion Services for Offenders with Mental Disorders: A Review' (2013) 64(9) Psychiatric Services 843; Frank Sirotich, 'The Criminal Justice Outcomes of Jail Diversion Programs for Persons with Mental Illness: A Review of the Evidence' (2009) 37(4) Journal of the American Academy of Psychiatry and the Law 461; Samir Srivastava et al, 'Developing Criminal Justice Liaison and Diversion Services: Research Priorities and International Learning' (2013) 23 Criminal Behaviour and Mental Health 315; Tamara Walsh, 'Diverting Mentally Ill Women away from Prison in New South Wales: Building on the Existing System' (2003) 10(1) Psychiatry, Psychology and Law 227.
[8] Ronald Roesch, James R P Ogloff & Derek Eaves, 'Mental Health Research in the Criminal Justice System: The Need for Common Approaches and International Perspectives' (1995) 18(1) International Journal of Law and Psychiatry 1, 7.

diversion. To explain, while individuals are moved out of the space of the criminal *justice system* through diversion, it is through the compulsion of criminal *law* that they are non-voluntarily moved into and required to stay for a period in the space of community disability and mental health service system. Prima facie, while individuals are diverted out of the *criminal justice system*, they seem to stay *within* the structure of criminal law. In remaining *within* criminal law, they might in turn be subject to state control through criminal law, albeit in a different material and administrative space than the criminal justice system. What is missing from the existing scholarship on diversion is any critical reflection on the significance of *criminal legal* dimensions of diversion. Turning to these dimensions might offer a more complex picture of state control of people with disability through criminal law.

It is also the case that current scholarship on diversion does not critically reflect on the significance of *disability* with regard to diversion, and the consequent implications of state control by criminal law of people with disability through diversion. Diversion schemes typically apply specifically (and exclusively) to people with disability, and on the basis of diagnostic definitions of impairment, on the premise that there is a relationship between offending and disability, and that individuals will be engaging in treatment related to curing or managing their disability. In the course of supporting diversion's continued expansion, the scholarship on diversion has overlooked some important issues. The scholarship has not approached disability as a political category[9] and has not considered the role of the criminal justice system in the marginalisation of, violence against and oppression of people with disability.[10] The scholarship on diversion has not located the specific disability and mental health service techniques of diversion in a broader consideration of the post-deinstitutionalisation methods of regulation of people with disability in society,[11] including the harnessing of these techniques by law.[12] The

---

[9] See the large body of critical disability studies scholarship, e.g. Dan Goodley, *Dis/Ability Studies: Theorising Disablism and Ableism* (Routledge 2014).

[10] See, for example, Liat Ben-Moshe, Chris Chapman & Allison C Carey, *Disability Incarcerated: Imprisonment and Disability in the United States and Canada* (Palgrave Macmillan 2014); Chris Cunneen et al, *Penal Culture and Hyperincarceration: The Revival of the Prison* (Ashgate 2013).

[11] In the context of disability support services for people with intellectual disability, see, for example, Chris Drinkwater, 'Supported Living and the Production of Individuals' in Shelley Tremain (ed), *Foucault and the Government*

scholarship on diversion has not considered the complex ways in which people with disability in the criminal justice system might be subject to state control through diversion. If control *is* operating through diversion, then it is important to consider how particular understandings of disability and techniques of managing (and normalising) people with disability are utilised by criminal law to enable this control. It is important to critically reflect upon the *disability* dimensions of diversion, and their intersection with the *criminal legal* dimensions of diversion. While largely outside the scope of this chapter, exploration of the intersections between criminal legal and disability dimensions of diversion is also important for another reason. This reason is the broader significance of disability to criminal law notions of capacity and rationality which include and exclude people in criminal responsibility, and have an important function in legitimating the principles and processes of punishment following conviction ('conviction-based punishment').[13]

---

of Disability (University of Michigan Press 2005) 229; Jack Levinson, *Making Life Work: Freedom and Disability in a Community Group Home* (University of Minnesota Press 2010); Karl Nunkoosing and Mark Haydon-Laurelut, 'Intellectual Disability Trouble: Foucault and Goffman on "Challenging Behaviour"' in Dan Goodley, Bill Hughes and Lennard Davis (eds), *Disability and Social Theory: New Developments and Directions* (Palgrave Macmillan 2012) 195. In the context of mental health treatment provided pursuant to community treatment orders, see, for example, Erick Fabris, *Tranquil Prisons: Chemical Incarceration under Community Treatment Orders* (University of Toronto Press 2011).

[12] Claire Spivakovsky, 'From Punishment to Protection: Containing and Controlling the Lives of People with Disabilities in Human Rights' 16(5) Punishment & Society 560; Claire Spivakovsky, 'Making Risk and Dangerousness Intelligible in Intellectual Disability' (2014) 23(3) Griffith Law Review 389; Claire Spivakovsky, 'Human Rights and the Governance of Cognitive Impairment and Mental Illness' in Leanne Weber, Elaine Fishwick, and Marinella Marmo (eds), *The Routledge Handbook of Criminology and Human Rights* (Routledge 2016) (forthcoming).

[13] See, for example, Alan W Norrie, *Crime, Reason and History: A Critical Introduction to Criminal Law* (Butterworths 2001). See similarly Hilary Allen, *Justice Unbalanced: Gender, Psychiatry and Judicial Decisions* (Open University Press 1987) 18–23; Nicola Lacey, 'Responsibility and Modernity in Criminal Law' (2001) 9(3) Journal of Political Philosophy 249, 254–5; Ngaire Naffine, *Law's Meaning of Life: Philosophy, Religion, Darwin and the Legal Person* (Hart Publishing 2009) 23, 60, 66–7, 69–75.

One of the few criticisms which has been made of diversion is that which is based on the critical criminology 'net widening' literature. The idea of net widening is based on Stanley Cohen's work on social control – the idea that community-based and human service-based criminal justice interventions extend and deepen the net of 'social control' typically facilitated by the criminal justice system through incarceration.[14] The net widening critique has been acknowledged in a cursory manner in the scholarship on diversion.[15] Certainly, the net widening approach is significant to an analysis of diversion for two reasons. One reason is that this approach highlights the possibility for state control through criminal law by different institutions and in different spaces than those typically associated with incarceration. The other reason is that the net widening approach opens up the community as a site for social control, where historically, in the context of disability, the institution was juxtaposed in absolute terms to the freedom of the community. For present purposes, the net widening approach does not sufficiently engage with criminal *law* and there is a lack of consideration of the ways in which criminal *law* shapes, authorises and legitimises this 'widening' of state control that is possible in the criminal law *jurisdiction*. This approach is focused on the institutions, relations and 'spaces' of punishment and social control *pursuant to and following* the making of a criminal legal order, as opposed to the criminal legal framing of the order itself. As a critical criminological

---

[14] Stanley Cohen, *Visions of Social Control: Crime, Punishment and Classification* (Polity Press 1985).

[15] See, for example, Elizabeth Richardson and Bernadette McSherry (n 5) 249; Ronald Roesch, James R P Ogloff and Derek Eaves, 'Mental Health Research in the Criminal Justice System: The Need for Common Approaches and International Perspectives' (1995) 18(1) International Journal of Law and Psychiatry 1. The concept of net widening has a long history of being considered in the context of other diversionary programs, notably juvenile diversion programs. See, for example, Scott H Decker, 'A Systemic Analysis of Diversion: Net Widening and Beyond' (1985) 13 Journal of Criminal Justice 207; Jeremy Prichard, 'Net-Widening and the Diversion of Young People from Court: A Longitudinal Analysis with Implications for Restorative Justice' (2010) 43(1) Australian and New Zealand Journal of Criminology 112; Lynne Roberts and David Indermaur, 'Timely Intervention or Trapping Minnows? The Potential for a Range of Net-Widening Effects in Australian Drug Diversion Initiatives' (2006) 13(2) Psychiatry, Psychology and Law 220.

(rather than *critical legal*) argument, this focus is to be expected.[16] The order itself and the process that precedes it is a significant (yet often rendered trivial, procedural and mundane) aspect of the exercise of coercion by the state,[17] and hence signals both the continued invisibility of the structural and assumed operations of criminal law and the ongoing authority of criminal law in punishment and social control. A further limitation of the net widening approach is that it does not specifically consider the significance of *disability* to the expansion of social control specifically over individuals with disability. Criminal legal and disability dimensions of control through diversion are yet to be investigated.

Considering criminal legal and disability dimensions of diversion and diversion's relationship to state control is timely, because at the international level, concerns are being raised about the appropriateness of diversion and other criminal legal mechanisms which apply specifically to individuals with disability (for example, detention following the defence of mental illness or a finding of unfitness[18]). These concerns are being raised in the light of the United Nations Convention on the Rights of

---

[16] See generally Nicola Lacey, 'Legal Constructions of Crime' in Mike Maguire, Rod Morgan and Robert Reiner (eds), The Oxford Handbook of Criminology (4th ed, Oxford University Press 2007) 179.

[17] See, for example, the literature around legal violence, notably Cover's discussion of the relationship between sentence and imprisonment: Robert Cover, 'Violence and the Word' (1986) 95 Yale Law Journal 1601. See also Rosemary Hunter, 'Law's (Masculine) Violence: Reshaping Jurisprudence' (2006) 17 Law and Critique 27; Austin Sarat, 'Situating Law between the Realities of Violence and the Claims of Justice' in Austin Sarat (ed), *Law, Violence, and the Possibility of Justice* (Princeton University Press 2001) 3; Austin Sarat and Thomas R Kearns, 'Introduction' in Austin Sarat and Thomas R Kearns (eds), *Law's Violence* (University of Michigan Press 1992) 1.

[18] In the context of the Australian jurisdiction of New South Wales (which is the focus of this chapter) see Mental Health (Forensic Provisions) Act 1990 (New South Wales) pt 2, pt 4; see also the recent review of the law in New South Wales Law Reform Commission, *People with Cognitive and Mental Health Impairments in the Criminal Justice System: Criminal Responsibility and its Consequences*, (Report No 138, 2013). In the context of England and Wales see Criminal Procedure (Insanity and Unfitness to Plead) Act 1991; see also the current review of the law in Law Commission, *Criminal Liability: Insanity and Automatism: A Discussion Paper* (Discussion Paper, 2013); Law Commission, *Unfitness to Plead: An Issues Paper* (Issues Paper, 2014).

People with Disabilities[19] (the 'Disability Convention'). The Disability Convention entered into force on 3 May 2008 and has been signed and ratified by Australia, Canada, New Zealand and the United Kingdom, among other nations.[20] Of particular significance to diversion is that the right to non-discrimination and equality is an overarching principle (as well as a specific human right). [21] Article 12 of the Disability Convention places obligations on States Parties to repeal laws which deny legal capacity to people with disability and introduce measures to support individuals with disability to exercise their legal capacity. In its General Comment on Article 12, the UN Committee on the Rights of Persons with Disabilities ('the Committee') states that it constitutes discrimination to deny legal capacity on the basis of disability, as do subsequent restrictions on liberty or forced medical or psychiatric treatment based on denial of legal capacity.[22] The Committee also noted that the practice of placing individuals in institutional settings without their specific consent, including by substituted decision makers such as through guardianship-based decision making (which, relevantly for present purposes, is utilised in diversionary orders to coerce some individuals to reside at disability-supported accommodation or engage in particular services or treatment), constitutes an arbitrary deprivation of liberty.[23] In the context of the Disability Convention, the Office of the United Nations High Commissioner for Human Rights has expressed concern about the discriminatory nature of criminal and civil legal mechanisms which enable the deprivation of liberty of individuals on the basis of their disability, and has gone so far as to suggest the abolition of the defence of mental illness and similar criminal legal mechanisms specific to individuals with

---

[19] *Convention on the Rights of Persons with Disabilities*, opened for signature 13 December 2006, 2515 UNTS 3 (entered into force 3 May 2008).

[20] The United States of America and Ireland have each signed but not formally ratified the Disability Convention. For full details, see: '15. Convention on the Rights of Persons with Disabilities' (United Nations Treaty Collection) <https://treaties.un.org/Pages/ViewDetails.aspx?src=TREATY&mtdsg_no=iv-15&chapter=4&lang=en> accessed 24 August 2015.

[21] See *Convention on the Rights of Persons with Disabilities*, (n 19) preamble para (h), Art 3(b), Art 5(1)-(2).

[22] Committee on the Rights of Persons with Disabilities, *General Comment No 1 (2014): Article 12: Equal recognition before the law*, 11th sess, UN Doc CRPD/C/GC/1 (19 May 2014), 10 [40] – 11 [42].

[23] ibid 10[40].

disability.[24] The Committee in its Concluding Observations on the Initial Report of Australia has urged Australia not to introduce diversion programs coercing individuals to engage with mental health services; 'rather, such services should be provided on the basis of the individual's free and informed consent'.[25] The emerging international human rights commentary on disability and criminal law, including diversion, signals the importance of considering the criminal legal framework that compels individuals with disability to engage in diversion, as well as the significance of disability to this framework.[26]

It is in the context of the extant scholarship on the social and political context of diversion and the growing international human rights concerns with diversion that this chapter turns to consider the question: is a diverted individual with disability still subject to state control through criminal law even if moved out of the criminal justice system, and what relevance does disability have to any such control? The chapter approaches this question through an examination of one diversionary scheme – diversion of individuals with disability from the NSW Local Court pursuant to section 32 of the *Mental Health (Forensic Provisions) Act 1990* (NSW). Pursuant to section 32, prior to conviction, individuals have their charges dismissed subject to engaging in a six-month court order centred on engagement with disability services and mental health treatment. It is appropriate to focus on section 32 because this provision is increasingly being viewed both within New South Wales and across other Australian jurisdictions as a model provision (albeit in need of some fine tuning). Ultimately, the chapter argues that section 32 enables state control through criminal law of

---

[24] Office of the United Nations High Commissioner for Human Rights, *Thematic Study by the Office of the United Nations High Commissioner for Human Rights on Enhancing Awareness and Understanding of the Convention on the Rights of Persons with Disabilities*, UN Doc A/HRC/10/48 (26 January 2009) 15–16 [48]–[49]. See also Committee on the Rights of Persons with Disabilities, *Concluding Observations on the Initial Report of Australia*, 10th session, UN Doc CRPD/C/AUS/CO/1 (21 October 2013) 4–5 [32] ('*Concluding Observations on Australia*').

[25] ibid 4 [29].

[26] Though see the scholarship on diversion that frames diversion as a way to realise the human rights of people with disability in the criminal justice system: Priscilla Ferrazzi, Terry Krupa and Rosemary Lysaght, 'Mental Health Courts, Court Diversion, and Canada's Obligations under the United Nations Convention on the Rights of Persons with Disabilities' (2013) 32(4) Canadian Journal of Community Mental Health 43; Elizabeth Richardson and Bernadette McSherry (n 5) 249.

individuals with disability who are otherwise beyond such control by criminal law because they exceed the limits of trial, conviction and sentence and, ultimately, the limits of conviction-based punishment. In doing so, section 32 both furthers state control of individuals with disability in the criminal justice system *and* contributes to the ordering of the criminal law jurisdiction and the legitimation of conviction-based punishment.

This chapter is structured in four parts. The first part gives a brief introduction to section 32 and briefly discusses the relevance of an analysis of section 32 to other jurisdictions, with a particular focus on England and Wales. The second part locates section 32 in a criminal legal context and establishes that section 32 has coercive and punitive effects beyond those typically possible through criminal law via conviction-based punishment. The third part then draws out the disability dimensions of control through section 32. The fourth part then identifies some points for further consideration.

The Legal Framework of Diversion: Section 32

Pursuant to section 32, an individual with disability appearing in the NSW Local Court on criminal charges can have his or her charges dismissed either unconditionally or on the condition that he or she engages with community disability services or mental health services for six months, on the basis that this is considered more appropriate than dealing with the individual through trial, conviction and sentence.[27] A magistrate can make a section 32 order following a three staged inquiry based on section 32(1)-(3) of the *Mental Health (Forensic Provisions) Act 1990* (NSW) and laid out in the New South Wales Court of Appeal decision of *DPP (NSW) v El*

---

[27] Mental Health (Forensic Provisions) Act 1990 (NSW) ss 32(1)–(3), 3(1) (definition of 'Magistrate'). Section 32 also applies in the NSW Children's Court. This chapter is focused on the application of section 32 in the Local Court. For a discussion of issues specifically relating to people appearing in the Children's Court, see New South Wales Law Reform Commission, *People with Cognitive and Mental Health Impairments in the Criminal Justice System: Diversion* (Consultation Paper No 7, 2010) 365–97 [14.1]–[14.133]; New South Wales Law Reform Commission, *Young People with Cognitive and Mental Health Impairments in the Criminal Justice System* (Consultation Paper No 11, 2010).

Mawas[28] (the '*El Mawas* inquiry'). The first stage of the inquiry is that 'it appears to the Magistrate' that the defendant is 'developmentally disabled', 'suffering from a mental illness' or 'suffering from a mental condition for which treatment is available in a mental health facility'.[29] The second stage of the inquiry is that it 'appears to the Magistrate' that it is 'more appropriate' for the defendant to be dealt with by section 32 than 'otherwise than in accordance with law'.[30] The third stage of the *El Mawas* inquiry is that an appropriate section 32 order can be made. An order can be interlocutory[31] or final,[32] and a final order can be conditional[33] or unconditional.[34] At the third stage of the *El Mawas* inquiry, the Magistrate considers whether an unconditional or conditional order is appropriate, and whether there are the necessary services and treatment available to form the basis of a conditional order. In relation to an individual with cognitive impairment, a section 32 order is generally conditional on the individual's engagement with community-based disability services such as case management, behaviour intervention and support, supported accommodation, participation in day programs and psychological treatment.[35] A conditional section 32 order made in relation to an individual with mental illness usually involves seeing a psychologist or psychiatrist, following all reasonable directions in relation to prescribed medications and engaging with case management through a community mental health service. A breach of a conditional section 32 order can result in the recipient of the order being brought back before the court to have his or her charges heard afresh and dealt with through the usual process of trial, conviction and sentence.[36]

---

[28] *DPP (NSW) v El Mawas* (2006) 66 NSWLR 93, 109–110 [75]–[80] (McColl JA) ('*El Mawas*').

[29] Mental Health (Forensic Provisions) Act 1990 (NSW) s 32(1)(a).

[30] Mental Health (Forensic Provisions) Act 1990 (NSW) s 32(1)(b).

[31] Mental Health (Forensic Provisions) Act 1990 (NSW) s 32(2).

[32] Mental Health (Forensic Provisions) Act 1990 (NSW) s 32(3).

[33] Mental Health (Forensic Provisions) Act 1990 (NSW) s 32(3)(a),(b).

[34] Mental Health (Forensic Provisions) Act 1990 (NSW) s 32(3)(c).

[35] Intellectual Disability Rights Service Inc, *Step By Step Guide to Making a Section 32 Application for a Person with Intellectual Disability* (Intellectual Disability Rights Service Inc 2011) 28–9; Intellectual Disability Rights Service, Coalition on Intellectual Disability and Criminal Justice and NSW Council for Intellectual Disability, *Enabling Justice: A Report on Problems and Solutions in Relation to Diversion of Alleged Offenders with Intellectual Disability from the New South Wales Local Courts System* (n 4) 46.

[36] Mental5 Health (Forensic Provisions) Act 1990 (NSW) ss 32(3A)–(3D).

The International Relevance of an Analysis of Section 32

Diversionary schemes differ greatly between jurisdictions, particularly in those jurisdictions where there is no legislative framework specific to diversion, and differ within a jurisdiction. [37] In England and Wales, for example, there are over 100 different diversion schemes in operation.[38] In this jurisdiction, there are multiple regional variations of diversion (or 'diversion and liaison schemes' as they are collectively known) and the precise nature of diversion and liaison schemes in a particular geographical area depends on the local health service (including available resources) and the circumstances of the individuals appearing at the courts in that area. There is no single legislative framework specific to diversion and liaison schemes in the same way there is in the context of section 32 in New South Wales, Australia. Instead, in England and Wales, diversion and liaison schemes are governed at a local level by policy and operational factors[39] and the legal force for diversion of an individual comes from various criminal *and* civil laws: sentencing legislation (in relation to individuals who have been convicted), forensic mental health legislation (in relation to individuals who have been found unfit) or civil mental health legislation (in relation to individuals who have not been convicted or individuals who have been found unfit but whose alleged offences are not considered serious).[40] Similar to section 32 in New South Wales, the flavor of the discussion of and scholarship on diversion and liaison schemes in England and Wales is focused on description and evaluation of schemes with the aim of fine-tuning and expanding diversion.

Recently, there has also been growing momentum from law reform to move towards more uniform and improved diversion practices, yet this is very much focused on the health and criminal justice service delivery of diversion with no indication of introduction of a legislative scheme

---

[37] See (n 5).

[38] Keith Bradley, *The Bradley Report* (n 3) 81.

[39] This is identified as one of the key limitations of diversion and liaisons schemes in England and Wales: Wendy Dyer (n 7) 36.

[40] For an overview of court diversion in England and Wales, see Wendy Dyer (n 7); David V James, 'Court Diversion in Perspective' (n 7); David V James, 'Diversion of Mentally Disordered People from the Criminal Justice System in England and Wales: An Overview' (n 5); Michael Parsonage, *Diversion: A Better Way for Criminal Justice and Mental Health* (n 5); Richard D Schneider, 'Mental Health Courts and Diversion Programs (n 5) 201, 204.

specifically on diversion. In 2009, *The Bradley Report* on people with disability in the criminal justice system identified that there was a lack of consistency in relation to what constitutes diversion and the absence of a centralised strategy on diversion.[41] This report recommended that every court should have access to a diversion and liaison scheme.[42] Subsequently, in 2014, the Government 'announced an additional £25 million spending on liaison and diversion services for police stations and magistrates' courts in ten areas across England, with a view to rolling out the scheme nationwide in 2017'.[43] Most recently, the Law Commission, in its review of unfitness to plead, is considering whether diversion should be a legal option for individuals found unfit to plead.[44]

It is anticipated that the findings in this chapter which are derived from an analysis of a specific diversion scheme (section 32) will have relevance to analysis of different diversionary schemes in other jurisdictions, regardless of jurisdictional variation. This is by reason of two interrelated aspects: one legal and one cultural. First, there are still likely many legal similarities between diversionary schemes, notably their disability-specific nature and their use of some kind of legal order (whether civil or criminal, or a mixture of both) to coerce individuals to engage in services (as is evident in the context of the England and Wales diversion and liaison schemes outlined above). Second, these legal and disability dimensions of diversion (which culminate in the provision of individualised 'treatment') generally point to common underlying *cultural* dimensions related to disability in terms of diagnosed impairment and the coupling of 'care' and 'treatment' with 'control'. This chapter elaborates on these aspects in the context of section 32 and provides the foundations for more critical reflection on diversion in other jurisdictions. Analysis might diverge, however, on the nuances of the precise relationship between the legal and the cultural aspects of disability and law – thus contributing to a more theoretically, legally and materially enriched understanding of diversion's various formations and operations vis-à-vis people with disability.

---

[41] Keith Bradley, *The Bradley Report* (n 3) 81.
[42] ibid 130-132.
[43] Law Commission, *Unfitness to Plead: An Issues Paper* (n 6) 2 [1.2(5)]. See NHS England, *Operating Model for Liaison and Diversion Services Across England* (September 2013).
[44] ibid 46 [5.33].

Section 32 and State Control?

Across the discussion by law reform organisations, disability advocacy organisations and criminal justice and forensic mental health and disability service providers and (a relatively small body of) scholarship by legal scholars and forensic mental health and disability scholars, section 32 is supported with the focus being on evaluating its operation in order to enhance its operation.[45] Section 32 is approached as humane because it moves an individual with disability away from exposure to the negative effects of the court process and imprisonment and to community-based disability and mental health services that will enhance the individual's ability to live in the community (in contrast to the historical legacy of institutionalization and segregation). Section 32 is viewed as therapeutic because it provides a clear pathway to disability and mental health services which are presumed to be needed to address the offending behaviour of individuals with disability (which is presumed to be linked to a presentation of their disability in an individualised diagnostic and clinical manner: as a 'diagnosed impairment'). Associated with this characterisation of section 32 as a humane and therapeutic diversionary

---

[45] See, for example, David Greenberg and Ben Nielsen, 'Court Diversion in NSW for People with Mental Health Problems and Disorders' (2002) 13(7) NSW Public Health Bulletin 158; David Greenberg and Ben Nielsen, 'Moving Towards a Statewide Approach to Court Diversion Services in NSW'(2003) 14(11-12) NSW Public Health Bulletin 227; Dan Howard and Bruce Westmore, *Crime and Mental Health Law in New South Wales: A Practical Guide for Lawyers and Health Care Professionals* (2nd ed, LexisNexis Butterworths 2010); Intellectual Disability Rights Service, Coalition on Intellectual Disability and Criminal Justice and NSW Council for Intellectual Disability, *Enabling Justice: A Report on Problems and Solutions in Relation to Diversion of Alleged Offenders with Intellectual Disability from the New South Wales Local Courts System* (n 4); Peter McGhee and Siobhan Mullany, 'Keeping People with Intellectual Disability out of Jail' (2007) 83 Precedent 16; Peter McGhee and Lee-May Saw, 'Chiselling the Bars: Acting for People with an Intellectual Disability' (2005) 43(9) Law Society Journal 61; New South Wales Law Reform Commission, *People with Cognitive and Mental Health Impairments in the Criminal Justice System: Diversion*, (n 27); New South Wales Law Reform Commission, *People with Cognitive and Mental Health Impairments in the Criminal Justice System: Diversion* (n 3); Nick Rushworth, 'Out of Sight, Out of Mind: People with an Acquired Brain Injury and the Criminal Justice System' (Brain Injury Australia 2011); Karen Weeks, 'To Section 32 or Not?: Applications under s 32 Mental Health (Forensic Provisions) Act 1990 in the Local Court' (2010) 48(4) Law Society Journal 49.

mechanism, section 32 is increasingly recognised as a significant component of criminal law's role in addressing the issues facing individuals with disability in the criminal justice system. This is most evident in the recent New South Wales Law Reform Commission ('NSWLRC') review of people with cognitive and mental health impairments in the criminal justice system which devotes an entire consultation paper and final report to diversion.[46]

There has been an absence of any sustained consideration by scholars and practitioners of diversion of how state control of people with disability might operate through section 32. While there is some recognition of the coercive and punitive effects of section 32 in the scholarly literature and law reform discussion,[47] this is generally framed in terms of cursory references to net widening which, as discussed above, does not engage sufficiently with criminal legal or disability dimensions of section 32. Disability and criminal law are presented in simple and apparently self-evident terms. Disability is portrayed narrowly in terms of diagnosed impairment. The link between diagnosed disability and offending, as well as the link between diagnosed impairment and the necessity of non-voluntary treatment-based interventions are each unquestioned. The approach to section 32 in the existing scholarship reflects the limiting spatialisation of diversion which was discussed above in the introduction to this chapter. Section 32 is approached as shifting individuals out of the criminal justice system and into different material and administrative spaces (community support services),[48] such that criminal law is equated with the material and administrative spaces of the criminal justice system (e.g. court and prison) from which individuals are being moved. This spatialisation of section 32 dislocates individuals who receive section 32 orders from criminal law and in turn locates these individuals (and section

---

[46] New South Wales Law Reform Commission, *People with Cognitive and Mental Health Impairments in the Criminal Justice System* (n 27); New South Wales Law Reform Commission, *People with Cognitive and Mental Health Impairments in the Criminal Justice System: Diversion* (n 3).

[47] See, for example, New South Wales Law Reform Commission, *People with Cognitive and Mental Health Impairments in the Criminal Justice System: Diversion* (n 3) 41–5 [3.59]–[3.77]; Elizabeth Richardson and Bernadette McSherry (n 5).

[48] In the broader context of diversion generally see, for example, Michael Parsonage, 'Diversion: A Better Way for Criminal Justice and Mental Health' (Sainsbury Centre for Mental Health 2009) 8.

32) at the margins of criminal law – moving individuals from the inside to
the outside of the presumed material spaces of criminal law. Within this
spatial ordering of section 32, criminal law is viewed in technical terms as
the mechanism for shifting individuals with disability out of the criminal
justice system; but this characterisation of section 32 ignores the political
and anti-therapeutic effects of criminal *law* itself (as opposed to the
criminal justice space).[49] Comprehending the possibility of and
appreciating the nuances of any state control that operates through section
32 requires, as a first step, the shifting of focus from the material and
administrative spatialities of section 32 to the criminal legal dimensions of
section 32.

Diversion's Coercive and Punitive Effects

The starting point to drawing out criminal legal dimensions of section 32
is to acknowledge that prima facie section 32 *is* a criminal legal
mechanism because it is in the Local Court's criminal jurisdiction; it deals
with individuals who come before the court on criminal charges; and
section 32 orders relate to criminal charges. More specifically, while
section 32 might shift individuals out of material spaces of the court and
the prison, the individuals still remain bound to criminal law. This is the
case because, while a section 32 order *does* involve dismissal of a
defendant's charges,[50] when the order is conditional, dismissal of the
defendants' charges is coupled with conditions that are backed up by
supervision and enforcement provisions.[51] The effect is that a conditional
section 32 order coerces individuals to engage with disability and mental
health services under the threat of the individuals' criminal charges being
brought back before the court and hence the possibly of being subject to
conviction-based punishment, and depending on the charges, possibly also
imprisonment. The individuals who receive section 32 orders are punished
because engagement with these services has restrictive and possibly
negative effects, and, if the order is breached, individuals additionally risk
being subjected to conviction-based punishment. The coercive and

---

[49] A similar point has been made by Arrigo in the context of a critique of
therapeutic jurisprudence: Bruce A Arrigo, 'The Ethics of Therapeutic
Jurisprudence: A Critical and Theoretical Enquiry of Law, Psychology and Crime'
(2004) 11(1) Psychiatry, Psychology and Law 23.

[50] Mental Health (Forensic Provisions) Act 1990 (NSW) s 32(3).

[51] Mental Health (Forensic Provisions) Act 1990 (NSW) ss 32(3A)–32(3D).

punitive effects of section 32 are clearly acknowledged in the leading decision on section 32, *DPP (NSW) v El Mawas*,[52] in which McColl JA stated:

> [A]dopting the diversionary route *does not mean that a defendant is not exposed to punishment*. While an order under s 32(3) is not custodial in the strict sense, it may involve the imposition of conditions restricting a discharged defendant's freedom of movement and actions. Compliance with those conditions is ensured by the Magistrate retaining a supervisory jurisdiction for 6 months.[53]

While section 32 might shift individuals out of the material and administrative spaces of the court and the prison (or other criminal justice system spaces such as the probation and parole office), this movement is necessarily provisional and subject always to the possibility of return to these spaces. More to the point, for present purposes, putting to one side the material and administrative spatialisation of criminal law, in an abstract legal sense (and drawing on critical legal geography scholarship[54]), through section 32, individuals still remain *within* the criminal law's *jurisdictional space* because the coercive and punitive effects of section 32 on individuals with disability are related to the dismissal (or, in reality, the suspension of the consideration) of the individuals' criminal charges which can be brought back if these individuals resist the coercive effects of section 32 by breaching their order.

While it is outside the scope of this chapter,[55] it is important to note that the *coercive* and *punitive* dimensions of section 32, as embodied in the supervision and breach elements of section 32, have gained increasing

---

[52] *El Mawas* (n 28).

[53] ibid 108-109 [73] (McColl JA) (emphasis added).

[54] See generally Nicholas Blomley, 'From "What?" to "So What?": Law and Geography in Retrospect' in Jane Holder and Carolyn Harrison (eds), *Law and Geography* (Oxford University Press 2003) 17; Nicholas Blomley, *Law, Space, and the Geographies of Power* (The Guilford Press 1994); Lawrence Douglas, Austin Sarat and Martha Merrill Umphrey, 'At the Limits of Law: An Introduction' in Lawrence Douglas, Austin Sarat and Martha Merrill Umphrey (eds), *The Limits of Law* (Stanford .University Press, 2005) 1.

[55] For a detailed discussion of the historical development of section 32, see Linda Steele, 'Disability at the Margins: Diversion, Cognitive Impairment and the Criminal Law' (PhD thesis, University of Sydney, 2014) 47-69.

prominence and acceptability over time. Section 32 has its legislative origins in section 428W of the *Crimes Act 1900* (NSW), which was inserted into the *Crimes Act 1900* (NSW) in 1983[56] and came into force in 1986.[57] In its original form, s 428W did not have any 'breach' and 'supervision' provisions, these being introduced in 2002.[58] An earlier suggestion to introduce similar provisions in the mid-1990s was met by disability rights advocates, criminal lawyers and law reformers as problematic and ultimately did not occur at that time. Since these provisions were introduced in 2002, these provisions have become part of the assumed landscape of section 32, with a recent law reform review not even considering abolishing the breach provisions but instead focussing on how the supervision and breach provisions could operate more effectively to maximise treatment efficacy and compliance with orders.[59] Related to these observations of the section's development over time, it would be interesting to consider how these developments towards *greater* coerciveness might parallel (or be related to) the contemporary developments in the preventive turn in criminal law, more broadly including through greater use of bail and continuing detention orders.[60] In the context of this chapter's critique of diversion and state control through criminal law, it is important to note this trend *towards greater coerciveness* and *greater complacency towards coerciveness*, and that this is sitting comfortably with the assumed benefits of section 32 for individuals with disability.

The discussion above has focused on *conditional* section 32 orders. It should be noted that section 32 also provides for unconditional orders. An

---

[56] The Crimes (Mental Disorder) Amendment Act 1983 (NSW) inserted a new Part XIA, 'Unfitness to be Tried for an Offence', into the Crimes Act 1900 (NSW). This part included s 428W, which was in similar terms to the current s 32.

[57] The amendments made to the Crimes Act 1900 (NSW) by the Crimes (Mental Disorder) Amendment Act 1983 (NSW) were assented to on 31 December 1983 and commenced on 22 August 1986.

[58] Crimes Legislation Amendment Act 2002 (NSW) sch 9 cl 3.

[59] See, for example, New South Wales Law Reform Commission, *People with Cognitive and Mental Health Impairments in the Criminal Justice System: Diversion* (n 3) 37–48 [3.44]–[3.73].

[60] See, for example, David Brown, 'Looking Behind the Increase in Custodial Remand Populations' (2013) 2(2) International Journal of Crime, Justice and Social Democracy 80; Tamara Tulich, 'Post-Sentence Preventive Detention and Extended Supervision of High Risk Offenders in New South Wales' (2015) 38(2) UNSW Law Journal 823.

argument might be made that these orders do not have any coercive or punitive effects because the individual is not required to engage with disability and mental health services and their charges are dismissed outright. The reported cases, anecdotal evidence and empirical research all indicate that, in practice, there are few unconditional orders made, particularly in relation to individuals with cognitive impairment. Unconditional section 32 orders can still have some problematic effects, even if the orders themselves are not specifically coercive or punitive on each individual who receives such an order. Individuals might receive an unconditional order because the magistrate is of the view that the disability services or mental health services are sufficiently intensive that they effectively surpass the state control that is possible through the conviction-based punishment or because there is a civil guardianship or mental health order in place, rather than because the magistrate is of the view that it is unnecessary for the individual to be subjected to any legal regulation whether that be pursuant to section 32 or some other legal mechanism.[61]

A consideration of criminal legal dimensions of section 32 has illuminated some coercive and punitive effects of section 32 and signals the relationship of section 32 to state control through criminal law. There is further nuance to state control through section 32, because it is not subject to the same legal limits that delineate control through criminal law in relation to conviction-based punishment. Importantly, the coercive and punitive effects of section 32 are not bound by the principles and processes of conviction-based punishment, which typically limit the scope of the coercive and punitive effects of the criminal law jurisdiction. Section 32 refers to dealing with a defendant 'otherwise than in accordance with law'.[62] Prima facie this might suggest that an individual who receives a section 32 order is not dealt with by criminal law and hence is not subject to any further coercive or punitive effects of criminal law. It has been argued that 'law' refers specifically and only to the principles and processes of criminal law relating to conviction-based punishment, as opposed to the criminal law jurisdiction in an exhaustive and broader sense. That is, pursuant to section 32, an individual is still dealt with by *criminal law* even though he or she is not dealt with through the legal processes of conviction-based punishment.

---

[61] Linda Steele (n 55) 76.
[62] Mental Health (Forensic Provisions) Act 1990 (NSW) s 32(1)(b).

Here, I suggest that section 32 has coercive and punitive effects which are not bound by the principles and processes associated with conviction-based punishment. This occurs in a number of specific ways which I will now identify. Section 32 applies to defendants who have not been convicted of a criminal offence and sentenced in relation to that offence or even tried for the offence. This is because a section 32 application can be made 'at the commencement or at any time during the course of the hearing of proceedings before a Magistrate'.[63] Furthermore, a successful section 32 application results in the dismissal of the defendant's charges[64] and section 32(4) states that '[a] decision under this section to dismiss charges against a defendant does not constitute a finding that the charges against the defendant are proven or otherwise'.[65] Section 32 may apply to defendants who are incapable of forming the necessary *mens rea* for an offence or performing the *actus reus* (the latter being more relevant to those Local Court matters involving strict liability). The magistrate is not bound by the rules of evidence that would typically apply in a criminal trial[66] (with the exception that the magistrate must not inform him or herself in a way that would be self-incriminating to the defendant).[67]

Section 32 may apply to defendants who are unfit to be tried. The legal framework for unfitness consists of common law and legislative dimensions. The common law provides that individuals cannot be tried when they are unfit,[68] and legislation then provides for the subsequent regulation of individuals found unfit in the forensic mental health system.[69] When both of these dimensions are present in a particular jurisdiction, they work in tandem such that, upon a finding of unfitness, an individual is channeled into the forensic mental health system. Even where there are no legislative provisions, it has been held that the common law unfitness rule must apply regardless of the absence of the legislative framework for regulating those found unfit, or a system for the extra-criminal confinement of those found unfit, because the common law

---

[63] Mental Health (Forensic Provisions) Act 1990 (NSW) s 32(1).

[64] Mental Health (Forensic Provisions) Act 1990 (NSW) s 32(3).

[65] Mental Health (Forensic Provisions) Act 1990 (NSW) s 32(4).

[66] Evidence Act 1995 (NSW).

[67] Mental Health (Forensic Provisions) Act 1990 (NSW) s 36.

[68] *Presser v R* [1958] VR 45.

[69] See, for example, Mental Health (Forensic Provisions) Act 1990 (NSW) pt 2.

principles are grounded in ideas of fairness of trial.[70] Even though, in the context of New South Wales, the *Mental Health (Forensic Provisions) Act 1990* (NSW) only provides for post-unfitness legislative procedures in the District and Supreme Courts and there is no legislative scheme in the Local Court jurisdiction,[71] it has been held that proceedings can still be stayed on the basis of unfitness.[72] The application of section 32 to individuals who are unfit is further supported by the New South Wales Law Reform Commission ('NSWLRC') in its recent recommendations which seek to formalise section 32's role in dealing with unfit defendants. This remains a contentious issue in the scholarly literature and law reform discussion.[73]

---

[70] *Pioch v Lauder* (1976) 27 FLR 79, 85–6 (Forster J); *R v Ngatayi* (1980) 147 CLR 1, 7–8 (Gibbs, Mason and Wilson JJ) (in obiter). These two decisions concerned the Northern Territory criminal jurisdiction, interestingly both concerning Indigenous defendants with a combination of intellectual, linguistic and cultural difficulties. The accused in *Ngatayi* was a 'full-blooded aboriginal who did not speak or understand English' and the accused in *Pioch* was a 'deaf mute', 'a full blood aboriginal brought up in a tribal community', who 'had not absorbed the cultural or moral values of either tribal or European society' and 'was at least of average intelligence with no evidence of mental incapacity': *R v Ngatayi* (1980) 147 CLR 1, 1; *Pioch v Lauder* (1976) 27 FLR 79 (1976) 27 FLR 79, 79.

[71] Mental Health (Forensic Provisions) Act 1990 (NSW) pt 2.

[72] *Mantell v Molyneux* (2006) 68 NSWLR 46, 54 [28]–[29], 56 [33]–[34], 56 [36]. The section 32 decision of *Mantell* can be compared to the earlier decision of *Perry v Forbes* (Unreported, Supreme Court of New South Wales, Smart J, 21 May 1993) where parties agreed that a Magistrate could not consider the question of fitness in the Local Court. This latter case concerned indictable offences triable summarily and the issue of fitness was raised in the context of a request that the charges be dealt with summarily.

[73] On the argument that an individual cannot be dealt with as unfit in the Local Court because of the absence of legislative provisions *and* that section 32 is the only option available to a Magistrate in these circumstance, see New South Wales Law Reform Commission, *People with an Intellectual Disability and the Criminal Justice System: Courts and Sentencing Issues* (Discussion Paper No 35, 1994) [5.3]–[5.5]; New South Wales Law Reform Commission, *People with an Intellectual Disability in the Criminal Justice System* (Report No 80, 1996) [5.66]–[5.75]; New South Wales Law Reform Commission, *People with Cognitive and Mental Health Impairments in the Criminal Justice System: Criminal Responsibility and Consequences* (Consultation Paper No 6, 2010) [1.46]–[1.48]. On the alternative argument that an individual can be dealt with as unfit in the Local Court, but in light of the available legislative provisions for regulation in section 32, only if a section 32 application has been unsuccessful (i.e., fitness and

Section 32 is also not limited by the principles of sentencing (which is particularly relevant in the Local Court context where there is a high proportion of guilty pleas); that is, the terms of the section 32 order are not determined by principal reference to the defendant's liability for a criminal offence, nor by reference to the sentencing principle of proportionality. The six month compliance period for a section 32 conditional order is arbitrary and cannot be altered by a magistrate – the period of compliance is not calculated by reference to the particular offence. The punitive effects of criminal law can therefore be disproportionate to the alleged offence that initially brought the individual before the court, which can actually enable longer or more intensive punishment of the defendant including in relation to minor offences which might have been disposed of by way of dismissal without proceeding to conviction, conviction with no other penalty or a minor fine.[74] The period of the order also does not need to be set by reference to the sentencing aims of rehabilitation and deterrence.[75] On the point of section 32's relationship to the principles of sentencing, the NSWLRC has noted that:

> While the intentions of the court may be rehabilitative, compliance with the requirements of a diversionary order may be understood or experienced by the defendant as punitive and going beyond that which would be imposed on a person without impairments. Indeed intervention or diversionary programs which are undertaken prior to any finding of guilt have been criticised 'for creating quasi-punitive orders, similar to sentencing powers but without the same protections'.[76]

---

stay of proceedings / no regulation as a last resort), see Tom Gotsis and Hugh Donnelly, 'Diverting Mentally Disordered Offenders in the NSW Local Court' (Monograph No 31, Judicial Commission of NSW, March 2008) viii, 22–3; Dan Howard and Bruce Westmore, (n 45) [5.95]–[5.96]. On the further argument that an individual can be dealt with as unfit in light of the common law principles of unfitness, regardless of the absence of legislative provisions, see Mark Ierace, *Intellectual Disability: A Manual for Criminal Lawyers* (RLC Publishing 1989) 39–40; Greg James, *Consultation Paper: Review of the* Mental Health Act 1990 *and the* Mental Health (Criminal Procedure) Act 1990 (Department of Health (NSW) 2006) 11.

[74] See, for example, the sentencing options in Crimes (Sentencing Procedure) Act 1999 (NSW) pt 2 divs 3–4.

[75] Crimes (Sentencing Procedure) Act 1999 (NSW) s 3A.

[76] New South Wales Law Reform Commission, *People with Cognitive and Mental Health Impairments in the Criminal Justice System: Diversion* (n 3) 44 [3.71], quoting Michael King et al, *Non-Adversarial Justice* (Federation Press 2009) 175.

A section 32 order also does not restrict the administration of the order to corrective services, as is largely the case with conviction-based punishment,[77] and instead implicates disability and mental health services and professionals in the administration of the order (a point returned to in the next part of this chapter).

To this point, this chapter has demonstrated in this part that section 32 has coercive and punitive effects on individuals with disability, specifically in a manner that is not bound by the principles and processes around conviction-based punishment that typically limit the scope of state intervention through the criminal law jurisdiction. This signals the importance of section 32's *relations with* other dimensions of criminal law, rather than its exclusivity from these, and opens up section 32 to analysis in two key respects (which are outside the scope of this chapter, but which provide important directions for future research on diversion). One respect in which this insight opens up section 32 to analysis is that it reveals that there are *multiple* criminal legal pathways for state control of individuals with disability in the criminal justice system, and specifically, that there is a pathway for *non-convicted* individuals with disability which is not available to non-convicted individuals without a diagnosis of cognitive impairment or mental illness. This directs analysis to the ideas about disability that underline state control through criminal law of people with disability. The second respect in which section 32 is now opened up to analysis is that section 32 locates individuals *inside* the criminal law jurisdiction but *outside* of the typical limits of state control through the criminal law jurisdiction through conviction-based punishment. This is an important observation because it signals the need for analysis of the relationship between section 32 and conviction-based punishment, and a consideration of what legitimises state control through section 32, if not these principles. The legal limits to conviction-based punishment have an important role in supporting conviction-based punishment's coercive and punitive effects, such that the perceived legitimacy of state intervention through section 32 must have an alternative grounding.

In discussing the coercive and punitive effects of section 32, so far this part has drawn out section 32's location inside criminal law's jurisdictional space and the complexities of this location. This discussion has provided a basis for appreciating *criminal legal* dimensions of the state

---

[77] Crimes (Administration of Sentences) Act 1999 (NSW).

control that operates through section 32. Discussion now turns in the next part to the significance of *disability* to the coercive and punitive effects of section 32 and the relationship of disability to the criminal legal dimensions which have just been discussed.

The Discriminatory Nature of Diversion's Coercive and Punitive Effects

In the introduction to this chapter, the disability-specific nature of diversion and other criminal legal mechanisms was identified as potentially discriminatory by reason of recent developments in international human rights. This part will consider how section 32's coercive and punitive effects discussed above are discriminatory by reason of *who* they apply to and *how* they apply. A section 32 order applies only to defendants with disability. The first stage of the *El Mawas* inquiry, the 'jurisdictional question' of section 32, is that the defendant is 'developmentally disabled', 'suffering from a mental illness' or 'suffering from a mental condition for which treatment is available in a mental health facility'.[78] A jurisdictional question has been described as follows: 'the court's power to make an order in favour of an applicant under [a legislative provision] is conditional upon the court being satisfied of affairs predicated in [the legislation]'.[79] On a more general level, section 32 is located in the *Mental Health (Forensic Provisions) Act 1990* (NSW) which is an Act for 'the care, treatment and control' of those appearing in criminal proceedings who are 'affected by mental illness and other mental conditions'.[80] An individual cannot even be considered eligible for a section 32 order if that individual does not have the relevant diagnosed impairment, and hence section 32's coercive and punitive effects are dependent upon the presence of impairment.[81] Mindful of the fact that section 32 applies to *non-convicted* individuals, it is arguable that section 32 is discriminatory because it subjects *non-convicted* individuals with disability to greater detriment by reason of the additional opportunities for

---

[78] Mental Health (Forensic Provisions) Act 1990 (NSW) s 32(1)(a); *El Mawas* (n 28) 109, [75] (McColl JA).

[79] *Singer v Berghouse* (1994) 181 CLR 201, 208–209 (Mason CJ, Deane and McHugh JJ).

[80] Mental Health (Forensic Provisions) Act 1990 (NSW) long title (emphasis added).

[81] *El Mawas* (n 28).

them to be subject to criminal law's coercive and punitive effects when compared to *non-convicted* individuals who *do not* have disability who are beyond criminal law's jurisdictional scope.

Generally, criminal law presents itself as applying equally to individuals regardless of any particular individual's membership of a particular racial or other identity-based group.[82] In the context of conviction-based punishment, subjective factors are generally not acknowledged – are even denied – by criminal law until sentencing (except where there is a *psychological* basis for these factors negating the *actus reus* or *mens rea* of an offence or where they relate to a specific defence).[83] At the sentencing stage, a variety of subjective factors including diagnosed impairment,[84] age[85] and social deprivation in childhood[86] can be considered in determining the sentence. In section 32, diagnosed impairment is taken into consideration even before the sentencing stage and in a broader sense than in relation to its relevance to trial or conviction as it does not need to relate to unfitness to be tried, to the *actus reus*, the *mens rea* or a defence. McColl JA drew attention to this in *DPP (NSW) v El Mawas*[87] where she stated that:

> [T]he significance of mental illness of an offender in the sentencing exercise has long been accepted. Pt 3 is clearly intended to permit the Magistrate, if it is appropriate, to divert a defendant from being exposed to sentence, with his or her mental condition being taken into account at that comparatively late stage.[88]

Here, McColl JA depicts the relevance of disability to section 32 in humanitarian terms as an advantage to the disabled defendant, and this sentiment is shared in the existing literature and discussion of section 32. The singling out of disability as a relevant characteristic on which to (a) not convict an individual (the McColl JA reading) is also at the same time

---

[82] See the recent discussion by the High Court in *Bugmy* (2013) 249 CLR 571.

[83] Nikolas Rose, *The Politics of Life Itself: Biomedicine, Power and Subjectivity in the Twenty-First Century* (Princeton University Press 2007) 229–30. See also Alan W Norrie (n 13).

[84] Crimes (Sentencing Procedure) Act 1999 (NSW) s 21A(3)(j); *Hemsley* [2004] NSWCCA 228 (7 July 2004).

[85] Crimes (Sentencing Procedure) Act 1999 (NSW) ss 21A(3)(h), 21A(3)(j).

[86] *Bugmy* (82).

[87] *El Mawas* (n 28).

[88] ibid 93, 108 [72] (McColl JA), citing *R v Israil* [2002] NSWCCA 255, 97 [21] (Spigelman CJ).

the basis on which to (b) coerce and punish those non-convicted individuals with disability who might otherwise *not* be convicted or receive a harsh sentence. Therefore there is a tension between the general exclusion of subjective factors prior to consideration of the sentence in the context of conviction-based punishment's coercive and punitive effects, and the inclusion (despite this) of, specifically, disability in relation to section 32 where the recognition of these factors provides an additional means for criminal law as a jurisdiction to have coercive and punitive effects. No other subjective factors of an individual are given this status.[89] Singling out disability has the effect of providing a means for criminal law to have coercive and punitive effects exclusively on this specific group of non-convicted individuals.

In applying exclusively to non-convicted individuals with disability, section 32 describes this category of individuals in negative terms such as 'risk' and 'need for management'. At a general level, the *Mental Health (Forensic Provisions) Act 1990* (NSW) refers to the 'care, treatment and control' specifically of people with cognitive and mental health impairment – there is a coupling of 'care' and 'treatment' with 'control'. In specific relation to section 32, McColl JA in *DPP (NSW) v El Mawas*[90] states of the legislative scheme:

> Part 3 of the Act requires a Magistrate to balance the public interest in those charged with a criminal offence facing the full weight of the law against the public interest in treating, or regulating to the greatest extent practical, the conduct of individuals suffering from any of the mental conditions referred to in s 32(1) or mental illness (s 33) with the object of ensuring that the community is protected from the conduct of such persons.[91]

Accordingly, the overarching purpose of section 32 is to protect the public from defendants with disability, and only this group. Section 32's application specifically to individuals with disability attaches exclusively to people with disability the notions of risk ('community is protected') and

---

[89] This is with the exception of age in relation to children, although in the context of children, their age results in the inability for them to be held criminally responsible and hence to be tried and punished through criminal law. See Children (Criminal Proceedings) Act 1987 (New South Wales); *C (A Minor) v DPP* [1994] 3 WLR 888.

[90] *El Mawas* (n 28).

[91] *El Mawas* (n 28) 108 [71] (McColl JA).

the need for legal management ('regulating to the greatest extent practical'), and echoes the longstanding link between disability and risk in the case law in relation to unfitness, the mental illness defence and automatism.[92] In the excerpt from McColl JA's judgement above, there is also a link drawn between disability, treatment and coercion, compounded with the focus on treatment in the 'public interest' rather than in the interests of the individual, which is also seen in numerous civil legal mechanisms such as involuntary mental health admission, detention and treatment of people with disability and court-authorised sterilization of girls and women with disability.

Drawing out the disability dimensions of section 32 suggests the discriminatory nature of the state control that operates through section 32, because it directs analytical attention to the meaning of disability in the context of section 32 (notably links between disability with criminality, and the necessity and permissibility of criminal law's coercive and punitive effects on these individuals regardless of the absence of conviction) and the importance of locating these reflections in a broader question of why disability is significant to criminal law as compared to other aspects of identity (for example, race, gender, social deprivation). Furthermore, recalling the earlier discussion of section 32's characterisation as humane and beneficial, a further consideration related to section 32's disability-specific nature is why section 32 *evades* being viewed as discriminatory, and the significance of the discourses of humanity and therapy (which juxtapose section 32 to a history of injustice and mistreatment) to the positive (rather than detrimental) construction of section 32.

Section 32 orders are administered through the use of disability and mental health services, as opposed to corrective services. The orders are also administered in the community rather than in a custodial setting. Section 32 orders can be more resource intensive than sentences as they are linked to supported accommodation, behaviour intervention support and mental health case management. On a related note, the orders set up ongoing service relationships which can continue beyond the six month

---

[92] This is most vividly apparent in the case law delineating the distinction between sane automatism and insane automatism: *Bratty v A-G for Northern Ireland* [1963] AC 386; *R v Falconer* (1990) 171 CLR 30. See also Arlie Loughnan, *Manifest Madness: Mental Incapacity in Criminal Law* (Oxford University Press 2012) 128–31.

enforcement period of a section 32 order. The services involved in section 32 orders are institutionally, geographically and materially distinct to those involved in criminal law's coercive and punitive effects via conviction-based punishment through corrective services. While it was observed in Part I above that this distinction is what gives section 32 its positive 'diversionary' character in the existing literature and discussion, here it is argued that this distinction means that section 32 involves an extension of the agencies and strategies involved in state control through criminal law, and in a manner that is specific to the institutions, professions and material spaces exclusive to individuals with disability and historical trajectories of disability rights. This points to a specific feature of the discriminatory nature of section 32 because the operation of section 32 through services exclusively available on the basis of diagnosed-impairment causes greater detriment to non-convicted individuals with disability as opposed to non-convicted individuals without such diagnoses who are ineligible to access such services (and hence to experience criminal law's coercive and punitive effects through such services).

One particular issue with the coercive and punitive effects of section 32, which occurs in part through the use of disability and mental health services, is the perceived therapeutic and empowering nature of these services. Community-based mental health services are typically depicted as focused on balancing therapeutic outcomes for individuals with the perceived risks of living in the community, whereas disability services focus on teaching life skills or providing supported accommodation are purportedly aimed at encouraging the independence and community inclusion of persons with disability. These community-based services gain their beneficial meaning in part from the historical legacy of institutionalisation against which they are positioned. The use in section 32 of these services in a context where section 32 has coercive and punitive effects on individuals with disability seems prima facie contrary to the underlying sentiments of mental health and disability services because here their punitive and coercive use is counter to the wellbeing, autonomy, independence and inclusion of the individual, and additionally their use is discriminatory. This might be understood in reference to critical disability studies scholarship. Critical disability scholars have explored the disciplinary regulative effects of disability support services.[93]

---

[93] See generally Chris Drinkwater (n 11) 229; Jack Levinson (n 11); Scott Yates, 'Truth, Power, and Ethics in Care Services for People with Learning Difficulties'

It has been argued that contemporary approaches to disability support services – group homes, case management, life skills training, community access and counselling – have characteristics of disciplinary regulation. This is held to be the case in a material and a discursive sense. In the material sense; while individuals are not repressively detained and isolated from the community (as they were in an earlier era of institutionalisation), they are instead supported to live freely and inclusively within the community yet they are still regulated through the highly structured and supervised nature of their living environments, daily routines and lifestyles which contours their available choices, relationships and spatial location. In a discursive sense; critical disability scholars also note the significance of discourses of empowerment, rights and freedom to the framing of these services. The significance of these discourses is peculiar to disability support services because of the historical legacy of the institutionalisation of individuals with cognitive impairment. Critical disability scholars argue that these discourses actually serve to mask the disciplinary nature of disability support services. Critical disability scholars have noted a core tension inherent in disability support services such that the characteristics of these services, which are typically valorised for their progressive and empowering nature, are the aspects that give these services their disciplinary character.

Contrary to the argument that section 32 provides a necessary pathway to disability and mental health services which is central to the characterisation of section 32 as humane and therapeutic, the services the subject of section 32 orders could generally be accessed by individuals voluntarily in the community and hence there is no need for them to have to be accessed through criminal law. While section 32 is seen as beneficial because it provides access to disability and mental health services in a criminal legal context, it is problematic that this access must necessarily be associated with coercive and punitive effects.

The perceived therapeutic and humane character of the disability and mental health services, the basis of section 32 orders, points to a further dimension of the discriminatory nature of section 32. The use of community-based disability and mental health services in criminal legal orders might unintentionally be 'humanising' criminal law more broadly

---

in Shelley Tremain (ed), *Foucault and the Government of Disability* (University of Michigan Press 2005) 65.

through promoting the assumption that state control through criminal law in the lives of individuals can possibly achieve therapeutic benefits. This is particularly evident in the linkages made elsewhere between section 32 and 'therapeutic jurisprudence'.[94] Therapeutic jurisprudence risks depoliticising state control through criminal law, pathologising and individualising a person's presence in the jurisdictional space of criminal law and negating the marginalising and violent dimensions of criminal law.[95] On a related note, section 32 still puts the expectation on the individual to change (through involvement with disability and mental health services) rather than focusing on changing society, notably through the fact that section 32 orders cannot bind anyone or any service other than the diverted individual him or herself.[96]

This part has discussed the ways in which section 32's coercive and punitive effects on individuals with disability apply *specifically* to people with disability and *on the basis* of their disability, and are possible in part because of the *use* of disability and mental health services. Drawing out the disability dimensions of the state control that operates through section 32 directs analytical attention to the coupling of diagnosed impairment, coercion and treatment and the significance of discourses of empowerment, therapy and community to the necessitating and legitimating of these specific forms of state control through criminal law of (non-convicted) individuals with disability.

Diversion and Disability: Control Inside Criminal Law

This chapter set out to consider whether through diversion, individuals with disability are still subjected to state control through criminal law and, if so, what the relevance was of disability to any such control. Confronted with the accepted view that diversion of individuals with disability is a humane and beneficial practice, central to the very comprehensibility of control through diversion was shifting the analytical focus from the material and administrative spatialisation of the *operation* of diversion to

---

[94] New South Wales Law Reform Commission, *People with Cognitive and Mental Health Impairments in the Criminal Justice System: Diversion* (n 47) 27–8 [3.8]–[3.9].

[95] Bruce A Arrigo (n 49).

[96] *Minister for Corrective Services v Harris* (Unreported, Supreme Court of New South Wales, Brownie J, 10 July 1987).

criminal legal and disability dimensions of the *legal framework* for diversion's operation. Through a detailed analysis of the legal framework of one diversion scheme – section 32 – the chapter identified the coercive, punitive and discriminatory effects of section 32 which demonstrates the complex ways in which diversion enables state control *exclusively* of *non-convicted* people with *disability inside criminal law*. Identifying the state control that operates through diversion does not require a wholesale denial of the possibility that diversion has any benefits (including in comparison to incarceration). Rather, any possible purported benefits of diversion and any claims of its place in broader social justice and disability rights agendas must now be assessed in the context of diversion's social and political context *and* by reference to a range of *non-coercive and non-punitive* alternatives *outside of criminal law* through which similar individual services, treatment and social outcomes (as well as systemic change) might be achieved. This analysis of the legal framework of a specific diversion scheme has provided new openings for the analysis of diversion in other jurisdictions (including in England and Wales, as discussed in the first part of this chapter) which is attentive to the nuances of the relationships between the legal and the cultural aspects of disability and law which circulate in a particular legal framework of diversion which enables state control of individuals with disability in ways different to that possible through conviction-based punishment.

This chapter concludes by flagging two areas for further exploration. First, the analysis of section 32 highlights the constitutive role of diversion in conviction-based punishment. While the perceived legitimacy of criminal law's authority is largely contingent on the limits on conviction-based punishment, the analysis of section 32 has demonstrated how diversion operates outside of these limits. This raises the question of diversion's relationship to the legitimacy of criminal law. That is, whether diversion undermines the legitimacy of criminal law in both operating in the criminal law jurisdiction but outside the principles and processes that typically gives criminal law's coercive and punitive effects (through conviction-based punishment) their perceived legitimacy, or alternatively whether diversion supports conviction-based punishment by operating in a manner exceptional to the limits on conviction-based punishment. Building on the existing scholarship on disability and the legal construction of capacity and rationality, more research is required on the important roles that diversion (and disability) have in the legitimacy of state control through conviction-based punishment. Second, the analysis of section 32 has highlighted the significance of individualistic, pathologised and medicalised understandings of disability as diagnosed impairment to non-voluntary and violent interventions in the lives of individuals with disability *through law*. The explicit coupling of control with care and treatment suggests that the specific use of disability services in diversion falls into a pre-existing and deeply embedded approach by criminal law to people with disability in the criminal justice system. Thinking beyond criminal law, there are *other* ways in which individuals with disability are subjected to coercive state interventions in a manner that would not be possible but for their diagnosed impairment. These include detention and treatment pursuant to civil mental health legislation and guardianship legislation, and sterilization (which are being characterized on an international human rights level as forms of violence and of torture[97]). It seems that there is a relationship between law, disability and coercion (and *consent and incapacity*) which is central to the way in which the state intervenes in the lives of individuals with disability. It is necessary to unpack this approach (and its link to the meaning and significance of disability), rather than take it for granted.

---

[97] See, for example, Juan E Méndez, *Report of the Special Rapporteur on Torture and Other Cruel, Inhuman or Degrading Treatment or Punishment, United Nations, Human Rights Council* 22nd session, agenda item 3, UN Doc A/HRC/22/53.

CHAPTER FOURTEEN

SEX OFFENDERS WITH AUTISTIC SPECTRUM CONDITIONS

ANN CREABY-ATTWOOD AND CHRIS INCE

The Sex Offender with High Functioning Autism and the Suitability of Sex Offenders Treatment Programmes[1]

Background

In recent years, the spotlight has increasingly fallen upon those who perpetrate contact and non-contact offences of a sexual nature, perhaps

---

[1] The UK Ministry of Justice (MOJ), relying upon the research of Hanson et al (2009) have indicated that sexual offender programmes which follow the risk, need and reponsivity of offenders will lead to the greatest reduction in criminogenic recidivism. In light of this, the MOJ provide Sex Offenders Treatment Programmes which can be offered as part of a custodial sentence or as a requirement of a community penalty. Mainstream treatment programmes use a cognitive-behavioural approach concentrating upon the person's offending behaviour by restructuring attitudes that support or permit sexual offending, and addressing 'previous dysfunctional behaviours'. This work takes place within small groups and utilises pro-social modelling and victim empathy interventions. In 2011, an adapted suite of programmes were accredited by the MOJ to meet the needs of 'intellectually disabled sexual offenders' (MOJ 2013). These programmes were specifically developed for men with IQ 60-80 with associated adaptive functioning deficits. Whilst current empirical data would suggest that sex offenders who receive such treatment either in prison or in the community reduce their post-treatment reoffending, this approach is challenging for offenders with an Autistic Spectrum Condition. The recognised criteria for Asperger's of no significant delay in spoken or receptive language or cognitive development (ICD 10) would make it unlikely that without an additional low IQ, they could be included in an adapted programme. Additionally, a lack of socio-emotional reciprocity may impair utilisation of a programme, which is developed with an empathic intervention at its core.

influenced by the high profile historical cases involving television and media presenters.

Accordingly, there has been a similar focus upon assessment, punishment, rehabilitation, treatment and ongoing management to reduce the likelihood of recidivism.

There is, however, an understanding that the current treatment pathways available to offenders are generally generic in nature. From this, we believe there results a failure to address the criminogenic needs of specific groups. Whilst those convicted of sexual offences who have a learning disability may be offered support and treatment via an adapted suite of programmes, accredited by the Ministry of Justice, described as meeting the needs of 'intellectually disabled sexual offenders'[2], the needs of those convicted of sexual offences and who have an Autistic Spectrum Condition may not be being met.

It has been recognised that an Autistic Spectrum Condition remains, to a degree, an underdiagnosed condition, particularly in adulthood.

The National Autistic Society indicates that the latest prevalence studies of autism show that over 695,000 people in the UK may have autism, with this estimate taken from the 2011 UK census figures. Having carried out relatively recent research involving randomly sampled adults interviewed throughout England, Dr Brugha, Professor of Psychiatry at the University of Leicester, reported in 2012 that:

> [T]here were no tested methods for conducting epidemiological studies of autism spectrum disorders. (In light of this he and colleagues) compared the probability of respondents having an Autistic Spectrum Disorder across three survey phases. A random subset completed phase 2 utilising ADOS-4 assessments (n = 618); In phase 3, informant-based Diagnostic Interview Schedule for Social and Communication Disorders and Autism Diagnostic Interview Revised (ADI-R) developmental assessments were completed (n = 56). Phase 1 and 2 data were presented as vignettes to six experienced clinicians working in pairs. The probability of respondents having an Autistic Spectrum Disorder was compared across the three survey phases.

---

[2] Ministry of Justice, 'Freedom of Information Request -information regarding any new Sex Offender Treatment Programmes which are being developed and are scheduled to replace the existing SOTP programmes in the future. (2013) <https://www.gov.uk/government/uploads/system/uploads/attachment_data/file/25 9044/sex-offender-treatment-programmes.doc> accessed 28th November 2015.

There was moderate agreement between clinical consensus diagnoses and ADOS-4.[3] [ADOS being the Autistic Diagnostic Observation Schedule].

There is also is a profound geographical variation in the availability of diagnostic services and ongoing support from health, social care and third sector organisations throughout the United Kingdom.

We will explore these particular issues with specific reference to those individuals with a diagnosis of Autism Spectrum Conditions who sexually offend or display sexually offensive behaviours. We will then further focus upon phenotypic considerations in the provision of services, and specifically upon the availability, efficacy and suitability of existing Sex Offender Treatment Programmes.

Introduction

Diagnostic Overview

Autistic Spectrum Conditions are defined as a 'group of disorders characterised by qualitative abnormalities in reciprocal social interactions and in patterns of communication and by a restricted repertoire of interest and activities; these qualitative abnormalities are a pervasive feature of the individual's functioning in all situations'.[4]

Within a 'traditional' diagnosis of Childhood Autism, there would be evidence of abnormal or impaired development, prior to the age of three years, in at least one of the following areas: receptive or expressive language as used in social communication; the development of selective social attachments or of reciprocal social interaction; functional or symbolic play. Whilst not included in its entirety, the ICD-10 criteria – that is, the World Health Organisation Classification of Diseases – references difficulties or an inability to develop age-appropriate peer relationships that involve a mutual sharing of interest, activities and emotions; a lack of socio-emotional reciprocity as shown by impaired or deviant responses to other people's emotions; or a lack of modulation of behaviour according to social context; or a weak integration of social, emotional and communicative behaviours.

---

[3] Terry S Brugha et al, 'Autism, Study Findings from T S Brugha et al; to Broaden the Understanding of Autism, [2012] Psychology and Psychiatry Journal 363.

[4] World Health Organisation, ICD10, International Classification of Diseases – Tenth Edition.

Additionally, there are overarching themes that link conditions such as Childhood Autism, Disintegrative Disorder, Rett's Syndrome and Pervasive Developmental Disorder – Not Otherwise Specified (PDD-NOS); however, there are noted distinguishing features, which include cognitive ability, the level of adaptive functioning and differences in the range of communication skills.

It is estimated that the prevalence of autism in children is almost 40% per 10,000 and the prevalence of related Autistic Spectrum Conditions is 7% per 10,000. This is a conservative estimate from a 2006 study of a cohort of 56,946 nine to ten year olds in the South Thames area of England.[5]

In such individuals, those previously referred to as having Asperger's Syndrome, it is considered that there is a 'severe and chronic developmental disorder', much like autism and Pervasive Developmental Disorder – Not Otherwise Specified (PDD-NOS), which ties together with these other disorders along a 'continuum referred to as the autism spectrum disorders characterised by marked and enduring impairments within the domains of social interaction, communication, play and imagination, and a restricted range of behaviors or interests'.[6]

The term Asperger's Syndrome – whilst referencing the work of Dr Hans Asperger in which he observed a series of children who displayed deficits in significant and primarily non-verbal, communication skills; levels of motor clumsiness that could not be ascribed to their underlying global level of cognitive functioning; and a failure to develop 'empathy' – was described by Lorna Wing in 1981 as applying to 'some [who are] are over sensitive to criticism, suspicious of other people and a small minority have a history of bizarre anti-social acts perhaps because of their lack of empathy.[7]

Accordingly, Asperger's Syndrome was only relatively recently included within the respective diagnostic manuals of the International Classification

---

[5] Gillian Baird et al, 'Prevalence of disorders of the autism spectrum in a population cohort of children in South Thames: the Special Needs and Autism Project [2006] 368 The Lancet 210.
[6] James Mc Partland, Ali Klin, 'Aspergers Syndrome' [2005] (3) Handbook of Autism and Pervasive Development Disorders 88.
[7] Lorna Wing, 'Asperger's Syndrome: a clinical account' [1981](11)(1) Psychological Medicine 115.

of Diseases (ICD)[8] and the Diagnostic and Statistical Manual of Mental Disorders (DSM).[9]

Medical definitions of Asperger's Syndrome have seen a development thereafter, with Tantum later referring to it to as a neurobiological brain-based disorder.[10] It is generally recognised that those with what was described as Asperger's Syndrome, now more commonly referred to as an Autistic Spectrum Condition, display a qualitatively different, and thus impaired, understanding of non-verbal and other social cues, such as facial expressions and the reaction of others, when compared to individuals who would be deemed neuro-typical.

In 2007, Goddard[11] found, in a group of 18-35 year olds with an Autistic Spectrum Condition as against a control group of similar aged participants described as neuro-typical, that those with the diagnosis all had difficulties in social interaction and the understanding of social cues.

> Social problem-solving deficits in adults with Asperger's Syndrome were evident and characterised by deficits in generating detailed and effective solution[s] (...) whilst individuals with Asperger's Syndrome retrieved personal experiences in response to problem solving cues, (they) do not effectively use these experiences in response to problem solving.[12]

The terms 'Theory of Mind' and 'mind blindness' have also been used to describe this phenomenon, in which individuals with Asperger's Syndrome are described as having an inability to perceive other peoples' needs, desires or emotional distress due to their inability to correctly interpret other peoples' behaviour.[13]

---

[8] World Health Organisation, 'International Statistical Classification of Diseases and Related Health Problems' [2010] (10th revision).

[9] American Psychiatric Association, 'Diagnostic and Statistical Manual of Mental Disorders' [2013] (5th edition) APA.

[10] Digby Tantum, 'The challenge of Adolescents and Adults with Asperger's Syndrome' [2003] (1) Child and Adolescent Psychiatry Clinics of North America 143.

[11] Lorna Goddard, Patricia Howlin, Barbara Dritschel, Trishna Pate, 'Autobiographical Memory of Social Problem Solving in Asperger's Syndrome' [2007] 37 Journal of Autism and Developmental Disorders 291–300.

[12] ibid.

[13] Simon Baron-Cohen 'Mind Reading: the interactive Guide to Emotions' [1999] British Journal of Psychiatry 484.

The child with Asperger's Syndrome does not recognise or understand the cues that indicate the thoughts or feelings of the other person at a level expected for someone of that age.[14]

The Criminal Justice System and those with an Autistic Spectrum Condition

Specific Relevance of Criteria to Offending

The growing understanding of both Autistic Spectrum Conditions and the prevalence of Asperger's Syndrome, has led to increasing debate as to the extent by which the underlying diagnostic criteria may protect or predispose an individual to act in a manner that leads to contact with the Criminal Justice System.

Deficient social awareness of salient interpersonal and social constraints on behaviour coupled with the inability of an individual with an Autistic Spectrum Condition to appreciate the feelings and primarily non-verbal cues of others, may result in acts that are viewed as criminogenic.[15] Accordingly, and whilst not at all suggesting that all offending behaviours perpetrated by people with Autistic Spectrum Conditions can therefore be excused as a manifestation of their underlying disorder, it must be recognised that there will be cases where behaviour that, for a neuro-typical individual would be viewed as anti-social or deviant, may be perpetrated in ignorance.

Whether this leads to a defence or an argument as to the lack of the relevant criminal intent, or mens rea, is another debate for another article; however, perpetrators who display a lack of understanding of the underlying offensive nature or characteristics of the offence, undoubtedly raise questions about the validity of some convictions of defendants with behaviours demonstrating autistic tendencies. Indeed, Katz and Zemishalny assert that the inability to 'assess social situations and

---

[14] Tony Attwood, 'Asperger's Syndrome' [2006] (11) (4) Tizard Learning Disability Review 3.
[15] Barbara Haskins, Silva A, 'Asperger's Disorder and Criminal Behaviour: Forensic-Psychiatric Considerations' [2006] Journal of American Academy of Psychiatric Law 374.

appreciate others' point[s] of view may constitute the main cause for offending behaviours'.[16]

Previous studies have suggested that the prevalence of Autistic Spectrum Conditions and Asperger's Syndrome in selected samples of violent offenders is higher than that usually found in the general population. Silva et al reported a particular association between autism spectrum pathology and sexual serial homicidal behaviour.[17]

However, such studies of the prevalence of autism in the criminal justice system have tended to exhibit one or both of two problems: on the one hand, they conflate Asperger's Syndrome and autism as one diagnosis; and on the other hand, they focussed on the restricted population of the highly specialised institutions such as the high security psychiatric hospitals.
Scragg and Shah[18] carried out a study of 392 male patients in Broadmoor Psychiatric Hospital, finding a rate of prevalence for Asperger's Syndrome or autism at a rate of 1.5%. Hare et al,[19] carrying out a study in three English high security hospitals, found in Ashworth that 25.8% had autism; in Broadmoor, the rate was 32.26%; and in Rampton, it was 41.94%. 67% of patients met the criteria of Asperger's Syndrome.

Recent research questions whether Asperger's Syndrome is a risk factor to offending behavior at all. However, what is generally agreed upon is that sexual offences and arson are over-represented in the convictions of those within this client group. David Allen and his colleagues considered this in some detail when carrying out a study utilising quantitative data, with his study involving interviews with adults who had Asperger's Syndrome. They found:

> [V]iolent behaviour and threatening conduct were the most common types of offending, followed by destructive behaviour, drug offences and theft. Specific examples of offending included: (a) Violent assault against a couple with whom the participant had established a superficial relationship.

---

[16] Katz N and Zemishalny Z, 'Criminal Responsibility in Asperger's Syndrome' [2006] Israel Journal of Psychiatry and Relative Science 166.

[17] J Arturo Silva et al, 'A neuropsychiatric developmental model of serial homicidal behaviour' [2004] Behavioural Sciences and the Law 797.

[18] Peter Scragg and Amitta Shah, 'Prevalence of Asperger's Syndrome in a secure hospital' [1994] (5) British Journal of Psychiatry 165.

[19] Dougal Hare et al 'A preliminary study of individuals with autistic spectrum disorders in three special hospitals in England [1999] National Autistic Society at the Centre for Social and Communication Disorders.

The assault occurred after the couple failed to reciprocate further approaches; (b) placing a hidden camera in a stepchild's bedroom to monitor suspected self-harm and underage sexual activities. The participant had not discussed this action with their partner, and was oblivious to the concerns that other might have about his actions. The police became involved when he mentioned the camera to the child's grandparents; (c) sexual assault against children in the extended family. The parents concerned did not wish their children to have to go to court, and so the participant agreed to seek voluntary help as an alternative; (d) assault against a person that the participant thought was dealing drugs in his neighbourhood; (e) acting as an accomplice to another family member committing murder; (f) sending a knife with a red substance on it to a mental health professional and then subsequently being found in the possession of a number of petrol bombs.[20]

Sexual Behaviour

There is little research on the sexuality of adolescents with Autistic Spectrum Condition diagnosis, both in terms of their knowledge and their sexual preferences. However, what is being recognised in the Courts is that whilst sexual offending is a legal construct governed by the Sexual Offences Act 2003, it overlaps but is often not synonymous with the clinical constructs of mental disorders of a sexual nature.

In the case of *R v Thompson*,[21] the defendant had a history of sexual behaviour, most of which had led to convictions. The first accusation that brought him before the court occurred when Thompson was eighteen years old and he was accused of encouraging a six-year-old boy to masturbate him in a graveyard. Three years later, he was again brought before the court; his behaviour involved him rubbing a child's genitals outside of his clothing. Following periods of imprisonment, on release, complaints of sexual offences were again raised whereby young boys described mutual masturbation, him bathing with children and towelling dry thirteen year olds. Other behaviour resulting in criminal convictions involved smacking young boys, and holding their penises whilst drying them. There was also evidence on his computer of searches for underage rent boys in Sri Lanka.

The defendant generally admitted the behaviour; however, he later explained his behaviour stating he masturbated the young boy as he saw

---

[20] David Allen et al 'Offending Behaviour in Adults with Asperger's Syndrome' [2008] 38 Journal of Autism and Developmental Disorder 748.
[21] *R v Thompson* [2014] EWCA Crim 836.

him doing it and he wanted to show him how to do it correctly; 'it wasn't the way my cousin showed me how to do it'. He explained drying the boys to speed up the process. He stated that he was looking up 'rent boys in Sri Lanka' as a computer search, as he was going on holiday in the area, and in light of TV coverage of famous pop stars being arrested for such behaviour, he wanted to find out how to avoid getting into trouble.

Whether this seems fantastical or honest, what is important is that a psychologist and later a psychiatrist described his behaviour as 'rigid, very ordered and mechanical in social relationships. Anxious to maintain the order he had imposed upon his life.' She goes on in the court report to describe him as having a 'lack of emotional understanding which would make him seem at times, callous, selfish because he would be unaware of the impact of his behaviour on others'.

What is interesting about this case is that his first appearance in Court was in 1982, and it was not until 2008, during a parole hearing, that a formal diagnosis of Asperger's Syndrome was raised by the prison consultant clinical psychologist.

In 2012, Thompson was once again before the court charged with historical sexual offences, primarily against young boys. The jury were furnished with evidence relating to the defendant's diagnosis. The jury returned verdicts of not guilty on all counts.

In light of this, a subsequent appeal hearing took place relating to the earlier convictions. It was held that:

> (…) the expert evidence upon which the appellant relied in 2012 was both relevant and of some probative importance (…) The jury in the 2007 trial was very much concerned with the interpretation of the appellant's alleged conduct, partly admitted and partly denied. We cannot conclude the decisions made by the jury in 2007 would undoubtedly have survived their consideration of the new evidence admitted in the appeal. For this reason, we take the view that the verdicts were unsafe and must be quashed.

It is recognised that individuals with an Autistic Spectrum Condition have a propensity for repetitive and ritualised activities, and therefore it is possible that sexual actions could become one of their 'special activities'.[22]

> (What needs to be understood is) that teenagers with Asperger's Syndrome do not process social cues in the same way as neuro-typical peers. They do not understand how to fit sexual urges into the context of interpersonal relationships (…) [W]hen they act in sexually abusive or inappropriate ways, they may be doing so for reasons that are distinctively their own, unlike the pattern of regular juvenile offenders.[23]

However, behaviour that includes near obsessional interests, dismissal of social conventions, a poor ability to decode social gestures and language, and a limited repertoire of appropriate behaviour, is frequently recognised in those diagnosed with an Autistic Spectrum Condition. This may result in inappropriate sexual behaviours such as aggression, excessive self-stimulation, and sexual compulsivity.

There is extensive evidence to suggest that social skills acquisition and generalisation of skills often form the most significant challenges for children and adolescents with high-functioning autism spectrum disorders. It can therefore be expected that, based upon the developmental phenotype described above, adolescents with an Autistic Spectrum Condition who experience major difficulty with social interactions and perhaps a lack of sexual knowledge will often experience impairment in their ability to appropriately interact in the sexual world of adolescence; and as such, inappropriate sexual behaviour may result.

As such, difficulties in non-verbal and verbal communication clearly impair those individuals' abilities to have meaningful social interactions. There is a conspicuous lack of facial expressions or a reduction in the diversity of expressions, limitations in the use of gesture, and difficulties in understanding others' non-verbal cues.[24]

It is further noted that those with Autistic Spectrum Conditions often display difficulties in social circumstances where, as intelligent and often

---

[22] Francis Ray et al 'Challenges to Treating Adolescents with Asperger's Syndrome who are Sexually Abusive' [2010] Sexual Addiction and Compulsivity 270.

[23] ibid 282.

[24] Ali Klin et al, 'Asperger Syndrome' in Fred Volkmar et al (eds) Handbook of Autism and Pervasive Developmental Disorders Diagnosis, Development, Neurobiology and Behaviour (3rd edn, John Wiley & Sons 2005) (3)(1) 88.

high-functioning people, the social expectations are for them to naturally perceive and understand social customs.

The case of *R v Chapman*[25] captures this well. The basic facts of the case are that at the time of the offence, Chapman was a sixteen-year-old adolescent who had attended an eighteenth birthday party with school friends. He and his friends were drinking alcohol and he left with a young girl, with the intention of sharing a taxi home. In the taxi, Chapman offered the young girl money for sex and she declined. The taxi dropped off the girl, but ten minutes later, returned to her house with Chapman. The girl, assuming there was a problem with the taxi, invited Chapman in whilst she telephoned for another. However, at the door, he grabbed her, dragged her to the garden, put his fingers down her throat and sexually assaulted her. A chase ensued, with Chapman running after her in a state of undress and was only stopped when the taxi driver returned and contacted the police.

At Luton Crown Court, he was sentenced to twelve months' imprisonment to be served in a Young Offenders Institution, having pleaded guilty to section 3 of the Sexual Offences Act 2003. This sentence was passed following the submission of a pre-sentence report from the Probation Service and a court ordered medical report from a Consultant Forensic Psychiatrist. Additionally, the defence team had also requested a medical report from another Psychiatrist.

The reports indicated that the defendant's medical history included a diagnosis of Autistic Spectrum Disorder alongside Attention Deficit Hyperactivity Disorder and Developmental Dyspraxia. One of the reports, that from Dr Gralton, the defence funded psychiatrist, noted:

This is a combination of developmental disorders which often cluster together, and cumulatively produce a very significant disability for the person even within this normal IQ range (...) There can be a reduction in some obsessional symptoms but there is evidence of very significant social impairment. By this I mean an inability to understand non-verbal social cues, like facial expressions and body language, as well as the meaning inferred by non-literal communication like vocal intonation. This can mean that a person can misinterpret a variety of verbal and non-verbal communications and can significantly impair everyday social interaction, but is particularly more problematic negotiating the subtleties of more intimate and sexual communication.

---

[25] *R v Chapman* [2010] EWCA Crim 565.

In 2010, the defendant appealed against the sentence on the grounds that it was manifestly excessive and wrong. The appeal notice also noted that as the reports all outlined his mental health difficulties – alongside the pre-sentence report recommending a community disposal – it could be argued that over the eight month period from case management hearing to sentence, the appellant had every expectation of a non-custodial sentence.

On 26th February 2010, the appeal was successful. The sentence was quashed and a community order was imposed. Conditions were attached to the order. These included supervision under the care of a probation officer, alongside a non-residential mental health treatment requirement and a prohibitive activity requirement to stay away from a stated address and to not contact the victim.

The Role of Sex Offender Treatment Programmes

The UK Ministry of Justice has considered the implementation of more than four treatment approaches for those convicted of offences of a sexual nature.[26]

The low intensity Sexual Offender Treatment Programme (hereafter SOTP) has a target population of offenders who are convicted of non-contact sexual offences. This is generally the downloading, making or distributing of images.

The high intensity programme is a specific programme with a target group of adult men who have been convicted of contact or attempted contact offences. The Ministry of Justice indicate that this programme is only suitable for those who accept that they have committed a sexual or sexually motivated offence. Importantly, the programme is not suitable for those who are:

> (…) intellectually disabled, with an IQ of less than 80, or those who are appealing against conviction.[27]

---

[26] Ministry of Justice, 'Freedom of Information Request – information regarding any new Sex Offender Treatment Programmes which are being developed and are scheduled to replace the existing SOTP programmes in the future (2013) found at <https://www.gov.uk/government/uploads/system/uploads/attachment_data/file/25 9044/sex-offender-treatment-programmes.doc> accessed 28th November 2015.
[27] ibid.

There are, however, specialist programmes for those convicted sex offenders who are described as having an intellectual disability. It can therefore be presumed that those people who do not fit into the above criteria – that is, those who do indeed have an IQ below 80 – are recommended for such specialist programmes.

Additionally, there is a suite of SOTPs designed to specifically meet the needs of men with an IQ within the 60 to 80 range, which were fully accredited in 2011.

Where does this leave a person convicted of a sexual offence who has an Autistic Spectrum Condition alongside an IQ that is well over the 80 threshold? Are they to be advised to take part in the high intensity programmes?

As we have stated, it is recognised that despite conviction and despite confession, often the defendant with an Autistic Spectrum Condition does not accept that they have committed a sexually motivated act. The case of *R v Thompson*[28] clearly demonstrated behaviour which matched the sexual offences alongside his confession to the acts. However, he explained his actions in a way that would not be accepted within the confines described for admittance and progress on a sex offender treatment programme.

There is also a further sex offender treatment programme called the Healthy Sex Programme. This involves interventions utilising individual treatment, focussing upon the offenders' sexual interests and fantasies and how to manage them.

Again, this raises a similar dilemma for a participant with an Autistic Spectrum Condition. The case of *R v Jamie Aaron Stewart*[29] describes how the defendant's behaviour may present as difficult if not impossible to manage in such a way. In this case, Mr Stewart was convicted of causing or inciting a child under thirteen to engage in sexual activity. It was held that the conviction was unsafe owing to a number of failings in the Judge's summing up; particularly the lack of reference to the Stewart's Autistic Spectrum Disorder. Briefly, the case involved Stewart being left with a three-year-old boy and the prosecution case was such that he had exposed his penis and invited the boy to touch it. In explaining his actions, Stewart

---

[28] *Thompson* (n 22).
[29] *Chapman* (n 26).

described being concerned for the welfare of the child. He said his brother had been sexually abused and he wanted to educate the boy in 'appropriate and inappropriate sexual touching'.

In light of this case and the consequences of the Court not dealing with the crucial issue of sexual motivation, and the previously described recognised distorted thinking sometimes associated with an Autistic Spectrum Condition, it becomes a challenge to comprehend the appropriateness of programmes focussing upon the offenders' sexual interests and fantasies and how to manage them.

In 2010, the Ministry of Justice's Rehabilitation Services Group of the National Offender Management Service (NOMS) devised targeting criteria that considered the risk, needs and responsivity of offenders. This document instructs Probation Service staff who prepare court reports to accurately place offenders into specific group-work programmes.

It states:

> One of the key focusses of effective intervention is appropriate targeting. An offender is more likely to benefit from participation if he or she demonstrates levels of risk and need that are appropriate for the particular intervention. Offenders who are unsuited in terms of risk and / or need will be less likely to benefit.[30]

Conclusion

It is recognised that some individuals with an Autistic Spectrum Disorder may innocently engage in inappropriate or intrusive behaviours in relationships, in an attempt to develop close interpersonal contact (Stokes and Newton[31]). Others may explain their sexual behavior in a way which does not sit with the criminal definitions within the relevant statute. Likewise, there will be defendants with an Autistic Spectrum Condition who will understand that their sexual behavior is wrong, recognize fantasy thoughts linked with such behavior, and be totally responsive to treatment via sex offender treatment programmes.

---

[30] Ministry of Justice, National Offender Management Service 'Suitability for Accredited Interventions' (Rehabilitation Services 2010).

[31] Mark Stokes, Naomi Newton, Autistic spectrum disorders and stalking [2004] 8(3) Autism 337-339.

Medical diagnosis is now sitting as an uncomfortable bed-fellow with criminal law and sentencing in such cases. Examples have been provided in this chapter where, on appeal, such sentences have been quashed in light of new information regarding the diagnosis of an Autistic Spectrum Condition. Nevertheless, such evidence remains missing form cases such as the provided case of Stewart, which was before the court as recently as December 2015.

It is our understanding that sex offender treatment programmes may face challenges for participants with Autistic Spectrum Conditions and may benefit from including 'training specifically concentrating upon social skills that are designed for those with Asperger's Syndrome, Autistic Spectrum Conditions and related PDD syndromes', suggested as early as 1995 by Klin and Volkmar.[32]

---

[32] Ali Klin, Fred Volkmar, Asperger's Syndrome: Guidelines for treatment and intervention (Learning Disabilities Association of America 2005).

CHAPTER FIFTEEN

CONSENT, COMPULSION AND SEX OFFENDERS: AN ETHICAL AND RIGHTS BASED APPROACH TO THE TREATMENT AND MANAGEMENT OF SEX OFFENDERS

KAREN HARRISON AND BERNADETTE RAINEY

Introduction

The treatment and management of sex offenders is an area of penal law and policy that encompasses the use of compulsion to control and manage risk, whilst recognising the principles of consent and dignity with regard to the individual. This chapter will focus on the legal frameworks in place, using a rights based approach to examine compulsion and consent in the treatment and management of those who sexually offend.[1] The political discourse on sexual offending has focused on public protection, and the need to control offenders both, through draconian sentencing regimes and greater control through management in the community. The prescription of sexual offending as a medical issue[2] has led to different treatment options which can include pharmacotherapy, more commonly known as chemical castration. When an offender is released back into the community, there

---

[1] Some practitioners working to prevent recidivism prefer the term 'those who sexually offend' to 'sex offender' in order to avoid labeling that may have a negative impact on the offender with regard to positive outcomes for offender programmes. However, this chapter will use the term sex offender as the term in common parlance at present.

[2] Karen Harrison, Kieran McCartan and Rachel Manning, 'Paedophilia: definitions and aetiology' in Karen Harrison (ed), *Managing High-Risk Sex Offenders in the Community* (Willan Publishing 2010).

are numerous measures to reduce recidivism. This chapter will examine the treatment and management of sex offenders in two areas: the use of drugs such as libidinal suppressants as a treatment option, and measures taken to manage offenders who are in the community. The focus will be on the legal regulation in England and Wales against the background of European Human Rights law, although some reference will be made to the approach in the United States (US). The chapter will take a rights based approach to the issue of compulsion in treatment and management, and will examine the debate over the nature of consent to treatment. A rights based approach in the United Kingdom (UK) must be cast against an increasingly political and media-led animosity towards rights, with the UK government planning to repeal the Human Rights Act 1998 and replace it with a British Bill of Rights that emphasises responsibilities as well as rights. [3] The government has used the development of rights for the 'undeserving' such as offenders, as a reason for limiting rights protection. This development is alongside the public protection agenda. However, at the same time, professionals in the area of sex offender treatment are attempting to move towards a model of intervention that is inclusive and respectful of the offender's dignity, using language familiar to human rights lawyers. [4] The language of rights and risk, of dignity and dangerousness are not mutually exclusive and thus the chapter will examine tensions between these policy objectives.

Sexual Offending, Risk and Rights

Although interpreting trends in the volume of sexual offences that are recorded can be difficult, [5] the number of reported sexual offences in

---

[3] Conservative Party 'The Conservative's Proposals for Changing Britain's Human Rights Laws' <https://www.conservatives.com/~/media/files/downloadable%20Files/human_rights.pdf> accessed 24 July 2015. See also The Guardian 'Michael Gove to proceed with Tory plans to scrap the Human Rights Act' <http://www.theguardian.com/politics/2015/may/10/michael-gove-to-proceed-with-tories-plans-to-scrap-human-rights-act> accessed 24 July 2015.

[4] See Tony Ward and Gwenda Willis, 'Ethical Issues in Sex Offender Research' in Karen Harrison and Bernadette Rainey (eds), *The Wiley-Blackwell Handbook of Legal and Ethical Aspects of Sex Offender Treatment and Management* (Wiley-Blackwell 2013).

[5] Levels of recorded sexual crimes are usually relatively low compared to other crimes. However, figures may have increased due to recent changes in methods of recording and an increased willingness from victims to report offences, in the light

England and Wales has increased and there has been a rise in the number of convicted prisoners in the prison population.[6] The public debate on sex offending often portrays a person who is seen by society as a 'folk devil',[7] labeled as undeserving of the legal protections given to other offenders and society as a whole.[8] Penal policy has shifted from welfarism to public protection[9] and successive UK governments have maintained this policy.[10] The public protection agenda means the focus has shifted from a subjective view of the offender who can be transformed,[11] to a dehumanising view of dangerousness and risk. Beck[12] argues that risk has

---

of historical abuse inquiries in the UK. See Office for National Statistics (ONS) Crime in England and Wales, year ending March 2015 <http://www.ons.gov.uk/ons/rel/crime-stats/crime-statistics/year-ending-march-2015/stb-crime-march-2015.html#tab-Sexual-offences> accessed 4 September 2015.

[6] The number of recorded sexual offences has risen from just under 60,000 in 2002/03 to just under 90,000 in 2014/15. Office for National Statistics (ONS) Crime in England and Wales, year ending March 2015 <http://www.ons.gov.uk/ons/rel/crime-stats/crime-statistics/year-ending-march-2015/stb-crime-march-2015.html#tab-Sexual-offences> accessed 4 September 2015. At the end of June 2015, there were 11,490 sentenced sex offenders in the prison population, which is 10% higher than June 2014, and 33% higher when compared to June 2010. See Ministry of Justice Statistical Bulletin, Offender Management Statistics, England and Wales, Quarterly, January to March 2015, 30th July 2015 <https://www.gov.uk/government/uploads/system/uploads/attachment_data/file/449528/offender-management-statistics-bulletin-jan-mar-2015.pdf > accessed 4 September 2015.

[7] Hazel Kemshall and Gill McIvor, 'Sex offenders: policy and legislative developments' in Hazel Kemshall and Gill McIvor (eds), *Managing Sex Offender Risk* (Jessica Kingsley Publishers 2004).

[8] Peter Brown, 'Castrate 'em!': Treatments, Cures and Ethical Considerations in the UK Press Coverage of 'Chemical Castration' in Karen Harrison and Bernadette Rainey (eds), *The Wiley-Blackwell Handbook of Legal and Ethical Aspects of Sex Offender Treatment and Management* (Wiley-Blackwell 2013).

[9] David Garland, 'The culture of high crime societies, Some preconditions of recent law and order policies' (2000) British Journal of Criminology 347.

[10] Hazel Kemshall, *Understanding the Community Management of High Risk Offenders* (Open University Press 2008); Karen Harrison and Bernadette Rainey, 'Suppressing human rights? A rights-based approach to the use of pharmacotherapy with sex offenders' (2009) Legal Studies 29 (1) 47, 51-53; See also government statements on the need to allow review of sex offender registration, see text to (n 171).

[11] Garland (n 9).

[12] Ulrich Beck, *World at Risk* (Polity Press 2007).

become the predominant rationale of governmental policy in the modern era. The idea of a 'risk society' has led to a 'precautionary logic'[13] that has impacted on regulatory regimes. [14] However, the concept of risk is malleable, complex and value laden.[15] Risk can be interpreted against the cultural norms of the political, social and legal context in which it is used, leading to different interpretations between practitioners, policy makers and lawyers.[16]

This risk penology is in contrast to a rights based approach. Traditional human rights discourse has been based on the principle of human dignity, where rights are applicable to all, 'no matter how unpopular or unworthy she may be.' [18] The application of this concept is more akin to the welfarism approach[19] where the focus was on the transformation of the offender, but with additional protections that mean any attempt at transformation should be rooted in the principle of human dignity. [20] Human dignity can provide a foundational value for ethical practice as well as legal regulation.[21] In this way, it can go further than practitioner codes of practice by filling in gaps caused by 'ethical blindness' where research or treatment issues are not covered by a professional code. [22] Human dignity is also the central principle of human rights law. The principle flows from the Kantian categorical imperative, which states that no person may be used as a means to an end.[23] The Kantian approach has been developed by modern jurisprudence with a focus on human agency and rationality.[24]

---

[13] Bill Hebenton and Toby Seddon, 'From dangerousness to precaution: managing sexual and violent offenders in an insecure and uncertain age' (2009) British Journal of Criminology 49(3) 343.

[14] Jenny Steele, *Risks and Legal Theory* (Hart Publishing), see also Richard V Ericson, *Crime in An Insecure World* (Polity Press 2007).

[15] Mary Douglas, *Risk and Blame: Essays in Cultural Theory* (Routledge 1992).

[16] Kemshall (n 10).

[18] *R (Adam and others) v Secretary of State for the Home Department* [2005] UKHL 66, [76] (Lady Hale).

[19] See discussion on shift from welfarism to risk, text to (n 8).

[20] Ward and Willis (n 4).

[21] ibid 100.

[22] ibid 98.

[23] Immanuel Kant, *Grounding for the Metaphysics of Morals* (James W Ellington, ,Hackett Publishing 1981); Christopher McCrudden, 'Human dignity and judicial interpretation of human rights' (2008) European Journal of International Law 19(4) 655.

[24] Alan Gerwith, *Reason and Morality* (University of Chicago Press 1978).

As a legal concept, dignity has been described as one of the principles of adjudication for the application of human rights law[25] and the right to human dignity is explicit in international human rights instruments and several domestic constitutional documents.[26] However, dignity as a legal concept is difficult to apply in legal decision-making given its malleable nature.[27] Like risk, dignity is open to cultural interpretation.[28] McCrudden notes that dignity can be divergent in different legal cultures. However, he argues that there is a minimum core of universal meaning[29] that can be applied. Legal regulation should reflect this minimum core and reflect 'an expression of something that gives particular point and poignancy to the human condition'.[30] However, as noted, dignity can be applied differently dependent on the circumstances and Feldman has differentiated two different forms of dignity applicable to legal issues.[31] Subjective dignity focuses on the autonomy and self-determination of the individual. The importance of autonomy is highlighted in medical law cases with the need for free and informed consent.[32] However, objective dignity recognises the need to protect the dignity of humanity as a collective. This would justify limitations on individual autonomy. The 'dwarf tossing' case in France is often cited as an example of the restriction of autonomy for the protection of objective dignity. Even though the participants seemed to consent, the French Court still found that individual consent did not legitimise

---

[25] Conor Gearty, *Principles of Human Rights Adjudication* (Oxford University Press 2004).

[26] See Bernadette Rainey, 'Dignity and Dangerousness: sex offenders and the community-human rights in the balance? The use of pharmacotherapy with high risk sex offenders' in Karen Harrison (ed), *Managing High Risk Sex Offenders in the Community* (Willan Publishing 2010); See also Bernadette Rainey, 'Human Rights and Sexual Offenders' in Karen Harrison and Bernadette Rainey (eds), *The Wiley-Blackwell Handbook of Legal and Ethical Aspects of Sex Offender Treatment and Management* (Wiley-Blackwell 2013).

[27] David Feldman, 'Human Dignity as a Legal Value: Part 1' (1999) Public Law, Winter 682.

[28] Jack Donnelly, *Universal Human Rights in Theory and Practice* (2nd edn, Cornell University Press 2003).

[29] According to McCrudden, the three core elements are the recognition of the intrinsic worth of every human being, that this intrinsic worth is recognised and respected by others, and that the state should recognise and exist for the sake of individual worth McCrudden (n 23) 679.

[30] David Feldman (n 27); David Feldman, 'Human Dignity as a Legal Value: Part 2' (2000) Public Law, Spring: 61.

[31] ibid.

[32] See text to (n 104).

behaviour that undermined the dignity of human beings.[33] The vitiation of consent by a Court has implications for sex offender treatment.[34]

The concepts of risk and rights premised on dignity have similarities in that they are both culturally contingent and open to various interpretations.[35] The assessment of risk has led to the development of risk assessment tools in order to differentiate and manage risk. Different tools have been used including clinical assessment tools based on the individual and actuarial risks assessment focusing on the context and statistical data. [36] The problem with actuarial measurement is the removal of individual characteristics from the measurement, objectifying the offender and violating the Kantian notion of dignity. A combination of these methods has developed into dynamic risk assessment, which is arguably more effective, but difficulties remain as to who is a high-risk offender.[37] The uncertainties surrounding the measurement of risk in a penal system are concerning to rights advocates as risk penology has arguably moved the treatment and management of offenders away from rational notions of proportionate punishment.[38] Proportionate punishment is the measurement for rights protection under the European Convention on Human Rights (ECHR). The European Court of Human Rights (ECtHR) has not attempted to define the notions of dignity or risk. However, it has increasingly used human dignity within its judgments to justify its decision-making. In the *Pretty* case,[39] the ECtHR noted that the meaning

---

[33] David Feldman (n 30).

[34] See reference to surgical castration, text to (n 110).

[35] See Murphy and Whitty who argue that traditionally, criminologists examining risk have left rights discourse to expert lawyers, whilst lawyers have been reluctant to engage in risk analysis as risk is seen as a scientific inquiry, However, they argue that both risk and rights discourse operate in 'different institutional and cultural settings.' Therese Murphy and Noel Whitty, 'Risk and human rights in UK prison governance' (2007) British Journal of Criminology 47(5); See also Rainey (n 26) 19.

[36] Don Grubin et al, 'A Convergent approach to sex offender risk management' in Karen Harrison and Bernadette Rainey (eds), *The Wiley-Blackwell Handbook of Legal and Ethical Aspects of Sex Offender Treatment and Management* (Wiley-Blackwell 2013).

[37] Hazel Kemshall, *Understanding Risk in Criminal Justice* (Open University Press 2003).

[38] Andrew Von Hirsch, *Past or Future Crimes: Deservedness and Dangerousness in the Sentencing of Criminals* (Manchester University Press 1985).

[39] *Pretty v UK* (2002) 35 EHHR 1.

of private life under Article 8 ECHR encompasses respect for human dignity.[40]

It is argued that a rights based approach to the treatment and management of sex offenders should be premised on human dignity, whilst acknowledging the risk of harm and the undermining of the dignity of potential victims. Human Rights law allows permissible limitations to rights that may be premised on risk. However, permissibility depends upon the nature of the right concerned and the state's justifications for limiting rights. The right not to be ill-treated under Article 3 is an absolute right. Once the ECtHR has decided that the ill treatment reaches a threshold of severity to engage Article 3, no limitation on the protection given by Article 3 is permitted. Article 3 applies to all, irrespective of the risk posed by the offender [41] as severe ill-treatment by its nature undermines human dignity. It could be argued that this encompasses both the subjective dignity of the individual and the importance of maintaining the dignity of humanity as a collective. However, under qualified rights such as the right to family and private life under Article 8 ECHR, a balancing exercise between risk and rights may take place. An interference with the rights guaranteed by Article 8 can be justified by the state on grounds such as public good and criminal law, as long as any state measure is in accordance with law and necessary in a democratic society. The measure has to be proportionate to the legitimate aim.[42] It should also be noted that risk can also be used to place positive obligations on states to take measures to protect those who may be at risk of harm. A state may be responsible for protecting potential victims of sex offenders if the *Osman* test[43] is met: the state knows or ought to know of a real and immediate risk of serious harm and can take reasonable steps to prevent that harm. The

---

[40] ibid [65] 'The very essence of the Convention is respect for human dignity and human freedom'; See *McDonald v UK* App no 4241/12 (20 May 2014) [47] for a discussion of the importance of dignity to protection from ill treatment under Article 3; See *Bouyid v Belgium* App no 23380/09 (28 September 2015) which explicitly underlines the importance of the protection of human dignity [89].

[41] *Chalal v UK* (1996) ECHR 54 [80]; Bernadette Rainey, Elizabeth Wicks and Clare Ovey, *The European Convention on Human Rights* (6th edn, Oxford University Press 2014) 169–170.

[42] Council of Europe European Convention on Human Rights and Fundamental Freedoms, ETS No.005, Article 8(2) <http://www.echr.coe.int/Documents/Convention_ENG.pdf> accessed 29 August 2015.

[43] As formulated in *Osman v UK* (2000) 29 EHRR 245; for further discussion on positive obligations see Rainey, Wicks and Ovey (n 41) 153-158.

ECtHR has not attempted to define or measure risk but considers whether there is a risk of serious harm on all the evidence available to the Court.[44] Inherent in the balancing act under the qualified rights is the application of the different forms of dignity described by Feldman above.[45] Rights and risk are interrelated and foundational to a rights based discussion of compulsion and consent in sex offender treatment and management.

Compulsion or Consent in Sex Offender Treatment: Pharmacotherapy

As noted, sex offenders elicit more draconian responses than other offenders. Intervention in an attempt to treat sexual deviance has a long history. [46] Intervention can include different cognitive-behavioural programmes[47] and medical interventions using pharmacotherapy such as libidinal suppressants. The use of libidinal suppressants is commonly known as chemical castration, although this is inaccurate as the use of these drugs does not permanently castrate the offender and is normally reversible.[48] Libidinal suppressants are used in order to reduce and in some cases eradicate testosterone levels, leading to a reduction in sexual potency and sperm production. [49] Studies examining the use of libidinal suppressants have been positive in regard to reducing recidivism. [50] However, these studies have also been controversial, with some reviewers questioning the reliability of the data given the absence of double-blind, placebo-controlled studies.[51] Libidinal suppressants are only effective for

---

[44] *Chahal v UK* (1996) ECHR 64.

[45] See text to (n 33).

[46] Phil Fennell, 'Sex Offenders, Consent to treatment and the Politics of Risk' in Karen Harrison and Bernadette Rainey (eds), *The Wiley-Blackwell Handbook of Legal and Ethical Aspects of Sex Offender Treatment and Management*, (Wiley-Blackwell 2013).

[47] Sarah Brown, 'An introduction to sex offender treatment programmes and their risk reduction efficacy' in Karen Harrison (ed), *Managing High-Risk Sex Offenders in the Community* (Willan Publishing 2010).

[48] Harrison and Rainey (n 10) 48.

[49] Jackie Crassati, *Managing High Risk Sex Offenders in the Community: A psychological Approach* (Routledge 2004) 150.

[50] Harrison and Rainey (n 10) 49-50.

[51] Raephaele Basdekis-Jozsa, Daniel Turner and Peer Briken, 'Pharmacological Treatment of Sexual Offenders and its Legal and Ethical Aspects' in K Harrison and B Rainey (eds), *The Wiley-Blackwell Handbook of Legal and Ethical Aspects of Sex Offender Treatment and Management* (Wiley-Blackwell 2013) 308.

certain types of sex offenders,[52] so the use of such treatment without considering the type of offender may cause it to be ineffective.[53] There are also side effects of pharmacotherapy which can be severe. Side effects of MPA (used widely in the USA) and CPA (used in European States) can include thrombosis, osteoporosis, diabetes, weight gain, hypertonus, high cholesterol, gynaecomastia (breast growth), liver damage, depression, fatigue and in some cases permanent infertility.[54] It has been argued by some studies that CPA has fewer side effects than MPA, and that fertility is more likely to return after cessation.[55] The side effects caused by the use of these drugs is relevant to the efficacy of treatment in terms of the best interests of the patient,[56] although this may also include safeguarding the offender from the commission of future offences.[57] Side effects are also relevant to the impact of the rights of the offender. Do the side effects amount to ill-treatment under Article 3 ECHR? Can these be justified under Article 8 ECHR?

Pharmacotherapy: Punishment or Treatment?

There is an ongoing debate as to whether pharmacotherapy and other treatment options are a component of punishment or part of a separate treatment package. If pharmacotherapy is part of a punishment regime, then this has consequences for the ethical position of professionals and legal implications in terms of rights protection. Traditional theories of punishment describe punishment as an intentional state sanction on a person who has violated societal norms by committing a crime, which

---

[52] ibid; it is thought that they will only be effective for those offenders who offend due to sexual desire and have an inability to control this rather than for those who are motivated by power.

[53] ibid 305-307; Harrison and Rainey (n 10) 47.

[54] Basdekis-Jozsa, Turner and Briken (n 51) 303–305; Larry Helm Spalding, 'Florida's 1997 Chemical Castration Law: a return to the Dark Ages' (1998) Florida State University Law Review (25) 117.

[55] Thomas S Davis, 'Cyproterone acetate for male hypersexuality' (1974) International Medical Research 159, as cited in AJ Cooper, 'A placebo-controlled trial of the anti-androgen Cyproterone Acetate in deviant hypersexuality' (1981) Comprehensive Psychiatry 458, 463.

[56] ibid 314. This issue is especially important to medical professionals given the practitioner's Hippocratic oath of 'do no harm'.

[57] Daniel T Wilcox, 'A Forensic Psychologist's Involvement in Working with Sex offenders' in K Harrison and B Rainey (eds), *The Wiley-Blackwell Handbook of Legal and Ethical Aspects of Sex Offender Treatment and Management* (Wiley-Blackwell 2013) 265.

inflicts harm.[58] The aim of punishment may be retributive, focusing on the crime and holding the offender accountable. It encompasses the idea of just deserts; which also means that if the Kantian idea of dignity is being considered, the punishment should be proportionate to the harm caused.[59] Another theory of punishment focuses on deterrence. Unlike retributive punishment, deterrence looks at the impact of punishment on future offending by deterring the offender and potential offenders from future offences. It is consequentialist rather than Kantian, as the focus is on the benefits to society rather than the offender.[60] More inclusive views of punishment have developed, such as the communicative theory of punishment that includes the offender as a moral agent in the process of punishment, leading to reconciliation between the offender and the community.[61] Elements of this theory may be seen in restorative justice programmes[62] and in therapeutic interventions such as the Good Lives Model,[63] which focuses on the offender as an individual. However, rehabilitation is often seen as separate from the imposition of the punishment. Punishment is followed by expiation.[64] This expiation may include pharmacotherapy as a treatment option, separate from the original punishment. A separate treatment regime would also open up the

---

[58] R Anthony Duff, *Punishment, Communication and Community* (Oxford University Press 2001).

[59] Andrew Von Hirsch, *Past of Future Crimes: Deservedness and Dangerousness in the Sentencing of Criminals* (Manchester University Press 1985); Morris J Fish 'Proportionality as a moral principle of punishment' (2008) Oxford Journal of Legal Studies 28(1) 5.

[60] Christopher Bennett, *The Apology Ritual: A Philosophical Theory of Punishment* (Cambridge University Press 2008).

[61] Tony Ward and Chelsea Rose, 'Punishment and Rehabilitation of Sex Offenders: An Ethical Maelstrom' in Karen Harrison and Bernadette Rainey (eds), *The Wiley-Blackwell Handbook of Legal and Ethical Aspects of Sex Offender Treatment and Management* '(Wiley-Blackwell 2013); Tony Ward and Karen Salmon, 'The ethics of punishment: implications for correctional practice' (2009) Aggression and Violent Behaviour 14, 239; Duff (n 58).

[62] Anne-Marie McAlinden, 'Reintegrative and Disintegrative Shaming: Legal and Ethical Aspects' in Karen Harrison and Bernadette Rainey (eds), *The Wiley-Blackwell Handbook of Legal and Ethical Aspects of Sex Offender Treatment and Management* '(Wiley-Blackwell 2013).

[63] Tony Ward and Theresa A Gannon, 'Rehabilitation, etiology and self-regulation: The good lives model of sex offender treatment' (2006) Aggression and Violent Behaviour, 11, 77-94.

[64] John Braithwaite, *Crime, Shame and Reintegration* (1st edn Cambridge University Press 1998); Iain Crow, *Treatment and Rehabilitation of Offenders* (Sage 2003).

possibility of a person who has not committed an offence accessing treatment programmes.[65] Therefore, a question arises as to whether the use of pharmacotherapy in the criminal justice system is part of a punishment package. Glaser[66] argues that interventions within the criminal justice system are, by their nature, part of the punishment regime. Some treatments may cause harm; the aim is public protection; confidentiality may be breached; and there is a lack of consent. Glaser points out that these features of intervention add up to a punishment package. This impacts on the ethics of using such interventions. Glaser argues further that traditional ethical codes for therapy and other interventions are not applicable within the criminal justice system. He argues that practitioners should recognise this and be open with their patients, making sure that human rights are respected within a punishment framework.[67] However, others argue that interventions are separate from the punishment regime. Prescott and Levenson[68] argue that present ethical codes are applicable and that some of the issues addressed by Glaser are already faced by practitioners when giving treatment. When discussing these arguments, Ward and Rose conclude that ethically complex interventions in the criminal justice system contain aspects of both punishment and treatment. This has consequences for ethical practice and practitioners need to be aware of the complex and competing values they must deal with:

> Practitioners are both moral agents with duties to the state and the community, and therapists working side by side with quite damaged individuals in order to help them lead personally more fulfilling, and socially responsible lives.[69]

The lack of clarity as to whether pharmacotherapy is treatment or punishment has legal implications. In the US, the Eighth Amendment[70] is

---

[65] Harrison and Rainey (n 10) 56.

[66] Bill Glaser, 'Distinguishing Moral and Clinical Decisions in Sex Offender Programs: The Good Lives Model and Virtue Ethics' in Karen Harrison and Bernadette Rainey (eds), *The Wiley-Blackwell Handbook of Legal and Ethical Aspects of Sex Offender Treatment and Management* (Wiley-Blackwell 2013); Bill Glaser, 'Sex offender programs: new technology coping with old ethics' (2010) Journal of Sexual Aggression 16, 261.

[67] ibid.

[68] David Prescott and Jill Levenson, 'Sex offender treatment is not punishment' (2010) Journal of Sexual Aggression 16, 275.

[69] Ward and Rose (n 61) 285.

[70] Eighth Amendment of the Constitution of the United States (Bill of Rights 1791) 'Bill of Rights: Primary Documents of American History'. Library of Congress

limited to the prohibition of cruel and unusual punishment. It does not cover treatment. Article 3 of the ECHR proscribes the use of torture, inhuman and degrading *treatment and punishment*.[71] The ECHR does not define treatment or punishment. However, the approach of the ECtHR has been different in cases that clearly involve punishment or treatment.[72] The Court has noted that it is permissible for the state to punish, but only if the punishment is proportionate to the crime. In this way, the Court takes a traditional approach to punishment. However, it has recognised Duff's argument[73] that there should be an element of rehabilitation.[74] Punishment that is so severe it amounts to ill-treatment will be held to be disproportionate by the ECtHR, irrespective of the crime that an offender has been found guilty of committing.[75] However a different approach has been taken to medical treatment based on issues of consent and medical necessity.[76]

Punishment or Treatment: Compulsion or Consent?

As noted above, it can be argued that pharmacotherapy should be part of a treatment package that helps a sex offender to reintegrate into society once punishment has been completed. One of the issues that arise is the nature of consent. In some jurisdictions, compulsion is involved in the sentencing regime as pharmacotherapy is a part of the sentencing process. It is clear, here, that consent is not seen as necessary and that the use of the treatment is more akin to punishment. For example, in some US states that have court ordered treatment, treatment may be given as long as the offender poses a risk of re-offending and pharmacotherapy may be ordered for a

---

<http://www.loc.gov/rr/program/bib/ourdocs/billofrights.html>   accessed   29 August 2015.

[71] Council of Europe European Convention on Human Rights and Fundamental Freedoms, ETS No.005, Article 3 <http://www.echr.coe.int/Documents/Convention_ENG.pdf > accessed 29 August 2015.

[72] See Rainey, Wicks and Ovey (n 41) 172-176.

[73] R Anthony Duff, *Punishment, Communication and Community* (University Press Oxford 2001).

[74] See *Vinter and Others v UK* App no 66069/09 (9 July 2013) [119] where the Court noted that the primary aim of punishment should be rehabilitation and see concurring opinion of Judge Power-Forde who noted that the offender should retain some hope of release.

[75] See for example the controversial case of *Gafgen v Germany* App no 22978/05 (1 June 2010).

[76] See text to (n 80–88).

range of sexual offences where the use of the drugs may not be medically suitable for the offender.[77] The mandated use of pharmacotherapy is not widespread in Europe. However, Poland and Moldova have introduced legislation on compulsory chemical castration and Russia has recently passed legislation on the use of pharmacotherapy.[78] Other European states such as the UK offer pharmacotherapy on a voluntary basis.[79]

In the US, the courts have held that surgical castration does violate the Eighth Amendment,[80] but no case on the use of chemical castration has reached determination in the US Courts. In Europe, there has not been a case at the ECtHR dealing with the compatibility of *compulsory* treatment. However, if a case did come before the ECtHR, it would more than likely be argued under Article 3, which prohibits torture, inhuman and degrading punishment or treatment.[81] The Court's first question would be whether the ill-treatment is severe enough to be at least degrading. Degrading punishment or treatment is an action that 'arouses in the victim feelings of fear, anguish and inferiority capable of humiliation and debasement and possibly breaking physical or moral resistance'.[82] Inhuman punishment or treatment is an act causing severe suffering, whilst torture is an aggravated form of inhuman punishment or treatment.[83] When deciding if an act is at least degrading, the Court will contextualize the situation by examining the age, sex, health and mental and physical effects on the applicant as

---

[77] For example in Florida, the Court may order treatment for any period of time including the life of the offender see Spalding (n 54) 117.

[78] BBC 'Poland castration law takes effect' BBC News (8 June 2010) <http://www.bbc.co.uk/news/10269055> accessed 3 Sept 2015 BBC 'Moldova introduces chemical castration for paedophiles' BBC News (6 March 2012) <http://www.bbc.co.uk/news/world-europe-17278225> accessed 3 Sept 2015; RT 'Russia introduces chemical castration law for paedophiles' RT (4 October 2011) <https://www.rt.com/news/pedophilia-russia-chemical-castration-059/> accessed 3 Sept 2015.

[79] Home Office (2007) 'Review of the Protection of Children for Sex Offenders' (London).

[80] *State v Brown* 326 SE.2d 410, the Supreme Court found that surgical castration is a form of mutilation and so prohibited it as a sentencing option.

[81] Council of Europe European Convention on Human Rights and Fundamental Freedoms, ETS No.005, Article 3 <http://www.echr.coe.int/Documents/Convention_ENG.pdf > accessed 29 August 2015.

[82] *Ireland v UK* (1978) 2 EHRR 25.

[83] ibid.

well as the duration and circumstances of the punishment or treatment.[84] Given this threshold, in a hypothetical application on the use of pharmacotherapy as part of a punishment package, the ECtHR would consider the side effects of the drugs on the offender. The side effects described above are dependent on the types of drugs used. However, any long-term impacts such as feminization may at a minimum be seen as humiliating by the offender.[85] It is likely the side effects as well as the length and duration would go beyond what would be considered proportionate with regard to punishment.

Where the intervention is labeled as treatment, it should be noted that in an English case examining the nature of consent to pharmacotherapy in the Czech Republic, the Court noted that non-consensual treatment using pharmacotherapy would in their view amount to a violation of Article 3.[86] However, case law on the use of non-consensual drug therapy as treatment for patients with a mental disorder has held that even severe side effects may not violate Article 3.[87] Furthermore, the ECtHR stated in *Herczegfalvy*[88] that 'as a general rule a measure which is a therapeutic necessity cannot be regarded as inhuman or degrading'.[89] A question arises as to what would be therapeutically necessary. The Court has not expanded on this, except to state that treatment should be based on established principles of medicine.[90] Given the absolute nature of Article 3, it is argued that it should be narrowly construed and that it should not include non-medical issues such as crime prevention.[91] The use of pharmacotherapy needs to be justified based on medical reasons. In *Dvoracek*,[92] the Court applied the *Herczegfalvy* test for the first time to treatment concerning pharmacotherapy. Even though it found that there was consent in this case, it went on to state that it believed that under the circumstances, the treatment was a therapeutic necessity.[93] However, there

---

[84] ibid.

[85] In *Tyrer v UK* (1979-1980) 2 EHRR 1, [30] the Court found that the effects of the ill treatment did not have to be seen as humiliation by others, but it is enough if humiliation is only in the eyes of the victim.

[86] *Janiga v Czech Republic* [2011] EWHC 533 (Admin).

[87] *Grare v France* (App No. 18835/91).

[88] *Herczegfalvy v Austria* (1992) 15 EHRR 47.

[89] ibid [82].

[90] ibid.

[91] See Harrison and Rainey (n 10).

[92] *Dvoracek v Czech Republic* (2014) App no 12927/13 (6 November 2014).

[93] ibid [92] The ECtHR also found that the 'protective treatment' order by the Court was not punishment

is a lack of detail or clarity in the judgment on this point. The Court found there was necessity based on the fact that medical opinion demonstrated that it was the best treatment for the applicant in the circumstances as alternative treatment would be longer *and* may not prevent reoffending.[94] However, it is arguable that in this case, the need to protect human dignity trumps risk given the importance of protection from ill treatment. Crime prevention should not be part of a test focusing on medical necessity.[95] Both *Herczegfalvy* and *Dvoracek* are concerned with incompetent applicants. Forcible treatment in these circumstances can be justified under mental health legislation based on necessity and the best interests of the patient,[96] although safeguards must be in place and the necessity of consent may not always be removed altogether.[97] As noted in *Janiga,* forcible treatment used on competent persons would be extremely difficult to justify. The ECtHR has applied the *Herczegfalvy* test to competent persons, but in these cases,[98] has found a violation of Article 3. It is suggested that the use of medical necessity in cases involving competent persons should be severely circumscribed by the Court. The Court has noted the need for medical necessity to be convincingly demonstrated,[99] and considering the powerlessness of a person in custody, this is especially important where treatment is mandatory.

Pharmacotherapy may also be a violation of Article 8 on family and private life.[100] As noted above, Article 8 is a qualified right, so any

---

[94] ibid [102].

[95] See criticisms of the possible expansion of 'therapeutic necessity' into crime prevention in Harrison and Rainey (n 10) 66-68; See also Andrew Ashworth, 'Case comment, human rights: Article 3-Article 6' (2007) Criminal Law Review Sept. 717.

[96] See Fennell (n 46) 59–63.

[97] For a discussion concerning restorative justice with sex offenders see Anne-Marie McAlinden; Stephen Hanvey and; Mechtild Höing, 'A More Ethical Way of Working: Circles of Support and Accountability' in Karen Harrison and Bernadette Rainey (eds), *The Wiley-Blackwell Handbook of Legal and Ethical Aspects of Sex Offender Treatment and Management* (Wiley-Blackwell 2013); Anne-Marie McAlinden, *The Shaming of Sex Offenders: Risk, Retribution and Reintegration* (Hart Publishing 2007).

[98] *Jalloh v Germany* (2006) EHRR 721; *Nevmerzhitsky v Ukraine* (2005) ECHR 210.

[99] *DD v Lithuania* App No. 13469/06 (February 14, 2012) [173].

[100] Council of Europe European Convention on Human Rights and Fundamental Freedoms, ETS No.005, Article 8

interference with the private or family life of the offender can be justified by the state under certain circumstances. The punishment or coercive treatment would have to be proportionate to a legitimate aim such as public protection. The greater the side effects, the less likely that punishment would be proportionate. The Court would also examine the procedural safeguards in place.[101] It should also be noted that the impact on the family of the offender would also be taken into account.[102] In a report to the Council of Europe Parliamentary Assembly Committee on Social Affairs, Health and Sustainable Development,[103] the Rapporteur argued that:

> '[C]hemical' castration, when it is coerced (or mandated by law) is a violation of human rights and human dignity, made worse by its inefficacy. The recent legislation mandating 'chemical' castration of certain sex offenders (…) in Poland and Moldova is thus clearly the wrong way to go. As a Parliamentary Assembly committed to human rights, we must work with the parliaments of these countries to repeal these laws now, and should not wait for a ruling of the European Court of Human Rights which may come too late to right the wrong.[104]

However, pharmacotherapy may also be used as treatment on a consensual basis in a criminal justice setting. A question arises as to the validity of consent in this context. The approach of the courts has been based on a medical model. Consent is valid where a person is competent and has the

---

<http://www.echr.coe.int/Documents/Convention_ENG.pdf> accessed 29 August 2015.

[101] Procedural safeguards play an important role in Article 8 case law. If there is a lack of procedural safeguards when a state implements a measure that interferes with Article 8(1), the ECtHR has found that this can be a factor in a finding of a disproportionate interference with an applicant's right, See Rainey, Wicks and Ovey (n 41) 365

[102] *Dickson v UK* (2007) 34 EHRR 21, where it was held that the prohibition on a prisoner using a private IVF clinic was disproportionate. The ECtHR took the impact of the prohibition on his partner into account.

[103] Council of Europe Parliamentary Assembly Report of the Committee on Social Affairs, Health
and Sustainable Development, 'Putting an End to Coerced Sterilisations and Castrations' Rapporteur: Ms Maury Pasquier (Doc 13215) 28 May 2013 <https://www.tbmm.gov.tr/ul_kom/akpm/2013_akpm_genel_kurul/3/Putting%20a n%20end%20to%20coerced%20sterilisations%20and%20castrations.pdf> accessed 10 September 2015.

[104] ibid [44].

capacity to make a decision that is free and fully informed.[105] Consent is a 'transformative concept capable of legitimizing as treatment what might otherwise be viewed as assaults, inhuman or degrading treatment or punishment or breaches of the right to physical integrity'.[106] In English common law, failure to fully inform a patient can lead to a claim for negligence against the professional.[107] At the European level, the Council of Europe has made clear the need for free and informed consent in medical interventions.[108] It has developed guidelines for sex offenders who are offered treatment in prison. The offender should retain the right to refuse treatment, be given information on the side effects of treatment and the consequences of refusal.[109] In several reports on visits to the Czech Republic, the European Committee for the Prevention of Torture (CPT) has been critical of the use of treatments on sex offenders.[110] It noted that

---

[105] Council of Europe Parliamentary Assembly Resolution 1945 (2013) 'Putting an End to Coerced Sterilisations and Castrations'
<http://assembly.coe.int/nw/xml/XRef/X2H-Xref-ViewPDF.asp?FileID=19984&lang=en> accessed 10 September 2015.
[106] Fennell (n 46) 59.
[107] *Chatteron v Gerson* [1981] 1 QB 432; *Sidaway v Board of Governors of the Bethlem Royal Hos*pital [1985] 1 All ER 643.
[108] Council of Europe Convention for the Protection of Human Rights and the Dignity of the Human being, with regard to the application of Biology and Medicine 1997 article 6, states: An intervention in the health field may only be carried out after the person concerned has given free and informed consent to it. The person shall beforehand be given appropriate information as to the purpose and nature of the intervention as well as on its consequences and risks. The person concerned may freely withdraw consent at any time.
<http://conventions.coe.int/Treaty/en/Treaties/Html/164.htm>   accessed   10 September 2015.
[109] Council of Europe European Committee on Crime Problems. The State of Work on the Text of a Draft Recommendation on the 'Treatment of Sex Offenders in Penal Institutions and the Community' CDPC-BU (2006) 02 E. See also Council of Europe (2007) Convention on the Protection of Children Against Sexual Exploitation and Sexual Abuse ETS No. 201.
[110] Council of Europe European Committee for the Prevention of Torture and Inhuman and Degrading Treatment 'Report to the Czech Government on the Visit to the Czech Republic of the European Committee for the Prevention of Torture and Inhuman and Degrading Treatment' 27 March – 7 April, 21-24 June 2006 CPT/Inf (2007) 32; Council of Europe, European Committee for the Prevention of Torture and Inhuman and Degrading Treatment Report to the Czech Government on the Visit to the Czech Republic of the European Committee for the Prevention of Torture and Inhuman and Degrading Treatment CPT/inf (2009) 8; Council of Europe European Committee for the Prevention of Torture and Inhuman and

medical interventions on those deprived of their liberty, where the effects are irreversible, should only be given where there was free and informed consent. The CPT concluded that surgical castration should not be used, even where the offender may have consented.[111] When commenting on the use of libidinal suppressants, it concluded proper procedures were not in place to ensure free and informed consent.[112] In 2015, the CPT reiterated its opinion from the 2009 report, emphasising that the use of pharmacotherapy:

> (...) should be based on a thorough individual psychiatric and medical assessment and that such medications should be given on a purely voluntary basis (...) the patient should be fully informed of all the potential effects and side effects.[113]

However, the validity of consent has been questioned where the offender may be offered early release if he/she consents to a treatment programme, or an offender may have the length of their incarceration increased for failure to consent to such programmes.[114] Miller argues that the 'fact the offender is incarcerated at the time of consent and that such consent would bring about release factors (...) do not render voluntary choices impossible.'[115] Others have argued that such consent cannot be valid as the choice between prison and treatment is constrained.[116] A Council of Europe Parliamentary Assembly Resolution[117] noted:

Degrading Treatment Report to the Czech Government on the Visit to the Czech Republic of the European Committee for the Prevention of Torture and Inhuman and Degrading Treatment 1–10 April 2014 CPT/inf (2015) 18.

[111] ibid.

[112] ibid.

[113] ibid CPT/inf (2015) 18 [158].

[114] For example, in the Czech Republic, the length of incarceration may be extended if a prisoner refuses treatment. See *Janiga v Czech Republic* [2011] EWHC 533 (Admin).

[115] Wilbur R Miller, 'Chemical castration of sex offenders: treatment or punishment' in Bruce J Winick and John Q Le Fond (eds), *Protecting Society from Sexually Dangerous Offenders, Law Justice and Therapy* (American Psychological Association 2003) 255.

[116] Harrison and Rainey (n 10) 57; see also William Green, 'Depo-Provera, castration, and the probation of rape offenders: Statutory and constitutional issues' (1986) University of Dayton Law Review 12(1) 1.

[117] Council of Europe Parliamentary Assembly Resolution 1945 (2013) 'Putting an End to Coerced Sterilisations and Castrations'
<http://assembly.coe.int/nw/xml/XRef/X2H-Xref-ViewPDF.asp?FileID=19984&lang=en> accessed 10 September 2015.

The concept of 'coercion' is currently evolving in human rights law, based on the definition of the lack of free and informed consent. Thus, even where consent is ostensibly given – also in written form – it can be invalid if the victim has been misinformed, intimidated or manipulated with financial or other incentives. New concepts of 'emotionally coerced sterilisation' and 'pressure that diminishes a patient's autonomy' are currently emerging. Some of these concepts go as far as considering as coercion the lack of freedom from any bias introduced, consciously or unconsciously, by health-care providers, and power imbalances in the patient–care provider relationship which may impede the exercise of free decision making.[118]

Despite this statement and the CPT's opinion that consent given to interventions that cause irreversible harm should not be 'directly or indirectly given under duress',[119] the idea of conditional consent has been accepted in litigation. The premise that the offender still consents freely even though that consent is given to achieve prison release reflects the theory of responsibilisation. Offenders are expected to play a role in their rehabilitation in return for greater freedom:

Individuals – theoretically in return for greater individual freedom and reduced regulation – are expected to a large extent to 'manage their own risks' by both refraining from criminal behavior and protecting themselves against crime.[120]

As Fennell[121] notes, consent in medical law protects the integrity and autonomy of the patient, whereas in relation to those in the criminal justice

---

[118] ibid [2]. This reflects case law of the ECtHR involving the sterilisation of Roma women when giving birth, The Court in these cases has found that the consent obtained was not valid given the circumstances under which it was obtained (for example; in the course of childbirth, in a language that was not familiar to the applicants, and with no explanation of the procedures). See, for example, *VC v Slovakia* App. No. 18968/07, Dec (16 June 2009).

[119] Council of Europe European Committee for the Prevention of Torture and Inhuman and Degrading Treatment Report to the Czech Government on the visit to the Czech Republic of the European Committee for the Prevention of Torture and Inhuman and Degrading Treatment 27 March – 7 April, 21-24 June 2006 CPT/Inf (2007) 32 [109].

[120] Hazel Kemshall and Jonathan M Maguire, 'Sex offenders, risk penalty and the problem of disclosure in the community' in Amanda Matravers (ed), *Sex Offenders in the Community, Managing and Reducing the Risks* (Willan Publishing 2003) 107. In mental health parlance, this can also be referred to as compliance with treatment or possession of 'insight'. See Fennell (n 46) 41.

[121] Fennell (n 46) 59.

system, it is 'a sign, a token of good faith, that the person is taking responsibility for managing their own risk by complying with prescribed treatment'.[122] In the English Courts, conditional consent has been accepted as valid. In *Freeman*,[123] the Court of Appeal found that incarceration does not negate the prisoner's consent. However, it is a question of fact, not law. The Court must consider the circumstances to be sure the consent is real. In *Re (SH)*,[124] the applicant was under a conditional discharge from a hospital order. One of the conditions of the discharge was compliance with taking prescribed medication. SH argued that this amounted to compulsion and so invalidated his consent. The Court found that SH still retained the choice as to whether he took the medication. Any pressure on SH came from the conditional discharge and not from the condition requiring treatment. Refusal to take medication would not in itself lead to recall. His will 'had not been overborne'.[125] Despite safeguards being in place concerning recall from a conditional discharge,[126] Fennell argues that the fact that refusal may lead to recall means the right to refuse treatment in such cases is 'illusory'.[127]

In *Janiga*,[128] the appellant argued that his consent was illusory. Janiga was appealing against a decision to extradite him to the Czech Republic under a European Arrest Warrant. He had been convicted of serious sexual offences and sentenced to prison as well as preventative sexual treatment in a hospital. Libidinal suppressants were available as part of the treatment, although it could only be given with consent. Janiga argued that there was a real risk that consent would not be valid. He relied on the CPT reports, which were critical of the system.[129] It was noted that all but one patient in the wards visited by the CPT had undergone pharmacotherapy.

---

[122] It has been argued that an offender taking responsibility for treatment that prevents further offending may enhance his/her autonomy; see Tom Douglas et al, 'Coercion, Incarceration and Chemical Castration: An argument from autonomy' (2013) Bioethical Inquiry 10, 393.

[123] *Freeman v Home Office No 2* (1984) QB 524.

[124] *R (SH) v Mental Health Review Tribunal* (2007) EWHC 884 (Admin).

[125] ibid [35] (Holman J); See also *R(MM) v Secretary of State for the Home Department* [2007] EWCA Civ 687.

[126] Ministry of Justice (2009) 'Guidance on Recall of Conditionally Discharged Restricted Patients' (Ministry of Justice). Safeguards include a requirement for medical evidence and procedural safeguards once recalled including a review of detention.

[127] Fennell (n 46) 57.

[128] *Janiga* [2011] EWHC 553 (Admin).

[129] See CPT reports, text to (n 110.)

If a patient refuses treatment, then a court may prolong the original sentence.[130] However, the Court found that despite the CPT's criticisms, the appellant's consent could still be valid. It also noted that there is domestic court supervision of the regime, which can be entrusted to protect the appellant's rights concerning treatment.[131] The Court in *Janiga* followed the reasoning of previous cases such as *R (SH)*. It accepted that conditional consent can still be consent. However, as noted,[132] *Freeman* found that consent is a question of fact and the Court should be cognisant of the circumstances that may invalidate consent. It could be argued that the Court in *Janiga* gave a lack of consideration to the numbers of patients undergoing pharmacotherapy under hospital orders, and may have been reluctant to interfere in the Czech Republic's chosen methods for treatment and public protection. In the first case to come before the ECtHR concerning the use of pharmacotherapy, the ECtHR was also asked to examine the system for protective treatment in the Czech Republic. In *Dvoracek*,[133] the applicant argued that the anti-androgen treatment he had been taking was given without valid consent and that 'one cannot talk about a free and informed consent in a situation where the choice takes place only between a medical intervention and unlimited detention'.[134] However, the Court, whilst acknowledging the difficult decision that the applicant had to make given the pressure he may have been under, still found that the consent was valid. It noted that he was able to withdraw from the treatment and alternatives were offered. The Court agreed with the CPT report on the Czech Republic that there was a lack of procedural safeguards in place and a written form for consent with information was recommended.[135] However the absence of these safeguards was not enough to amount to degrading treatment under Article 3. The outcome is not surprising given the previous case law on conditional consent in domestic law. However, it can be criticised for underplaying the concerns of the CPT, a Council of Europe body working within the human rights framework. It should also be noted that on a practical level, conditional consent may be detrimental if it undermines the motivation of an offender to engage with a treatment package and so undermining the desired outcomes of public protection.[136]

---

[130] *Janiga* (n 128) [7].

[131] ibid [21].

[132] text to (n 122)

[133] *Dvoracek v Czech Republic* App No 12927/13 (6 Dec 2014).

[134] ibid [78].

[135] ibid [104].

[136] Harrison and Rainey (n 10) 57–58.

It is clear that consent in sex offender treatment is complicated by the use of treatment in a criminal justice setting. Fennell[137] argues that over time, treatment and punishment models have converged to create a regime where consent is being used to transform control into treatment underlined by the politics of risk. Fennell argues that 'treatment and consent play key roles in the developing apparatus of risk management which over 30 years has brought about a near merger of the penal and psychiatric systems'.[138] The initial case law before the ECtHR appears to demonstrate evidence of this and suggests deference to institutional systems for treating sex offenders. What is medically necessary has not been fully explored by the Court but it is clear it is adopting objective dignity in accepting treatment as therapeutically necessary. However, the Court should not lose sight of its supervisory function and its role in upholding the absoluteness of protection against serious ill treatment, regardless of the status of the applicant.[139] Necessity should be narrowly construed.

It is argued that the separation of treatment and punishment is the appropriate structure for the criminal justice regime in order to facilitate a rights based approach. A clear legal delineation may make it easier for practitioners working under their own ethical codes. Clear legal guidelines should be in place. An effective rights based approach would include accessible procedures for giving and withdrawing consent, clear understanding of the benefits and side effects of treatment, an independent body to review treatments being used, a timetable for the length of treatment and guidelines on suitability of offenders for a treatment programme. There is also an issue surrounding the efficacy of detaining an offender who is high risk without having a proper treatment plan in place. It may be that a state has a positive obligation to provide treatment if an offender asks for it in the knowledge that he/she may reoffend without it, or may have to access it in order to prove that he/she no longer poses a risk and so can be released. In England and Wales, the Supreme Court noted that a failure to provide programmes that allow an offender to demonstrate that he/she is no longer a risk may violate Article 5 of the ECHR.[140] In the

---

[137] Fennell (n 46).

[138] ibid 59.

[139] For discussion on the supervisory function of the ECtHR, see Rainey, Wicks and Ovey (n 41) 21-54.

[140] Article 5 ECHR prohibits the arbitrary deprivation of liberty. See *Wells v Secretary of State for Justice (Parole Board Intervening)* [2009] UKHL 22; See also *James, Wells and Lee v UK* App no 25119/09 (18 September 2012) where the

US, civil commitment[141] in Minnesota has been found to be unlawful where there was a failure to provide treatment programmes for those committed after serving a prison sentence.[142] In both situations, the Courts were concerned about the lack of procedural protections for offenders. The US court noted the civil commitment of elderly, intellectually disabled and juvenile offenders with no appropriate treatment programmes or clear guidelines.[143] This undermined the efficacy of practitioner's work and the rights of the offender, with no clear evidence that risk has been measured appropriately or that public protection has been enhanced. The Minnesota Court observed that:

> [I]n light of the current state of Minnesota's sex offender civil commitment scheme, it is not only the 'moral credibility of the criminal justice system' that is at stake today, but the credibility of the entire system, including all stakeholders that work within the system, and those affected by the system, not forgetting those who have been convicted of sex crimes, their victims, and the families of both.[144]

Controlling and Managing Sex Offenders in the Community

There are a number of measures to control and manage offenders in the community, usually after a conviction for a sexual offence. These control measures include registration, disclosure, sexual harm prevention orders,[145] sexual risk orders,[146] the use of polygraphs[147] and various community measures for those with a recognised mental disorder who

---

ECtHR found the lack of access to treatment programmes was a violation of article 5.

[141] For an analysis of civil commitment in the US, see, for example, Rebecca L Jackson and Christmas N Covell, 'Sex Offender Civil Commitment' in Karen Harrison and Bernadette Rainey (eds), *The Wiley-Blackwell Handbook of Legal and Ethical Aspects of Sex Offender Treatment and Management* (Wiley-Blackwell 2013).

[142] *Karsjens v Jesson* US District Court CASE 0:11-cv-03659-DWF-JJK, 17 June 2015, for links to case see <https://www.aclu.org/news/federal-district-court-finds-minnesotas-sex-offenders-program-unconstitutional> accessed 5 August 2015.

[143] ibid, conclusion.

[144] ibid, conclusion.

[145] Sexual Offences Act 2003 c.42, s 103A.

[146] ibid s 122A.

[147] See Daniel T Wilcox, 'Ethical Practice and the Use of the Polygraph in Working with Sex Offenders' in Karen Harrison and Bernadette Rainey (eds), *The Wiley-Blackwell Handbook of Legal and Ethical Aspects of Sex Offender Treatment and Management* (Wiley-Blackwell 2013).

have been conditionally discharged from a hospital setting.[148] As noted, the development of these measures has been driven by risk penology and preventative governance.[149] McAlinden[150] argues that these measures amount to disintegrative shaming which sets out to restrain and control a sex offender with little regard for the reintegration of the offender into society or for the appropriate balancing of rights. Two of these measures will be examined: sex offender notification requirements, and the disclosure of information to the public. The focus will be on the law in England and Wales, but similar concerns have been raised in other jurisdictions.[151]

Sex Offender Registration: Notification
Requirements in England and Wales

Sex offender registration in England and Wales was introduced in 1997[152] and was modeled to some degree on similar registration schemes in the US.[153] The legislation meant that all offenders who had been convicted or cautioned for a listed sexual offence or found not guilty by reason of insanity had to submit their details to the police. The relevant sexual offences were listed in Schedule One of the Act. The register is now governed by the Sexual Offences Act 2003[154] and is known as the violent and sex offenders register (ViSOR). Trigger offences are found under Schedule 3 of the Act. ViSOR is held on a national police database. Within three days of conviction, the offender must provide the authorities with his/her name; home address and any other address where he/she resides; date of birth; National Insurance number; and, any other

---

[148] For an account of the restrictions put in place after discharge see Fennell (n 46)

[149] Adam Crawford, 'Contractual governance of deviant behaviour' (2003) Journal of Law and Society 30, 479.

[150] McAlinden (n 62); See also McAlinden (97).

[151] Terry Thomas, *The Registration and Monitoring of Sex Offenders: A Comparative Study* (Routledge 2011); for an example of the Scottish approach, see Peter W Ferguson, 'Sex Offender Registration' Scots Law Times (2012) 20, 121.

[152] Sex Offenders Act 1997 c.51

[153] Terry Thomas (n 151); See also Terry Thomas, 'Sex Offender Registration in the United States and the United Kingdom: Emerging Legal and Ethical Debates' in Karen Harrison and Bernadette Rainey (eds), *The Wiley-Blackwell Handbook of Legal and Ethical Aspects of Sex Offender Treatment and Management* (Wiley-Blackwell 2013) 356.

[154] Sexual Offences Act 2003 (n 145) c 42. Notification requirements have been further modified by The Sexual Offences Act 2003 (Notification Requirements) (England and Wales) Regulations 2012 S.I. No 1876.

prescribed information which is deemed to be relevant. An offender is also photographed and fingerprinted and may have to give notification of foreign travel. Powers of forced entry by police into registered sex offenders' premises exist and the use of polygraphs may also be mandatory.[155] The offender also has a duty to notify the police of any changes to this information within three days. It is a separate criminal offence to either fail to notify the police or provide the police with false information;[156] the onus being on the offender to notify the police. There are different relevant time periods for remaining on the register (notification period).[157] A sliding scale exists which is dependent on the relevant offence and on the time spent in a custodial setting. The scale ranges from an indefinite notification period to seven years.[158] Where the offender is under 18, the notification period is half of the adult equivalent.[159]

Although the notification requirements have become increasingly draconian, both the UK domestic court and the ECtHR have found that they are an administrative tool rather than part of a punishment regime.[160] However, it has been acknowledged that the more draconian notification requirements become, the more likely a court in the future will categorise registration as punitive.[161] The predominance of risk and control raises a question about the compatibility of the register with human rights. The main right engaged would be the right to family and private life under Article 8 of the ECHR.[162] As noted above, Article 8 is a qualified right. Even a minor interference with a person's physical or moral integrity will

---

[155] The Offender Management Act 2007 c.21, ss 28-30, where the offender has served a custodial sentence of 12 months or more.

[156] Punishable by up to five years in prison.

[157] Sexual Offences Act 2003 (n 145) s 82.

[158] ibid s 82(1). Where a person has been sentenced to a determinate sentence of 30 months or more, the notification period is indefinite. Where the period in custody is between six months and 30 months, registration is for ten years and where the custodial term was for a term of six months or less the period is for seven years

[159] ibid s 82(2).

[160] *Attorney General's Reference (No 50 of 1997)* [1998] 2 Cr App R (S) 155; *Adamson v United Kingdom* (1999) 28 EHRR CD209.

[161] Home Office/Scottish Executive 2001, 'Consultation Paper on the Review of Part 1 of the Sex Offenders Act 1997' July; See Rainey (n 26).

[162] Council of Europe European Convention on Human Rights and Fundamental Freedoms, ETS No.005, Article 8 <http://www.echr.coe.int/Documents/Convention_ENG.pdf> accessed 29 August 2015.

engage it. The registration requirements clearly do engage Article 8.[163] Therefore the decisive question focuses on the justifications of the state for limiting the right. Any justification has to be in accordance with law, meet a legitimate aim and be necessary in a democratic society. In these circumstances, the measures will have to be proportionate to the aim of public protection. [164]

Several challenges to the notification requirements have reached the Courts. In particular, several cases challenged the indefinite retention of notification requirements with no right to review. In *Re Gallagher*,[165] the applicant used Article 8 to argue that the automatic nature of the register requirements failed to consider the individual circumstances of the claimant and denied him the right to review of his indefinite registration. However, the Court found that 'the gravity of sex offences and the serious harm (…) must weigh heavily in favour of a scheme designed to protect potential victims of such crime'.[166] Individual rights were held to be of secondary importance to risk. It can be argued that the court was 'deferring to parliament and reflecting governmental and public attitudes'.[167] Subsequent case law followed this reasoning.[168] However, in *F and Thompson*,[169] the Supreme Court found that indefinite registration without any chance of review was disproportionate and so incompatible with Article 8. The Court disagreed with *Gallagher* and found that where an offender believes he/she is no longer a risk, in principle he/she should have a chance to establish this. The Court also noted that one of the appellants was a child when he committed the offence. The legislation failed to treat juveniles differently. [170] It noted that it was within the purview of the government as to how a review should be established. In

---

[163] See Thomas (n 153).

[164] Council of Europe European Convention on Human Rights and Fundamental Freedoms, ETS No.005, Article 8(2) <http://www.echr.coe.int/Documents/Convention_ENG.pdf> accessed 29 August 2015.

[165] *Gallagher* [2003] NIQB 26.

[166] ibid [24].

[167] Rainey (n 26).

[168] *Forbes v Secretary of State for Home Department* [2006] 1 WLR 3075; *H v The Queen* [2007] EWCA Crim 2622; *A v Scottish Ministers* [2007] CSOH 189.

[169] *F and Thompson v Secretary of State for Justice* (2009) EWCA Civ 792.

[170] The Court considered the judgment in *S and Marper v UK* (2008) Application No.30562/04, in which the ECtHR criticised the UK for a blanket penal policy that failed to consider children.

response, the government was critical of the judgment[171] but amended the legislation to allow for review.[172] However, the changes reflect the government's desire to prioritise public protection. A review of indefinite detention can be requested by an adult after 15 years, and a juvenile after 8 years.[173] When reviewed by a police officer, the test is one of 'risk of sexual harm'.[174] This has been criticised as vague[175] and there is also no obligation on the reviewer to contact relevant bodies such as MAPPA[176] for further information. The efficacy of the review can be questioned if risk is not sufficiently assessed.

The decision in *F and Thompson* did not interfere with the requirements of the register but requires minimum procedural safeguards and the consideration of the individual. The reluctance of the Court to interfere in the substantive provisions of the register is further demonstrated in *Prothero*[177] where the Court found that requiring notification of the use of credit and debit cards was proportionate under Article 8. Similarly, informal visits by the police to a registered sex offender were held not to violate Article 8.[178] Although the Court accepted that the informal visits may be intrusive, risk alerting neighbours to past offending and refusal may lead to warranted searches,[179] the Court found that the visits furthered the aim of preventing further harm.[180] There was also a question surrounding whether the appellant's consent to police entry was valid. He argued that he only allowed entry as he was concerned about the consequences if he did not. However, like conditional consent above, the Court found the appellant still had a choice whether to refuse entry or not.[181]

---

[171] Theresa May, HC 16 Feb 2011, Vol 523, Col 955, 959.

[172] For details see Rainey (n 26).

[173] Sexual Offences Act 2003 (n 145) s 91B

[174] ibid.

[175] Parliamentary Joint Committee on Human Rights (2012) Draft Sexual Offences Act 2003 (Remedial) Order: second report HL Paper 8/HC 165.

[176] Multi-Agency Public Protection Panels.

[177] *R (on the application of Prothero) v Secretary of State for the Home Department* [2013] EWHC 2830 (Admin).

[178] *R(M) v Chief Constable of Hampshire Constabulary* [2014] EWCA 1651

[179] ibid [19].

[180] ibid [26].

[181] ibid [17].

Disclosure

Following Megan's Law, US states introduced public disclosure schemes. Despite public pressure, the UK has resisted similar schemes.[182] There is no general duty on the police to disclose the whereabouts of registered sex offenders, though there was a discretionary policy in place for several years.[183] In 2008, however, new public disclosure duties were enacted.[184] A new presumption to disclose was introduced, involving child sex offenders who pose a risk of serious harm to particular children.[185] If the named person is considered to be a risk, the police will disclose information on that person. Anyone providing false information, in an attempt to find out whether a neighbour is on the register or who passes on information will be subject to police action. There is thus recognition that disclosure can impact on the rights of the offender by circumscribing information and penalising if this is misused. Such disclosure may also force offenders underground and so undermine the public protection aims of the register.[186] As noted above, the state has a positive obligation to protect under the ECHR if it knows of a credible threat and does not take steps to prevent harm to the offender.[187] The state also has a positive obligation to protect victims and potential victims of a sex offender if there is a real and immediate risk of harm. A victim would have to demonstrate that the threat was immediate and that the supervisory regime in place was not providing effective protection. This may be difficult to prove; especially since the rights of the offender will be part of the analysis.[188]

In legal challenges to public disclosures, the Court has tended to uphold the right to disclose in particular circumstances. However, courts have found that disclosure engages Article 8(1) and must be justified under

---

[182] Terry Thomas, *The Registration and Monitoring of Sex Offenders: A Comparative Study* (Routledge 2011).

[183] Kemshall, (n 10).

[184] Criminal Justice and Immigration Act 2008 c 4, s 140 which created a new s.327A of the Criminal Justice Act 2003.

[185] Criminal Justice Act 2003 c 44, s 327A(3).

[186] McAlinden (n 62) 116.

[187] See text to (n 41). See also H Power, 'Disclosing Information on sex offenders: the human rights obligations' in Amanda Matravers (ed), *Sex Offenders in the Community: Managing and Reducing the Risks* (Willan Publishing 2003)

[188] ibid; Rainey (n 26).

Article 8(2). In *XX*,[189] the Court held that although the scheme allowed for police to seek representations from the offender before disclosure, a failure to do so did not make the scheme unlawful. It also held that the disclosure in this case was proportionate given the aim of public protection. Based on case law, any challenge to a disclosure may lead to careful scrutiny of the necessity of such disclosure. The Court has demonstrated greater vigor when scrutinising disclosures than the compatibility of the register and this may be due to the serious consequences of disclosure. In *Re C*,[190] the Court carefully weighed the need to protect others with privacy, the danger to C from vigilantes and dangers in controlling sensitive information.[191] The Court also carefully weighed up disclosure through an enhanced criminal records check for employment applications. In *L*,[192] L had applied for a job as a children's worker. The enhanced records check had disclosed that his father was on the register and his uncle had been convicted of sex offences during a trial in which charges against L had been dropped. Suspicions about L were therefore based on his family history. The Court found that the suspicions concerning L were unfounded and the disclosure disproportionate. The Court made it clear that the police were under a duty to act proportionately when disclosing such information.[193] The Court has also given protection to an offender's privacy rights by awarding damages and an injunction against Facebook when a Facebook page listed details about convicted sex offenders.[194] The Court found that the misuse of the information created a risk of reoffending, risk of incitement to violence and was an attempt to expose the offender to vilification.[195]

These two examples of management strategies in the community underscore the dominance of risk penology over rights in a community

---

[189] *(R on application of XX) v Secretary of State for the Home Department, Chief Constable of South Yorkshire Police, Association of Chief Police Officers, The Secretary of State for Justice* [2014] EWHC 4106 (Admin).

[190] *Re C* (unreported, 15 Feb 2002).

[191] Power (n 187) 84.

[192] *R (on the application of L) v the Chief Constable of Kent Police* [2014] EWHC 463 (Admin).

[193] This reflects case law, which found the scheme for criminal records checks in general needed modification to comply with Article 8. See Rainey, B and Harrison, K 'Criminal records checks and human rights compatibility update' (2013) National Organization Treatment of Sexual Abusers news, No.70, July/August 12.

[194] *CG v Facebook Ireland Ltd.* [2015] NIQB 11.

[195] ibid [98]; See Lorna Skinner, 'Case Comment: CG v Facebook Ireland - harassment of sex offenders and a Facebook injunction' (2015) Entertainment Law Review 145.

setting. [196] These forms of disintegrative shaming clearly focus on compelling the offender not to reoffend by constraining movement, lifestyle and allowing for disclosure under certain circumstances. Unlike in the US, the shaming of sex offenders publicly is not part of the governmental policy in the UK. It is argued this makes it more compatible with the dignity of the offender whilst still maintaining protection for potential victims. Risk and rights are clearly interrelated in these schemes, although the more draconian the register becomes, the more it is in danger of becoming punitive; with less chance of the offender being able to reintegrate back into society. [197] The Courts have provided scrutiny for the register and have been prepared to interfere when it considers procedural safeguards are flawed and in the case of disclosure, does take seriously the risk to the offender as well as to potential victims.

Conclusions

The treatment and management of sex offenders demonstrates the complex relationship between rights and risk. A risk-led penal policy is in danger of objectifying the offender by focusing on assessment of risk as a reason for treatment and control in the community. There can be a clear tension between the need to protect potential victims, especially children, from those who would cause sexual harm and at the same time maintaining the protection of rights in a democratic society governed by the rule of law. However, these are not mutually exclusive and it may be a false dichotomy to think so. [198] For example, the due process rights scrutinised by the courts are applicable to all and it would undermine the justice system if certain groups were excluded from its purview. Guaranteeing the review of indefinite registration does not necessarily impact on the risk to potential victims. In fact, it can be argued that a review process that re-examines effectively the risk of re-offending enhances protection as those who are no longer a risk can be removed from the register, freeing up resources to put towards the management of those classified as high risk. [199] There is also a need to be clear about when treatment is used and how far a state can go to undermine the basic tenets of consent. It is well

---

[196] Kemshall (n 10) 110.

[197] This would move registration towards the idea of punishment as retribution rather than having a rehabilitative element; see text to n 58.

[198] Rainey (n 26).

[199] Liberty 'Liberty's submission to the Joint Committee on Human Rights Report on the Draft Sexual Offences Act 2003 (Remedial order) 2011' (n 175); Rainey (n 26) 46.

established that to perform medical treatment without consent may violate the dignity of the offender/patient[200] and this can cause ethical as well as legal problems for practitioners. The acceptance by courts of conditional consent allows the state and practitioners to be able to carry out treatment, which they believe is in the interest of the patient (and so autonomy in decision making can be constrained for the greater autonomy to be achieved through treatment)[201] as well as of society as a whole (objective dignity). However, there is a concern that this may lead to coercion, especially in institutional settings.[202] The courts in the future may take greater cognisance of this when examining whether consent is valid. There is also a growing body of literature that highlights the need to move away from the shaming policies of community control, and the need to move towards re-integrative policies such as restorative justice schemes like Circles of Support and Accountability.[203] This is alongside the Good Lives Model for treatment[204] and a growing literature examining offender desistence from offending.[205] It may be that, despite the anti-rights rhetoric, government approaches to treatment and management need to be more nuanced to consider strategies that minimize risk through engaging with rights and furthering the reintegration of the offender.

---

[200] See text to (n 105).

[201] See (n 122).

[202] See text to (n 118).

[203] McAlinden (n 62); Hanvey and Hoing (n 97).

[204] Ward and Gannon (n 63) 77-94.

[205] Richard Laws and Tony Ward, *Desistance from Sex Offending: alternatives to throwing away the keys* (Guildford Publications 2011).

CHAPTER SIXTEEN

CONSENT *VERSUS* COERCION:
OFFENDER RIGHTS *AND* COMMUNITY RIGHTS
IN SEXUAL OFFENDER REHABILITATION

ASTRID BIRGDEN

Introduction

Principles of sentencing in Western legal systems simultaneously deliver punishment, deterrence, retribution, community protection, incapacitation, and rehabilitation. As a sentencing principle, offender rehabilitation aims to identify causes for offending and reduces re-offending by changing the thoughts, feelings, and behaviours of individuals.[1] The dominant paradigm regarding offender rehabilitation is cognitive behavioural therapy (CBT) which aims to change anti-social thoughts, feelings and behaviours. Usually, CBT procedures include developing an offence cycle (understanding how the thoughts–feelings–behaviour chain leads to re-offending) followed by a relapse prevention plan (practical strategies to manage high-risk thoughts, feelings, and behaviours in the community). Within prisons, sexual offender rehabilitation tends to be delivered as group therapy programmes as this approach is considered more effective and efficient.[2]

Sexual offenders may be subjected to rehabilitation in prisons that can be considered intrusive and coerced. While traditional treatment in the

---

[1] Andrew Ashworth, *Principles of Criminal Law* (5th edn, Oxford University Press 2006).

[2] See Don Andrews and James Bonta, *The Psychology of Criminal Conduct* (5th edn, Matthew Bender & Co 2010).

community is essentially negotiated with the client, in the correctional system, the offender is given little real choice. In particular, participation may be a way of avoiding indefinite detention in a prison or as a means to obtain parole from prison. In encouraging sexual offenders to engage in programmes in correctional settings, the power of coercion lies in the consequence of a conviction that incarcerates an individual for the offence, and combined with rehabilitation, is offered as a means of gaining parole for community reentry. The correctional system cannot apply 'coercive authority' to compel treatment of a competent adult, as can occur in the civil commitment setting, as this becomes a threat to autonomy. Concern regarding preying upon a sexual offender's vulnerability in order to coerce consent to participate in a rehabilitation programme can arise when making a connection between engagement in offender rehabilitation and the prospect of release.[3]

Sexual Offender Rehabilitation: A Contemporary Example

A contemporary example of sexual offender rehabilitation within the correctional system is as follows. A critical ethnographic analysis of CBT with a child sexual offender (Mr S) who appeared before the Parole Board of Canada after completing treatment in the Correctional Services of Canada in 2000 was conducted by Lacombe, a programme that the Department confidently reported to her would reduce re-offending.[4] Mr S had served four years for sexual interference, the index offence being against a 10-year old boy. The policy of Correctional Services of Canada is described as 'active encouragement' in which participation in programmes is explicitly linked to prospects of release or a transfer to a lower security facility. Lacombe described the situation of Mr S as '[he] must attend treatment programmes as part of his correctional plan otherwise he has no chance in front of the Parole Board'.[5] This approach can be described as 'psychological pressure' although sexual offenders have the right to refuse and Correctional Services of Canada is obliged to

---

[3] Jeremy Rigg, 'Measures of Perceived Coercion in Prison Treatment Settings' (2002) 25 International Journal of Law and Psychiatry 473.
[4] Dany Lacombe, '"Mr S. You do have sexual fantasies?" The parole hearing and prison treatment of a sex offender at the turn of the 21st century' (2013) 38 Canadian Journal of Sociology 33.
[5] ibid 37.

ensure that participation is voluntary.[6] Although the rehabilitation programme followed by the two Parole Board of Canada hearings that Lacombe observed occurred in 2000, the following example is still typical of contemporary sexual offender rehabilitation and the goals of correctional services throughout the United Kingdom, the United States, Australia, and New Zealand.

Rehabilitation with Mr S entailed the development and presentation of an offence cycle regarding the link between sexual fantasies, arousal, and offending, and a relapse prevention plan to manage his arousal.[7] The programme emphasised cognitive distortions that justify, minimise, and deny harm to victims, and focused on 'self-policing' by Mr S in his keeping a sexual fantasy log and enrolling family members in the community as 'social control agents' with whom he was to share high-risk thoughts, feelings, and behaviours. The Parole Board of Canada hearings (described by Lacombe as 'an interrogation') tested what Mr S had learned in treatment regarding his offence cycle – that he had planned or 'engineered' to 'get a victim', that he was able to list his high risk situations which were to be avoided (e.g., not watching TV shows or reading books that include children), and whether he had fantasised prior to his offence or presently fantasised about children. The Parole Board members and the treating clinicians became frustrated when Mr S indicated that he had not 'groomed' the victim after all and that he would just 'block out' sexual thoughts about children in the future. Lacking in the treatment programme was consideration of the social, economic, and individual circumstances of the participants (e.g. two First Nations sexual offenders were strongly dissuaded from discussing their early experiences of abuse in residential schools). Lacombe noted that treatment had evolved from a humanist philosophy addressing broad psychological, social, and economic needs (i.e. a transformative experience addressing the root causes of offending) and toward equipping offenders with individualistic strategies to control dynamic risk factors statistically correlated to re-offending (i.e. a punitive and managerial approach). Lacombe ultimately concluded that Mr S was considered an identity overwhelmed by desires and forever at risk of re-offending: 'the parole hearing and treatment programme exist in a symbiotic relationship that fabricates the sex offender into a species larger than life, one at risk of offending all the

---

[6] Rigg (n 4).
[7] Lacombe (n 5).

time',[8] 'the sex offender internalises a criminal identity as a sex offender, an identity that constitutes the pivot around which all other aspects of his personality revolve',[9] and therefore 'it boggles the mind why we would want to try to reintegrate him into our community.'[10]

The following chapter will take this typical example of contemporary sexual offender rehabilitation to consider the implications of coercion versus consent for reducing re-offending in sexual offenders, and where each approach endorsed by correctional services may lead. First, an overview of the legal theory of therapeutic jurisprudence (TJ) as a framework to consider the balance between coercion and consent will be provided. Second, coercion (both legal and psychological) and consent as applied to sexual offenders will be compared. Third, TJ combined with human rights will be considered in order to balance sexual offenders as both rights-violators and rights-holders. Fourth, two contemporary theories of offender rehabilitation – Risk–Need–Responsivity (RNR) and the Good Lives Model (GLM) – will be contrasted with TJ and human rights principles to assess how Mr S may have been more successfully engaged in offender rehabilitation. Finally, the case of Mr S is provided to demonstrate how the principles of human rights, TJ, and GLM can be applied to minimise the anti-therapeutic effects of legally coerced offender rehabilitation.

Therapeutic Jurisprudence

The current public policy debate about community protection is weighted toward managing offender risk as opposed to meeting offender needs, as if the two constructs are mutually exclusive.[11] Consent *or* coercion to engage in programmes highlights the tension between community rights (justice principles) and offender rights (therapeutic principles). While obtaining consent to rehabilitation supports offender rights, coercing offenders into rehabilitation overrides their human rights. Therefore, coercing sexual offenders to engage in rehabilitation brings with it ethical, social, and

---

[8] ibid 33.
[9] ibid 52.
[10] ibid 53.
[11] Astrid Birgden, 'Therapeutic jurisprudence and sex offenders: A Psycholegal Approach to Protection' (2004) 16 Sexual Abuse: A Journal of Research and Treatment 351.

political challenges.

A legal framework that can assist in considering the balance between consent and coercion is the legal theory of TJ; a theory that actively promotes therapeutic objectives by balancing justice principles and therapeutic principles. TJ is useful in considering consent and coercion as the framework is concerned with autonomy and due process, not punishment'.[12] TJ is a humanistic theory that is concerned with well-being. TJ determines that the law can function as a therapeutic agent in substantive law (where the law actively promotes therapeutic objectives through the balance of community rights against individual rights), legal procedure (where the legal system maximizes therapeutic effects and minimizes anti-therapeutic consequences), and legal roles (where the behaviours of legal actors are therapeutic or anti-therapeutic).[13] While the normative stance of TJ is that it aims to maximise the existing overarching aims of the law, therapeutic effects are considered desirable and should generally be the aim of the law, and anti-therapeutic effects are undesirable and should be avoided or minimised by the law.[14] In the context of offender rehabilitation, TJ is not only applicable to courts and parole boards, but can be extended to the correctional system in considering the role of correctional staff as therapeutic or anti-therapeutic agents.[15]

In terms of the role of the law within the correctional system, autonomy is a fundamental prerequisite for participation in programmes, particularly for those sexual offenders who are unlikely to be seeking help. Whether a legal system should be concerned with autonomy is a normative

---

[12] David B Wexler and Bruce J Winick, 'Introduction' in David B Wexler and Bruce J Winick (eds.), *The Law in a Therapeutic Key: Developments in Therapeutic Jurisprudence* (Carolina University Press 1996).

[13] David B Wexler, (1990). 'An Introduction to Therapeutic Jurisprudence'. In David B Wexler (ed.), *Therapeutic Jurisprudence: The law as a Therapeutic Agent* (Carolina Academic Press, 1990).

[14] Bruce J Winick, 'The Jurisprudence of Therapeutic Jurisprudence' (1997) 3 Psychology, Public Policy, and Law 184.

[15] Astrid Birgden, 'Therapeutic Jurisprudence and Responsivity: Finding the will and the way in offender rehabilitation' [2004] 10 Crime, Psychology & Law 283; *Birgden* (n 12).

question. [16] However, autonomy is a basic human need which can maximise individual *and* community well-being from both a legal perspective[17] and a psychological perspective,[18] and treating individuals as '(...) competent adults who are able to make choices rather than as incompetent subjects of paternalism predictably has a therapeutic effect'.[19]

Therapeutic Jurisprudence and Social Science

When the law allows a degree of coercion, it does so on the assumption that offender rehabilitation is effective.[20] A social science question that TJ can pose is: *Does coerced treatment of sexual offenders improve community well-being and offender well-being or is it anti-therapeutic?*

Oddly, there has been very little literature regarding this question, unlike the drug treatment literature that has considered compulsory, quasi-compulsory, and voluntary treatment in detail.[21] The sexual offender literature considers the effectiveness of programmes in reducing re-offending (community well-being), but does not identify the level of coercion applied to participants (whether it is ethical) and does not consider offender well-being outcomes (whether it works). Based on contemporary public policy toward managing the risk of serious sexual offenders, it will be assumed that most participants have experienced some form of coercion to participate in programmes. A review of the literature regarding reduced re-offending noted that definitive conclusions about effectiveness were hampered by methodological problems resulting in conflicting conclusions ranging from treatment being ineffective to

---

[16]Astrid Birgden, 'Offender Rehabilitation: A Normative Framework for Forensic Psychologists' (2008) 15 Psychiatry, Psychology & Law 1.

[17] Bruce J Winick, 'On Autonomy: Legal and Psychological Perspectives' (1992) 37 Villanova Law Review 1705.

[18] Tony Ward and Claire Stewart, 'Criminogenic needs and human needs: A theoretical model' (2003) 9 Psychology, Crime & Law 125; Tony Ward and Claire Stewart, 'The relationship between human needs and criminogenic needs' (2003) 9 Psychology, Crime & Law 219; *Winick* (n 15).

[19] Bruce J Winick, 'The MacArthur Competence Treatment Study: Legal and Therapeutic Implications' (1996) 2 Psychology, Public Policy, and Law 161.

[20] Bruce J Winick, 'A Therapeutic Jurisprudence Approach to Dealing with Coercion in the Mental Health System' (2008) 15 Psychiatry, Psychology, and the Law 25.

[21] Birgden (n 17).

treatment (particularly CBT) being effective, and meta-analyses showing that treated sexual offenders are less likely to re-offend than untreated sexual offenders.[22] Burdon and Gallagher concluded that the expectation of rehabilitation should be to control sexual offending behaviour by reducing the risks associated with relapse and re-offending (a risk management approach).

The effect on re-offending rates in a sample of sexual offenders who volunteered for a programme, some of whom participated (n=161) and some who did not (n=282), was compared with a matched sample of participants who did not volunteer for the programme and therefore did not commence (n=443).[23] There was no difference in re-offending rates between offenders who volunteered and non-volunteers, but those that volunteered were assessed as less likely to re-offend on an actuarial test than non-volunteers who were less treatment ready. However, once risk factors were controlled, there was no effect of volunteering. That is, merely volunteering does not in and of itself protect an offender from future risk of re-offending, so the question of whether to accept volunteers or non-volunteers may be moot. In other words, rehabilitation programmes should not only be offered to those who seek treatment.

As to whether coercion improves community and individual well-being, this remains unanswered. A second TJ question is: *What evidence-based therapeutic strategies can be put into place to increase the likelihood of engaging coerced sexual offenders in rehabilitation programmes?* TJ supports social science research on strategies that support autonomy in sexual offenders. These include the constructs of perceived coercion, procedural justice, and treatment readiness.

Perceived coercion in general was first considered within the context of psychiatric treatment, civil commitment settings, and drug treatment. Subsequently, perceived coercion was measured amongst a sample of 30 sexual offenders in Canadian prisons, with a focus on the right of

---

[22] William M Burdon and Catherine A Gallagher, 'Coercion and Sex Offenders: Controlling Sex-Offending Behaviour through Incapacitation and Treatment' (2002) 29 Criminal Justice and Behaviour 87.

[23] Melissa D Grady et al, 'Does Volunteering for Sex Offender Treatment Matter? Using Propensity Score Analysis to Understand the Effects of Volunteerism and Treatment on Recidivism' (2012) 25 Sexual Abuse: A Journal of Research and Treatment 319.

participants to refuse rehabilitation programmes. [24] The questionnaire administered considered self-motivation, amotivation, motivation by non-specific external factors, and the extent to which parole and transfer to lower security was a motivator for treatment, as well as the MacArthur Admission Experience Interview Scale (AEIS)[25] designed for psychiatric patients. On the AEIS, the majority (n=19 or 63%) of sexual offenders indicated little or no perceived coercion, combined with high levels of self-motivation and low levels of amotivation, although pressure to engage was acknowledged even though the decision to refuse or accept was considered their own. The minority (n=11 or 37%) scored higher on the AEIS and felt they had not been afforded a full or meaningful right to refuse treatment. Those offenders who were closer to, or had passed parole eligibility or statutory release dates, were more likely to perceive coercion in the treatment process.

In this study, Rigg noted that those sexual offenders who lacked motivation, and who were more likely to resent pressure for treatment, were in more need of coercion as a motivator, begging the question about how to motivate them while respecting autonomy (therapeutic) and not fostering resentment (anti-therapeutic). However, such sexual offenders were not present in this particular sample. Rigg also noted that the prospect of release or parole was no greater a motivator than those serving a longer sentence being transferred to a lower security facility, indicating that these motivators may not be perceived as the coercive elements that are assumed to be, although it is more of a motivator at the beginning 'to bring inmates to the treatment table',[26] but then less important toward the end of treatment. However, note that almost half of the sample of offenders were serving life or indeterminate sentences, so there would have been less likelihood of release. Rigg considered the relationship between perceived coercion and actual coercion and concluded that linking programme engagement to prospects of release was not inherently coercive or unfair; more often, participants commented on the anti-therapeutic effects of correctional staff attitudes and Correctional Services of Canada's use of treatment information.

---

[24] Rigg (n 4).

[25] Charles W Lidz et al, 'Factual Sources of Psychiatric Patients' Perceptions of Coercion in the Hospital Admission Process' (1998) 155 American Journal of Psychiatry 1254.

[26] Jeremy Rigg (n 4) 486.

Procedural justice supports autonomy by allowing freedom of choice without intrusion on individual liberty and the pursuit of happiness; where the State does intervene, the decision needs to be rationally justified rather than being arbitrary or unreasonable.[27] Procedural justice was analysed by Tyler, who reviewed social science evidence regarding the psychological consequences of judicial procedures and concluded that procedural justice is made up of participation (inclusion in decision-making), dignity (acknowledged rights and values as a competent, equal citizen and human being), and trust (evidence is presented and decisions clearly explained). In turn, being treated with respect translates into greater compliance with the law.[28] Put another way, procedural justice entails 'three Vs' – voice, validation, and voluntariness.[29] Procedural justice was more recently considered regarding offenders.[30]

Assessing treatment readiness or what stage of change an individual is experiencing and then matching it with motivational strategies to engage change is useful. Prochaska and others have developed a general explanatory model of how individuals change health-related behaviour.[31] Individuals are assisted to change with a goodness of fit between the right thing (process) at the right time (stage). In essence, the model can be described as a CBT approach commencing with verbal processes followed by environmental or behavioural management processes, which underpin progress through the stages of change. Motivational interviewing techniques have been devised by Miller and others to increase the likelihood that individuals will enter, continue, and comply with active

---

[27] Tony Ward and Astrid Birgden, 'Human Rights and Clinical Correctional Practice' (2007) 12 Aggression and Violent Behaviour 628; Bruce J Winick (n 15).

[28] Tom R Tyler (1996), 'The Psychological Consequences of Judicial Procedures: Implications for Civil Commitment Hearings' in David B Wexler and Bruce J Winick (eds), *The Law in a Therapeutic Key: Developments in Therapeutic Jurisprudence* (Carolina University Press 1996).

[29] Amy D Ronner, 'The Learned-Helpless Lawyer: Clinical Legal Education and Therapeutic Jurisprudence as Antidotes to Bartleby Syndrome' (2008) 24 Touro Law Review 601.

[30] Tom R Tyler, (2010) 'Legitimacy in Corrections' (2010) 9 Criminology and Public Policy 127.

[31] For example, James O Prochaska and Carlo C DiClemente, 'Transtheoretical Therapy: Toward a More Integrative Model of Change' (1982) 19 Psychotherapy: Theory Research and Practice 276.

change strategies.[32] As with the transtheoretical model, the techniques are based on health-related behaviour change. In motivational interviewing, the clinician expresses empathy, encourages reasons for change, avoids arguments, rolls with resistance, and supports self-efficacy (i.e. displays an ethic of care or therapeutic alliance). Motivational interviewing techniques can be applied at different stages of the change readiness model.[33]

The factors that were predictive of sexual offenders volunteering to engage in programmes were considered.[34] They compared sexual offenders who were accepted for treatment (n=251), rejected from treatment (n=66), and those who refused treatment (n=87). Jones et al found that motivation was an important predictor for volunteering and then entering programmes, and that internal motivation (i.e. recognition of a problem with sexual deviance and readiness to change sexual behaviours) as well as external motivation (i.e. recommendation by a judge at time of sentencing) increased a person's likelihood of volunteering. This indicates that motivational programmes using stages of change and motivational interviewing may encourage increased participation. Both stages of change and motivational interviewing have been applied to offenders.[35]

Further, treatment readiness in offenders can be described as the presence of characteristics within the person or their environment which are likely to enhance engagement in programmes and therefore likely to enhance change.[36] To be treatment ready, a sexual offender needs to be ready, and therefore willing (motivated) and able (capable). The Multifactor Treatment Readiness Model (MORM) addresses person, programme, and context factors in order to best enhance a 'goodness of fit' between

---

[32] William R Miller and Stephen Rollnick, *Motivational Interviewing: Preparing People for Change* (The Guilford Press 2002).

[33] James Prochaska and Carlo C Norcross, *Systems of Psychotherapy: A Transtheoretical Model* (Brooks/Cole 1994).

[34] Nicole Jones, Bernadette Pelissier, Jody and Klein-Saffran, 'Predicting Sex Offender Treatment Entry Among Individuals Convicted of Sexual Offence Crimes' (2012) 18 Sexual Abuse: A Journal of Research and Treatment 83.

[35] Birgden (n 12); James O Prochaska and Daniel A Levesque, 'Enhancing Motivation of Offenders at Each Stage of Change and Phase of Therapy' in Mary McMurran (ed) *Motivating Offenders to Change: A Guide to Enhancing Engagement in Therapy* (John Wiley & Sons 2002).

[36] Tony Ward et al, 'The Multifactor Offender Readiness Model' (2004) 9 Aggression and Violent Behaviour 645.

offenders and rehabilitation programmes. Based on the MORM, the Corrections Victoria Treatment Readiness Questionnaire was devised to assess: (1) attitudes and motivation (attitudes and beliefs about the desire to change); (2) emotional reactions (emotional responses to offending behaviour); (3) offending beliefs (beliefs about personal responsibility for offending); and (4) efficacy (belief that they can participate in programmes).[37]

Considering the constructs of perceived coercion, procedural justice, and treatment motivation or readiness, the lack of research regarding the methods by which treatment compliance is obtained in sexual offenders and how perceptions of coercion may impact upon treatment motivation has been noted.[38] Self-report measures in 116 sexual offenders incarcerated within the Texas Department of Criminal Justice were administered early in programme entry and later within the programme. Participation was required in order to obtain parole (although participation was considered voluntary) and participants were within two years of release, making the consequences of programme refusal more salient. Barcharz found significant results in terms of a positive correlation between treatment motivation and perceived procedural justice, a negative correlation between perceived coercion and perceived procedural justice, and a negative correlation between perceived coercion and treatment motivation, both at onset of treatment and later in treatment. Interestingly, there was no significant difference between those sexual offenders who were earning conditional release and those with mandatory release dates. Perceived procedural justice was found to be the most significant predictor of treatment motivation in that it mediated the effects of perceived coercion on treatment motivation. Feelings of being coerced could lead to feelings of being treated unjustly that in turn may have impacted upon treatment motivation.

---

[37] Sharon Casey et al, 'Assessing Suitability for Offender Rehabilitation: Development and Validation of the Treatment Readiness Questionnaire'. (2007) 34 Criminal and Justice Behaviour 1427.

[38] Caroline A Barchaz, *Perceived Coercion, Procedural Justice, and Treatment Motivation in a Sex Offender Treatment Programme* (San Houston State University 2008).

Coercion Versus Consent

In sexual offender rehabilitation, coercion is when a sexual offender is forced against their will to engage in offender rehabilitation, while consent is when a choice is freely given to engage in offender rehabilitation.[39] It is expected that feelings of coercion will undermine the effectiveness of rehabilitation programmes (anti-therapeutic) and feelings of voluntariness will enhance the effectiveness of rehabilitation programmes (therapeutic).

Coercion

As stated, the research literature is relatively silent regarding the coercive rehabilitation of sexual offenders. Coercion can incapacitate the sexual offender through imprisonment and/or ensure that the sexual offender accepts some form of rehabilitation as a condition of parole.[40] Mr S had presumably experienced both forms of coercion. In this context, coercion, as defined by Burdon and Gallagher, will be defined as external pressures applied to sexual offenders to engage in rehabilitation programmes. In a TJ analysis of civil commitment and coerced treatment, Winick noted that coercion is a complex concept, which is context dependent and normative, with both a legal and a psychological meaning.[41] Further, within a correctional context, coercion can be divided between coercive offers and coercive threats.[42]

Legal Coercion or Coercive Offer

Legal coercion is when a legally voluntary choice is forced[43] or when a coercive offer creates options that otherwise would not exist.[44] In other words, a choice should be provided in the absence of restriction on choice or the threat of an unpleasant consequence if a particular choice is not

---

[39] Bruce J Winick, 'The Judge's role in encouraging motivation to change' in Bruce J Winick and David B Wexler (eds) *Judging in a Therapeutic Key: Therapeutic Jurisprudence and the Courts* (Carolina Academic Press 2003).

[40] Burdon and Gallagher (n 23).

[41] Bruce J Winick, 'A therapeutic jurisprudence approach to dealing with coercion in the mental health system' (2008) 15 Psychiatry, Psychology and Law 25.

[42] John McMillan, 'The Kindest Cut? Surgical Castration, Sex Offenders, and Coercive Offers' (2014) 40 Journal of Medical Ethics 583.

[43] Winick (n 42).

[44] McMillan (n 43).

made (i.e. the sexual offender would be detained regardless of whether they engaged in offender rehabilitation). Legal compulsion would occur if Mr S is offered the choice by a parole board of indefinite detention or the possibility of release on parole upon completion of a rehabilitation programme, or by a clinician with an opinion of the suitability for the release of Mr S made to a parole board upon completion of a rehabilitation programme.

While McMillan noted that coercive offers are controversial as they undermine consent, [45] Winick viewed legal coercion as perhaps appropriately normative as once the sexual offender chooses the rehabilitation option, they do so knowing that future actions will be constrained as result of a choice voluntarily made.[46] In the correctional system, Rigg noted that the consequences of sexual offenders refusing rehabilitation programmes is not necessarily unfair as other factors are considered by the parole board regarding release, such as the level of risk of re-offending balanced against the need for community reintegration.[47]

Psychological Coercion or Coercive Threat

Psychological coercion occurs when negative pressure and improper inducements are applied.[48] Put another way, coercive threats attempt to remove options by making at least one of them undesirable, resulting in involuntary choices and so limits freedom.[49] Psychological coercion would occur if Mr S is told by a parole board that unless he engages in a rehabilitation programme, release will not occur until end-of-sentence, or if Mr S is told by a clinician that if he were to engage in a rehabilitation programme, his chances of being released on parole would be increased. This view is in contrast to Rigg, who stated that making it clear that release is not predicated upon involvement in offender rehabilitation *per se*, but that if successful, treatment could result in re-assessment as a lower risk, or as no longer dangerous, and would therefore enhance the prospects of release, this could be considered voluntary consent.[50] Even if there are

---

[45] ibid.
[46] Winick (n 40).
[47] Rigg (n 4).
[48] Winick (n 40).
[49] McMillan (n 43).
[50] Rigg (n 4).

several options provided to the sexual offender, and they have made an informed, rational, and voluntary choice, McMillan argued that coercive threats are likely to cause moral harm in that the sexual offender has not been accorded the moral respect as a fellow human being that they deserve.[51]

If it is made clear to a sexual offender that unless they agree to choose or accept an offer, then the state or clinician will do everything in their power to ensure that the sexual offender is not released, then this is a coercive threat,[52] and making a file notation that offender rehabilitation was refused, and so using it for other purposes, is also unnecessarily coercive.[53] According to Winick, psychological coercion is unethical.[54]

Clinician versus State Coercion

If a clinician mentions the possibility of offender rehabilitation to Mr S without any influence over whether he will be released if he refuses to participate, but notes that the state is unlikely to release him, then the clinician makes a coercive offer or uses legal coercion but the state imposes a coercive threat or psychological coercion. This approach provides Mr S with an implicit message of: 'either participate in offender rehabilitation or you will not be released'. Rigg indicated that in order to avoid this scenario, clear boundaries between programme delivery and the coercive, punitive correctional environment ought to be established without clinicians (as agents of the state) brokering between the sexual offender and judicial decision-making.[55]

Consent

Both legal coercion and psychological coercion intersect with consent. Non-coerced consent requires the sexual offender to have the capacity to consent, make a decision based upon a cost-benefit analysis of the information, and make a voluntary decision through the exercise of free

---

[51] McMillan (n 43).
[52] ibid.
[53] Rigg (n 4).
[54] Winick (n 40).
[55] Rigg (n 4).

will and autonomy without coercion or constraint.[56] Obviously, with the possibility of parole as an incentive to participate in offender rehabilitation as outlined above, the voluntariness prong is not met. In the United Kingdom, it was found that 41 per cent of sexual offenders interviewed stated that they would only participate in treatment in order to obtain parole.[57]

Rigg argued that clinicians must be able to ensure that sexual offenders make a voluntary choice to accept or refuse programmes, with the reassurance that their considerations are being handled fairly in order to prevent coercive authority from resulting in both perceived and actual coercion, to the detriment of offender rehabilitation.[58]

Coercion-Consent Continuum

The distinction between coercion and consent is not clear-cut. Coercion can be better understood as a continuum progressing from friendly persuasion, to interpersonal pressure, to control of resources, and then using force; where the law chooses to draw the line is a normative judgement.[59] A concrete example is that of the castration of sexual offenders. Ryberg indicated that if castration is offered as an alternative to a lengthy prison sentence, then it is psychological coercion, but if castration is offered as an option, it is legal coercion; either way it is coercion.[60] However, that castration was not coerced was the argument put forward by the Czech Republic in 2009 and Germany in 2012 in response to reports by the European Committee for the Prevention of Torture and Inhuman or Degrading Treatment or Punishment (CPT) criticising the surgical castration of sexual offenders as degrading treatment.[61] The rebuttals by both countries cited evidence that surgical castration was

---

[56] Astrid Birgden and Frank Vincent, 'Maximising Therapeutic Effects in Treating Sexual Offenders in an Australian Correctional System' (2000) 18 Behavioural Sciences & Law 479.

[57] Don Grubin and David Thornton, 'A National Programme for the Assessment and Treatment of Sex Offenders in the English Prison System' (1994) 21 Criminal Justice and Behaviour 55.

[58] Rigg (n 4).

[59] Winick (n 15).

[60] Jesper Ryberg, 'Is Coerced Treatment of Offenders Morally Acceptable? – On the Deficiency of the Debate' (2005) 9 Criminal Law and Philosophy 619.

[61] McMillan (n 43).

clinically effective (although no research evidence was provided regarding its effect on reducing re-offending or improving lives) and that castration needed to be requested by the sexual offender and could not occur in the absence of informed consent.[62] Note that a meta-analysis found that chemically or physically castrated sexual offenders had a 37 per cent lower re-offending rate than the control group.[63] However, when a more recent meta-analysis by the same authors excluded chemical castration (and pharmacological interventions), as its application did not meet the criteria of meeting therapeutic rather than punitive or deterrent effect, a smaller effect size on reducing sexual re-offending was found.[64] The question to be considered is at what ethical cost chemical castration occurs, however.

Considering ethics, coerced castration assumes that free and informed consent is able to be provided by an imprisoned sexual offender. McMillan considered the ethical problems underlying surgical castration and concluded that sexual offenders should not be coerced into castration via a coercive threat or a coercive offer, because of the seriousness of the outcome (and if they were, it should be via coercive offers).[65] Further, McMillan considered the role of consent. McMillan reported that the CPT had raised three concerns about the quality of consent in imprisoned sexual offenders in the Czech Republic. McMillan reported that several concerns were expressed by the CPT. First, there were no other treatment options available (e.g. anti-androgen medication that can be ceased was considered too costly), and one sexual offender in particular had received no treatment for 19 years, in contrast to Germany where there were more treatment options available and so less men had been surgically castrated. Second, the sexual offenders interviewed reported that they had not been adequately informed about the side effects of surgical castration such as osteoporosis (i.e. the cost-benefit analysis aspect of consent is lacking). Third, and most importantly, nearly all sexual offenders interviewed

[62] ibid.

[63] Friedrich Lösel and Martin Schmucker, 'The effectiveness of treatment for sexual offenders: A comprehensive meta-analysis' (2005) 1 Journal of Experimental Criminology 117.

[64] Martin Schmucker and Friedrich Lösel, 'The effects of sexual offender treatment on recidivism: An international meta-analysis of sound quality evaluations' [2015] Journal of Experimental Criminology. Can be found at <http://link.springer.com/article/10.1007%2Fs11292-015-9241-z#/page-1>.

[65] McMillan (n 43).

indicated that they had applied for surgical castration out of fear of long-term detention (i.e. the voluntariness aspect of consent is lacking). That is, if the sexual offender is given a choice:

> [B]etween an undesirable option and another option that is so undesirable that it is not an option at all, then [consent does not] exhaust all of the relevant moral considerations (…) if it's not a voluntary decision, it's not valid consent.[66]

McMillan noted that the possibility of castration can be presented in a non-coercive way if the sexual offender requests the treatment in a competent, informed, and rational manner in order to manage their life and be integrated back into the community.[67] In this way, voluntariness is not open to question (even if the possibility of early release is considered by the offender). McMillan accepted that coercive offers or coercive threats were not occurring in the Czech Republic or Germany as the request for castration had to be initiated by the sexual offender and therefore it was not degrading, inhumane, or cruel treatment; 'If sex offenders can use castration for broad psychological change and development, we should be less concerned about the fact that they have to make this choice against a background where their choices are limited'.[68] This opinion was despite the three concerns raised by the CPT regarding the informed and voluntary aspects of consent in practice. McMillan concluded that sexual offenders should have the choice between chemical castration (the medication has unpleasant side effects) and surgical castration, but if chemical castration is unavailable, then they should not be deprived of the option of surgical castration. Note that in the United States, because surgical castration is an irreversible procedure, it is not viewed as a viable treatment in the correctional system, although some states allow it to be voluntarily requested.[69] Again, whether informed consent can ever be obtained is questionable (unless release to the community occurs regardless of castration).

Therapeutic Jurisprudence and Offender Rights

A TJ principle is that autonomy is enhanced through consent to participate in rehabilitation programmes and failure to obtain consent is a threat to

---

[66] McMillan (n 43) 585.
[67] ibid.
[68] ibid 589.
[69] Burdon and Gallagher (n 23); Ryberg (n 61).

offender rights. Whether the criminal justice system should be concerned with autonomy is a normative question, but at present it is expected that individuals should have their autonomy protected as it is a basic moral obligation.[70] The International Bill of Rights lists both civil and political rights (that the State is to protect individuals from violation) and economic, social, and cultural rights (that the State is to provide certain good and services to individuals). Within a rights framework, there is no doubt that offenders have enforceable human rights protected by international law and codes.[71] Although obvious, Ward and Birgden have stated that offenders should be accorded the same rights as all human beings and should not be treated as means to an end (e.g. incapacitating or coercing sexual offenders to serve the purpose of garnering political support from the community).[72] Therefore, while prisoners consequently have some limitations applied to their rights, they have the same enforceable human rights as other citizens and ought to expect humane treatment from both the courts and corrections. A risk management culture in corrections can undermine the human rights principle of autonomy. As a humanistic theory, these principles are supported by TJ as normative values that include dignity, respect, and autonomy ought to support offender rights. From a TJ perspective, it is preferable if sexual offenders experience the opportunity to provide non-coerced consent (a therapeutic effect) or at the least legal coercion (a neutral effect) rather than psychological coercion (an anti-therapeutic effect) when considering engagement in programmes.

A human rights model to engage offenders in rehabilitation programmes has been proposed by Ward and Birgden, based on human rights principles rather than policies.[73] An individual's right can be moral (i.e. based on a moral theory or principle), social (i.e. guaranteed by a social institution), or legal (i.e. prescribed by particular laws). Human rights literature generally considers legal rights but this focus does not guide correctional systems in delivering services within a human rights framework. To

---

[70] Winick (n 20).

[71] Astrid Birgden and Michael Perlin, 'Tolling for the Luckless, the Abandoned and Forsaked': Therapeutic Jurisprudence and International Human Rights Law as Applied to Prisoners and Detainees by Forensic Psychologists (2008) 13 Legal and Criminological Psychology 231.

[72] Tony Ward and Astrid Birgden, 'Human Rights and Clinical Correctional Practice' (2007) 12 Aggression and Violent Behaviour 628.

[73] ibid.

practice ethically, correctional staff need to also consider moral and social rights. The human rights model is made up of core values, objects, and policies, which can be applied to sexual offenders and adapted to any local setting. First, it is argued that offenders have the moral right to the core values of autonomy and well-being in order to function as an autonomous and dignified agent. The core value of autonomy entails non-coerced situations and internal capabilities (e.g. the capacity for Mr S to formulate intentions, to imagine possible actions, and to form and implement his own valued plans). The core value of well-being entails meeting Mr S in terms of his physical needs (healthy physical functioning), social needs (family life, social support, and access to meaningful work opportunities and leisure activities), and psychological needs (autonomy, relatedness, and competence).

Second, the two core values ought to articulate human rights objects as outlined in international conventions and instruments (e.g. the United Nations Standard Minimum Rules for the Treatment of Prisoners, 1957). Autonomy is made up of personal freedom and social recognition, and well-being is made up of personal security, material subsistence, and elemental equality. In terms of autonomy, Mr S can expect personal freedom (the right to rely upon his own judgement when deciding how to live a life, although curtailed somewhat in prison) and social recognition (the right to direct the course of his own life, be treated in a respectful and dignified manner as an autonomous agent, and to experience self-respect and self-esteem). In terms of well-being, Mr S can expect personal security (procedural justice and the right to physical safety and welfare, which includes freedom from violence perpetrated by staff and other offenders), material subsistence (the right to basic levels of physical health and education), and elemental equality (the right to equality before the law and freedom from discrimination). While it is assumed that Correctional Services of Canada are meeting Mr S' well-being rights, the analysis provided by Lacombe implied that there may have been some problems meeting Mr S' autonomy rights.[74] Again, autonomy is enhanced through consent to participate in rehabilitation programmes, and coerced consent is a threat to offender rights and is likely to result in an offender who is either reluctant to engage in the process (the motivation or 'will') or cannot assimilate the information provided to their own case (the capacity or 'way'), as appeared to be the case with Mr S.

---

[74] Lacombe (n 5).

Third, local policies articulate legal rights based on the moral rights and the objects. TJ is particularly interested in the role of legal actors, which, in the correctional context, these could be defined as *psycho*legal roles. The staff of Correctional Services of Canada and members of the Parole Board of Canada are duty-bearers in that they have a moral obligation to ensure Mr S' core moral rights of autonomy and well-being. In turn, Mr S is simultaneously a rights-violator who has infringed on the rights of children when offending, a rights-holder who requires support from the state to function in a dignified manner, and a duty-bearer who should be able to pursue his life goals as long as he does not infringe upon the rights of others. Offender rehabilitation needs to respond to all three of Mr S' roles.

Sexual Offender Rehabilitation Models

The chapter to date has considered the continuum from coercion to consent that may be applied to sexual offenders to engage them in programmes. In 2009, a survey of 649 adult male and female sex offender treatment programmes in North America for The Safer Society was conducted, to which there were 1,349 service delivery respondents.[75] The findings regarding male sexual offenders were divided between the primary theory as well as the 'top three' theories that described the programme being delivered in the US or Canada. The findings were further divided between community programmes and residential programmes (mostly prison). In considering Mr S, only data for male sexual offenders in residential programmes will be considered. CBT was the primary theory in the United States (95%) but was applied less often in Canada (50%). Of the top three theories, residential programmes in Canada applied self-regulation (75%), followed by the GLM (50%), RNR (38%), and relapse prevention (13%). Of the top three theories, residential programmes in the United States applied CBT (95%), followed by relapse prevention (67%), the GLM (33%), and RNR (32%). These theories will be described in more detail below.

While offender rehabilitation models can be considered overarching rehabilitation theories (*what* to do), CBT is a treatment modality (*how* to

---

[75] Robert J McGrath et al, Current Practices and Emerging Trends in Sexual Abuser Management (The Safer Society 2009 North American Survey 2010).

do it).[76] Once in rehabilitation programmes, sexual offenders are generally subject to CBT that involves changing thoughts (identifying cognitive distortions or thinking errors that justify sexual offending), feelings (addressing negative and/or positive emotions that occur before, during and after sexual offending), and behaviours (defining sexual offending acts). Most often, CBT is applied in a deficit-based way in that treatment ensures that sexual offending behaviours are less reinforcing and more aversive. CBT treatment focuses on decreasing deviant sexual arousal while increasing or reinforcing normative sexual arousal, achieved through: (1) behavioural reconditioning of deviant sexual arousal; (2) victim empathy training; and (3) social skills training (Stinson & Becker, 2013 citing Marshall, Anderson, & Fernandez, 1999). This explains why the Parole Board of Canada was asking Mr S to demonstrate links between sexual fantasy, arousal, and sexual offending. However, few of the treatment targets for CBT – victim empathy, acknowledging the offence, or social skills training – have been significantly correlated with re-offending.[77]

Coercion or Coercive Threat: Risk–Need–Responsivity

The RNR model is a deficit-based approach that does not address the issue of coercion in sexual offender rehabilitation. RNR was initially established in Canada and is generally considered the most widely applied offender rehabilitation model. However, in practice, RNR is not applied as the primary theory in residential programmes in Canada and only 10 per cent of the time in residential programmes in the United States.[78] Based on Lacombe's critique,[79] RNR could be described as managerial, and at times punitive.

RNR is a framework in which to deliver CBT and Mr S' rehabilitation is described as an RNR approach applying CBT. RNR is based on a psychological theory of offender anti-social behaviour with a focus on

---

[76] Gwynn W Willis et al, 'How to integrate the Good Lives Model into treatment programmes for sexual offending: An introduction and overview' (2013) 25 Sexual Abuse: A Journal of Research and Treatment 123.

[77] Jill D Stinson and Judith V Becker, *Treating Sex Offenders: An Evidence-Based Manual* (The Guilford Press 2013).

[78] McGrath et al (n 76).

[79] Lacombe (n 5).

general personality and social psychology. [80] This risk management approach identifies risk factors for re-offending, targets higher risk offenders, focuses on those dynamic risk factors that are changeable, and reduces adverse outcomes. Risk factors are determined from empirically-derived research, rather than a theory base, and for sexual offenders include: sexual preoccupation; sexual preference for children; sexualised violence; multiple paraphilias; offence-supportive attitudes; emotional congruence with children; lack of emotionally satisfying adult relationships; lifestyle impulsiveness; resistance to rules and supervision; grievance/hostility; and negative social influences. [81] Dynamic risk factors are also described as 'criminogenic needs' which ought to be targeted in rehabilitation programmes, while 'non-criminogenic needs' (e.g. personal distress, distrust, low self-esteem, anxiety, and feelings of alienation) ought not to be targeted in treatment as they have not been found to be correlated with re-offending. While research has shown that RNR is useful in reducing violent re-offending, it has not yet been thoroughly evaluated with sexual offenders. [82]

Offence Cycle

CBT treatment in RNR entails unpacking the 'offence cycle'. The offence cycle focuses on immediate risk factors that precipitate and perpetuate repeated sexual offending and requires participants to consider the deviancy of their thoughts and decisions as maladaptive problem solving, negative emotions, and high-risk situations are expected to result in sexual re-offending. Participants are required to recount their offence cycle in terms of internal and environmental factors, understand the risks of lapse and relapse, and identify potential risk of re-offending and then develop a concrete relapse prevention plan to avoid or cope with high risk situations and pro-offending thoughts. Offence cycles have been criticised for focusing on 'cognitive distortions' and 'thinking errors' without supporting the moral agency in the offender's story that could harness any accountability, responsibility, and remorse. [83] Therefore, this approach

---

[80] Don A Andrews and James Bonta (2010). *The Psychology of Criminal Conduct* (5th ed, Anderson Publishing Co 2010).

[81] Ruth E Mann et al, 'Approach Versus Avoidance Goals in Relapse Prevention with Sex Offenders' (2004) 10 Sexual Abuse: A Journal of Research and Treatment 141.

[82] Stinson and Becker (n 78).

[83] Lacombe (n 5).

does not adequately explain what initially prompted sexual offending, other than that it was triggered by negative emotions, when sexual offending is complex and can be the result of multiple causes.

Relapse Prevention

The outcome of RNR treatment is a relapse prevention plan. Relapse prevention was originally adapted from the drug and alcohol treatment literature with an emphasis on high-risk behaviours and situations to be avoided by offenders. However, relapse prevention is only applied as the primary theory in community programmes in Canada (16%) but not in residential programmes (zero), and in community programmes in the United States (15%) and residential programmes (13%).[84] Research outcomes regarding relapse prevention and sexual offending have been inconsistent with little evidence of lasting behaviour change and the model has been criticised for being too confrontational.[85] There has also been little empirical evidence in support of the use of relapse prevention with sexual offenders.[86]

On an international basis, the application of relapse prevention to sex offenders has declined over time. The relapse prevention model has been critiqued on conceptual and empirical grounds.[87] Briefly, the problems with its application include: it is conceptually confusing when applied to sexual offenders; only one offence pathway is captured; offences are not necessarily triggered by negative emotions; it focuses more on covert planning; and the concepts of lapse and relapse are not clear cut.[88] Ward

---

[84] McGrath et al (n 76).

[85] Stinson and Becker (n 78).

[86] Pamela M Yates and Drew M Kingston, 'The Self-Regulation Model of Sexual Offending: The Relationship Between Offence Pathways and Static and Dynamic Sexual Offence Risk' [2006] 18 Sex Abuse 259.

[87] Stephen M Hudson and Tony Ward, 'Relapse Prevention: Assessment and Treatment Implications' in D Richard Laws, Stephen M Hudson, and Tony Ward (eds), *Remaking Relapse Prevention with Sex Offenders: A Sourcebook* (Sage Publications, Inc 2000).

[88] Tony Ward and Stephen M Hudson, 'A Self-Regulation Model of Relapse Prevention' in D Richard Laws, Stephen M Hudson, and Tony Ward (eds), *Remaking Relapse Prevention with Sex Offenders: A Sourcebook* (Sage Publications, Inc 2000); Robin J Wilson and Pamela M Yates, 'Effective Interventions and the Good Lives Model: Maximising Treatment Gains for Sex Offenders' (2009) 14 Aggression and Violent Behaviour 157.

and his colleagues subsequently revised relapse prevention for sexual offenders using self-regulation theory and had placed relapse prevention within a problem behaviour process with four distinct offence pathways. In other words, over time, the self-regulation model is replacing relapse prevention.

Despite the substantial likelihood of coerced treatment of sexual offending, the RNR literature is silent regarding its delivery. Recently, Andrews and Bonta acknowledged that they had failed to highlight offender autonomy:

> [R]espect for personal autonomy is a key aspect of ethical practice (…) we think respect for personal autonomy should be underscored in a field of practice in which so much emphasis is placed on structure, discipline, accountability, and state-sanctioned imposition of restrictions and punishment.[89]

And so autonomy has been included in a list of values, together with '(...) ongoing exploration and development of decent, humane, just, and [cost-]effective means of introducing human service for purposes of reducing antisocial conduct'. [90] However, it is difficult to determine how this newfound respect for offender autonomy translates into practice within RNR. RNR emphasizes the values of efficiency, objectivity, maximizing outcomes, universality, and reliability.[91] These values reflect some of the principles within international covenants requiring that the criminal justice system be fair, responsible, ethical, and efficient, but the approach in practice rests on managerialism and risk management. Put another way, Mr S' 'complexity as a human being has been reduced in treatment and at the parole hearing. "Have you sorted out your sexual life yet?" (…) [He] has become, as it were, his sexuality'.[92]

Consent or Coercive Offer: Good Lives Model

The GLM is a strength-based approach and is more sensitive to offender autonomy and consent. The GLM also applies CBT in that beliefs, expectations, and behavioural contingencies are seen to interact with

---

[89]Andrews and Bonta (n 81) 5,6.
[90] ibid 373.
[91] ibid 53.
[92] Lacombe (n 5).

values and goals that direct behaviour.[93] However, the GLM extends CBT into more therapeutic strategies, particularly relying upon a therapeutic alliance (or what would be described as an 'ethic of care' in TJ terms).[94] Therefore, as with TJ, the GLM emphasises the need to include offenders in decision-making to support the ethical value of autonomy. Recall, GLM is ranked more often than RNR in the top theories applied in North America and, although not applied as the primary theory in residential programmes in Canada (zero), it is applied in residential programmes in the United States 3 per cent of the time.[95] Based on Lacombe's critique,[96] the GLM could be described as humanistic in addressing broad psychological, social, and economic needs (and including non-criminogenic needs).

The GLM addresses the causes of offending, identifies treatment targets, guides treatment style, and considers the values underpinning the entire treatment programme – it aims to be holistic, positive, and ethical.[97] Six GLM principles for sexual offender treatment were provided[98] and are contrasted here to Lacombe's description of Mr S' treatment programme in the Correctional Services of Canada:[99] (1) many sexual offenders lack the capacities and supports to achieve a coherent good life plan due to adversarial developmental experiences – discussion of past trauma was discouraged in Mr S' treatment group; (2) sexual offenders lack many of the capacities and supports necessary to achieve a fulfilling life – little effort was made for Mr S to have supportive others in the community; (3) sexual offending is an attempt to achieve desired life goals, but where the capacities and supports are lacking, or to relieve conflict arising from failing to reach life goals – there was no discussion regarding Mr S' life goals; (4) the absence of certain life goals – autonomy, inner peace,

---

[93] Stinson and Becker (n 78).

[94] Warren Brookbanks, 'Therapeutic Jurisprudence: Conceiving an Ethical Framework' (2001) 8 Journal of Law and Medicine 328.

[95] McGrath et al (n 76).

[96] Lacombe (n 5).

[97] Pamela M Yates, David S Prescott and Tony Ward, *Applying the Good Lives and Self-Regulation Models to Sex Offender Treatment: A Practical Guide for Clinicians* (Safer Society Press 2010).

[98] Tony Ward, Ruth E Mann and Therese A Gannon, 'The Good Lives Model of Offender Rehabilitation: Clinical Implications' (2007) 12 Aggression and Violent Behaviour 87.

[99] Lacombe (n 5).

relatedness – are more strongly associated with sexual offending – the focus for Mr S was on sexual fantasies leading to re-offending; (5) assisting sexual offenders to develop capacities and social supports, and address autonomy, inner peace, and relatedness, will reduce sexual offending – Mr S was to be controlled through risk management strategies alone; and (6) treatment should add to personal repertoire, not simply remove or manage a problem – there was no effort for Mr S to experience as normal a level of functioning as possible.

Within the GLM, the dynamic risk factors for sexual offending (see above) are acknowledged, but viewed as 'red flags' for problem areas regarding ineffective or inappropriate strategies employed by the offender to achieve their life goals. This approach requires that the relationship between the problems areas and the offender's life goals are to be explored, rather than the sole goal of treatment being the management of dynamic risk factors. An example of the relationship between risk factors and achieving life goals, provided by Wilson and Yates, is that a child sexual offender seeking intimacy may turn to children but the sexual offending comes from the means used to meet his goal of intimacy, not the goal itself.[100] The aim of treatment is not to change the life goal of intimacy, but to consider the dynamic risk factors that act as obstacles to pro-social behaviour and to change the means of meeting the goal of achieving intimacy. Treatment may therefore include attention to non-criminogenic needs or what may be viewed as empirically unsupported dynamic risk factors.

Case Formulation

Lacking in RNR is a case formulation to guide offender rehabilitation. Being based on clinical principles, the GLM emphasises case formulation. A case formulation is a set of hypotheses framed around what may be causing, triggering, and maintaining offending.[101] A 'case formulation has

---

[100] Wilson and Yates (n 89).

[101] Arthur M Nezu, Christine M Nezu, and Elizabeth Lombardo, *Cognitive-Behavioural Case Formulation to Treatment Design: A Problem-Solving Approach* (Springer Publication Company 2004).

been part of, and a guide for, psychological treatment programmes since such interventions began'.[102]

A case formulation of the offender's pathway is initially devised from a clinical interview, a file search, and structured clinical judgement. A clinician develops a case formulation together with the offender to: (1) obtain a detailed understanding of the offender's problems; (2) identify the variables functionally related to the problem areas; and (3) define treatment targets, goals, and objectives. Importantly, case formulation is considered a dynamic process, from assessment to treatment.

A GLM case formulation: (1) weights life goals; (2) identifies past and current actions; (3) determines any flaws in the actions that have led to offending in order to achieve life goals; (4) highlights strengths (current and past appropriate actions); and (5) makes links to self-regulation.[103] The focus of a GLM case formulation is on increasing autonomy (informed decision-making), improving individual psychological well-being, and maximising opportunities to lead a good life'.[104] These principles align with TJ. The case formulation assists offenders in developing their good life plan.[105] If the offender is reluctant to address offence-specific issues, motivational strategies to engage treatment readiness are required first. Treatment is then individualised to manage dynamic risk factors (using CBT) and meet need by developing a good life plan (addressing self, family, community, employment, leisure, etc.) in which participants fashion a new identity and actively work toward achieving life goals.[106]

Self-Regulation and Offence Pathways

In the past decade, greater attention has been applied to self-regulation theory in sexual offender programmes. Self-regulation refers to internal

---

[102] William L Marshall et al, *Rehabilitating Sexual Offenders: A Strengths-Based Approach* (American Psychological Association 2011).
[103] Willis et al (n 77).
[104] Tony Ward and Therese A Gannon, 'Rehabilitation, Etiology, and Self-Regulation: The Comprehensive Good Lives Model of Treatment for Sexual Offenders' (2006) 11 Aggression and Violent Behaviour 77.
[105] Tony Ward, Ruth E Mann, and Therese A Gannon, The Good Lives Model of Offender Rehabilitation: Clinical Implications (2007) 12 Aggression and Violent Behaviour 87.
[106] Wilson and Yates (n 89).

and external processes that allow individuals to engage in goal-directed actions over time and in different contexts.[107] Self-regulation is currently popular in Canada as it is applied in residential programmes (40%) but less so in US residential programmes (3%).[108]

Self-regulation theory posits that dysfunctions in self-regulation result in maladaptive behaviours and may be overridden by the distorting effects of strong preferences or motives and/or a lack of capacity and knowledge (or 'the will and the way'). Self-regulation is a process through which sexual offenders control emotions, thoughts, interactions, behaviours, and physiological states such as sexual drive requiring attention to emotional, cognitive, interpersonal, and behavioural states. [109] Unlike relapse prevention, self-regulation theory is not merely focused on inhibiting maladaptive behaviour (e.g. repressing an emotion), but it also emphasises enhancing adaptive behaviour (e.g. coping or self-management skills). Self-regulation theory as applied by Ward and colleagues,[110] with its self-management CBT focus, is viewed as an appropriate model for sexual offenders because: it allows for multiple offence pathways; clarifies when and where the processes that mediate the transition points in the offence process may occur; knits together diverse theories; and is open-ended enough to be modified in response to empirical and theoretical developments.

Self-regulation theory to posit various offence pathways is an alternative to the single offence cycle.[111] Offence pathways are a combination of three dimensions: (1) offence-related goals that are *avoidant* (decrease behaviours or situations, and failure to achieve the offending goal is all-or-nothing) or *approach* (increase skills or situation, and failure to achieve the offending goal may increase the individual's efforts); (2) offence related strategies which are either *passive* (fail to implement strategies to avoid offending such as ignoring sexual urges and impulsive behaviours, absent strategies and poor planning) or *active* (prevents an offence from occurring by leaving a high-risk situation or coping with an emotional

---

[107] Tony Ward, Stephen M Hudson, and Thomas Keenan, 'A Self-Regulation Model of the Sexual Offence Process' (1998) 10 Sexual Abuse: A Journal of Research and Treatment 141.

[108] McGrath et al (n 76).

[109] Stinson and Becker (n 78).

[110] Hudson and Ward (n 88); Ward, Hudson and Keenan (n 108).

[111] Ward, Hudson, and Keenan (n 108).

state, <u>or</u> explicitly plans an offence to achieve the goal); and (3) the type of self-regulation that are *under-regulation* or disinhibition (loss of control of thoughts, emotions, and behaviours in which emotions may be positive or negative such as sexual urges); (2) *mis-regulation* or loss of control (ineffective or counterproductive strategies such as sexual fantasies to modulate negative mood states); or (3) *self-regulation* with the goal of offending (controlled offending with goals that are false, self-serving, or distorted such as 'all women enjoy forced sex'). Combined, these three dimensions then create four possible offence pathways that can be hypothesised based on the case formulation: (1) avoidant–passive pathway – a desire to avoid offending but failing to do so (under-regulation); (2) avoidant–active pathway – a direct attempt to unsuccessfully control deviant thoughts, fantasies, or emotions (mis-regulation); (3) approach–passive pathway – following overlearned behavioural scripts that lead to offending (under-regulation); and (4) approach–active pathway – conscious and well-crafted planning as an acceptable means to a valued end (controlled self-regulation).

The self-regulation model as proposed by Ward and his colleagues provides for self-management within CBT, motivational strategies in determining approach and avoidant goals, and identifying different treatment needs according to the hypothesised offence pathway. Most recently, the model has been revised by to include life goals and appropriate language and pro-social actions.[112] It is posited that Mr S may have been more amenable to considering what his self-management strategies were if he had been engaged in guiding what he viewed as his most likely offence pathway.

Several empirical studies of self-regulation and offence pathways developed by Ward and colleagues have been conducted. Eighty sexual offenders in treatment were reviewed and the authors were able to distinguish between offence pathways associated with offender risk factors in the expected direction.[113] Sexual offenders completing an avoidant-focused relapse prevention programme were compared to offenders completing an approach-focused relapse prevention programme.[114] The

---

[112] Pamela M Yates and Tony Ward, 'Good Lives, Self-Regulation, and Risk Management: An Integrated Model of Sexual Offender Assessment and Treatment' (2008) 1 Sexual Abuse in Australia and New Zealand 2.

[113] Yates and Kingston (n 87).

[114] Mann et al (n 82).

avoidant programme was the traditional application of identifying high risk situations, listing cues for each risk factor, and planning to manage the risk factors, as in the case of Mr S. The approach programme entailed identifying the difference between approach and avoidance goals, describing Old Me and New Me through art and written work, identifying obstacles to achieving approach goals, identifying goals to achieve New Me, and developing any additional skills required to meet goals. The authors found that the approach-focused participants were fully engaged in treatment (as measured by homework completion and willingness to disclose relapses) and were rated by the therapists to be more motivated. More recently, a relapse prevention version was compared to a GLM version of a community-based sexual offender treatment programme and found that while there was no difference between attrition rates or treatment progress between the two versions, both facilitators and participants reported that the GLM version was more positive and future-focused. [115] The self-regulation approach has been described by RNR proponents as having empirical support for sexual offenders, allowing for individualised offence cycles and treatment plans, and as congruent with the RNR risk and needs principles. [116]

Good Life Plan

The ultimate outcome of a GLM approach is the development of a good life plan. All humans have roadmaps or an implicit good life plan, which may be effective or ineffective. Life goals are human needs that apply to all humans, offender or not; they have been identified from psychological, social, biological, and anthropological research. The life goals that sexual offenders may be seeking to achieve through offending may include one or more of the following 11 life goals: (1) life – healthy living and functioning; (2) knowledge – how well informed one feels about things that are important to them; (3) play – hobbies and recreational pursuits; (4) work – mastery of work skills; (5) agency – autonomy, independence, and self-direction; (6) inner peace – freedom from turmoil and stress; (7)

---

[115] Leigh Harkins et al, 'Evaluation of a Community-Based Sex Offender Treatment Programme Using a Good Lives Model Approach' (2012) 26 Sexual Abuse: A Journal of Research and Treatment 519.

[116] J Steven Wormith et al, 'The Rehabilitation and Reintegration of Offenders: The Current Landscape and Some Future Directions for Correctional Psychology' (2007) 34 Criminal Justice and Behaviour 879.

relatedness – intimate/familial/social relationships; (8) community – connection to wider social groups; (9) spirituality – in the broad sense of finding meaning and purpose in life; (10) happiness – feeling good in the here and now; and (11) creativity – expressing oneself through alternative forms.[117] A good life plan for offenders should build capacities and allow them to achieve personal goals to reduce their risk.

Conclusion: Minimising Anti-Therapeutic Effects of Coercion

The style of rehabilitation of Mr S, as described by Lacombe, generally occurs through the United Kingdom, the United States, Australia, and New Zealand with sexual offenders. [118] This chapter has considered the principles of human rights, TJ, and the GLM in the context of an individual such as Mr S being coerced into offender rehabilitation programmes. Accepting that Mr S will be experiencing some level of legal coercion while under the management of the Correctional Services of Canada, the task is to balance his individual rights to dignity against the community's rights to remain safe. From a human rights perspective, Mr S' moral rights are to be protected. As noted, while his well-being rights may have been met, his autonomy rights were less likely to be met because of the potential for psychological coercion, resulting in Mr S lacking 'the will and the way' to change his behaviour. A TJ analysis would conclude in relation to Mr S that: the current law is anti-therapeutic rather than therapeutic; the legal rules, procedures, and roles have an anti-therapeutic effect on him, demonstrated by his resistance despite rehabilitation; and psycho-legal actors within Correctional Services of Canada and the Parole Board of Canada should harness the law to be therapeutic rather than anti-therapeutic. From a TJ perspective, a rehabilitation model is required to at least minimise the anti-therapeutic effects of coercion. The GLM is a theory of offender rehabilitation that supports the principles of human rights and TJ, and in the case of Mr S, may have assisted to minimise the anti-therapeutic effects of the rehabilitation programme and the subsequent parole board hearing.

---

[117] Mayumi Purvis, Tony Ward, and Gwynn W Willis, 'The Good Lives Model in Practice: Offence Pathways and Case Management' (2011) 3 European Journal of Probation 4.
[118] Lacombe (n 5).

The following, but rather simplistic, application of GLM principles regarding Mr S are based on what is known of Mr S as described by Lacombe.[119] A GLM assessment of Mr S would have hypothesised an offence pathway and posed a case formulation that would have been actively tested with Mr S throughout the rehabilitation programme (i.e. continually supporting his agency). Mr S had experienced paedophilic fantasies since he was 14 years of age but had not acted upon them until he was over 40 years of age. It could be hypothesised that Mr S' offence pathway was most likely to be an avoidant-passive pathway: he was avoidant in that his offence-related goals were trying to avoid high risk situations such as being with children or thinking about them, but passive in that he failed to manage sexual fantasies about children that then ultimately led to offending. The avoidant-passive pathway results in under-regulation, which means that Mr S desires to avoid re-offending (the will) but does not have the capacity to do so (the way). Feeling anxious and fearful that he would offend caused Mr S to abandon his avoidant goals when he was in a high risk situation (whether he groomed the child first was unclear). That Mr S is motivated to change is a rehabilitative opportunity that ought to be harnessed therapeutically. A case formulation approach means that more distal vulnerability or non-criminogenic factors such as Mr S being a victim of child abuse himself at the hands of his uncle and doctor, and lacking self-efficacy in confidently mastering new skills. Protective factors or current strengths, such as Mr S being able to express himself well, being sociable, and having a supportive family, are also considered. In weighting the 11 life goals within the group rehabilitation programme, it could have been determined that in offending, Mr S was seeking relatedness (intimacy with children) and happiness (feeling good in the here and now to manage feelings of depression and loneliness).

Because he is most likely to be under-regulated, Mr S' rehabilitation requires an emphasis on capacity (the way). Mr S' good life plan requires both avoidant and approach treatment goals. Mr S has avoidant treatment goals in place in avoiding high-risk situations such as watching TV shows or reading books that include children, not attending malls or public pools, and not socialising with women with children so as not to fantasise about children and then re-offend. However, more likely to engage his motivation, are approach treatment goals to encourage Mr S to develop

---

[119] ibid.

alternative pro-social means of attaining relatedness and happiness. Mr S chose to engage with a group of like-minded adults who share his interests and hobbies (unknown as these were not described) in addition to support from the agreed Christian-based restorative justice ministry, with both strategies building on his strength of sociability.

In combining the principles of human rights, TJ, and the GLM, the anti-therapeutic effects of legal coercion are more likely to be minimised than risk management alone. In this approach, Mr S ought to be engaged as a rights-violator (with *agreed* avoidant treatment goals), a rights-holder (with *agreed* approach treatment goals), and most importantly as a duty-bearer (he is an autonomous adult who has the capacity to pursue his *agreed* life goals as long as he does not infringe upon the rights of children and others). As duty-bearers, correctional staff, parole board members, and other psycho-legal actors need to balance community rights *and* offender rights. In this way, Mr S is more likely to be engaged in meeting his life goals in different ways and, in turn, community protection will be enhanced.

NOTES ON CONTRIBUTORS

Chris Ashford
Chris Ashford is Professor of Law and Society at Northumbria University where he is Director of Research at the Law School. He is Editor of *The International Journal of Gender, Sexuality and Law*, and the award-winning journal, *The Law Teacher: The International Journal of Legal Education*, and is on the editorial board of *Porn Studies*. He is also Chair of the Association of Law Teachers. A queer theorist, he has published widely on legal education as well as the law and sex(uality).

Vera Bergelson
Vera Bergelson is a Professor of Law and the Robert E. Knowlton Scholar at Rutgers University School of Law, USA.

Vera Bergelson specializes in criminal law theory. She has written widely about consent, provocation, self-defense, necessity, victimless crime, and human trafficking. Her book *Victims' Rights and Victims' Wrongs: A Theory of Comparative Criminal Liability* (SUP 2009) raises questions about comparative liability in criminal law.

Vera Bergelson has served as a chair of the Association of American Law Schools' Section on Jurisprudence. She is on the editorial boards of *BdeF* and *Edisofer* (Buenos Aires and Madrid) as well as *Law and Philosophy*.

Astrid Birgden
Dr Birgden is a Consultant Forensic Psychologist, Just Forensic and an Adjunct Clinical Associate Professor at Deakin University, Australia. She has 30 years of experience developing policy and delivering services regarding the assessment, treatment, and management of serious offenders and offenders with intellectual disabilities. She has established a statewide sexual offender treatment program and a statewide offender rehabilitation framework, designed services for forensic disability clients, established family violence courts, and established and managed a compulsory drug treatment prison. As a consultant, Dr Birgden has also been involved in torture prevention with military and police in Sri Lanka and Nepal, established a citizen-police mediation program in New

Orleans, and was a moderator for an online course on problem solving courts through the National Institute of Canada, training judges from Canada, the US, Puerto Rico, New Zealand and Australia. Dr Birgden is published in the areas of risk assessment, offender rehabilitation, therapeutic jurisprudence, and human rights. In addition to a Masters in Forensic Psychology and a PhD, Dr Birgden has completed a Masters in Advanced Disability Law through the New York Law School.

Ann-Creaby Attwood

Ann Creaby-Attwood is a Senior Lecturer in Law at Northumbria University where she teaches in criminal law and forensic mental health law. Along with undergraduate teaching, professional solicitor training and external CPD training, Ann leads the mentally disordered offender module on the LLM mental health.

Ann's research primarily concentrates upon defendants with undiagnosed autism. Her current research focuses on detainees with an ASC in police custody. Ann has expertise in forensic mental health law, following over twenty-five years of experience in working with people with mental illness and learning disabilities within the criminal justice system. Ann has worked as a lawyer, social worker and probation officer.

Ann established and led a unique medico-legal team based at Newcastle Crown Court, and provided specialist legal advice to advocates and judiciary regarding complex forensic mental health law. This team received awards and nominations both from the Ministry of Justice and the NHS. Prior to this, Ann was seconded to NHS England's Health and Justice Commissioning Team.

Ann has spoken at conferences both nationally and internationally and was a panel-speaker at an event hosted by the Law Commission.

Jesse Elvin

Jesse Elvin graduated with a PhD in law from the University of London in 2005. He is a Senior Lecturer in Law at the City University London, where criminal law is one of his specialist fields. He has published in a number of leading journals, including the *Cambridge Law Journal*, the *Law Quarterly Review* and the *Modern Law Review*, and is a regular conference speaker.

Ben Fitzpatrick

Ben Fitzpatrick is a Senior Lecturer at York Law School at the University of York, UK. He has also worked at the University of Leeds, the Open University and the University of Derby. His research and teaching specialisms include criminal justice and legal philosophy. He has published on a range of issues relating to criminal law, the law of evidence, and policing. He has taught at both the undergraduate and postgraduate level and has participated in the delivery of training to criminal justice professionals. He blogs on criminal justice issues at *Crim up North*, and on issues relating to legal education at *Ed Lines*.

Natalia Hanley

Dr Natalia Hanley is a Senior Lecturer in Criminology at the University of Wollongong. is a criminologist with particular expertise in community corrections, street gangs and criminal justice policy. More broadly, Natalia has also published on the fear of crime, forensic mental health policy, the use of research evidence in rape law reform and public and policy constructions of male sexual victimisation. Natalia completed an ESRC funded PhD on probation service responses to street gangs in Manchester, UK.

Primarily a qualitative researcher, Natalia's research interests coalesce around a central concern with the contemporary experience of criminal justice. In particular, she is interested in the ways in which different actors experience criminal justice and the punishment process. To this end she has explored the changing nature of the former Probation Service in England and Wales from the perspective of staff members and street gang members. Her forthcoming work extends this interest to consider victims of crime in the justice process.

Karen Harrison

Karen Harrison is Senior Lecturer in the School of Law at the University of Hull, UK. She has published several articles on the sentencing, treatment and management of high-risk sex offenders and is the author of *Dangerousness, Risk and the Governance of Serious Sexual and Violent Offenders* (2011). She is the editor of *Managing High Risk Sex Offenders in the Community* (2010) and, co-edited with Dr. Bernadette Rainey, *The Wiley-Blackwell Handbook of Legal and Ethical Aspects of Sex Offender Treatment and Management* (2013). Dr Harrison is an editorial board member of the *Journal of Sexual Aggression* and the *Prison Service Journal* as well as associate editor of *Sexual Offender Treatment*.

Jonathan Herring

Jonathan Herring is a fellow in law at Exeter College, Oxford University and Professor of Law at the Law Faculty, Oxford University. He has written on family law, medical law, criminal law and legal issues surrounding care and old age. His books include: *Caring and the Law* (2014); *Older People in Law and Society* (Oxford University Press, 2009); *European Human Rights and Family Law* (Hart, 2010) (with Shazia Choudhry); *Medical Law and Ethics* (Oxford University Press 2014); *Criminal Law* (Oxford University Press 2014); *Family Law* (Pearson, 2015); and *The Woman Who Tickled Too Much* (Pearson, 2009).

David Hughes

David Hughes is a Senior Lecturer at Teesside University. He attained a First Class Honours LLB with Business Law from Sunderland University and a Distinction in LLM Criminal Law and Procedure, as well as a Commendation for the LPC at Northumbria University, and subsequently a PhD with his thesis addressing a Comparative Analysis of the Criminal Transmission of HIV. His work was cited extensively in the recent Law Commission Paper on Reform of Non-fatal Offences, notably within the contextualisation of Transmission of Communicable Diseases, and David's work in this regard has also been published in *The Journal of Criminal Law* and *Medical Science and the Law*.

Chris Ince

Dr Ince currently works as a Consultant in Forensic and Forensic Learning Disability Psychiatry for the Northumberland Tyne and Wear NHS Foundation Trust. He has previously worked within Mental Health and LD Forensic Services throughout the North East of England and also the High Secure Estate at Rampton Hospital. His clinical work is primarily based at Northgate Hospital, Morpeth, where he has responsibility for an in-patient caseload detained across a variety of levels of security. He is the Psychiatric Lead for the Women's Forensic Service and Chair of the Forensic Service Referrals and Admissions Panel. Furthermore, Dr Ince is the Psychiatric Lead for the National Referral Specialist In-Patient Autism Service. He was, until its closure, a longstanding member of the Newcastle-based Sexual Behaviour Unit.

Aside from his clinical work, Dr Ince is a Core and Higher trainer on the Northern Deanery Rotational Training Schemes and further lectures at the regional universities and a variety of other learned societies. He has current research interests in offending in Autism Spectrum Disorders and the physical healthcare needs of patients with learning disabilities.

He is a Care Quality Commission Clinical Expert, participating in the inspection of Mental Health Trusts and informing the current review of the inspection process. He previously sat on the Royal College of Psychiatry CCQI Advisory Group for Medium Secure Care, authoring the standards for women in such settings, and further supervised the preparation of similar guidance for Medium Secure LD services.

Ben Livings

Ben Livings is a Senior Lecturer in Law at the University of New England, Australia, and has previously held academic posts in the UK and in France. He is interested in normative problems posed to the criminal law by concepts such as consent, and in the discretionary elements of the criminal justice system. In 2013, he co-organised a UK conference on "Mental Disorder and Criminal Justice", and in 2014, he co-edited a *Northern Ireland Legal Quarterly* Special Edition on the same subject.

Rajan Nathan

Professor Rajan Nathan (MB, BCh, MMedSc, DipFBSc, MD, MRCPsych) completed his undergraduate medical studies at the University of Wales College of Medicine in 1991, and moved to Yorkshire to undertake junior psychiatric training. He then completed higher training in forensic psychiatry in Merseyside, and since 2001, he has held the post of Consultant Forensic Psychiatrist at the Scott Clinic Medium Secure Unit and more recently at the Saddlebridge Low Secure Unit. As a Consultant Forensic Psychiatrist, Dr Rajan Nathan has gained extensive clinical experience of the management of offenders with mental disorder in a range of settings, including secure hospitals, prison and the community. Professor Rajan Nathan has remained academically active and he was awarded a doctorate for research in the area of developmental pathways to serious violence by the University of Liverpool. Since 2005, he has held the honorary post of Senior Research Fellow at the University of Liverpool, and in 2015, he was additionally awarded the title of Visiting Professor at the Medical Institute at the University of Chester. Professor Rajan Nathan has developed a national profile in the field of forensic personality disorder and he has led the development of a range of innovative service models in this area, including a prison-based intervention service. Professor Nathan has considerable experience working within a range of legal forums as an independent expert. He has developed and delivered medical jurisprudence training and led academic work in this area. His expert practice is predominantly in Family and Criminal proceedings, but he has also provided expert testimony in the areas of Coroner's Court inquiries, civil litigation, prison law, and Mental Health Review Tribunals.

Tanya Palmer

Dr Tanya Palmer is a lecturer in Law and co-director of the Crime Research Centreat the University of Sussex. Prior to this, she held an ESRC post-doctoral research fellowship at the University of Bristol. Tanya's research interests are primarily in the legal regulation of sexual encounters, particularly through the substantive criminal law. She is the author of *Re-Negotiating Sex and Sexual Violation in the Criminal Law* (Hart, forthcoming), which advocates a rethinking of legal and ethical distinctions between sex and sexual violation, centred around a concept of 'freedom to negotiate'. Tanya is also interested in developing novel socio-legal research methodologies that draw together theoretical, doctrinal and empirical work.

Bernadette Rainey

Dr. Bernadette Rainey is a Senior Lecturer in Law at Cardiff Law School. She is also Director of the Law School's Centre for Human Rights and Public Law. Bernadette did her law degree and PhD at Queen's University, Belfast before taking up posts as a researcher at Aberystwyth and Swansea, and as a lecturer at Queen's University, Belfast. Bernadette's research interests include human rights especially offender rights, equality, and asylum and refugee law. She has published widely, including *The Wiley-Blackwell Handbook of Legal and Ethical Aspects of Sex Offender Treatment and Management* (Wiley Blackwell, 2013) (co-editor with Dr. Karen Harrison). Bernadette is also a co-author of the leading textbook on the European Convention on Human Rights (Rainey, Wicks and Ovey, *The European Convention on Human Rights* (Oxford University Press, 2014)).

Senthorun Raj

Senthorun Raj is a scholar and advocate with a passion for popular culture, social justice, and law. He has just submitted his PhD at Sydney Law School. His thesis, titled "Reading Emotion: Queer Injury, Intimacy, and Identity in Pro-LGBTI Cases," examines the way emotion has shaped legal responses that address the marginalisation of sexual and gender minorities. In 2017, Senthorun will take up a Lectureship in Law at Keele University.

Senthorun is a former Churchill Fellow and most has been a Scholar in Residence at New York University's Center for Human Rights and Global Justice.

Senthorun is a contributing writer for *The Guardian*. He has published numerous articles and academic papers on topics ranging from refugee law to social networking. Senthorun is also an advisory board member of the sexuality, gender and diversity studies journal *Writing from Below*.

In a governance capacity, Senthorun has served on the boards of Amnesty International Australia and ACON Health. He has also worked as the Senior Policy Advisor for the NSW Gay and Lesbian Rights Lobby.

Alan Reed

Alan Reed graduated from Trinity College, Cambridge University with a First Class Honours Degree in Law, and was awarded the Herbert Smith Prize for Conflict of Laws and the Dr Lancey Prize. Cambridge University awarded him a full Holland Scholarship to facilitate study in the United States, and he obtained an LLM Masters of Law (Comparative Law) at the University of Virginia. After completion of the Law Society Finals Examinations, he spent three years in practice in London at Addleshaw Goddard, and also acted as a Tutor in Criminal Law at Trinity College, Cambridge. He spent seven years as a Lecturer in Law at Leeds University, before working as Professor of Criminal and Private International Law at Sunderland University. Since April 2012, he has acted as Associate Dean of Research and Innovation in the Faculty of Business and Law at Northumbria University. For the last 10 years, he has been the editor of the *Journal of Criminal Law*.

Keith JB Rix

Keith Rix (BMedBiol (Hons), MPhil, LLM, MD, FRCPsych) is an Honorary Consultant Forensic Psychiatrist in the Norfolk and Suffolk NHS Foundation Trust. His involvement in the forensic field began in the 1960s when he lived in hostels in London with ex-offenders and assessed prisoners for hostel admission. He qualified in medicine in Aberdeen in 1975 and trained in psychiatry in Edinburgh and Manchester. In Manchester, he was a Lecturer in Psychiatry and carried out his doctoral research under the supervision of Professor Sir David Goldberg.

In 1983, he moved to Leeds as Senior Lecturer in Psychiatry and became a Visiting Consultant Psychiatrist at HM Prison, Leeds. He established the

Leeds Magistrates' Court Mental Health Assessment and Diversion Scheme and the city's forensic psychiatry service. His research has included studies of drunkenness offenders in a Scottish burgh police court as well as arson and psychiatric disorder in prisoners. He is the author of case reports on capacity to litigate, privilege and prison medical records, Mental Health Act restriction orders, wrongful arrest, out of court silence and the adverse inference, provocation and battered woman syndrome, hypothyroidism and grievous bodily harm, and intent. He provided expert evidence to the courts for over thirty years, including evidence on a *pro bono* basis in capital cases in the Caribbean and Africa, and he is the author of *Expert Psychiatric Evidence*. He is also editor of *A Handbook for Trainee Psychiatrists* and co-author, with his wife, Elizabeth Lumsden Rix, of *Alcohol Problems*. He is a former Chairman of the Fitness to Practise Panel of the Medical Practitioners Tribunal Service and a part-time Lecturer in the Department of Law, De Montfort University, Leicester. He continues to be Visiting Professor of Medical Jurisprudence at the Institute of Medicine, University of Chester. He also has an interest in medical ethics and has recently published on the subject of the involvement of health professionals in capital punishment.

Philip N Rumney

Professor Rumney is Professor of Criminal Justice at the University of the East of England, Bristol. He has been engaged in research concerning criminal justice responses to rape for two decades. Much of this work has involved doctrinal and socio-legal analysis of adult male rape, rape sentencing, and the policing and courtroom treatment of rape complainants, false allegations and the impact of social attitudes on rape law enforcement. He has authored or co-authored over 55 articles, book chapters, reports and reviews.

Linda Steele

Linda Steele is a lecturer in the School of Law and a member of Legal Intersections Research Centre, University of Wollongong, Australia. She holds a BA(Gender Studies) and LLB(Hons) from University of Wollongong, a Masters of Public and International Law from University of Melbourne and a PhD from University of Sydney. Linda's research explores the intersections of disability, law and injustice. Her research is interdisciplinary, drawing on diverse critical theories and empirical research methods to provide new approaches to understanding and responding to contemporary disability law and policy issues. Her current research projects focus on: (1) punishment of people with disability, and

(2) violence against people with disability. Linda has co-edited the following special issues: 'Disability at the Peripheries: Legal Theory, Disability and Criminal Law' (2014) *Griffith Law Review* and 'Medical Bodies: Gender, Justice and Medicine' (2016) *Australian Feminist Studies*, and is currently co-editing the following two special issues to be published in 2017: 'Normalcy and Disability: Intersections Among Norms, Law, and Culture' *Continuum* and 'Disability, Rights and Law Reform in Australia – Recent Trends' *Law in Context*. Linda is active in policy and law reform debates related to disability rights and her submissions and scholarship have been cited and used in domestic and international law reform contexts. Linda has a professional background in the community legal and social justice sector. She was a solicitor at the Intellectual Disability Rights Service (2006-2009) and is a member of the Executive Committee of the Women in Prison Advocacy Network (2008-present).

Claire de Than
Claire de Than is Co-Director of the Centre for Law, Justice and Journalism at City University, London, having previously held appointments at 2 London University colleges. She is a Law Commissioner (Jersey).The author or co-author of more than 15 books, including de Than, Criminal Law (OUP 2016), de Than and Heaton, Criminal Law (OUP 2014) and de Than and Shorts, International Criminal Law and Human Rights (Sweet and Maxwell 2004), she has over 80 legal publications in total, including chapters in leading legal monographs and edited collections, such as Reed and Bohlander, Substantive Issues in Criminal Law (Ashgate, 2011) and articles in a variety of national and international journals, including the Modern Law Review. Her research fields include criminal law, human rights law, media law, and disability law. She has been an expert for the Law Commission of England and Wales on two recent criminal law projects. A regular keynote speaker at legal and medical conferences, she has advised several governments and many organisations on criminal law, human rights and law reform issues, with specialisms in comparative human rights, the law of British Overseas Territories and Crown Dependencies and in the law of consent.